AF560218

TAXATION OF INCOME
An International Comparison

TAXATION OF INCOME
An International Comparison

A Select Study of
U.S. • U.K. • Australia • Malaysia • Pakistan • India

INDU JAIN

MANOHAR
2004

First published 2003
Revised edition 2004

ISBN 81-7304-559-3

Published by

Ajay Kumar Jain for
Manohar Publishers & Distributors
4753/23 Ansari Road, Daryaganj
New Delhi 110 002

Typeset at

Digigrafics
New Delhi 110 049

Printed at

Lordson Publishers Pvt. Ltd.
Delhi 110 007

Contents

Tables

FIGURES

Preface

Income tax, being an integral part of fiscal policy, is a unique instrument in the hands of the government to raise resources. It is also an important tool to promote social welfare and achieve desired economic objectives. Frequent changes in the income tax law and their impact on the tax liability of the assessees and the revenue of the government keep the subject alive for discussion and debate. Liberalisation and globalisation of world economies have opened the doors for foreign investment, transfer of goods, capital and human resources from one country to another. Any change in the income tax law of a country affects not only the investment decisions of its citizens, but also the decisions of the rest of the world whether to invest or not in that country. Hence, a critical and analytical study of the income tax systems of different countries becomes relevant.

This book explains and compares the income tax provisions of six countries, three developed—the U.K., the U.S., and Australia, and three developing ones, namely, Malaysia, Pakistan and India.

The book is divided into ten chapters. Chapter 1 introduces the relevant tax concepts. Chapter 2 examines various aspects of income tax system including the income base, tax unit, residential status, tax rate structure and tax-free threshold in the selected countries. Chapter 3 compares provisions relating to salary income including retirement benefits, fringe benefits, taxability of car benefits and rent-free accommodation. Chapter 4 analyses provisions relating to the computation of depreciation allowance in respect of plant and machinery and buildings, balancing adjustments and carry-forward of unabsorbed depreciation. Chapter 5 evaluates the provisions relating to the computation of capital gains, indexation allowance, capital loss adjustments and capital gains tax reliefs. Chapter 6 deals with various types of income tax incentives, namely, social-welfare reliefs, investment-related and business-related incentives. Chapter 7 makes an appraisal of the provisions relating to corporate tax rates, chargeability of dividend income and minimum alternate tax. Chapter 8 focuses on various aspects of assessment procedures, including filing of tax returns, self-assessment, regular assessment, negotiated settlement, appeal procedures, income-escaping assessment and search procedures. Chapter 9 examines the provisions relating to the payment of interest, penalty and prosecution applicable in selected countries. Chapter 10 draws conclusions from the study.

The completion of this project was made possible through the continued support of several persons and institutions from all over the world. I express my deep sense of gratitude to Professor D.P.S. Verma of the Department of

Commerce, Delhi School of Economics, University of Delhi, for his constant guidance and valuable suggestions.

I consulted several authors and tax experts for clarifications during the course of the project. I was fortunate to receive prompt and helpful response from them. In particular, I am grateful to Dr. Veerinderjeet Singh, Executive Director of Arthur Andersen HRM (Tax Services), Malaysia; Mr. T.N. Pandey, formerly Chairman, Central Board of Direct Taxes, India; Mr. Mark Winter, Board of Inland Revenue, U.K.; Mr. M. Hendy, Manager, Corporate Reporting Systems, Australian Taxation Office and Mr. Umar Wahid, Deputy Director, Central Board of Revenue, Pakistan.

I owe a special word of appreciation to my husband, Mr. Ved Jain for his support and understanding during the course of the work. Lastly, a word of appreciation for my son Ankit and daughter Shilpi who provided lighter moments during long hours of this tedious work.

Delhi INDU JAIN
January 2003

Abbreviations

ACRS	Accelerated Cost Recovery System
ADR	Asset Depreciation Range
ADS	Alternative Depreciation System
AGI	Adjusted Gross Income
AMT	Alternative Minimum Tax
AO	Assessing Officer
ATO	Australian Taxation Office
CBDT	Central Board of Direct Taxes
CBR	Central Board of Revenue
CGT	Capital Gains Tax
CII	Cost of Inflation Index
DBM	Diminishing or Declining Balance Method
DG	Director General
DVM	Diminishing Value Method
ETP	Eligible Termination Payment
FBT	Fringe Benefits Tax
FMV	Fair Market Value
FRV	Fair Rental Value
FTB	Family Tax Benefit
FTP	Family Tax Payment
FTZ	Free Trade Zone
FYA	First Year Allowance
GDP	Gross Domestic Product
HUF	Hindu Undivided Family
IA	Indexation Allowance
IRB	Inland Revenue Board
IRS	Internal Revenue Service
ITAA 36	Income Tax Assessment Act, 1936 (Australia)
ITAA 97	Income Tax Assessment Act, 1997 (Australia)
ICTA	Income and Corporation Taxes Act, 1988 (U.K.)
LTCG	Long-Term Capital Gain
LTCL	Long-Term Capital Loss
MACRS	Modified Accelerated Cost Recovery System
MAT	Minimum Alternate Tax
MCA	Married Couple Allowance
MIR	Mortgage Interest Relief
NIC	National Insurance Contributions
NLTCG	Net Long-Term Capital Gain
NLTCL	Net Long-Term Capital Loss
NSTCG	Net Short-Term Capital Gain
NSTCL	Net Short-Term Capital Loss
NTN	National Tax Number
OASDI	Old-Age, Survivors And Disability Insurance
PA	Personal Allowance
PAYE	Pay As You Earn
POA	Payment on Account

PPR	Principal Private Residence
RFA	Rent-Free Accommodation
RPI	Retail Price Index
RPS	Reportable Payment System
RSA	Retirement Savings Accounts
Sec.	Section
SLM	Straight-Line Method
STCG	Short-Term Capital Gain
STCL	Short-Term Capital Loss
TAA	Taxation Administration Act
TCGA	Taxation of Chargeable Gains Act, 1992 (U.K.)
TDS	Tax Deduction At Source
TIN	Taxpayer Identification Number
TMA	Taxes Management Act
U.K.	United Kingdom
U.S.	United States of America
VCT	Venture Capital Trusts
WDA	Written Down Allowance
WDV	Written Down Value

CURRENCY

AUD	Australian Dollar
PKR	Pakistan Rupee
RM	Malaysian Ringgitt
Rs.	Indian Rupee
£	U.K. Pound
$	U.S. Dollar

CURRENCY CONVERSION FOR 1997-98

1 U.K. Pound	=	64 Rupees
1 U.S. Dollar	=	39 Rupees
1 Australian Dollar	=	25 Rupees
1 Malaysian Ringgitt	=	11 Rupees
1 Pakistan Rupee	=	0.90 Rupee

FOR 2000-01

1 U.K. Pound	=	69 Rupees
1 U.S. Dollar	=	46 Rupees
1 Australian Dollar	=	25 Rupees
1 Malaysian Ringgitt	=	12 Rupees
1 Pakistan Rupee	=	0.80 Rupee

CHAPTER 1

Introduction

Business and investment operations of individuals and companies are becoming increasingly international in scope in the wake of current wave of globalisation and openness sweeping across the countries of the world. Industralisation has led to an increase in international trade which has brought the world closer and made the countries dependent upon each other. Faster communication and frequent exchange of information has helped the countries in knowing their relative position in the world, whether it is related to industrial growth, technological advancement, sports, infrastructure development or any other field. At the end of the twentieth century, globalisation has already demonstrated that economic decisions, wherever they are made in the world, must take international factors into account.[1]

Tax is a unique instrument of mobilisation of resources available with any government. Apart from raising revenue for the government, income tax provisions are being used extensively to promote social welfare and fighting the economic evils such as health care, education, recession and fiscal deficit.

Growing internationalisation of economics has made it imperative that taxation policy in a country be formulated not only keeping in view the internal factors, but also the circumstances prevailing and policy being adopted in other countries of the world. Fiscal policy, like any other governmental policy, derives its meaning and direction from the aspirations and goals of the society within which is operates, and of the people whom it serves.[2] Each country has a history marked by different internal and external environments that surround it. As a country passes from one set of circumstances to another, the pattern of its public finances typically changes.[3] Developing countries are facing the continued problem of fiscal deficit and outstanding public debt thus resulting in macroeconomic imbalances. The basic causes of fiscal imbalances in these countries are the narrow and punctured tax base, poor tax compliance and weak tax administration.

Taxation policy, which is an integral part of fiscal policy, helps in achieving social and economic objectives, removing inequality and in providing resources necessary for infrastructure development. Taxes may be either direct or indirect. Direct taxes which are payable directly by those on whom they are charged, ensures equity, are straight forward and easy to administer. Indirect taxes, on the other hand, are usually shifted and often increase the cost of goods and have to be borne by the people without knowing the burden of such taxes on their income. With the globalisation of economy, a country cannot live in isolation. A country gets directly and indirectly affected by the tax rates, tax incentives, and tax administration in other countries.

Considering these facts tax administrators are in the look out for those provisions of income tax in the other countries of the world which have been more successful in achieving its objectives whether it be better mobilisation of revenue, better tax administration, compliance and social welfare. Multinational enterprises on the other hand are evaluating the system of taxation such as tax rates, exemptions, compliance cost in different countries of the world for locating its branches and production facilities. Hence a comparative analysis of income tax provisions and practices becomes relevant.

Difference in the economic conditions and stages of development in different countries are bound to result in different income tax systems being adopted by countries. Accordingly, the system of levying tax on income in different countries differ in terms of meaning and scope of definition of income, exemptions, rates and collection procedures. Yet it is important to know how and in what manner the income tax system of one country is different from another. Also, how frequently a country changes its tax policy to solve the economic and social problems such as increase in the number of retiring people, the upcoming of more and more nuclear families. Similarly, changes are also observed in the income tax policies to revive and give boost to the stock market, to promote certain industries, and to prevent tax evasion by the people. Although a country can not follow the policy of other country without looking into the circumstances prevailing there, it can definitely make an attempt to bring changes which fulfills the requirements of the country as well as conform to the best international tax practices.

A sound tax policy is one where income tax charged from the people serves both the objectives, namely equity and revenue generation, gets the support and confidence of the people, and which brings harmony in achieving various social and economic goals. Keeping this in view, the present book compares and analyses taxation of income in India with a select developed and developing countries of the world.

The overall growth of an economy depends upon several factors including savings, investment, production, export surplus, and political stability. Direct taxes encourage savings through tax incentive schemes. These incentives help in promoting industries in those areas which are not very profitable but at the same time are important for the overall development of a country. While framing the tax policy, the government takes into account the following factors:

Social Factors. Taxation is widely used to fulfil social responsibility. The increase in the number of aged persons, changes in the family system, rise in the number of single-parent families, all these affect the taxpayer and taxable income.

Economic Factors. The overall economic growth of a country in terms of agricultural production, industrial production, and infrastructure development affects tax measures largely. While designing the tax policy, growth in GDP, per capita income, price index, inflation rate-all these factors are taken into consideration.

Political Factors. Political stability is very important for any successful tax reform. Frequent changes in the government are not desirable. Every new government introduces changes in tax rates, deductions and exemptions, partly to prove more efficient than the previous government and partly to give benefit to a particular group or a particular community to take some political advantage.

Technological Factors. Tax policy is also affected by technological advancement. The growing use of computers and internet has helped in making calculations faster, in maintaining accurate records and in communicating with the taxpayer.

Apart from these factors, there are certain income tax concepts which are frequently used and are part of a tax policy.

Income Tax Concepts

Major concepts pertaining to taxation are briefly introduced in the following paragraphs.

Tax Equity

It is possible to achieve both vertical equity and horizontal equity through income taxation. Vertical equity refers to unequal treatment of unequals. It is concerned with the distribution of tax burden among persons in different economic circumstances. Progressive taxation is considered as an equitable method of distributing the tax burden by income classes. Horizontal equity refers to equal treatment of equals, i.e. treatment of persons in essentially the same economic circumstances. Differentiation of tax liability on the basis of family responsibilities is ordinarily made through a system of personal exemptions, special exemption for the aged, and preferential treatment of capital gain.

Tax Base

Tax base basically refers to taxable income and is affected by the amount of the exemption limit, items included in taxable income, items excluded from taxable income, as well as allowances, deductions, and reliefs. It has a direct bearing on tax revenue. The wider the tax base, the larger will be the collection of tax revenue and vice versa.

Global and Scheduler Tax System

Scheduler taxation is a system where each source of income is subject to a separate treatment of rate and base. A global taxation system is one where all income from whatever sources is aggregated and one rate schedule is applied.

Actual and Effective Tax Rates

The rates given in any tax rate schedule generally show actual or nominal tax rates. These do not reflect effective tax rates. The average rate of tax on the other hand represents the effective tax rate and is found by dividing the taxable income by the total tax liability and shows the real burden imposed on the taxpayer.

Tax Administration and Tax Compliance

A sound tax policy along with efficient tax administration can produce the desired results. The method of collecting income tax affects the amount of tax revenues. The speed with which tax is collected and the collection cost-to-yield ratio are also important aspects of any tax administration. In some countries, the tax authorities assess the taxpayer's liability, whereas in others, the taxpayer makes self-assessment.

Strong administration, better management and efficient compliance mechanisms ensure higher collection. A mechanical approach to tax administration based entirely on the logistics of tax administration, that excludes effect on taxpayer's motivations is unlikely to be useful.[4] To ensure better compliance of tax law, it is important that law should be simple, equitable and easy to administer.

Tax Reforms and Personal Income Tax

Tax reform has been an integral part of the structural adjustment programme undertaken by several developing countries.[5] Successful tax reform might be defined as a change in the system, which results in the final outcomes intended by the government. Although a tax reform might seem a straightforward process, the final result frequently fails to achieve the desired outcomes.[6]

Tax reform, like other aspects of public policy in developing countries, does not lend itself readily to generalisation. Markets tend to be more segregated and imperfect than in industrialised countries, mobility tends to be lower, dependence on foreign markets for particular products is greater, and political and administrative constraints are more powerful.[7] These factors must be considered while formulating a tax policy.

The reduction in income tax rate and elimination or substantial reduction of incentives in many countries are probably the most dramatic manifestation of the wave of the tax reforms that were introduced during the mid-1980s.[8]

Personal income tax is considered the fairest method of taxation. It is the major element of progression in modern tax systems and permits differentiation of tax burdens on the basis of family responsibilities and other personal circumstances of taxpayers. The yield of tax expands or contracts more rapidly than personal income, thus imparting built-in flexibility to government revenue systems.[9] While progression in the personal income tax helps government in achieving its main objective of removing inequality, reliefs and allowances are the other alternatives at the government's disposal to consider personal circumstances of the family responsibilities of the taxpayer. A careful analysis of the social, economic, political, and technological factors is a pre-requisite to any tax reform.

Although a few studies are available on comparative income taxation, most of these comprise contribution by authors of different countries. While a comparison of income tax systems of different countries is useful, it is by no means an easy exercise. The manner of calculating taxable income and tax liability in different countries differ in many respects. While in some countries, reliefs and incentives are allowed by way of deductions from gross income, these are allowed by way of tax rebates and are deductible from tax liability in other countries.

Since taxable income is usually regarded as the income tax base, it is not comparable as in some countries it represents income after deduction of reliefs, while in others, it is income before deduction of reliefs. Similarly, the conditions for the grant of relief differs from country to country.

While some countries compile comprehensive data on income tax including the amount of reliefs, incentives, such detailed information is not available in respect of other countries.

The present work evalutes the income tax prorisions of the six selected countries, namely, the U.K., the U.S., Australia, Malaysia, Pakistan and India.

An analysis of the income tax data of the selected countries has been done. This includes the ratio of tax revenue to GDP, the ratio of individual tax payers to total population, the ratio of tax reliefs to total tax liability and the ratio of capital gains tax to total tax liability.

The book also highlights the areas where the income tax provisions of the developed countries are different from the developing countries. The income tax provisions of the selected countries are analysed on the basis of whether or not the provisions are equitable, administratively convenient and are helpful in generating more revenue.

NOTES

1. The World Bank, *World Development Report* 1999/2000 (New York: Oxford University Press, 2000), p. 31
2. Walter W. Heller, 'Fiscal Policies for Under-developed Countries', in Richard M. Bird and Oliver Oldman (eds.), *Readings on Taxation in Developing Countries* (Baltimore: The Johns Hopkins Press, 1967), p. 5
3. Arnold C. Harberger, 'Principles of Taxation Applied to Developing Countries: What We Have Learned', in Michael J. Boskin and Charles E. McLure, Jr. (eds.), *World Tax Reform: Case Studies of Developed and Developing Countries* (California: ICS Press, 1990), p. 25
4. Arindam Das-Gupta and Dilip Mookherjee, *Incentives and Institutional Reform in Tax Enforcement: An Analysis of Developing Country Experience* (Delhi: Oxford University Press, 1998), p. 19
5. Raja J. Chelliah, *Towards Sustainable Growth: Essays in Fiscal and Financial Sector Reforms in India* (Delhi: Oxford University Press, 1996), p. 138

6. Simon James, 'Self Assessment and the U.K. Tax System', *Australian Tax Forum*, Vol. 13, No. 2 (1997), pp. 205-26.
7. Richard Musgrave, 'Tax Reform in Developing Countries', in David Newbery and Nicholas Stern (eds.), *The Theory of Taxation for Developing Countries* (Washington, D.C.: Oxford University Press, 1987), p. 242
8. Charles E. McLure, Jr., 'Appraising Tax Reform', in Michael, J. Boskin and Charles E. McLure, Jr. (eds.), *World Tax Reform: Case Studies of Developed and Developing Countries* (San Francisco: ICS Press, 1990), pp. 279-88
9. Joseph A. Pechman, *Tax Reform: The Rich and the Poor* (New York: Harvester Wheatsheaf, 1989), p. 41

CHAPTER 2

Structure of Taxation of Income

The computation of taxable income and tax liability forms the most important part of any income tax structure. While formulating a tax policy, the government faces conflicting objectives. A change in the tax provisions to promote one objective may have secondary effects, which may help or hinder another objective. Although the main function of taxation is to provide revenue in order to finance public expenditure, concessions to meet social and economic policy may clash with this aim by reducing tax yields. There may also be a conflict between equity and efficiency objectives or between economic efficiency and simplicity, in that a particular measure, which promotes one of these objectives, may have a detrimental effect on the other.[1]

Tax rates, tax-free threshold, and personal allowances are the most important components of any tax structure. Inevitably, there are variations in this. While many countries provide tax-free threshold in the tax rate structure, others allow deduction on account of personal allowance from the gross income or total income. Many social changes, such as increase in the number of women earning income separately, increase in the number of one-parent family, and increase in the number of aged persons have compelled the government of many countries to change the tax structure accordingly.

Variation in the value of currency of different countries and their socio-economic environment and the overall growth make international comparison of the income tax structure a formidable task. The total income tax revenue of any country is determined on the basis of the taxable income and tax rates of that country. The ratio of the income tax revenue to the total tax revenue or Gross Domestic Product (GDP) of that country will therefore, be a sound basis to compare the adequacy or sufficiency of tax revenue of one country with that of another.

While necessary expenses incurred in earning the income are allowed for deduction everywhere, some countries even allow deduction of personal expenses or losses to find out the taxable income. There are provisions for allowances and exemptions that take into account personal circumstances as well as allow the taxpayer to retain a certain minimum income to enable him to meet his basic needs. These include personal allowance, dependent allowance, and single-parent allowance. While some allowances are deducted to find out the taxable income, others are deducted at a certain rate or percentage from the tax liability and are called tax reducers or tax rebates.

Considering the relevance of income tax structure, especially the tax rate and the taxable income components, which together determine the income tax revenue collection, various aspects of the income tax structure of the selected countries, including three developed; the U.K., the U.S., Australia and three developing; Malaysia, Pakistan and India, have been examined in this chapter. The chapter is divided into nine parts:

1. Historical background
2. Income base
3. Tax unit
4. Residential status and scope of taxable income
5. Income year
6. Tax rate structure
7. Tax-free threshold or exemption limit
8. Computation of taxable income
9. Income tax base.

HISTORICAL BACKGROUND

A brief account of the historical developments in the income tax system in the selected countries is given below.

THE U.K.

In the U.K., income tax was introduced for the first time by William Pitt in the year 1799 to provide help in the financing of war against France. The tax charged was at 10 pence in the pound on all incomes over £200 with a graduated rate between £60 and £200 and exemption below £60. Among permitted deductions were allowance for children, interest payments, and life insurance.

The tax system was, however, changed completely in 1803 with the introduction of the scheduler system backed up by an extensive system of withholding at source. In 1842, the tax was revised by Sir Robert Peel initially for a three-year period. The levy was extended a number of times and came to be accepted, becoming more or less a permanent tax in 1860, when tariff reduction made its revenue essential. The tax was gradually reduced in 1860, but was again raised during the South African war of 1899-1902.

These early taxes had been levied with minor exceptions at proportional rates. In 1909, however, the graduated rates were permanently established through the introduction of a surcharge. The tax rates were again reduced during the World War II. The exemptions were also reduced somewhat during World War II and raised after 1945. A separate tax on profits, primarily on those distributed as dividends, was introduced for the first time in 1937, largely replaced by excess profit tax during World War II and reinstated at relatively high rates in 1946.

Capital gains tax was introduced in the U.K. for the first time in 1965 as a measure to prevent taxpayers from converting their income into capital gain and thus avoiding income tax. Till the tax year 1988-89, the income of the wife was aggregated with that of her husband. From the tax year 1989-90, married couples have been taxed separately. If a married couple receives joint income, then the income is normally divided between them equally.

In the 1996-97 tax year, a self-assessment system was introduced in the U.K, thus shifting the responsibility from the inland revenue authorities to the taxpayer. The *Finance Act,* 1994 introduced major change in the basis period. In respect of business, which commenced operation, on or after April 6, 1994, the basis of assessment has been changed from the preceding year basis to the current year basis from the tax year 1997-98 onwards.

THE U.S.

The U.S. first adopted a tax on the income of individuals during the period 1864-72 to finance the civil war.[2]

The first enactment of an income tax law for individuals required the adoption of the 16th Amendment to the Constitution, which was ratified by the states in 1913. The amendment had to be adopted because the U.S. Constitution, which required that income tax be apportioned among the states in proportion to their populations, was challenged in the courts.[3] In 1895, the Supreme Court ruled that the tax was in violation of the U.S. Constitution. Thus, in 1913, the Sixteenth Amendment was ratified, which read as follows:

> The Congress shall have power to levy and collect taxes on incomes, from whatever source derived, without apportionment, among the several states and without regard to any census or enumeration.

The *Revenue Act* of 1913 imposed a flat 1 per cent tax on corporations, and tax rates ranging from 1 per cent to 7 per cent for individuals. However, very few individuals paid federal income taxes because a $3,000 personal exemption ($4,000 for married individuals) was allowed, which in many cases exceeded the taxable incomes of the individuals. In 1939, the separate Revenue Acts were codified into the *Internal Revenue Code* of 1939. The Congress replaced the 1939 Code with the *Internal Revenue Code* of 1954. This new Code introduced several new deductions and provided more accelerated depreciation rates. In 1981, the Congress substantially reduced individual rates and adopted extensive new tax incentives for savings and investment. The *Tax Reform Act* of 1986 broadened the tax base, substantially eliminating many incentive provisions and reducing individual rates further. The deduction for personal interest was eliminated, as was the preference for capital gains. Since then there have been a number of amendments increasing the maximum rate for individuals, and the reintroduction of preferential treatment of capital gains.

AUSTRALIA

Income tax was first introduced in Australia by individual states, commencing with South Australia in 1884, and in New South Wales and Victoria in 1895.[4] The first federal income tax was levied by the commonwealth in 1916 to finance Australia's participation in World War I. As a result, taxes at different rates were collected by the states and the federal government. To minimise the duplication of administrative facilities, a uniform tax system was introduced in 1923, whereby it was agreed that the federal income tax was to be collected by the state officials. The system however failed to harmonise state and federal income tax. From 1923 to 1936, there was substantial co-operation between the commonwealth and the state governments on the levying and collection of state and federal income taxes. However, significant differences appeared between the various states and the commonwealth in the make-up of the income tax legislation and in tax rates. After World War II, the federal government decided to take over the state income taxes, and levied a single federal income tax. It was agreed that the federal government would collect all income tax revenues, but hand over a proportion back to the states for their own use. States now rely on other taxes, i.e. payroll tax, stamp duty, land tax and other taxes for half of their revenue, the remaining half coming in the form of grants from the federal government.

Major changes in income tax were made in mid-1980, when the federal government introduced capital gains tax, a fringe benefit tax, and the imputation system. The maximum tax rates in this decade were reduced from 60 per cent to less than 49 per cent.

The income tax system in Australia is affected through a variety of separate Acts of Parliament. These include:

1. The Income Tax Assessment Act, 1936
2. The Income Tax Assessment Act, 1997
3. The Income Tax Regulations, 1936
4. The Income Tax Rates Act, 1986
5. The Income Tax Act, 1986
6. The Medicare Levy Act, 1986
7. The Taxation Administration Act, 1953

Australia's income tax system is based on the principle of self-assessment. Tax return forms are generally accepted at face value and are not individually reviewed. To support this approach, education and information services have been provided, enhanced post-assessment audit process has been introduced, and systematic computerised income checks for interest and certain other sources of income have been strengthened.

MALAYSIA

In Malaysia, the *Income Tax Ordinance*, 1947, was the first comprehensive Income Tax law to be introduced, though an early attempt to tax income was made in 1918 in the Straight Settlements by the War Ordinance 1918, which was repealed in 1922.[5] The 1947 Ordinance was retained, with minor changes, throughout the period leading to independence in 1957, the inclusion of Sabah and Sarawak in 1963 and the departure of Singapore in

1965. In 1967, the 1947 Ordinance as well as the separate ordinances which had applied to Sabah and Sarawak were repealed and the *Income Tax Act*, 1967, introduced with effect from the year of assessment, 1968 and subsequent years.

The Malaysian tax system is based on the U.K. tax system. Most of the appeals were carried to the Privy Council earlier. Since 1994, the Federal Courts have replaced the Supreme Court in Malaysia. From 1985, the right of appeal to the Privy Council in London was abolished.

There has not been much change in the income tax law in Malaysia. However, tax rates have been reduced in the last decade: effective rates of tax on income and on real property gains have been almost halved. Also, capital gains have been extended to cover gains from the disposal of shares in real properties.

PAKISTAN

Pakistan as an independent country came into existence in 1947 on the partition of India. The undivided India was under the British rule. The income tax law as was applicable to the undivided India continued to be applicable to the independent Pakistan. At that time, the 1922 Income Tax Legislation which was most detailed in its manifestations and legal provisions was applicable. This law continued to be applicable until 1979, when it was replaced by the *Income Tax Ordinance*, 1979. However, during this period, frequent adjustments were made to the rate structure and exemptions. A number of direct taxes have, however, been in place since its existence. Estate duties were introduced in 1950 but have since been withdrawn. The gift tax was imposed in 1963 as a federal charge but was made a provincial tax in 1973 and was abolished later on in 1985.

The *Income Tax Ordinance,* 1979 is similar in principle to the *Income Tax Act of 1922* which it replaces. The tax is intrinsically global and applies to the total income of a person from all sources unless specifically exempted, at rates to be specified in the Annual Finance Acts.

INDIA

The income tax was introduced in India from July 1, 1860, as a temporary measure to meet a financial emergency attendant upon the first war of Indian independence in 1858.[6] This was to last for five years. It applied to all income, viz., income from land, or other property, business and profession, interest as well as from salary. The assessment was to be annual. It was levied at the rate of 2 per cent on income between Rs.200 and Rs.500 and at 4 per cent on income above Rs.500. While there were over 1 million taxpayers, the administrative costs imposed by bringing in small taxpayers were thought to have contributed to the experiment's administrative and financial failure.[7] This tax came to an end on July 31, 1865. It was re-experimented with during 1869-1872 and it became a permanent measure in 1886. However, agriculture income was exempted on the grounds that the land tax and cesses already constituted a sufficient burden. In 1914, income tax accounted for 4 per cent of the total tax collection. During the First World War, the rates were increased, the highest rate being 6 per cent applicable on income above Rs.25,000. In 1922, the *Income Tax Act*, 1922 was enacted based on the English income tax system. This Act consolidated all the previous Acts. The 1922 Act is a landmark in the history of Indian income tax system. This Act was based on firm and scientific foundations. It was amended from time to time. The *Income Tax Amendment Act*, 1939 made certain major changes. These included the introduction of slab system in place of step system, abolition of exemption limit and the graduation for the purposes of corporation tax. Capital gains tax was levied in the beginning of the year 1947-48. The *Income Tax Act*, 1922 continued to be applicable to independent India and Pakistan. In India, the 1922 Act was replaced by the *Income Tax Act*, 1961, and is a comprehensive legislation. It brought changes in all aspects of income taxation, i.e. administration, procedure of assessment, and compliance to curb tax evasion. The Act of 1961 continues to be applicable till date in India, though many amendments have been made through various Finance Acts.[8]

INCOME BASE

The determination of the items to be included in the tax base is a central question in all tax systems. The tax base of income tax is the income of a person. It is therefore necessary that the tax base of income tax be elaborated and clarified in the taxation gamut. The concept of income is not amenable to any definitive articulation. It is indeed a multidisciplinary concept. Like many other concepts of general familiarity, income is still a controversial subject. However, different countries have defined the scope of income liable to tax in their Income Tax laws.

THE U.K.

In the U.K., an individual is liable to pay income tax on all his or her income for that year. The main kinds of income on which income tax is levied are ay, pension payments upon retirement, unemployment benefit, profits rom business, income from property, bank and building society interest and dividend on shares. However, certain types of income are specifically exempt from income tax in the U.K. These are interest on National Saving Certificates, interest on special savings accounts, income from scholarship, dividends on shares held in venture capital trust, certain social security benefits, winnings from betting, competition prizes, income up to £4,250 per annum received under the rent-a-room scheme, commissions, discounts and cash backs received by ordinary retail customers when purchasing goods, investments or services.

The definition of income is based on a number of categories or schedules and to be taxable a particular item must fall within any one of these schedules.

The schedules have evolved historically. Some schedules have broad coverage and other are very narrow. Each schedule is viewed as a separate source. As such, all income arising in the hands of a taxpayer is taxable except as stated above.

THE U.S.

The U.S. income tax legislation levies tax on all income regardless of source or type. The U.S. has the most extensive definition of income which is essentially a tautological statement that income is income 'from whatever source'. The starting point for calculating the tax is the gross income. The term *gross income* is defined to include all accession to wealth with well-defined exclusions. In the U.S., gross income includes wages and salaries, taxable interest, dividends, capital gains, rents, royalties, pension income including distribution of individual retirement accounts, business income from sole proprietorships, income from partnerships, income from estates and trusts, farm income, refunds of state and local income taxes, alimony received, and unemployment benefits. Gifts, bequests and proceeds from life insurance policies have been excluded from gross income. Certain employers provided benefits like health insurance to the employees, and contribution to pension plans, scholarship paid to degree seeking students, have been excluded from the gross income. In the U.S., winnings from gambling are taxable whether they arise from occasional transactions or are received by a professional gambler as compared to the U.K., where winning from gambling or lottery type prizes are not taxable unless the activity amounts to business.

AUSTRALIA

Australia has a global income tax system. However, there is no definition of the word *income* in either the *Income Tax Assessment Act*, 1936 (ITAA 36) or the *Income Tax Assessment Act*, 1997 (ITAA 97). To establish its meaning one has to look at the accepted usage. As such, income consists of income according to ordinary usage and other amounts which are included under the provisions of ITAA 36 or ITAA 97, but excluding income which is expressly or impliedly made exempt from income tax by a provision of ITAA 36 or ITAA 97. The main exemptions are scholarships, certain social security payments, bequests and gifts.

Despite the apparently global nature of the income tax system, the Australian courts have adopted a fairly narrow approach to what income is. Though the Australian system is structured quite differently from the explicit schedular nature of the U.K. system, nonetheless, the U.K. concept in cases have often been applied in determining whether specific items are income. That is why gambling and lottery winnings are not included in the general concept of income. Fringe benefits provided to the employees are not considered part of income of employees. Fringe benefits are taxed in the hands of employers under a separate legislation called the *Fringe Benefits Tax Assessment Act*, 1986 (FBTA).

MALAYSIA

The Malaysian Income Tax Act has not defined the term 'income'. However, the meaning of the term *income* has been described by the courts as a gain derived from capital, labour or both combined that is received by a taxpayer for his separate use, benefit and disposal. It is not necessarily a recurrent return. In Malaysia, the income is computed under various heads. The tax is levied on the total of the income derived under each heads. As such, an income to be taxable must fall in any of the heads. Malaysia does not levy tax on capital gains except on certain properties and on shares of companies engaged in real property business. As such, it is important to evaluate whether a receipt is a capital or a revenue receipt. If a receipt is of capital nature it is excluded from income for tax purposes. In Malaysia, as in some other countries, certain incomes are excluded from the income liable to tax. The items of income excluded in Malaysia includes, gift, scholarship, interest from savings certificates, and security and bonds issued by the government. In Malaysia also, like the U.K., certain benefits provided to the employees are exempt whereas certain benefits are valued at concessional rates.

As in the U.K. and Australia, gambling gains are not taxable in Malaysia unless one systematically carries on activities of gambling and betting with profit making intentions. Any gain made by way of prizes and awards, lotteries, and crossword puzzle are also not deemed to be income.

PAKISTAN

In Pakistan, the term *income* has been defined in the *Income Tax Ordinance*, 1979. The definition is inclusive and not exhaustive. Hence, the term not only includes those things which are stated in the definition, but also includes such things which the term signifies according to its general and natural meaning. As per Sec. 2(24) of the Ordinance, the term *income* includes any income, profit or gains from whatever source derived, chargeable to tax under any head specified and any loss of such income, profits or gains and any sum deemed to be income.

In Pakistan also, like Malaysia, income is computed under different heads of income. Any income to be taxable has to fall in any of the specified heads of income. There are six such heads. The sixth head of income is residual called 'income from other sources' and under this head income of every kind is chargeable if it is not included under any other head. As such, all kinds of income are included in Pakistan except those which are specifically excluded. The items specifically excluded are scholarship, pension to government and armed forces employees, pensions of person over 60 years of age, social security payments, such as provident fund, and contributions made by the employer. Any casual income up to PKR24,999 was specifically exempt in Pakistan till the assessment year 1995-96. This specific exemption, however, stands withdrawn from the assessment year 1996-97. Accordingly, windfall receipts, winnings from gambling, lottery and prizes may be included in the income liable to tax under the head income from other sources as specific exemption provided in the law stands withdrawn though the taxpayer can take the plea that windfall receipts are not income, hence not chargeable to tax.[9] Fringe benefits provided to the employees in Pakistan are considered part of income of the employees. In Pakistan, the face value of any bonus shares issued by a domestic company to its shareholder is specifically excluded from income. Dividend is considered part of income in the hands of the recipient but is taxed at a concessional rate.

The most noticeable exclusion in Pakistan is agriculture income. This is a general exemption available to all taxpayers except those who are having income from business or profession or who are directors of a company where this income is included in other income only to find out the average rate of tax on income other than agriculture income, although no tax is directly levied on agricultural income. This exclusion of agricultural income is the most peculiar feature of Pakistan's income tax law as it is in India.

INDIA

In India, the term *income* has been defined in the *Income Tax Act*, 1961. The definition of the term *income* is inclusive and not exhaustive. As per Sec. 2(24) of the Act, 'income' includes profits and gains, dividends, perquisites in lieu of salary, any capital gains, and winnings from lotteries, crossword puzzles, races including horse races, card games, gambling, betting of any form or nature whatsoever. In India, as in the U.K., Malaysia and Pakistan, income is computed under different heads of income. There are five such heads. The last head of income is 'income from other sources' which is a residual head. Income of every kind which is not specifically excluded from the total income under the Act shall be chargeable to income tax under this head if it is not chargeable to income tax under any other heads of income. As such, in India, income is taxable unless specifically excluded. In India, income from gambling, betting, lottery winnings are part of income liable to tax as compared to the U.K., Australia and Malaysia, where income from gambling, betting, prize winning is not considered part of income. In India, the items of income which are excluded from income liable to tax are scholarship, interest on certain securities, bonds issued by the government and public sector undertakings. Fringe benefits are taxable in the hands of employees, though at concessional rates. Contributions by employers to certain retirement plans and social security schemes are not considered income in the hands of employees. In India, as in Pakistan, agricultural income has been specifically excluded from income liable to tax irrespective of its amount. But agriculture income is considered for rate purposes where the taxpayer has income other than agriculture income. This means a higher rate of tax on income other than agriculture income but no direct tax on agriculture income. Prior to June 1, 1997 dividend income was takable in the hands of shareholders. From June 1, 1997, any dividends distributed by domestic companies do not form part of income of the shareholders. However, domestic companies are required to pay tax (at concessional rate) at the time of distribution of dividend. In India, income from export of merchandise, computer software, films and income from industrial units set up in certain notified areas and states are also exempt from the income liable to tax and as such do not form part of the income base.

TAX UNIT

Tax has to be levied on some entity. This entity is the 'tax unit'. Equity demands that equal treatment is meted out to equals in the tax system. But this equality can be achieved only if the tax structure of the society is such that the composition of tax units is the same. 'Individual' and 'company' are the common tax units in all the selected countries. In both, Pakistan and India, partnership is a tax unit, called 'firm' and taxed independently. In the U.K., U.S., Australia and Malaysia, though 'partnership' is required to submit returns, it is not considered as a separate tax entity for levying income tax. The profit or loss in a partnership is allocated to the partners. The 'partnership' as a tax unit is not being examined here. 'Company' as a tax unit has been examined in Chapter 7. This chapter examines the individual as a tax unit.

The choice of an individual as an appropriate taxable unit involves complex issues of social and economic policy and has been the subject of much discussion in many of the countries.[10] A decision to treat the individual as a tax unit will mean that married couples with the same amount of income will pay different amounts of tax depending upon how much income is earned by each partner. At the same time, a decision to treat the married couples as a tax unit will mean that such couples are treated differently from other couples whose economic and social arrangements are functionally similar. In deciding whether an individual or a couple or a family (spouses and minor children) should constitute the unit, two points must be taken into consideration, which are:

1. The tax liability should be unaffected by marital status.
2. Couples with equal means should pay the same taxes.

Arguments have been advanced both for individual as a tax unit and family as a tax unit. Arguments in favour of the former are that the tax liability is independent of the marital status, it is independent of earnings of other family members and also because the taxation of the individual as a tax unit is simpler. The argument against the individual as a tax unit is that in the case of unequal income of partners, the tax liability is more as compared to the tax liability where the income of partners is equal. The individual unit basis ignores the basic fact that families are the units in which civilised societies are organised. If the family is the tax unit then there will be equal tax liability both when a couple has an equal income or an unequal income. On the other hand, the drawback of the family as a tax unit relates to the privacy of financial matters and proper compliance in the absence of complete information. However, different countries have adopted different methods and have enacted various provisions to resolve these issues.

The position of six selected countries with respect to whether an individual is considered as tax unit or a couple or a family or a combination of any of these is given below.

THE U.K.

In the U.K., till 1972, a married couple was treated as a 'tax unit'. The wife's income was attributed to the husband who used to be the technical taxpayer. However, in 1972, this was changed when an option was given to the couple to elect to have the income taxed separately as a separate tax unit. However, this option was beneficial to higher income taxpayers. Hence, in 1990, the U.K. switched over to the individual tax unit system. Both earned and unearned income are now taxed individually. Separate annual exemption for both spouses is allowed. Children are also treated as separate taxpayers.

THE U.S.

In the U.S., the development of tax unit has been in sharp contrast to the U.K. Till 1948, the individual was a 'tax unit'. However, in 1948, couples were permitted to file 'joint' returns and to aggregate income and compute their tax under a tax rate structure which had income brackets twice as wide as the corresponding brackets used by an unmarried person. This was optional and was available to married couples only. However, with this option, the couples could pay tax lower than the individual with the same amount of income in case a spouse was having a much higher income as compared to his spouse. To overcome this problem, this system has been modified from time to time. Presently, individuals may file returns under four different rate schedules, applying to different forms of household composition. The width of the tax brackets is wider for the joint filers of return than for single filers. There is separate rate schedule for married couples filing returns separately. There is a separate rate schedule which applies to heads of households which is used by unmarried individuals having a dependent child. In this schedule, brackets are wider than the rate schedule for single filers, but narrower than the rate schedule for joint filers. As such, there are four 'tax units', i.e. 'single', 'head of household', 'married filing jointly', and 'married filing separately'.

In the U.S., dependent children are treated as separate taxpayers. However, the unearned income of children under 14 is taxed at the parents' highest marginal rate.

AUSTRALIA

In Australia, the tax unit is an 'individual' only. Separate returns have to be filed by wife and husband. However, there is a system of family tax assistance whereby the tax-free threshold is increased by AUD1,000 or more depending upon the number of children in a family. There are two types of family tax assistance. The first, known as Part A benefit applies where there is at least one dependent child and the family income is less than AUD70,000 (increasing by AUD3,000 for each dependent child after the first). Where this benefit applies, the standard tax-free threshold for one member of a couple or for a single parent, is increased by AUD1,000 for each dependent child. The second type of family tax assistance known as Part B benefit applies when there is one primary breadwinner of the family and at least one dependent child under 5 years. When this benefit applies, the standard tax-free threshold is further increased by AUD2,500.

In Australia, the income of children is treated separately. However, special rules apply in calculating tax payable on the income of minors to discourage income-splitting by means of diversion of income to children. Under these rules, the unearned income of minors over a certain level (AUD416 for the year 1998-99) is taxed at the highest marginal rate of tax (47 per cent for the year 1998-99). The rules apply to income including capital gains derived by minors directly or through a trust. Unearned income includes dividend, rent, royalties, but excludes 'business' income and employment income. These rules in Australia are different from the rules in the U.S., where the unearned income of children under 14 is taxed at a special rate and that too at the highest marginal rate applicable to the parents, not at the maximum marginal rate given in the tax rate structure.

MALAYSIA

In Malaysia, prior to the year of assessment 1991, only a married woman who derived her income from employment, pension or a qualifying profession could elect to be assessed separately from her husband. From the year of assessment 1991, a married woman is assessed separately on her income from all sources. However, a married woman can still elect that her total income be aggregated with the total income of her husband. This option is to be exercised for each year. The option is to be exercised by the wife only. No separate rate schedule is applicable in such cases of joint returns as is in the U.S. However, a relief of RM3,000 is allowed to the husband if his wife elects for joint assessment.

The income of children is taxable in the same way as an adult and his (the child's) obligation to file an annual return and his right to claim personal relief are the same as that of an adult. Thus, in Malaysia, unlike the U.S., Australia, both earned as well as unearned income are taxed separately in the hands of children at ordinary rates.

PAKISTAN

The 'tax unit' in Pakistan is the individual. Joint returns cannot be filed by wife and husband. The husband and wife have to pay tax on their own income, both earned and unearned. However, to discourage the transfer of income, there are provisions whereby the income of a spouse from an asset transferred to the other spouse without adequate consideration is deemed as the income of the transferor. As such, if a husband transfers any property or asset to his wife without adequate consideration, the income from such property or asset will be deemed as the income of the husband, not of the wife. However, this provision is applicable only on those assets which are transferred after marriage. Assets, transferred before marriage, are not subject to these clubbing provisions.

In Pakistan, properties are often transferred by husbands to their wives in lieu of Haq-Mehar which is a legal obligation of the husband in Muslim marriage. As such, asset or property transferred to the extent of Haq-Mehar is considered as adequate consideration. However, if the value of the property exceeds the amount of Haq-Mehar, the income proportionate to the amount exceeding, is deemed and added to the total income of the husband. Income from a partnership firm where both husband and wife are partners, is clubbed and taxed in the hands of either of the spouses.

The Pakistan income tax law is, however, presently not clear in whose hands this clubbing is to be done. There were similar provisions in India till the income year 1991-92 when it was clarified that this clubbing would be done in the hands of the spouse whose income is higher.

In Pakistan, the income of minor children is taxed separately. However, as in the case of transfer between spouses, income from assets transferred by parents to the minor children without adequate consideration is deemed as the income of the parent who transferred the asset and is clubbed with his or her income. However, when the children obtain the age of majority such income is considered as the income of such children. Income of minor from the business or profession except from the business acquired through inheritance is also deemed to be the income of the parents.

The tax officer has the option to decide whether the same will be clubbed with the income of the father or the mother. Similarly, the income of a minor from a partnership firm in which his/her father or mother is partner or from a partnership firm where capital contribution, in any form, of the minor has not been provided out of inheritance passed on to the minor, is deemed to be income of the parents.

INDIA

As in the U.K., Australia and Pakistan, the tax unit is the individual. Wife and husband are both assessable to tax in their individual capacity on their income, earned as well as unearned. Both wife and husband can claim separate reliefs, and rebates available under the law. Up to the income year 1991-92, there were provisions for the clubbing of income of wife and husband as in Pakistan if both were partners in the same partnership firm. However, from the income year 1992-93, income from a partnership firm is not considered as income in the hands of partners and consequently this provision for the clubbing of income of the partnership firm has been withdrawn. However, like Pakistan, income from assets transferred without adequate consideration by one spouse to another is considered income of the transferor. Moreover, any salary or commission, fee paid to the spouse (except to a spouse who possesses technical or professional qualifications for the application of his or her knowledge and experience) by a concern in which the other spouse has a substantial interest is clubbed with the income of other spouse.

In India, prior to the income year 1992-93, the income of minor children was considered separately though there were clubbing provisions almost similar to the present clubbing provisions in Pakistan as stated above. A minor was entitled to all the reliefs and deductions provided under the law. However, from the income year 1992-93 the income of a minor child is not considered separately. All income of minor children (other than on account of any manual work or activity involving the application of his skill, talent or specialised knowledge and experience) is included in the income of the parent whose total income excluding the income includible of minor is greater. Minor children suffering from permanent physical disability are excluded from the above provisions.

Conclusion

In a progressive tax structure, which is being followed in all these countries, both the individual unit and family unit basis are bound to result in anomalies and problems. Which one of these is more acceptable is a matter of social choice. All the countries under study have made provisions taking into account their social structure and to achieve the objectives of equity and administrative convenience. In the U.K., Australia, Pakistan and India, the tax unit is the 'individual'.

In Malaysia also, the tax unit is the individual although an option has been given to the wife to get her income aggregated with that of her husband. However, in the U.S. there are still options. Among all the selected countries, the U.S. is the only country which has taken into consideration the family responsibility in its rate structure and has thus provided separate tax rates for different category of taxpayers depending mainly upon how much responsibility one normally bears. In Pakistan and India, though the tax unit is the 'individual', various provisions have been enacted to check the transfer of income between spouses to reduce tax liability.

As regards the income of children, it is treated separately in all these countries except India. In the U.K. and Malaysia, both the earned and the unearned income of children are taxed in the hands of children only, whereas in the U.S. and Australia, though both are taxed in the hands of children, the unearned income is taxed at a higher rate. In Pakistan, the income of minor from business and assets transferred by parents is aggregated with that of the parents and taxed with the income of the parents.

In India, all income of minor (except the income earned by minor from his own skill and talent) is aggregated with that of parents and taxed with the income of the parents. Provisions in India and Pakistan regarding clubbing of the income of spouse and minors show that engagement of children in any business and women in family business is mainly for tax saving purposes and thus need to be discouraged by aggregating their income in the hands of the husband or the parents as the case may be.

Residential Status and Scope of Taxable Income

The incidence of taxation varies with the residential status. Various countries have laid down the technical test of territorial connection for determining the status of the taxpayer. In some countries the test of stay for a particular number of days is applied, in others, the test of domicile is applied, and further in some others, the test of citizenship is applied. Not only that, the scope of income liable to tax for different categories of taxpayers also differs in different countries. As such, it is important to examine the division of taxable entities in different categories and then to examine the income chargeable to tax for each category of taxpayers.

The manner in which residential status is determined and accordingly, the types of income which are taxable based on the residential status in the selected countries have been examined below.

THE U.K.

In the U.K., the extent to which an individual taxpayer's income is chargeable to tax depends upon that individual's residence, ordinary residence and domicile. Here, for an individual there are three categories; resident, ordinary resident and non-resident. The term *residence* is not defined in the tax legislation. Accordingly, the ordinary meaning is considered. The term *to reside* means 'to dwell permanently or for a considerable time, to have one's usual or settled abode, to live in or at a particular place'.[11]

Resident

An individual is a resident if he fulfils any of the following conditions:

1. If he is physically present in the U.K. for at least 183 days during a given tax year (excluding days of arrival or departure); or
2. If he is in the habit of making regular visits to the U.K. (averaging at least 91 days per tax year). In that circumstance, two situations may arise as follows.

   (a) an ex-resident who has now left the U.K. but who makes regular visits as described above is deemed to be a U.K. resident for the whole of each tax year during which the visits continue.

   (b) an individual not previously a U.K. resident but who begins making regular visits as described above is deemed to be a U.K. resident from the fifth year of the visits. However, if the visits are going to be regular, the individual may be regarded as a U.K. resident with effect from the first year of the visit.

The concept of the U.K. residence applies for a full tax year. An individual is either a U.K. resident for the full year or none of it and it is not possible to divide a tax year into periods of residence and non-residence. However, apportionment of a tax year is permissible in the following situations:

1. if, in the year of arrival an individual takes up permanent residence in the U.K or comes to stay in the U.K. for at least 2 years.
2. if, in the year of departure an individual leaves the U.K. in order to take up permanent residence abroad or to live abroad for at least 3 years.
3. if, in the years of departure and return, an individual leaves the U.K. in order to take up employment abroad under a contract of employment for at least a full tax year.

Personal allowances are allowed for a full year despite apportionment of a year into two periods of resident and non-resident status.

Ordinarily Resident

The term *ordinary residence* is also not defined in the tax legislation. In ordinary terms, an individual is an ordinarily resident in the U.K. if he is habitually a U.K. resident, i.e. resident year after year. As such, the term *ordinary residence* has a narrower meaning than residence and indicates a greater degree of permanence. An ordinarily resident is deemed to be a resident even if he is temporarily abroad during a tax year (i.e. not present for at least 183 days but not absent for the entire tax year).

The extent of taxability of income in the U.K. also depends upon an individual's domicile. Domicile is usually acquired at birth. A child takes the domicile of the father or legal guardian. Individuals over 16 years of age can take a domicile of choice. The intention of the individual must be proved by way of severing all ties with his domicile of origin and his actions to demonstrate his intention to settle permanently in the domicile of his choice. As such, while an individual may have a dual residence i.e. residences in two countries, one can only have one domicile at any one time.

Non-resident

Individuals other than residents, and residents but not ordinarily residents, are classified as non-residents.

Scope of income liable to tax

Individuals who are resident in the U.K. for a tax year are liable to pay tax on all of their income including both the U.K. income and the overseas income.

Individuals who are residents but not domiciled in the U.K. are liable for tax on the U.K. income and the overseas income only to the extent it is remitted to the U.K.

Individuals who are non-residents are liable to pay tax on the U.K. income only. Personal allowances are not allowed to non-residents except to those who are citizens of European Economic Area or the Commonwealth or Isle of Man, Channel Islands and persons who used to reside in the U.K. but now reside abroad for health reasons. Interest on the U.K. Government Securities is generally exempt if the recipient is other than an ordinary resident, i.e. non-resident and resident but not ordinarily resident. Income of non-residents is computed and taxed at the same rate as that of residents.

Residents and ordinarily residents are liable to capital gains tax on all disposals of chargeable assets wherever the assets are situated. Non-residents are not liable to capital gains tax even in relation to disposals of assets situated in the U.K. However, capital gains arising from business assets situated in the U.K. are liable to capital gains tax.

In the case of apportionment of tax year into two periods of residence and non-residence, the income rules are applied for each period as if each period were a separate tax year. To mitigate the hardship of double taxation of overseas income in the hands of the taxpayer, the U.K. law provides for a double tax relief. This relief in the case of a country where double taxation agreement exists is either by way of exemption of certain categories of income in either of the countries or by way of tax credit paid in another country. Where there is no double taxation agreement, the foreign income received net of foreign tax is grossed up and charged to the U.K. income tax and relief is given to the taxpayer of the lower of the amount of foreign tax suffered and the amount of the U.K. tax due on such foreign income. The tax due on the foreign income is the difference between the tax due on the taxpayer's total income including foreign income and the tax which would be due if this foreign income were ignored. However, for obtaining this relief, the taxpayer concerned must take all reasonable steps to minimise the amount of foreign tax liability.

THE U.S.

The scope of the total income chargeable to tax in the U.S. depends upon whether the taxpayer is a U.S. citizen, or an alien. There are three categories of taxpayers: U.S. citizen, resident alien, and non-resident alien.

The rules regarding the determination of resident alien in the US are detailed and complicated. These rules are discussed in brief and are as follows:

Resident Alien

An individual is a resident alien for income tax purposes if he:

1. is a lawful permanent resident of the U.S. at any time during the calendar year;
2. meets the requirement of the 'substantial presence' test; or
3. makes the first year election under Code Sec. 7701(b)(4).

An individual meets the substantial presence test if:

(a) such individual was present in the U.S. on at least 31 days during the calendar year; and

(b) the sum of number of days on which such individual was present in the U.S. during the current year and the two preceding calendar year (when multiplied by the multiplier determined under the following table) equals or exceeds 183 days)

In the case of days in:	*The applicable multiplier is:*
Current year	1
1st preceding year	1/3
2nd preceding year	1/6

Similarly, an individual can make election to be treated as resident provided he fulfils the condition of stay of some minimum number of days during the current year and the preceding year. (A detailed explanation of these two conditions is not given here.)

Non-resident Alien

An individual who is neither a citizen of the U.S. nor a resident alien is a non-resident alien.

Scope of Income Liable to Tax

The U.S. citizens and resident aliens are taxed on their world-wide income without regard to whether or not the income arose from a transaction or an activity originating within or outside the geographical borders of the country.

However, a qualified individual[12] (U.S. citizen and resident alien) working in a foreign country is allowed to exclude up to $74,000 (for the calendar year 1999) of foreign earned income[13] attributable to the period of residence in the foreign country as well as certain employer-provided housing costs.

In the U.S. also, to mitigate the hardship of double taxation, a taxpayer has the option either to deduct the foreign income tax paid or claim tax credit in respect of the foreign income tax paid against the U.S. income tax. The credit is allowed for the income tax imposed by a foreign country on a U.S. citizen, whether a resident or non-resident, both including the domestic corporation. A resident alien is allowed credit of the foreign income tax paid if the country of which such resident alien is a citizen, allows a similar credit to the citizens of the U.S. residing in such country while levying income tax. However, there is a limit to the amount of the foreign tax credit. This credit cannot be used to reduce tax liability on income from sources within the U.S. The foreign tax credit is limited to the tax liability on the foreign income at the average rate of U.S. tax liability on world-wide taxable income.

Non-resident aliens are however taxed only on income that is effectively connected with a trade or business conducted within the U.S. and on a fixed and determinable annual or periodic income from sources within the U.S.

Non-resident aliens are taxed in the same manner as the U.S. citizens. A non-resident alien who performs personal services within the U.S. during the tax year is considered engaged in a U.S. trade or business except when he is temporarily present in the U.S. for 90 days or less during the tax year and the compensation does not exceed $3,000 for services performed for a non-resident individual or for foreign corporation or a firm, not engaged in a U.S. business. The non-resident alien engaged in the U.S. trade or business is allowed to make deductions to the extent that they relate to income effectively connected with the U.S. trade or business and the deduction for charitable contributions. He can claim personal exemption except for the residents of certain countries. The U.S. source fixed or determinable periodical income[14] is taxed at a flat rate of 30 per cent unless a lower rate is fixed under tax treaty entered into by the U.S. The U.S. source capital gains net income is subject to tax if effectively connected with the conduct of a U.S. business. Other capital gains are not taxed unless the non-resident alien is present in the U.S. for at least 183 days. If the other capital gains are taxed because the non-resident alien was present in the U.S. for 183 days period, the tax rate applicable on other capital gains is 30 per cent.

In the U.S., change of residence during the year is possible. An alien who settles or abandons his residence during the tax year is taxable for that year as if it consists of two periods, one that of residence and the other that of non-residence. Thus, in the U.S., the status of a taxpayer is more linked to his citizenship, unlike all other selected countries, where the status depends upon the residence and the domicile. The credit of foreign tax paid is allowed to all residents irrespective of the citizenship of the taxpayer and whether or not there is any corresponding concession available to the U.S. citizen in the country of which the taxpayer is a citizen.

AUSTRALIA

In Australia, the liability to income tax is decided on the basis of residence and the source of income of the taxpayer. There are only two kinds of status for fixing the liability to tax in Australia, resident and non-resident.

In Australia, the status of an individual whether he is resident or non-resident is decided by applying the primary or ordinary test of residence, besides applying three statutory residence tests. While applying the primary test of residence, the domicile, nationality and citizenship are not considered.

Resident

Individuals are considered residents if their behaviour shows a degree of continuity, routine or habit over a considerable period that is consistent with residing in Australia. Six months is considered a considerable time. If a person is not resident in Australia within the ordinary meaning stated above, then three statutory tests are considered and an individual is considered a resident, if he satisfies any one of these three tests:

The first is *'the domicile and permanent place of abode'* test. A person whose domicile is in Australia, is deemed to be a resident of Australia under this test, unless the person's permanent place of abode is outside the country. Permanent abode means, that which is not a temporary or transitory abode. The factors which are considered for this test include the intended and actual length of stay overseas, whether a home has been established outside

Australia, and the durability of the person's association with a place outside Australia.

The second test is called '*the constructive residence*' test. Under this, an individual is a constructive resident if he is actually present in Australia continuously or intermittently for a total period of more than half the year of income, except in those cases where the person's usual place of abode is outside Australia and there is no intention to take up residence in Australia. The test is applied with reference to the relevant income year of the taxpayer.

The third test is of '*the contributing member of the superannuation fund for Commonwealth government officers*'. Even the spouse or child under 16 of such a person is considered resident under this test.

In Australia, it is possible for an individual to be a resident for part of the year. The tax-free threshold is available pro rata for the period for which the taxpayer is resident in Australia.

Non-resident

An individual who does not qualify to be a resident under any of the above tests is considered a non-resident.

Scope of Income Liable to Tax

In Australia, a resident taxpayer is taxable on income derived from all sources whether in or out of Australia, i.e. world-wide income. Income includes both the ordinary income and the statutory income. On the other hand, a non-resident taxpayer is taxable on income from the Australian sources.

Income derived by a resident taxpayer from employment in a foreign country is not included in the total income if it is from a continuous employment of at least 91 days, and the taxpayer is an Australian resident at that time. This exemption to the resident is not available if there is no income tax on this income in the foreign country.

Non-residents are taxed on income from Australian sources only. Non-residents are not taxed on the foreign source income. However, capital gains arising from the capital gains tax event that occurs in relation to an asset with an Australian connection, is taxable in Australia even though the gain does not have an Australian source.

Income in the hands of a non-resident taxpayer is generally taxed in the same manner as in the case of a resident. The non-resident taxpayers are entitled to exemptions and business deductions and special incentive against gross income as are available to residents. Non-residents are exempt from medical levy but cannot claim concessional rebates for dependants and medical expenses.

In Australia, the tax rates applicable to non-residents are different from those applicable to residents. For the purpose of tax rates, the non-resident is called a prescribed non-resident[15] (Sec. 3 (1) of the *Income Tax Rates Act, 1986*). As such, a person in receipt of social security or veteran entitlement is excluded from the non-resident category without applying the test of residency. There is no tax-free threshold for prescribed non-residents and thus, the prescribed non-residents pay tax on the very first dollar of taxable income. The tax rates applicable to the prescribed non-resident individual taxpayer are higher than those applicable to resident taxpayers. The minimum rate is 29 per cent up to AUD20,000 of taxable income and the maximum rate is 47 per cent on income exceeding AUD60,000 (for the income year 2000-01). Dividends, interest and royalties paid to non-residents are subject to final withholding tax. Amounts which have been subject to withholding tax are excluded from the assessable income of non-residents. The rate of withholding tax on dividends and royalty is 30 per cent. However, in the case of payment to residents of countries with which Australia has a double taxation agreement, the withholding rate is 15 per cent for dividends and 10 per cent for royalty. The withholding rate on interest is a flat 10 per cent on gross amount without deducting expenses incurred to earn that interest. This rate is unaffected by the double taxation agreement.

Australia has entered into double taxation avoidance agreements with many countries. These agreements are to prevail in the event of conflicting provisions in ITAA 36 and ITAA 97 (other than ITAA 36, Sec. 160AO and the general anti-avoidance provisions of ITAA 36, Pt. IVA). These agreements contain rules to classify a person as a resident of Australia or of the other country and also contain rules on taxing rights over certain class of income to the country of residence only.

Resident taxpayers are also entitled to a credit of the foreign tax paid on the foreign income. The credit is allowed at the average rate of Australian tax on the foreign income. The maximum foreign tax credit paid on foreign income is the Australian tax payable on that income. The foreign tax paid in excess of the Australian tax credit is ignored.

MALAYSIA

In Malaysia, as in Australia, the liability to income tax depends upon the residential status of the taxpayer and the source of income. In Malaysia, a taxpayer may be either a resident or a non-resident.

The residential status in Malaysia is dependent upon the stay of taxpayer in Malaysia and his status in the preceding or the succeeding year. Citizenship has no relevance while deciding the residential status.

Resident

There are four situations in which an individual can acquire the status of a resident. These are:

1. An individual is a resident if he is in Malaysia in the basis year (income year) for a period or periods which in total are 182 days or more. Part of a day is counted as a full day. This period need not be continuous.
2. An individual is a resident if he is in Malaysia for a period of less than 182 days in the basis year, but such a period is linked to a period of 182 or more consecutive days throughout which he is in Malaysia (the qualifying period) either immediately preceding or immediately succeeding that

income year. Temporary absences from Malaysia in connection with his services in Malaysia or attending conferences, studies abroad or due to ill health and social visits not exceeding 14 days in total are treated as part of the qualifying period.

3. When an individual is in Malaysia in the basis year for 90 days or more and in any 3 out of 4 years immediately preceding the basis year he was either resident in Malaysia or was in Malaysia for 90 days or more. The period of 90 days need not be consecutive.
4. An individual may not be in Malaysia in the income year but still become a resident if he is resident in the basis year immediately following the basis year and was resident for the 3 years immediately preceding year, he is deemed a resident for that particular year.

Non-resident

An individual who does not fall within the above four categories is 'non-resident'.

Scope of Income Liable to Tax

The Malaysian income tax is territorial in jurisdiction. Unlike other countries, world-wide income is not taxed in Malaysia. The income which has a Malaysian source is taxed both in the hands of residents and non-residents. Where its source is outside Malaysia it is taxed only in the hands of residents only when it is remitted into Malaysia. However, the source of income from employment is the location where the services are rendered. The place where remuneration is paid is not relevant. There is no definition of the remittance. However, the general principles of taxation on income are applied in Malaysia. The remittance which is taxed in Malaysia in the hands of residents must come out of income which has accrued or derived from overseas sources and is not out of capital. The remittance must belong to the resident taxpayer and must be actually received or brought into Malaysia and unless that happens there is no question of taxing the income. Moreover, if the accumulated overseas income is capitalised by the taxpayer then remittance of such capital is not taxable because the income has changed its nature to capital before being remitted. The remittance of such income which is not taxable as per Malaysia Income Tax Law, is not taxed. Non-residents in Malaysia are not entitled to personal reliefs except residents of a country with which there is double taxation agreement and the reciprocal relief is provided to the residents of Malaysia in that country. The tax rate applicable to non-resident individuals is a flat 29 per cent (from the year of assessment 2000) as against the progressive tax rate structure applicable to resident individuals. The income of non-resident persons consisting of interest derived from Malaysia is taxed at 15 per cent of the gross amount. Royalty incomes are taxed at 10 per cent on the gross amount. The income of non-residents by way of remuneration or other income in respect of services performed or rendered in Malaysia by a public entertainer are taxed at the rate of 10 per cent of the gross amount. Dividends paid to non-resident taxpayers by a Malaysian company are not taxable as they are paid out of the paying company's taxed income.

In Malaysia, income earned abroad is taxed only when it is remitted in the hands of residents. It does not tax income on a world-wide basis As such, residents of Malaysia have double taxation problem only when their overseas income is remitted into Malaysia. The double taxation agreement entered into by Malaysia with various countries provide relief in such cases by providing an exemption in the country of origin on income or by granting tax credit against the tax suffered on that income in the other country.

PAKISTAN

In Pakistan, taxpayers have been classified into two categories as in Australia on the basis of their residential status, i.e. 'resident' and 'non-resident'.

Resident

An individual is a resident in Pakistan in an income year if he is in Pakistan in the said year for a period of 182 days or more or he is in Pakistan in the income year for 90 days or more and was in Pakistan for 365 days or more during the 4 years preceding the said income year.

It is not essential that the individual's stay in Pakistan is continuous. Residential status is determined in respect of each income year and it may vary from year to year.

Non-resident

An individual who does not fulfil the conditions stated above is a 'non-resident'.

Scope of Income Liable to Tax

A resident is chargeable to tax for his total world-wide income. The total income of a resident includes all income from whatever source derived, which is received, deemed to be received, or which accrues or arises or is deemed to accrue or arise to him in Pakistan and also which accrues or arises to him outside Pakistan.

A non-resident is taxed on income which is received, deemed to be received or which accrues or arises or is deemed to accrue or arise[16] to him in Pakistan. A non-resident is not taxed on income which accrues or arises to him outside Pakistan. Receipt of income refers to receipt on the first occasion when the recipient gets the money under his control. Once an amount is received as income, any further remittance or transmission to another place does not result in receipt but is treated as transfer of money.

Income from salary is deemed to accrue or arise in Pakistan if it is earned in Pakistan, irrespective of where it is paid. Income for services rendered in Pakistan is regarded as income earned in Pakistan. Any salary paid by the Pakistan Government or a local authority to its employees is deemed to accrue or arise in Pakistan, no matter where the employees are working and at which place the salary is paid. Similarly, any income which accrues or arises outside Pakistan by virtue of any business connection in Pakistan, shall be deemed to accrue or arise in Pakistan. Income through or from any property, asset or source of income in Pakistan is deemed to accrue or arise in Pakistan. Property includes any tangible or immovable property and the term 'asset' would include all intangible rights and consequently interest, dividend, patents, copyrights, royalties, and rental income etc. Capital gains earned by a non-resident by transfer of any capital asset situated in Pakistan is deemed to accrue or arise in Pakistan. Interest payable by a resident or a government (except where interest is payable in respect of any debt used for the purpose of a business outside Pakistan) or a non-resident (in respect of any debt used for the business in Pakistan) is deemed to accrue or arise in Pakistan. The dividend paid by a Pakistan company to any shareholder outside Pakistan is deemed to accrue or arise in Pakistan. Income once included in the total income on the accrual basis, is not included again on the receipt basis when such income is later on received by the taxpayer.

Income of a non-resident is taxed at a flat rate of 30 per cent without any tax-free threshold limit or tax payable on the total income as a resident, whichever is greater. As such, the minimum rate of tax is 30 per cent but in case the total income falls in a higher bracket as a resident, then that rate is applicable. However, a non-resident taxpayer has an option to be taxed according to the proportionate share of his total income in Pakistan to his total world-wide income if he exercises his option when he becomes assessable in Pakistan for the first time through a notice in writing to the tax officer in the year of assessment. The option once exercised is final and applicable to all assessments thereafter. Non-residents in Pakistan like residents are covered by the presumptive taxation of certain types of income such as dividends, income from contracts and imports. The tax withheld on such income is treated as final tax liability on the whole of such amount, which is deemed to be income. The tax rate on dividend income is 10 per cent of the gross amount.

Pakistan's Income Tax Law also provides for relief from double taxation like other countries. This relief is available to resident taxpayers of Pakistan only. The credit for the double taxed income depends upon the nature and the extent of the provisions contained in the double taxation agreement of the concerned country. The amount of credit to be allowed for foreign tax against Pakistan tax in respect of any income cannot exceed the amount which would be arrived at by applying the average rate of such tax to the double taxed income. Foreign tax credit relief is available in Pakistan in respect of those countries also where there is no bilateral agreement to avoid double taxation. In Pakistan, unilateral relief is allowed for foreign tax if the resident taxpayer proves to the satisfaction of the tax officer that he has paid income tax on the income, which has accrued or arisen to him during the income year outside Pakistan in any country. The foreign tax credit allowed is a sum equal to the tax calculated on such double-taxed income at the average rate of tax of Pakistan or the average rate of tax of the said country whichever is lower.

INDIA

In India, the taxability of an individual is decided on the basis of the residence of the individual. On this basis of residence, there are three categories of taxpayers in India, i.e. resident, non-resident and not ordinarily resident. Whether a taxpayer falls in one category or the other depends mainly upon his stay in India during the income year and/or the earlier years.

Resident

An individual is 'resident' if he fulfils any one of the following conditions:

1. He has been in India for a period or periods amounting in all to 182 days or more during the income year called 'previous year'; or
2. He has been in India for a period of 60 days or more in the income year, and has been in India for a period or periods accounting in all to 365 days or more in the 4 years preceding the previous year.

However, under the second test, a citizen of India who leaves India in the income year for the purposes of employment outside India or as a member of the crew of an Indian ship or if a person of Indian origin (a person is deemed to be of Indian origin if he or either of his parents or any of his grandparents was born in undivided India), who being outside India comes on a visit to India in the income year, will be resident when such individual is in India for a period or periods amounting in all to 182 days instead of 60 days. As such, the citizenship of India narrows the scope while determining the status as resident as compared to the U.S. where the citizenship of the U.S. extends the scope of income liable to the U.S. tax.

Not ordinarily Resident

An individual (though a resident as per the above test) who has not been a resident in India in 9 out of the 10 income years preceding the income year under consideration is not ordinarily resident for that income year. Similarly, an individual who has not been in India for 730 days or more during the 7 income years preceding the income year under consideration, is considered as not ordinarily resident. Not ordinarily resident is one who is resident but since he fulfils either of or none of the above two conditions is considered as resident but not ordinarily resident. In India, the status of 'not ordinarily resident' is different from the status of ordinarily resident in the U.K.

Non-resident

'Non-resident' means a person who is not a resident.

In India, it is not possible to have two kinds of status for the same income year. If an individual is a resident in respect any source of income in the income year, he is deemed to be a resident in India in that income year in respect of each of his other sources of income. However, a taxpayer can have different residential status for different years. It is possible that a taxpayer may be resident in more than one country at the same time for tax purposes.

Scope of Income Liable to Tax

A resident in India is also liable to pay tax on the world-wide income. A resident taxpayer is liable to tax in respect of income which is received, or deemed to be received, income which accrues or arises or is deemed to accrue or arise to him in India as well as outside India during the income year. A resident but not ordinarily resident is also liable to tax on all income stated above except that in respect of the income which accrues or arises outside India, he is liable to tax only on income from such business that is controlled from a place within India. A non-resident is liable to tax only in respect of income which is received or is deemed to be received in India or which accrues or arises or is deemed to accrue or arise in India. He is not liable to tax on income that accrues or arises outside India. The terms 'receipt', 'accrues or arises' have the same meaning under the Indian income tax law as mentioned while examining the tax provisions of Pakistan.

In India, the income of non-resident individual taxpayers is computed and taxed in the same manner as that of residents. Unlike Australia, Malaysia, and Pakistan, the tax rate applicable to non-residents in India is the same as that of residents. Non-residents are also eligible for the tax-free threshold available to residents. However, the income by way of dividend (other than the dividend declared by Indian companies on which dividend distribution tax has been paid by the company), interest received from the government or Indian concern on money borrowed in foreign currency and income from units of mutual funds purchased in foreign currency, are taxable at a flat rate of 20 per cent on the total amount without any deduction of expenditure incurred and without the benefit of allowances. Income by way of interest, dividend (other than that on which distribution tax has been paid), long-term capital gains[17] on bonds or shares of an Indian company issued under a scheme of the government of India or on bonds or shares of public sector company sold by the government and purchased by the non-resident in foreign currency are taxable at a flat rate of 10 per cent on the total amount without any deduction of expenses or allowances. Withholding of tax provisions are applicable on the above-stated income of dividends, interest, income from mutual fund and long-term capital gains. If a non-resident has income from the above-stated sources only and tax on such income has been withheld, then such resident is not required to file a return of income.

Non-resident Indians being citizens of India or persons of Indian origin, are taxed at a flat rate of 10 per cent in respect of income on investment and long-term capital gains from shares, debentures, deposits and security of the Central Government purchased or subscribed in convertible foreign exchange (foreign exchange treated by the Reserve Bank of India as convertible foreign exchange). The flat rate is applicable on the total amount without any deduction of any expense or allowance. In case the non-resident Indian has his total income only from investment income or income by way of long-term capital gains or both and tax on such income has been withheld, then such non-resident Indian need not file his return of income. However, option

TABLE 2.1. INCOME YEAR IN THE SELECTED COUNTRIES

Country	Normal Income Year	Other Year as Income Year	Commonly Known
U.K.	April 6 to April 5	For business and professional income, any other year ending between April 6 and April 5 following	Tax Year or Year of Assessment
U.S.	January 1 to December 31	The taxpayer may adopt a fiscal year of 12 months ending on the last day of the month other than December	Accounting Year
Australia	July 1 to June 30	In the case of a company, the 12 month period ending during the financial year for which income tax is charged	Income Year
Malaysia	January 1 to December 31	For business income, the accounting year may be a period of 12 months or less and need not necessarily end on December 31	Basis Year
Pakistan	July 1 to June 30	In some cases a special income year other than July 1, to June 30, may be adopted as the income year	Income Year
India	April 1 to March 31	Same accounting year in all cases	Previous Year

is the income year, in other countries it may be a 12-month period starting on any other date. The income year is the year, the income earned during which is charged to tax at the prescribed rates applicable for that year. In Malaysia, income year is known as the basis year. The income year of the selected countries is given in Table 2.1.

As shown in the table, in the U.K, for his income from business and profession, the taxpayer can choose any period other than April 6 to April 5 following, ending on any day during this period as the income/tax year. In the U.S., though the calendar year is the accounting year, the taxpayer may choose a fiscal year (a 12 month period that ends on the last day of any month other than December) as the accounting year.

In Australia, normally the financial year from July 1 to June 30 is the income year, but in certain circumstances, a substituted accounting period of 12 months closing on a date other than June 30 may be adopted. In Malaysia, for non-business income, the calendar year, from January 1 to December 31, immediately preceding the year of assessment is the accounting year and is known as the basis year. For business income, the accounting year may consist of 12 months or less which need not necessarily end on December 31.

In Pakistan, from the assessment year 1995-96 onwards, all assessees including those who earn income from business or profession may adopt financial year July 1 to June 30 immediately preceding the assessment year as the income year. Only in some cases, special income year may be adopted subject to the approval of Central Board of Revenue.

In India, a financial year from April 1 to March 31, immediately preceding the assessment year is the income year for all types of income.

Thus, there is no uniformity in the adoption of income year in any of the selected countries. While in India, a uniform income year known as the previous year is applicable for all types of assessees, in all other countries, the taxpayer has the option to choose any year other than the normal income year as the income year. Another major difference is that while in some countries like Malaysia, Pakistan and India, the income year is linked to the assessment year,[18] in the U.K., the U.S and Australia it is not so linked.

Tax Rate Structure

One of the most important aspects of any taxation system is the tax rate structure. It is the basis of calculation of tax liability and is an important tool in the hands of policy makers. The total tax revenue collection also gets affected by the tax rates. The old theory of levying a high rate to collect more tax revenue has now become redundant. From 1985 onwards, tax rates have been reduced in many parts of the world to build confidence among the taxpayers so that they do not conceal their income due to the fear that a large part of their income is taken away from them by the government in the form of income tax. However, tax rates have increased since then in some countries including the U.S.

The minimum and maximum tax rates of individual taxpayers in the selected countries have been analysed in Table 2.2.

TABLE 2.2. MINIMUM AND MAXIMUM TAX RATES FOR INDIVIDUAL TAXPAYER

Country	Amount of Taxable Income	Minimum Rate (in percentage)	Amount of Taxable Income	Maximum Rate (in percentage)	Relevant Income Year	No. of Slabs
U.K.	Up to £1,520	10	Income exceeding £28,400	40	2000-01	3
U.S.	Up to $26,250	15	Above $288,350	39.6	2000	5
Australia	Above AUD6,000 up to AUD20,000	17	Above AUD60,000	47	2000-01	4
Malaysia	Above RM2,500 up to RM5,000	1	Above RM150,000	29	2000	9
Pakistan	Up to PKR100,000	5	Above PKR1,000,000	35	2000-01	7
India	Above Rs.50,000 up to Rs.60,000	10	Above Rs.150,000	30	2000-01	3

Sources: 1. *The Inland Revenue Satistics*, 2000 (U.K.)
2. *The Internal Revenue Code*, 1986 as on December 1, 2000 (U.S.)
3. *W.W.W. ato. gov. au* (Australia)
4. *CCH, 2000, Malaysian Master Tax Guide*, 2000
5. *The Income Tax Ordinance*, 1979, upto July 10,2000 (Pakistan)
6. *The Income Tax Act*, 1961, as on June 1, 2000 (India)

As given in the table, the tax rates have been the highest in Australia with a maximum tax rate of 47 per cent followed by 40 per cent in the U.K. and 39.6 per cent in the US. Pakistan, which had the maximum tax rate of 20 per cent for one year, only, i.e. 1998-99 income year, has again raised it to 35 per cent from the income year 1999-2000. Malaysia and India with a maximum tax rate of 29 per cent and 30 per cent respectively have the lowest tax rates. However, in India, a surcharge of 10 per cent for the income year 1999-2000 was levied especially due to the super cyclone in Orissa, and further, the surcharge on high level income was raised to 15 per cent in the income year 2000-01, which was further increased from 15 per cent to 17 per cent in January 2001, when a severe earthquake rocked many areas in Gujarat. Thus, including the surcharge of 17 per cent, the maximum tax rate in India was 35.1 per cent for the income year 2000-01.

The number of tax slabs in these countries also differs. While Malaysia has the maximum number of slabs, i.e. 9, on the other hand, Pakistan has 7 slabs, which makes the tax structure complicated. The next is the U.S. with 5 slabs. Australia has 4 slabs, while India and the U.K. have 3 slabs each.

The tax rate structure of the U.S. has four separate tax rate schedules. Although tax rates are the same in all these schedules, the amount of income at which these rates are applicable differs. The taxable incomes at which the minimum tax rate of 15 per cent is applicable in the income year 2000 are as follows.

$21,925 for married persons filing returns separately
$43,850 for married persons filing returns jointly.
$26,250 for single persons and
$35,150 for the head of the household.

The amount of taxable income at which the maximum tax rate of 39.6 per cent is applicable is $288,350 for married persons filing returns jointly, for single persons and also for the head of the household, while the amount of taxable income at which 39.6 per cent rate is applicable is $144,175 for married persons filing returns separately.

It therefore emerges that married persons filing returns separately have to pay the maximum tax, while married persons filing returns jointly have to pay the minimum tax amongst all the taxpayers. Thus, the tax rate structure of the U.S. has been framed according to the personal circumstances of the taxpayer. The tax rates are not changed frequently in the U.S, but the income level at which these rates are applicable is adjusted according to the inflation level. In the US, if the individual income of couples is distributed unequally, and is high, they can save their tax by filing joint returns.

Though the tax rate structure for individuals shown in Table 2.2 indicates the minimum and the maximum tax rates as well as the level of income at which these rates are applicable, a proper analysis of the tax rate structure can be done only on the basis of the full tax structure. Considering this, the complete tax structure of individual taxpayers has been given in Table 2.3, which is divided into several parts to show the country wise distribution. Since the income level in the tax rate structure of each country is given in the currency of that country, these levels are converted into common currency, i.e. Indian rupees to give a comparable view of the structure.

TABLE 2.3. INDIVIDUAL INCOME TAX RATE STRUCTURE OF THE SELECTED COUNTRIES

TABLE 2.3(A). U.K.

(Income year 2000-01)

Income Level (in £)		Tax Rates (in %)	Income Level (in Rs.)		Tax Rates (in %)
Upto	1,520	10	Upto	104,880	10
1,520	28,400	22	104,880	1,959,600	22
Above	28,400	40	Above	1,959,600	40

TABLE 2.3(B). U.S.

(Income year 2000)

Income Level (in $)		Tax Rates (in %)	Income Level (in Rs.)		Tax Rates (in %)
Upto	26,250	15	Upto	1,207,500	15
26,250	63,550	28	1,207,500	2,923,300	28
63,550	132,600	31	2,923,300	6,099,600	31
132,600	288,350	36	6,099,600	13,264,100	36
Above	288,350	39.6	Above	13,264,100	39.6

TABLE 2.3(C). AUSTRALIA

(Income year 2000-01)

Income Level (in AUD)		Tax Rates (in %)	Income Level (in Rs.)		Tax Rates (in %)
Upto	6,000	0	Upto	150,000	0
6,000	20,000	17	150,000	500,000	17
20,000	50,000	30	500,000	1,250,000	30
50,000	60,000	42	1,250,000	1,500,000	42
Above	60,000	47	Above	1,500,000	47

TABLE 2.3(D). MALAYSIA

(Income year 2000)

Income Level (in RM)		Tax Rates (in %)	Income Level (in Rs.)		Tax Rates (in %)
Upto	2,500	Nil	Upto	30,000	nil
2,500	5,000	1	30,000	60,000	1
5,000	10,000	3	60,000	120,000	3
10,000	20,000	5	120,000	240,000	5
20,000	35,000	9	240,000	420,000	9
35,000	50,000	15	420,000	600,000	15
50,000	70,000	20	600,000	840,000	20
70,000	100,000	25	840,000	1,200,000	25
100,000	150,000	28	1,200,000	1,800,000	28
Above	150,000	29	above	1,800,000	29

TABLE 2.3(E). PAKISTAN

(Income year 2000-01)

Income Level (in PKR)		Tax Rates (in %)	Income Level (in Rs.)		Tax Rates (in %)
Upto	100,000	5	Upto	80,000	5
100,000	200,000	10	80,000	160,000	10
200,000	300,000	15	160,000	240,000	15
300,000	500,000	20	240,000	400,000	20
500,000	700,000	25	400,000	560,000	25
700,000	1,000,000	30	560,000	800,000	30
Above	1,000,000	35	Above	800,000	35

TABLE 2.3(F). INDIA

(Income year 2000-01)

Income Level (in Rs.)		Tax Rates (in %)	Income Level (in Rs.)		Tax Rates (in %)
Upto	50,000	Nil	Upto	50,000	nil
50,000	60,000	10	50,000	60,000	10
60,000	150,000	20	60,000	150,000	20
Above	150,000	30	above	150,000	30

Sources: Same as for Table 2.2

Two important observations emerge out of Table 2.3, which are as follows:

1. While the maximum marginal tax rate of 30 per cent in India is amongst the lowest, the level of income at which the maximum rate of 30 per cent is applicable in India is income above Rs.0.15 million which is much lower than the income levels at which the rate of 30 per cent is applicable in other countries. This level in the U.S. is around Rs.2.9 million to Rs.6.0 million, in Australia, it is Rs.0.5 million to around Rs.1.2 million and in Pakistan it is Rs.0.8 million which is higher than the income level of India.
2. In all the countries under study except India, there is a substantial difference in the level of income at which the maximum rate is applicable, i.e. approximately 10 times or more than the level at which the minimum tax rate is applicable. In India, however, the maximum marginal rate of 30 per cent is applicable on the income level of above Rs.0.15 million which is just three times the level at which the minimum tax rate is applicable. Thus, in India, the maximum tax rate of 30 per cent is payable by even those individuals who come in the medium income group category. The structure in India appears to be almost a flat type of structure and does not seem to be truly progressive.

Tax-free Threshold or Exemption Limit

While personal tax reforms emphasise a widening of the tax base, social requirements tend to limit its scope. It is recognised everywhere that some minimum income should be exempt from tax specially for taxpayers earning low income to enable them to fulfil their basic requirements. However, the mode of providing exemption differs in different countries. While in some countries, an exemption limit or a tax-free threshold is fixed, in others, a fixed allowance is deductible. The form in which some minimum income is exempt in the selected countries is given in Table 2.4

As shown in the table, amongst the developed countries, the U.K., and the U.S. allow deduction of personal allowances of £4,385, and $2,800 respectively. In the U.K., a higher allowance of £5,790 is allowed to taxpayers between 65 and 74 years of age and still a higher allowance of £6,050 is allowed to taxpayers aged 75 years or more. Australia provides a tax-free threshold of AUD6,000.

Malaysia is the only country, which provides both reliefs, i.e. a tax-free threshold of RM2,500 and personal allowance of RM5,000. Although, in Pakistan, the tax structure does not provide any tax-free threshold, as per Schedule 1, Part 1 of the *Income Tax Ordinance*, no tax is payable by the individual taxpayer, if his total income does not exceed:

1. PKR50,000 in case the total income consists of or includes salary income and such income is more than 50 per cent of his total income.
2. PKR60,000 in case of a working woman, whose salary income constitutes more than 50 per cent of her total income, and
3. PKR40,000 in other cases.

Besides this, rebate from income tax is also provided to the extent of PKR2,500, 3,000, and 2,000 respectively in all the three cases mentioned above.

Thus, in Pakistan, if the taxable income of an individual is upto PKR40,000, it is wholly exempt, or if it is more than PKR40,000, then a rebate of minimum PKR2,000 is allowed which means no tax is payable on income up to PKR40,000 as relief is given at the minimum rate of 5 per cent. In India however, the tax rate structure provides a tax-free threshold of upto Rs.50,000.

TABLE 2.4. EXEMPTION LIMITS/PERSONAL ALLOWANCES IN THE SELECTED COUNTERIES

Country	Exemption Limit	Personal Allowances	Income Year
U.K.	Nil	£4,385	2000-01
U.S.	Nil	$2,800	2000
Australia	AUD6,000	Nil	2000-01
Malaysia	RM2,500	RM5,000	2000
Pakistan	PKR40,000	Nil	2000-01
India	Rs.50,000	Nil	2000-01

Sources: Same as for Table 2.2

Per Capita GDP and Tax-free Threshold

Though it is apparent that all the selected countries allow some income to be kept outside the purview of income tax, the extent to which the tax-free threshold is related to the per capita GDP will help in knowing how strong the tax base can be in any country. With a view to analysing this, the per capita GDP and the tax-free threshold/personal exemption allowed in the selected countries during the income year 1997-98 are given in Table 2.5. The amount has been converted into a common currency for comparison purposes.

It appears from the table, that though the personal exemption in rupee value was maximum, i.e. Rs.258,880 in the U.K., followed by Rs.135,000 and Rs.103,350 in Australia and the U.S., respectively, the amount of personal exemption was much lower in developing countries. It was Rs.40,000 in India, Rs.36,000 in Pakistan and Rs.27,500 in Malaysia. However, in Malaysia, the effective exemption was more because besides this, a personal relief of RM5,000, i.e. Rs.55,000 was also allowed, thus increasing the total exemption to Rs.82,500.

In spite of the fact that a higher personal exemption was allowed in all the developed countries during 1997-98 income year, the amount of exemption in all these countries was much less than the GDP per capita. Even in Malaysia, the tax-free threshold and personal relief, together were less than the GDP per capita. It was only in Pakistan and India that the amount of exemption was much higher than the GDP per capita. This leads to the conclusion that where the personal exemption is higher than the GDP per capita, the income tax base is bound to be narrow. That seems to be one of the basic reasons for the low income tax revenue collection in Pakistan and India.

Computation of Taxable Income

Taxable income and tax rates together determine the tax revenue collection in any country. Taxable income represents the tax base of any country. It is affected by various inclusions, exclusions, allowances and deductions. While

TABLE 2.5. PER CAPITA GDP AND TAX-FREE THRESHOLD/PERSONAL EXEMPTION

(for the income year 1997-98)

Country	GDP (Country Currency)	GDP (Rs.)	Tax-free Threshold/ Personal Exemption	Tax-free Threshold/ Personal Exemption (Rs.)
U.K.	£13,762	880,768	£4,045	258,880
U.S.	$30,276	1,180,764	$2,650	103,350
Australia	AUD29,659	741,475	AUD5,400	135,000
Malaysia	RM13,113	144,243	RM2,500	27,500
Pakistan	PKR18,724	16,852	PKR40,000	36,000
India	Rs.16,370	16,370	Rs.40,000	40,000

Source: IMF: *International Financial Statistical Yearbook* 1999, *and Taxation Statistics and Income Tax Acts of Selected Countries.*

in some countries like India and Pakistan, gross income is the aggregation of income computed under the specified heads of income, different schedules are provided in the U.K and the gross income is the aggregate of income computed under these schedules. In the U.S. and Australia, the Income Tax law defines what is included in the gross income. Although in these countries specific incomes to be included in the gross income are mentioned, they are not taxable under different heads. The method of computation of taxable income, tax liability and tax payable in the relevant countries are analysed and examined in Table 2.6.

As shown in the table, the steps required in the computation of taxable income, tax liability and tax payable differ in the selected countries. Although almost all revenue receipts are part of gross income, capital gains also form part of such income in most of the selected countries. In some countries, including the U.S. and India, though capital gains are a part of gross income, tax is calculated at preferential rates on such capital gains.

In the U.K., certain charges on income, including contribution to charity, maintenance payment, mortgage interest are deducted upto a fixed limit from the gross income and then after deducting the personal allowance, the resulting amount is the taxable income. Where any payment allowed as charges on income is paid net after the deduction of tax, such payment is fully deducted (gross payment) from the total income. Then the tax withheld on such charges is added while calculating the tax liability. Another distinct feature of the U.K. income tax system is that while capital gains are charged at the tax rates applicable on individual taxpayers, they are taxable like savings income for the income year 1999-2000 and thus form part of the top slice of the income. Capital gains are taxable upto a certain level of income at a lower tax rate and above certain level at a higher tax rate in the U.K., but are never taxable at the basic tax rates.

While deductions from the total income reduce the taxable income that reflects the tax base, on the other hand, rebates and tax credits reduce the tax liability.

In the U.S., while the specified heads of income are not prescribed, the type of income to be included in the gross total income is given. The unique feature of the U.S. tax system is that after making deduction from the gross income, two further types of deductions are allowed from the Adjusted Gross Income (AGI). These deductions are:

1. Personal and dependent exemption.
2. Itemized or standard deduction.

Personal and dependent exemptions are allowed basically to provide relief to lower income earner and are phased out gradually and are reduced to nil if the AGI exceeds a certain limit. Besides personal exemption, a further deduction by way of itemized deductions can be claimed in respect of specified expenses, mainly personal expenses, including medical expenses, charitable contributions, casualty and theft losses, non-business taxes and

TABLE 2.6. COMPUTATION OF TAXABLE INCOME, TAX LIABILITY AND TAX PAYABLE IN THE SELECTED COUNTRIES

U.K.	U.S.	AUSTRALIA	MALAYSIA	PAKISTAN	INDIA
Gross Income	Gross Income	Gross Assessable Income	Gross Income	Gross Total Income	Gross Total Income
↓	↓	↓	↓	↓	↓
Schedule A–Income from House Property Schedule D, Case I–Profits of business Schedule D, Case II–Profits of a profession Schedule D, Case III–Interest received gross Schedule D, Case IV–Interest on overseas securities Schedule D, Case V–Income from overseas professions Schedule D, Case VI–Income from other sources Schedule E, Case I–Income from employment	Wages, salaries, gross business profits, rents and royalties, dividend, interest, capital gains, annuities, pensions, alimony received, commission, tips, fringe benefits, prizes and awards, farm income, trust and estate distribution, share of partnership income.	Salaries, wages, gross business and professional receipts and royalties, rent, dividend, Interest, capital gains, allowances, pensions, unused long service leave payment, net primary production, income share in partnership or trust, workers compensation	Gains or profits from a business, income from employment, dividend, interest income, rents, royalties or premium, pension or annuities, income from any other source	Salary, Interest on securities, Income from property, profits and gains from business and profession, capital gains, income from other sources (after making deductions under the specified heads)	Salary, Income from house property, profits and gains from business and profession, capital gain, Income from other sources, including dividend and interest income (Income under specified head is after making prescribed deductions)
↓	↓	↓	↓	↓	↓
Equals	Minus	Minus	Minus	Minus	Minus
↓	↓	↓	↓	↓	↓
Total Income	Deductions from Gross Income	Business Deductions	Expenses wholly and exclusively incurred in the production of gross income	Zakat Paid	Deductions including expenses incurred on medical treatment of handicapped dependents, donations to approved institutions, income from exports, income from industrial undertakings located in specified area, certain interest and dividend income and income of
	↓	↓	↓	↓	
	Trade or business expenses, expenses of producing rental or royalty Income, self employed retirement plan contribution, alimony paid contributions to Individual Retirement Accounts,	Expenses of carrying on business, car expenses, travel expenses, interest and dividend deductions, property and investment income expenses, self employed superannuation contributions, Film Industry incentives, environment protection	Adjusted gross income or loss	Equals	
			↓	↓	
			Plus	Total Income	
			↓	↓	
			Balancing charge, agricultural charge or any forest charge	Minus	
				↓	
				Allowances and donations to approved organizations	
				↓	

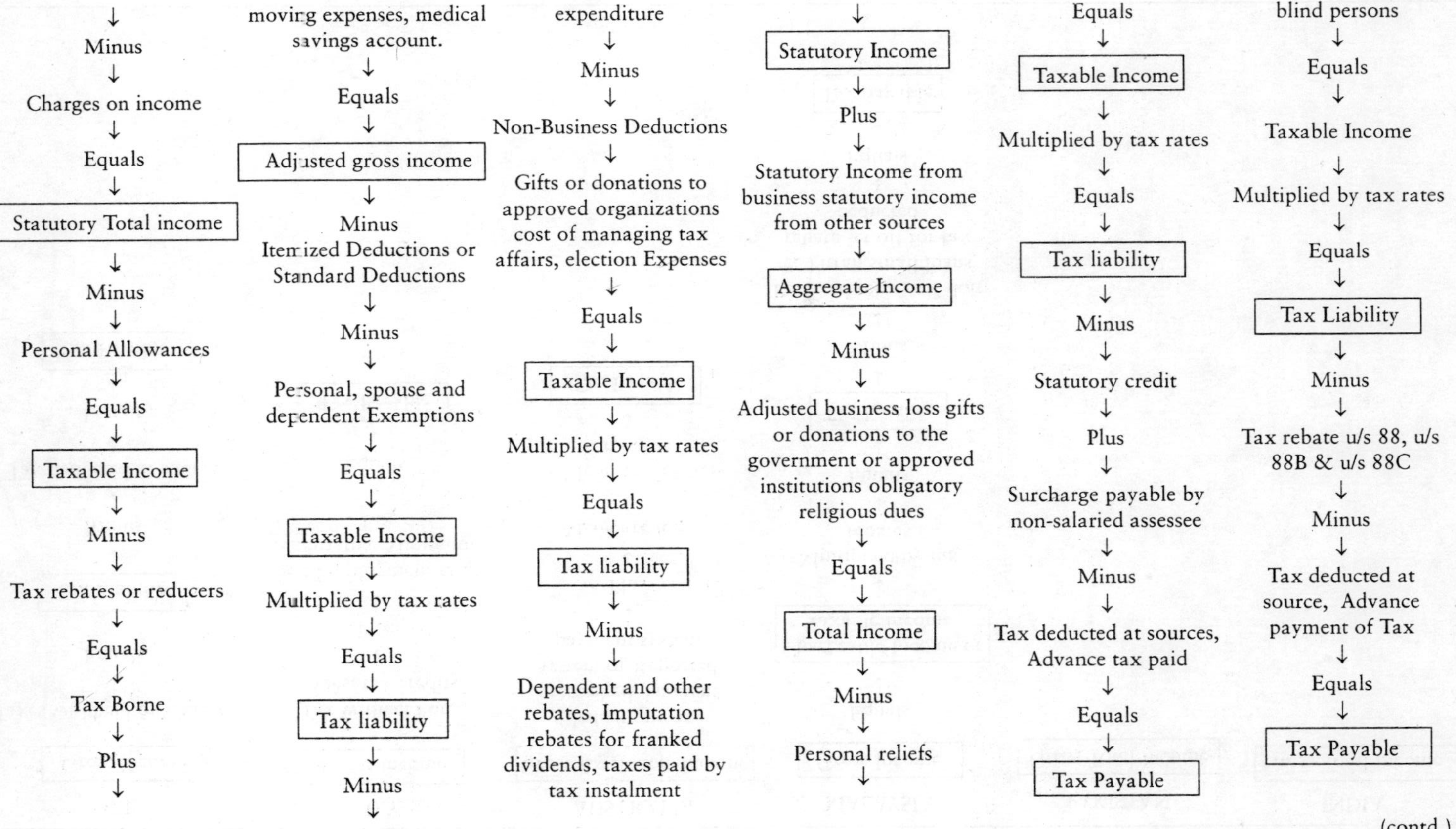
↓
Minus
↓
Charges on income
↓
Equals
↓
Statutory Total income
↓
Minus
↓
Personal Allowances
↓
Equals
↓
Taxable Income
↓
Minus
↓
Tax rebates or reducers
↓
Equals
↓
Tax Borne
↓
Plus
↓
moving expenses, medical savings account.
↓
Equals
↓
Adjusted gross income
↓
Minus
Itemized Deductions or Standard Deductions
↓
Minus
↓
Personal, spouse and dependent Exemptions
↓
Equals
↓
Taxable Income
↓
Multiplied by tax rates
↓
Equals
↓
Tax liability
↓
Minus
↓
expenditure
↓
Minus
↓
Non-Business Deductions
↓
Gifts or donations to approved organizations cost of managing tax affairs, election Expenses
↓
Equals
↓
Taxable Income
↓
Multiplied by tax rates
↓
Equals
↓
Tax liability
↓
Minus
↓
Dependent and other rebates, Imputation rebates for franked dividends, taxes paid by tax instalment
↓
Statutory Income
↓
Plus
↓
Statutory Income from business statutory income from other sources
↓
Aggregate Income
↓
Minus
↓
Adjusted business loss gifts or donations to the government or approved institutions obligatory religious dues
↓
Equals
↓
Total Income
↓
Minus
↓
Personal reliefs
↓
Equals
↓
Taxable Income
↓
Multiplied by tax rates
↓
Equals
↓
Tax liability
↓
Minus
↓
Statutory credit
↓
Plus
↓
Surcharge payable by non-salaried assessee
↓
Minus
↓
Tax deducted at sources, Advance tax paid
↓
Equals
↓
Tax Payable
blind persons
↓
Equals
↓
Taxable Income
↓
Multiplied by tax rates
↓
Equals
↓
Tax Liability
↓
Minus
↓
Tax rebate u/s 88, u/s 88B & u/s 88C
↓
Minus
↓
Tax deducted at source, Advance payment of Tax
↓
Equals
↓
Tax Payable

(contd.)

TABLE 2.6. (contd.)

U.K.	U.S.	AUSTRALIA	MALAYSIA	PAKISTAN	INDIA
Gross Income	Gross Income	Gross Assessable Income	Gross Income	Gross Total Income	Gross Total Income
Taxes withheld on charges	Tax withheld on wages, tax credits	deductions or prescribed payment system or Reported payment system	Equals		
↓	↓	↓	↓		
Equals	Plus	Plus	Chargeable Income or Taxable Income		
↓	↓	↓	↓		
Tax Liability	Self Employment tax, Alternative Minimum Tax	Medicare levy	Multiplied by tax rebates		
↓	↓	↓	↓		
Minus	Equals	Medicare levy surcharge	Equals		
↓	↓	↓	↓		
Tax deducted at source	Tax Payable	Tax Payable	Tax liability		
↓			↓		
Equals			Minus		
↓			↓		
Tax Payable			Personal rebates Zakat & Fitrah small loans rebate set off for tax deducted		
			↓		
			Equals		
			↓		
			Tax payable		

interest. An individual can claim a fixed standard deduction instead of itemized deductions without fulfilling any conditions.

Further, many tax credits are allowed from the tax liability. Though the tax base in the form of taxable income is not affected by these credits, the tax revenue is certainly reduced as a result of these credits. However, the loss of tax revenue as a result of these tax credits is reduced as Alternative Minimum Tax (AMT) is payable by higher income earners. While calculating the AMT, these tax credits except the foreign tax credit are not allowed. In other words, the benefit of tax credit in the U.S. can be availed of by those individuals who earn income upto a specified limit.

In Australia, a large number of incomes are specifically included in the gross assessable income. Expenses incurred in carrying on the business or in connection with the earning of rental income or other incomes are allowed either fully or subject to certain limits and conditions. Special incentives are allowed to primary producers. Deduction is also allowed in respect of film industry investments and expenditure on environmental impact studies and in respect of environment protection. Certain non-business deductions including gifts or donations to approved institutions, cost of managing tax affairs and election expenses are also deductible.

Similar to the U.S, many rebates including spouse and other dependent rebates, sole-parents rebate, medical expenses rebate, zone rebate, imputation rebate for franked dividends, foreign tax credits, averaging rebate for primary producers and many other rebates are deducted from the tax liability. After allowing tax rebates, further adjustment is made in respect of the tax paid under different schemes, namely the Prescribed Payments System (PPS), Reportable Payment System (RPS), Pay As You Earn (PAYE) and provision tax schemes. A resident taxpayer in Australia is also required to pay medicare levy of 1.5 per cent of the taxable income. The rate of medicare levy is less for low-income earners. The high-income taxpayers without adequate private patient hospital insurance are liable to pay medicare levy surcharge of one per cent of the taxpayer's entire taxable income in addition to 1.5 per cent of medicare levy.

In Australia, since AMT is not payable, even higher income taxpayers can claim rebates. However, some rebates, mainly dependent rebates are phased out gradually and reduced to nil if the dependant's net separate income exceeds a certain limit.

Gross income in Malaysia is the aggregate of income computed under six specified heads. Capital gains do not form part of the gross income and are taxable under the *Real Property Gains Act*. Besides a tax-free threshold of RM2,500, personal relief and wife relief are also deductible. Further, many more reliefs for children, the disabled, medical treatment of specified diseases, education fees and life insurance and medical insurance payments are allowed. Further, rebate is also allowed in respect of *Zakat*, *Fitrah* or other Islamic religious dues payment of which is obligatory. Small loan rebate and rebate in respect of personal computer are the other rebates.

In Pakistan, the gross total income is the aggregate of income computed under six heads. A large number of incomes, including agricultural income are exempt from tax. Donations to approved institutions are allowed within limits as tax rebate. Any *Zakat* or *Fitrah* paid is deductible from the total income. Neither a tax-free threshold nor any personal allowances is allowed in Pakistan. However, no income tax is payable by those persons whose total taxable income does not exceed Rs.40,000. Also a rebate of Rs.2,000 is allowed to all individuals. The limit of exemption and tax rebate is higher for those individuals and women whose salary income constitutes more than 50 per cent of their total income.

The gross total income in India is the aggregate of income computed under five specified heads including salary, income from business or profession, income from house property, capital gains and income from other sources. A large number of incomes are exempt from tax in India also. Agricultural income is wholly exempt from tax.

A large number of deductions based on socio-economic considerations are allowed to be deducted from the gross total income.

Apart from these deductions, tax rebate is also provided under Sec. 88 in respect of contribution to life insurance premiums, approved provident funds, annuity, units of Unit-linked insurance plan, specified government securities, on repayment of loan taken for the purchase or construction of house.

Income Tax Base

The base of the income tax structure is the most crucial factor affecting tax revenue. Wider the tax base, higher will be the tax collection. Since the beginning of tax reforms in the mid-1980s, many studies conducted all over the world have emphasised base broadening as a tool to increase revenue collection. In the Executive Summary based on the findings of World Development Report 1988, which dealt mainly with public finance, it was suggested that 'Broadening the base of the tax system should be a high priority. It further provided that in developing countries the tax base is often so narrow that the government must rely on relatively high tax rates to raise tax revenue. The higher the rate, the greater the distortion in private economic activity and greater the associated efficiency costs of taxation. Reducing rates in the presence of revenue constraints or raising additional revenue without aggravating economic distortions requires broadening the base.'[19] Base broadening, if designed carefully, can effectively address the objectives of revenue collection, efficiency and equity in a tax system. Base broadening through the elimination of exemptions and preferences can also help simplify tax administration.

A study of the Organisation for Economic Co-operation and Development (OECD) countries conducted by Ken Messere also highlights base broadening. According to him, 'Structural changes in the personal income tax which occurred in nearly all the OECD countries between 1985 and 1998 took the form of base broadening, reduction of top rates, flattening of the income tax schedule and increases in real terms of the tax-free threshold (i.e. the tax allowance given to all taxpayers)'.[20] According to Messere, widening the tax base has taken two forms:

1. bringing into the tax base the hitherto untaxed income or income equivalents. (In many countries, capital gains became taxable between 1958 and 1980, including in Canada, and the U.K.)
2. abolishing or reducing tax relief for certain expenditures.[21]

Developing countries are currently very deeply concerned at the appropriateness of their tax base within the overall economy. The tax base of a country is affected by the exempted incomes, tax-free threshold, personal allowances, business and non-business deductions, rebates and tax credits.

The study analyses various factors that shows the tax base of any country such as the number of taxpayers as percentage of total population, the raito of tax revenue to GDP and the percentage growth in income tax as compared to the growth in the GDP.

Taxpayers as Percentage of Total Population

The income tax base of any country is also reflected through the number of taxpayers of the country as compared to the total population of that country. The more is the number of taxpayers, the stronger will be the tax base.

In developing countries the narrow base of income tax is due to the reason that only a very small percentage of the total population is within the tax net framework. The ratio of individual taxpayers as percentage of the total population is given in Table 2.7.

As shown in the table, the ratio of taxpayers to the total population is quite high in developed countries, ranging from 45 per cent to 53 per cent. The ratio is very low in India, which is less than 2 per cent and approximately 7 per cent in Malaysia. The number of taxpayers at 52.92 per cent is highest in Australia amongst all the six countries. As shown in figure 2.1, in developing countries, especially in Pakistan and India, the ratio of taxpayers to total population is very low as compared to developed countries.

TABLE 2.7. NO. OF INDIVIDUAL TAXPAYERS AS PERCENTAGE OF TOTAL POPULATION

(for the year 1997-98)

Country	No. of Taxpayers (in millions)	Total Population (in millions)	No. of Taxpayers as % of Population
U.K.	27.9	58.2	47.94
U.S.	122.42	267.9	45.70
Australia	9.8	18.52	52.92
Malaysia	1.46	21	6.95
Pakistan	1.66	128.42	1.29
India	11.2	955.12	1.17

Sources: 1. For number of taxpayers, *Taxation Statistics of U.K., Australia and Malaysia and IRS Statistics of Income Bulletin*, Fall 1999.

2. For total population; IMF, *International Financial Statistics Year Book*, 1999.

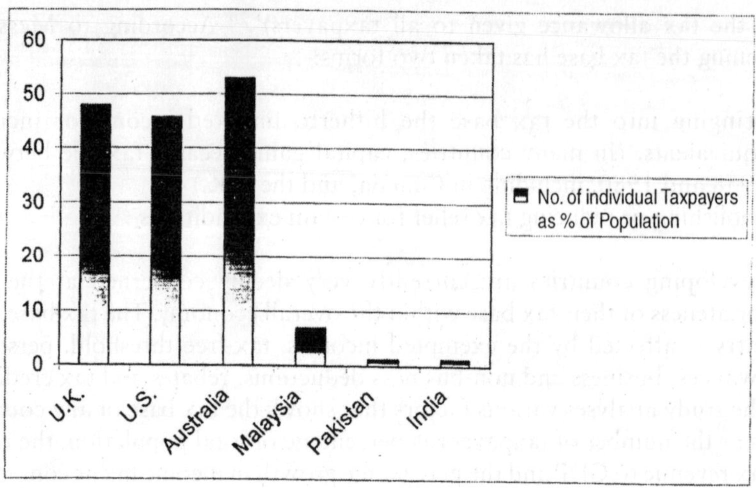

FIGURE 2.1: NO. OF INDIVIDUAL TAXPAYERS AS PERCENTAGE OF TOTAL POPULATION

Tax Revenue and GDP

Many developing countries including India are facing the severe problem of fiscal deficit. Amongst the many steps taken by the government to reduce the fiscal deficit, one such measure is to increase the tax revenue. However, the tax revenue as compared to GDP in the developing countries continues to be small. The ratio of tax revenue to GDP of these countries will reflect how much is the share of tax revenue in the GDP of these countries.

The ratio of tax revenue to the GDP during 1984—1997 is given in Table 2.8. The table and the Figure 2.2 shows that the ratio of tax revenue to GDP in Pakistan and India is much less than that of other countries. Also,

TABLE 2.8. RATIO OF TAX REVENUE TO GDP IN THE SELECTED COUNTRIES

(ratio is in percentage)

Year	U.K.	U.S.	Australia	Malaysia	Pakistan	India
1984	32.71	16.53	20.92	21.43	13.27	10.15
1985	33.10	17.01	22.29	17.57	12.33	10.93
1986	32.54	16.84	22.86	21.79	13.45	11.33
1987	31.90	17.69	22.65	17.05	n.a.	11.30
1988	32.04	17.51	22.46	17.51	13.17	11.24
1989	29.31	17.71	22.62	17.53	13.71	11.30
1990	35.46	17.40	23.13	19.63	13.32	10.75
1991	34.17	17.36	23.24	20.75	12.18	10.92
1992	33.59	16.97	21.04	20.71	12.93	10.57
1993	31.77	17.23	20.29	20.53	12.74	8.53
1994	32.72	17.72	20.16	20.91	12.65	8.89
1995	33.44	18.15	17.73	20.20	13.13	9.13
1996	33.80	18.61	22.18	20.07	13.53	9.13
1997	33.69	19.10	22.68	19.38	12.87	9.13

Sources: IMF, *Government Finance Statistics Yearbook*, 1991 *and* 1999; IMF, *International Financial Statistical Yearbook*, 1999.

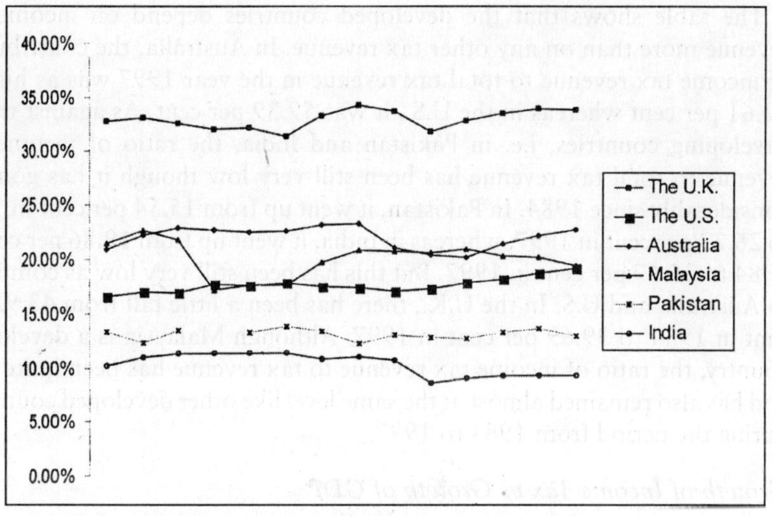

FIGURE 2.2: RATIO OF TAX REVENUE TO GDP

the ratio is not only decreasing in India, it is also less as compared to Pakistan. In the developed countries, there is marginal increase, whereas in all the three developing countries, it has gone down. In India, it went down from 11.33 per cent in 1986 to 9.13 per cent in 1997, while in Malaysia it went down from 21.43 per cent in 1984 to 19.38 per cent in 1997.

Income Tax Revenue as percentage of Total Tax Revenue

The ratio of income tax revenue to tax revenue over a period of time reflects the share of income tax revenue in the total tax revenue and also whether the share is decreasing or increasing. This is given in Table 2.9.

TABLE 2.9. RATIO OF INCOME TAX REVENUE TO TOTAL TAX REVENUE

(ratio is in percentage)

Year	U.K.	U.S.	Australia	Malaysia	Pakistan	India
1984	43.92	55.12	66.11	46.59	15.54	19.86
1985	44.56	55.71	66.71	64.68	15.67	18.94
1986	43.05	55.37	66.99	53.15	13.94	18.19
1987	42.80	57.42	68.91	45.15	n.a.	17.60
1988	43.01	56.05	69.23	44.85	13.09	19.45
1989	45.02	57.03	70.17	40.61	12.88	18.92
1990	43.23	56.08	70.86	42.49	12.76	18.60
1991	41.75	55.12	71.89	45.13	15.48	22.11
1992	39.76	54.43	72.18	46.76	18.02	23.45
1993	38.63	55.51	72.38	46.18	21.50	26.61
1994	38.84	55.54	71.11	43.76	36.07	28.88
1995	39.88	56.67	70.43	45.58	40.73	29.90
1996	39.85	58.09	71.40	45.26	26.02	29.91
1997	39.69	59.39	72.61	44.35	26.23	35.67

Source: IMF, *Government Finance Statistics Yearbook*, 1991 *and* 1999.

The table shows that the developed countries depend on income tax revenue more than on any other tax revenue. In Australia, the contribution of income tax revenue to total tax revenue in the year 1997 was as high as 72.61 per cent whereas in the U.S., it was 59.39 per cent. As against this in developing countries, i.e. in Pakistan and India, the ratio of income tax revenue to total tax revenue has been still very low though it has gone up considerably since 1984. In Pakistan, it went up from 15.54 per cent in 1984 to 26.23 per cent in 1997, whereas in India, it went up from 19.86 per cent in 1984 to 35.67 per cent in 1997. But this has been still very low as compared to Australia and U.S. In the U.K., there has been a little fall from 43.92 per cent in 1984 to 39.69 per cent in 1997. Although Malaysia is a developing country, the ratio of income tax revenue to tax revenue has been quite high and has also remained almost at the same level like other developed countries, during the period from 1984 to 1997.

Growth of Income Tax vs Growth of GDP

Over a period, the role of income tax as a major revenue source in the developing countries is gradually increasing. To find out this, the growth in income tax has been compared with the growth in the GDP during 1984-97 in the selected countries.

The ratio of growth of income tax to the growth of the GDP between 1984 and 1997 is reflected in Table 2.10 and Figure 2.3. The comparison reveals that income tax revenue as percentage of GDP has been high in developed countries as compared to developing countries. In the year 1997, it was as high as 16.46 per cent in Australia as against the low of 3.26 per cent in India. One of the reasons for the small share of income tax in the GDP in India appears to be that while the maximum tax in most of the selected

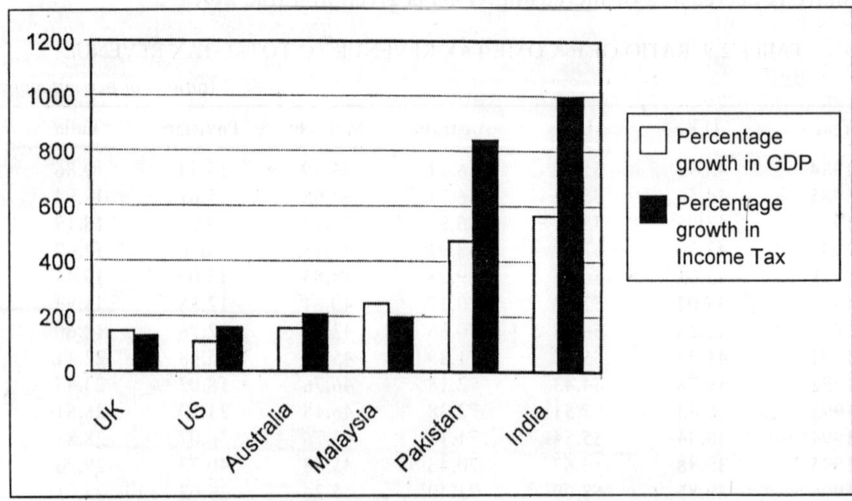

FIGURE 2.3: RATIO OF GROWTH IN INCOME TAX TO GROWTH IN GDP DURING 1984-97

TABLE 2.10. RATIO OF GROWTH IN INCOME TAX TO GROWTH IN GDP DURING 1984-97

Country	GDP (in billion) 1984	GDP (in billion) 1997	Percentage Growth in GDP	Total Income Tax in (in billion) 1984	Income Tax Revenue as percentage of GDP 1984	Total Income Tax in (in billion) 1997	Income Tax Revenue as percentage of GDP in 1997	Percentage Growth in Income Tax	Difference in percentage Growth in Income Tax and GDP
UK	325.850	800.940	145.80	46.806	14.36	107.097	13.37	128.8	(-) 17.0
US	3902.400	8,110.900	107.80	355.530	9.11	920.250	11.35	158.8	(+) 51.0
Australia	214.350	549.290	156.30	29.649	13.83	90.436	16.46	205.0	(+) 48.7
Malaysia	79.950	275.367	244.20	7.982	9.98	23.663	8.59	196.5	(-) 47.7
Pakistan	419.800	2,404.600	472.80	8.655	2.06	81.155	3.37	837.7	(+) 364.9
India	2313.400	15,635.500	564.20	46.600	2.01	509.100	3.26	992.5	(+) 446.3

Note: Amount is given in individual country currency.

Source: Same as given in Table 2.8

countries is payable by the high income taxpayers, the maximum tax in India is payable by the medium income group individuals. It seems that while the salaried class people who fall mostly in the medium group income are subject to compulsory taxation, the high income group individuals, especially self-employed individuals have been able to either avoid or evade tax. Another reason appears to be that the low per capita of GDP and the amount of exemption limit being higher than the per capita GDP, a major part of taxable income which is otherwise low or small is outside the purview of income tax.

The percentage growth in income tax between 1984 and 1997 as compared to the growth in GDP during the same period has been higher by 446.3 per cent in India and by 364.9 per cent in Pakistan, both developing countries. Similarly it is higher in the U.S. by 51.0 per cent and by 48.7 per cent in Australia but down by 47.7 per cent in Malaysia and by 17.0 per cent in U.K. The reason for high percentage growth of income tax in Pakistan and India as compared to the percentage growth in the GDP since 1984 onwards appears to be that in 1984, the income tax revenue in these two countries was very low as compared to the other countries. Thus, in comparison to that narrow base, the growth is substantial but the income tax revenue of other countries was already very high even in 1984 and that is why despite the growth in absolute terms being much higher in the U.K., the U.S. and Australia, the growth in percentage is less than the growth in Pakistan and India.

Thus, it is clear from the above analysis that in the developing countries, especially in Pakistan and India, the rise in income tax revenue is substantial but still it is far behind the level in the developed countries. In developing countries, the higher growth in income tax as compared to the growth in GDP is expected, as the growth in the GDP had increased the per capita income, which consequently had the effect of increasing the income liable to tax over and above the tax-free threshold allowed to individual taxpayers.

From the above, it appears that in the coming years if the above trends persists, then the percentage growth in income tax to percentage growth in GDP in both Pakistan and India may be much higher as the percentage of income tax to GDP is still very low and growth in the GDP per capita consequent to increase in the GDP will contribute in much larger proportion to income tax than what is being contributed presently.

Growth in Population, GDP Per Capita and Income Tax Per Capita

In many developing countries including Pakistan and India, the per capita GDP and income tax per capita are much less than that of developed countries due to over population. The ratio of growth in population, GDP per capita and income tax per capita between 1984 and 1997 have been shown in Table 2.11 and Figure 2.4.

The table reveals that in India, despite there being increase in population

TABLE 2.11. RATIO OF GROWTH IN POPULATION, GDP PER CAPITA AND INCOME TAX PER CAPITA DURING 1984-97

Country	Population (in millions) 1984	Population (in millions) 1997	Percentage Growth in Population	GDP per capita 1984	GDP per capita 1997	Percentage Growth in GDP per capita	Income Tax per capita in 1984	Income Tax per capita in 1997	Percentage Growth in per capita Income Tax
UK	56.51	58.20	3.00	5,766	13,762	138.7	828	1,840	122.2
US	236.37	267.90	13.30	16,510	30,276	83.4	1,504	3,435	128.4
Australia	15.56	18.52	19.00	13,776	29,659	115.3	1,905	4,883	156.3
Malaysia	15.27	21.00	37.50	5,236	13,126	150.7	523	1,127	115.5
Pakistan	93.29	138.16	48.10	4,500	17,404	286.7	93	587	531.2
India	736.00	955.12	29.80	3,143	16,370	420.8	63	533	746.0

Note: Amount is given in individual country currency.

Source: Same as given in Table 2.8

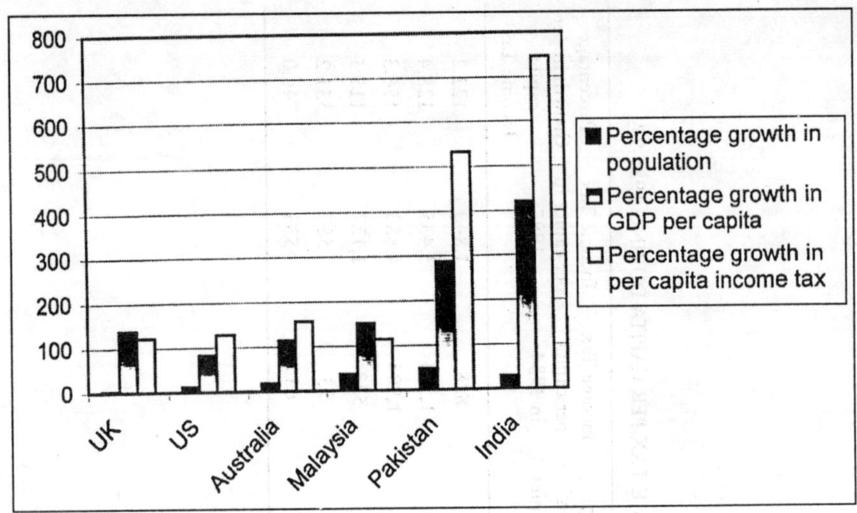

FIGURE 2.4: RATIO OF GROWTH IN POPULATION, GDP PER CAPITA AND INCOME TAX PER CAPITA DURING 1984 AND 1997

of 29.8 per cent between 1984 and 1997, the growth in the GDP per capita and income tax per capita has been the highest. Similarly, in Pakistan, though there was an increase of 48.1 per cent in population between 1984 and 1997, the growth in the GDP per capita and income tax per capita is next to India, but higher than in the other selected countries. In the U.K, there was small increase in population i.e. 3.0 per cent between 1984 and 1997, still the percentage growth in GDP per capita was only 138.7 per cent and whereas growth in income tax per capita has been 122.2 per cent which appears to be very low as compared to the growth in income tax per capita of 746.0 per cent in India. Though the percentage increase in income tax per capita has been higher in India and Pakistan, in absolute terms, the income tax per capita was much higher in developed countries as compared to two developing countries, i.e. Pakistan and India.

The analysis reveals that the percentage growth in the GDP per capita and the income tax per capita in the developing countries is much higher than the percentage growth in population. This indicates three things:

1. The base of per capita GDP and income tax per capita was very low in developing countries, especially Pakistan and India and therefore any increase in GDP and income tax per capita appears to be substantial.
2. The population in Pakistan and India was already high, and thus increase in population, over these years did not show much increase in percentage terms, in spite of substantial increase in population in real terms as compared to the developed countries.
3. There has been sufficient improvement in the income tax per capita and GDP per capita in these countries.

Taxable Income and Tax Liability

It is also important to analyse at which level of income the number of taxpayers are maximum in any country, and also at which level of income are the taxable income and the tax liability maximum. As the data of the different countries are given in different currencies, for comparison purposes the amount has been converted into equivalent in Indian rupees. The number of taxable returns, the taxable income and the tax liability at different levels of income in the selected countries are given in Table 2.12, which is divided into 5 parts.

The analysis of the data shown in Table 2.12 has been done under three heads:

1. *Number of Returns*: In the U.K., the maximum number of taxpayers, i.e. 4.26 million filed return in the income range of Rs.0.96 million to Rs.1.28 million and in the U.S., 15.18 million taxpayers filed their returns in the income range of Rs.1.95 million to Rs.3.66 million. In Australia, maximum number of taxpayers, 1.82 million filed returns in the income level of around Rs.0.62 to Rs.0.87 million, in Malaysia, around 0.53 million taxpayers filed returns in the income range of Rs.0.11 million to Rs.0.22 million and in India, the maximum number of taxpayers, i.e. 3.5 million filed returns in the income level of just Rs.50,000 to Rs.0.1 million. The data of Pakistan was not available. Thus, amongst all the selected countries, India is the only country where the maximum number of returns were filed at a very low level of income.

2. *Taxable Income*: The level of income at which the maximum amount of taxable income arose in the respected countries are given in Table 2.12 (F).

Thus, in Malaysia and India, the income becomes taxable at a comparatively much lower level of income than in any of the other developed countries.

3. *Tax Liability*: The level of income at which the maximum tax liability was payable in the respective countries is given in Table 2.12 (G).

The trend with regard to the tax liability is similar to that of taxable income in respect of developed countries and shows that the maximum tax liability arose at a high level of income. The trend in Malaysia is altogether different. While the maximum percentage of taxable income arose at around Rs.0.22 to .38 million of income, the maximum percentage of tax liability arose at income level exceeding Rs.4.4 million. The reason appears to be that the tax rates applicable on income level of Rs.0.22 to .38 million of income were much less than the tax rates applicable on income level exceeding Rs.4.4 million.

In India, not only is the level of income at which the maximum tax liability arose is the lowest amongst all these countries, but also the level at which the maximum tax liability arose was just Rs.0.1 million to Rs.0.2 million, which

TABLE 2.12(A). TAXABLE INCOME AND TAX LIABILITY IN THE U.K.

(for the income year 1997-98)

Total Income (Rs.)		Number of Individuals	Total Income (in million £)	Total Income (in million Rs.)	Taxable Income as % of Total Taxable Income	Total Tax Liability (in million £)	Tax Liability (in million Rs.)	Tax Liability as % of Total Tax
Upto 258,880		924,000	3,940	252,160	0.84	21	1,344	0.03
258,880	288,000	1,000,000	4,770	305,280	1.02	74	4,736	0.09
288,000	320,000	1,070,000	5,640	360,960	1.20	130	8,320	0.16
320,000	352,000	966,000	5,550	355,200	1.18	190	12,160	0.24
352,000	384,000	1,850,000	12,000	768,000	2.55	600	38,400	0.76
384,000	448,000	1,670,000	12,500	800,000	2.66	820	52,480	1.03
448,000	512,000	3,060,000	27,500	1,760,000	5.85	2,440	156,160	3.07
512,000	640,000	2,850,000	31,300	2,003,200	6.66	3,520	225,280	4.43
640,000	768,000	3,530,000	47,500	3,040,000	10.11	6,270	401,280	7.89
768,000	960,000	4,260,000	73,800	4,723,200	15.71	11,100	710,400	13.97
960,000	1,280,000	4,260,000	102,700	6,572,800	21.87	17,200	1,100,800	21.64
1,280,000	1,920,000	1,830,000	63,700	4,076,800	13.56	13,100	838,400	16.49
1,920,000	3,200,000	582,000	38,400	2,457,600	8.18	10,600	678,400	13.34
3,200,000	6,400,000	186,000	40,400	2,585,600	8.60	13,400	857,600	16.86
	Total	28,038,000	469,700	30,060,800	100.00	79,465	5,085,760	100.00

Source: Inland Revenue Statistics, 1999 (U.K.).

TABLE 2.12(B). TAXABLE INCOME AND TAX LIABILITY IN THE U.S.

(for the income year 1997)

Size of Adjusted Gross Income (Rs.)		Number of Returns	Taxable Income (in million $)	Taxable Income (in million Rs.)	Taxable Income as % of total taxable income	Total Tax Liability (in million $)	Total Tax Liability (in million Rs.)	Tax Liability as % of Total Tax Liability
No adjusted gross income		918,707				111	4,329	0.02
Upto 195,000		13,935,880	2,772	108,108	0.08	460	17,940	0.06
195,000	390,000	13,414,246	14,137	551,343	0.41	2,065	80,535	0.28
390,000	585,000	13,174,125	42,999	1,676,961	1.25	6,079	237,081	0.83
585,000	780,000	11,393,805	76,956	3,001,284	2.24	9,699	378,261	1.33
780,000	975,000	9,944,745	111,836	4,361,604	3.26	14,973	583,947	2.05
975,000	1,170,000	8,064,922	128,101	4,995,939	3.74	18,689	728,871	2.56
1,170,000	1,560,000	12,966,743	279,356	10,894,884	8.15	43,079	1,680,081	5.89
1,560,000	1,950,000	9,787,857	288,610	11,255,790	8.42	46,713	1,821,807	6.39
1,950,000	3,656,250	15,180,241	646,563	25,215,957	18.86	110,279	4,300,881	15.08
3,656,250	3,900,000	6,454,920	404,479	15,774,681	11.80	80,167	3,126,513	10.96
3,900,000	7,800,000	5,377,899	548,325	21,384,675	15.99	126,267	4,924,413	17.27
7,800,000	19,500,000	1,401,734	345,717	13,482,963	10.08	99,512	3,880,968	13.61
19,500,000	39,000,000	261,708	157,796	6,154,044	4.60	51,291	2,000,349	7.01
Above 39,000,000		144,459	381,459	14,876,901	11.12	121,936	4,755,504	16.67
	Total	122,421,991	3,429,109	133,735,251	100.00	731,321	28,521,519	100.00

Source: *IRS Statistics of Income Bulletin,* Fall 1999, Publication (Rev 12-99).

TABLE 2.12(C). TAXABLE INCOME AND TAX LIABILITY IN AUSTRALIA

(For the income year 1997-98)

Taxable Income (Rs.)		Number of Returns	Taxable Income (in million AUD)	Taxable Income (in million Rs.)	Taxable Income as percentage of Total Taxable Income	Total Tax (in million AUD)	Total Tax (in million Rs.)	Tax as percentage of Total Tax
Non-Taxable	1,554,455	5,616	140,400	2.03	576	14,400	0.89	
0	250,000	606,038	4,756	118,900	1.72	236	5,900	0.36
250,000	375,000	983,977	12,352	308,800	4.46	1,056	26,400	1.63
375,000	500,000	978,203	17,132	428,300	6.18	2,113	52,825	3.26
500,000	625,000	1,045,336	23,474	586,850	8.47	3,704	92,600	5.71
625,000	875,000	1,824,485	54,294	1,357,350	19.59	11,201	280,025	17.27
875,000	1,250,000	1,688,266	70,122	1,753,050	25.31	17,599	439,975	27.13
1,250,000	2,500,000	972,590	62,169	1,554,225	22.44	19,165	479,125	29.55
2,500,000	12,500,000	148,037	23,309	582,725	8.41	7,975	199,375	12.30
12,500,000	25,000,000	3,302	2,178	54,450	0.79	737	18,425	1.14
25,000,000	and above	906	1,693	42,325	0.61	496	12,400	0.76
Total		9,805,595	277,095	6,927,375	100	64,282	1,621,450	100

Source: Taxation Statistics 1997-98 (CD-ROM).

TABLE 2.12(D). TAXABLE INCOME AND TAX LIABILITY IN MALAYSIA

(for the income year 1997)

Taxable Income (Rs.)		Number of Returns	Taxable Income (in million AUD)	Taxable Income (in million Rs.)	Taxable Income as percentage of Total Taxable Income	Total Tax Liability (in million AUD)	Total Tax Liability (in million Rs.)	Tax Liability as percentage of Total Tax Liability
0	27,500	16,694	23,217	255,387	0.05	306	3,366	0.01
27,500	5,500	31,594	133,850	1,472,350	0.34	1,728	19,008	0.04
5,500	110,000	270,034	2,235,381	24,589,191	5.54	51,749	569,239	1.12
110,000	220,000	539,012	7,715,904	84,874,944	19.13	280,246	3,082,706	6.07
220,000	385,000	296,429	7,747,580	85,223,380	19.21	441,489	4,856,379	9.56
385,000	550,000	113,139	4,699,054	51,689,594	11.65	389,880	4,288,680	8.44
550,000	770,000	65,792	3,854,245	42,396,695	9.56	436,222	4,798,442	9.44
770,000	1,100,000	40,796	3,380,219	37,182,409	8.38	506,074	5,566,814	10.95
1,100,000	1,650,000	25,297	3,050,682	33,557,502	7.57	579,392	6,373,312	12.54
1,650,000	2,200,000	9,785	1,682,202	18,504,222	4.17	372,386	4,096,246	8.06
2,200,000	2,750,000	4,872	1,041,277	11,454,047	2.58	259,368	2,853,048	5.61
2,750,000	3,300,000	2,925	798,529	8,783,819	1.98	200,234	2,202,574	4.33
3,300,000	2,750,000	1,807	584,257	6,426,827	1.49	150,953	1,660,483	3.27
2,750,000	4,400,000	1,185	442,183	4,864,013	1.10	116,691	1,283,601	2.52
4,400,000	and above	3,549	2,935,394	32,289,334	7.28	833,012	9,163,132	18.03
Total		1,422,910	40,323,974	443,356,714	100	4,619,730	50,817,030	100

Source: Taxation Statistics, 1998 (Malaysia).

TABLE 2.12(E). TAXABLE INCOME AND TAX LIABILITY IN INDIA

(for the income year 1996-97)

Taxable Income (Rs.)		Number of Returns	Taxable Income (in million Rs.)	Taxable Income as percentage of Total Taxable Income	Total Tax Liability (in million Rs.)	Tax Liability as percentage of Total Tax Liability
0	40,000	1,083,346	26,472	3.44	514	0.46
40,000	50,000	2,487,851	109,702	14.24	1,842	1.67
50,000	100,000	3,568,286	247,259	32.10	19,466	17.61
100,000	200,000	1,641,864	216,717	28.13	39,613	35.83
200,000	300,000	121,350	29,320	3.81	7,988	7.22
300,000	400,000	56,939	19,482	2.53	5,711	5.17
400,000	500,000	29,062	12,976	1.68	3,998	3.62
500,000	1,000,000	40,642	27,988	3.63	8,792	7.95
1,000,000	and above	20,058	80,378	10.43	22,625	20.47
Total		9,049,398	770,295	100.00	110,549	100.00

Source: *All India Income Tax Statistics:* Assessment Year, 1997-98

TABLE 2.12(F)

Country	Maximum Percentage of Taxable Income	Size of Taxable Income at which maximum Taxable Income arose in any country (in million Rs.)
U.K.	21.86	0.96 to 1.28
U.S.	18.86	1.95 to 3.66
Australia	25.31	0.87 to 1.25
Malaysia	19.21	0.22 to 0.38
Pakistan	n.a.	n.a.
India	32.10	0.05 to 0.10

TABLE 2.12(G)

Country	Maximum Percentage of Tax Liability	Size of Taxable Income at which maximum Tax Liability was payable in any country (in million Rs.)
U.K.	21.64	0.96 to 1.28
U.S.	17.27	3.90 to 7.80
Australia	29.55	1.25 to 2.50
Malaysia	18.03	above 4.40
Pakistan	n.a.	n.a.
India	35.83	0.10 to 0.20

was not only the lowest but was in sharp contrast to Malaysia. This is due to the maximum tax rate applicable on income level of Rs.0.1 million to Rs.0.2 million.

Thus it can be concluded that compared to all the other countries for which data is available, India is the only country where maximum tax was payable at a very low level of income. It appears that high-income group individuals, especially self-employed persons have been able to escape from income tax net due to tax avoidance techniques or possibly through tax evasion.

Agricultural Income and Income Tax Base

Any discussion on income tax base shall be incomplete without any reference to the agricultural income. As mentioned earlier, agricultural income in Pakistan and India are exempt from income tax and therefore do not form part of the income tax base in these two selected countries. It is true that taxation of agricultural income has been a controversial issue. There are several issues connected with it. Firstly, any attempt to tax agricultural income will require amendment in the Indian constitution, because under the constitution, only states are authorised to levy tax on agricultural income. Secondly, it is presumed that the majority of farmers in India are those who take agriculture as activity to fulfil their basic necessities and in the absence of any statistics available on how many persons are earning sufficient or a high level of agricultural income which may provide revenue to the government, it may not be logical to impose tax on agricultural income. Thirdly, there is indirect or concealed taxation in the form of compulsory procurement of food grains by the government. One way in which agriculture is taxed through import tariffs and quotas, which restrict imports and therefore raise the exchange rate. This lowers the domestic price for potential exports, which will mean lowering the domestic price per agricultural outputs and in this sense is like a tax on output.[22]

Fourthly, in a majority of the cases the agricultural crop even in the twenty-first century is at the mercy of the rainfall and fifthly, the agricultural income tax will certainly lead to further increase in the prices of agricultural products many of which are used as raw materials in industries and will distort the overall economy.

On grounds of equity, it may be justified that agricultural income be treated at par with other incomes. However, considering the cost of collecting these taxes as well as administrative burden, it may not be desirable to tax agricultural income.

The position of Pakistan with respect to the taxation of agricultural income is similar to that of India. All other selected countries, besides India and Pakistan levy tax on agricultural income, which is a part of the income tax base in their countries. This is despite the fact the agriculture forms a very small part of the GDP in these countries, especially the developed countries.

The share of agricultural output in the GDP of the selected countries are given in Table 2.13

The share of agricultural output in the overall GDP of these countries is evident from Table 2.13. It is clear that the percentage share of agricultural output in the GDP in the developed countries is from 2 to 3 per cent. Though it is around 25 per cent both in Pakistan and in India in 1998, the percentage share in India has reduced substantially from 38 per cent, in 1980 to 25 per cent, in 1998.

TABLE 2.13. SHARE OF AGRICULTURAL OUTPUT IN THE GDP

Country	Share of Agricultural Output in GDP (Percent)	
	1980	1998
U.K.	2	2
U.S.	3	2
Australia	5	3
Malaysia	22	12
Pakistan	30	25
India	38	25

Source: World Development Report, 1999-2000

Share of Taxable Agricultural Income in the Total Taxable Income

The share of taxable agricultural income in the total taxable income of individual and corporate taxpayers of the selected countries is given in Table 2.14

The table reveals that even in the case of developed countries where agricultural income is taxable, the ratio of taxable agricultural income to the total taxable income is negligible. In the U.K., this ratio is 0.6 per cent. In the U.S., there is loss from the farm activity in the case of individual taxpayers. In Australia, not only is the share less than one per cent in the case of both kind of taxpayers, there are also past losses relating to primary production. The data with regard to past losses is not given. The share of taxable agricultural income in the total income in Malaysia is less than 1 per cent and 4 per cent respectively, in the case of individual and corporate taxpayers. It may be concluded that even in those countries where agricultural income is taxable, the share of taxable agricultural income is negligible and in some cases there is even loss. The share is even much less than the share of agricultural output in the GDP of these countries.

TABLE 2.14. THE RATIO OF TAXABLE AGRICULTURAL INCOME TO TOTAL TAXABLE INCOME

(for the income year 1997-98, amount is in millions)

Country	Individual Taxpayer			Corporate Taxpayer		
	Taxable Agricultural Income	Total Income	Agricultural Income as percentage of Total Income	Agricultural Income	Total Income	Agricultural Income as percentage of Total Income
U.K.	2,820	469,700	0.6	418	118,499	0.35
U.S.	–6,848	3,429,109	loss	2,674	915,397	0.29
Australia	1,440	277,089	0.52	729	99,737	0.73
Malaysia	400	40,324	0.99	3,064	69,763	4.4

Notes: 1. Amount is given in individual country currency.
2. Agricultural income is exempt in Pakistan and India and therefore no taxable agricultural income arises in these two countries.

Source: Same as given in Table 2.12(a-d)

Considering the overall picture, there does not seem to be any rationale behind imposing any tax on agricultural income. The income tax base in India is narrow not because agricultural income is exempt but because of low GDP per capita. Also, the high-income earners seem to be resorting to tax avoidance and tax evasion.

NOTES

1. Ken Messere, *Tax Policy in OECD Countries: Choices and Conflicts* (Amsterdam: IFBD Publications, 1993), p. 33
2. Hugh J. Ault, *Comparative Income Taxation: A Structural Analysis* (The Netherlands: Kluwer Law International, 1997), p. 131
3. Thomas R. Pope and John L. Kramer (eds.), *Prentice-Hall's Federal Taxation:* 1998, *Individual* (Upper Saddle River, N.J.: Prentice-Hall, 1997), pp. 2, 3
4. *CCH Australian Master Tax Guide* (Sydney: CCH Australia Ltd, 1999), p. 1
5. Richard Thornton, *MLJ Tax Handbook* (Kuala Lumpur: Malaysian Law Journal Sdn Bhd, 1998), p. 1
6. A.T. Pandey, 'A Study of Changing Dimensions of Taxation of Income in India' (an unpublished Ph.D. thesis, faculty of commerce: Amravati University, 1992), p. 66
7. D. Kumar, *The Cambridge Economic History of India,* Vol. II (Cambridge: Cambridge University Press, 1982) p. 924
8. In this study, unless otherwise stated reference of the Section is to the following Acts of the respective countries,
   The *Income and Corporation Taxes Act,* 1988 (U.K.)
   The *Internal Revenue Code,* 1986 (The U.S.)
   The *Income Tax Assessment Act,* 1936 (Australia)
   The *Income Tax Assessment Act,* 1997 (Australia)
   The *Income Tax Act,* 1967 *(Act 53)* (Malaysia)
   The *Income Tax Ordinance,* 1979 (Pakistan)
   The *Income Tax Act,* 1961 (India)
9. Ikramul Haq, *Practical Handbook of Income Tax* (Lahore: Lahore Law Publications, 1999), p. 317.
10. Hugh J. Ault, op. cit., p. 270
11. *Oxford English Dictionary.*
12. A qualified individual means, a U.S. citizen working abroad having a tax home in a foreign country and who meet either the bonafide residence test or physical presence test. A U.S. resident alien working abroad can qualify for either exclusion provided he meets the physical presence test. Bonafide residence test means a taxpayer must be a bonafide resident of foreign country or countries for an uninterrupted period that includes a full tax year. However, he will not be considered to be a bonafide resident if he files a non-residency statement with the foreign authorities and is held exempt from such country's income tax. (Physical presence test means that a taxpayer spends 330 full days out of any 12 consecutive month-period in a foreign country or countries. This requirement is unconditional with only one exception when an individual is required to leave the foreign country, because of war, or civil unrest. However, shortfall because of illness is not excluded.
13. Foreign earned income is considered received in the year in which services are rendered. The term 'earned income' means wages, salaries, professional fees and other amounts received as compensation for personal services actually rendered during the period in which bonafide residence test or physical presence test is met. If it is a trade or a business, in which both personal services and capital are material factors for producing income, a reasonable allowance not in excess of 30 per cent of its share of net profits of such trade or business is considered as earned income being compensation for

personal services. Foreign earned income does not include amounts paid by the U.S. or its agencies to its employees, amounts received as pensions, annuities and social security payments.

14. Fixed or determinable income includes interest dividends, rents, salaries, wages, premiums, annuities and other fixed or determinable amount or periodical gains, profits and income.
15. For rating purpose, a person is treated as resident if he was resident during the income year or was in receipt of a taxable Australian social security or veterans entitlement pension or benefit. Others are classified as a prescribed non-resident.
16. The words 'accrue and arise' denote the same idea, both the words mean a right to receive. When the right to receive the income becomes vested in the taxpayer, it is said to have accrued or arisen to him. The meaning of words 'deemed to accrue or arise', is where it does not actually accrue or arise but the law requires it to be treated as if it had accrued or arisen in Pakistan.
17. For a detailed discussion on the concept of long-term capital gains, see Chapter 5.
18. Assessment year is the year next to income year and is the year in which a return of income is filed and assessed.
19. The World Bank, *Lessons of Tax Reform* (Washington, D.C.: The World Bank, 1991), p. 5
20. Ken Messere, 'Half a Century of Changes in Taxation', *International Bureau of Fiscal Documentation*, Vol. 53, No. 8/9 (Aug.-Sept. 1999), pp. 347-8.
21. *Ibid.*
22. Ehtisham Ahmad and Nicholas Stern, *The Theory and Practice of Tax Reform in Developing Countries* (New Delhi: Foundation Books, 1991), p. 97.

CHAPTER 3

Taxability of Salary Income

Salary income, commonly known as income from employment, or compensation for services, constitutes a significant part of taxable income of individuals in many countries. Although income from salary and income from business and profession both are earned income, an important difference exists between both these two types of income. Any amount received for rendering services is known as salary, provided it is received by the individual from an employer. The relationship of employer and employee is must for any receipt to be treated as salary. While the salary is given by way of direct reward for services, the business income may not be a direct reward for services. Part of the business income may be due to the unexpected rise in prices or a sudden increase in the demand for the product. While the salaried employees work with the minimum risk, the businessman on the other hand, undertakes a lot of risk and, therefore, the business income may also be a reward for the risk taken.

Although the term 'salary' commonly refers to the amount received for non-manual work, and the term 'wages' refers to the amount received for manual work, these two terms are treated at par for tax purposes. The tax base of salary income in a country depends upon many factors including the following:

1. The extent to which different components of salary, including allowances, fringe benefits, pension contributions and retirement benefits, are exempt.
2. Whether any deduction is allowed in respect of expenses incurred in connection with the employment, and the conditions required to claim such deduction.

While salary income is one source where the tax compliance is maximum as tax is deducted at source in most of the countries, still ways and means are found to reduce the amount of taxable salary. The payment of a part of salary to the employee in the form of fringe benefit is a common way of tax evasion.

The income tax provisions related to income from salary are vast and complicated. Whether a component of salary is exempt or taxable, and whether a deduction is allowed in respect of the expenditure incurred in connection with employment purposes, depends upon various conditions and these conditions vary from one country to another country.

The provisions relating to the salary income of the selected countries are compared and evaluated under following heads:

1. Salary income in general

2. Taxability of retirement benefits
3. Taxability of fringe benefits
4. Taxability of car benefit
5. Taxability of rent-free accommodation
6. Deductions from salary income

SALARY INCOME IN GENERAL

In general, *Salary Income* includes wages, salaries, pension, gratuity, leave salary, allowances and fringe benefits. The base of salary income is narrowed down by exemptions granted fully or partly.

Salary income in the U.K. is chargeable to tax under Schedule-E of the *Income and Corporation Taxes Act*. Under Schedule E, the tax is charged on the emoluments of an office or employment. The term *emoluments* includes practically anything that could conceivably be received by an employee in respect of an employment. It includes wages, salaries, bonuses, commissions, fees, expense allowances, payments on the termination of employment, pensions arising from an employment and benefits-in-kind. Emoluments also include social security benefits such as retirement pension, incapacity benefit, maternity pay, invalid care allowance and industrial death benefit.[1]

In the U.K., emolument received as a result of the office or employment is taxable under Schedule E. Emoluments received from a source other than the employer such as a waiter's tips are also taxable as Schedule E income. Tax on salary income is payable under 'Pay As You Earn' (PAYE) system. The PAYE was introduced in the U.K. in an attempt to overcome many of the difficulties of assessment and collection that arose during the Second World War. At that time the rate of income tax was raised by 50 per cent and the value of the exempt allowances reduced. This brought a large number of people who were unused to paying income tax into the tax net.

In the U.S., Sec. 61 (a) of the *Internal Revenue Code*, 1986, provides a list of items to be included in the gross income. The first item in the list is compensation for services, including fees, commissions, fringe benefits, and similar items. Salary also includes tips, bonuses, the director's fees, jury fees, annuity and pension.[2] Wages and salaries are subject to withholding tax in the U.S. Exemption is granted from income tax withholding to certain employees, such as agricultural labourers, ministers, domestic servants, newspaper carriers under age 18 and earning tips of less than $20 per month. As regards annuity and pension, if they are received annually, they are subject to ordinary withholding rules. A 10 per cent withholding rate is used for lump sum distribution or payment. However, the individual may elect to have no tax withheld.

Earnings for personal services in Australia include salary, wages, overtime payments, commissions, long service leave pay, and the director's fees.[3] Any tax deducted at source, the employee's superannuation contributions deducted from his salary and any other payment such as health insurance and loan repayment deducted from salary on the employee's instruction is added in the income from salary. Salary and wages income is the primary source of individual income tax in Australia.

Earnings for personal services rendered are assessable in the year of receipt or constructive receipt, and not in the year earned, except where the services are rendered in the course of business and professional practice, which is subject to an accrual basis of accounting. A receipt is considered constructive when income is credited without restriction and made available to the taxpayer. Any voluntary payment or gift, if provided in connection with employment or a reward for services, is treated as salary, even if it is paid by a third party, such as tips.

Employment income in Malaysia in general includes:

1. wages, salary, leave pay, fee, commission, bonus, gratuity, perquisite, or allowance (whether in money or otherwise) in respect of having or exercising the employment,
2. an amount equal to the value of the use or enjoyment by the employee of any benefit or amenity (not being a benefit or amenity convertible into money),
3. Accommodation provided free, and
4. Compensation for the loss of employment.[4]

Employment income in Malaysia is assessed on a preceding year basis. The basis period runs from January 1, to December 31. Generally, employment income is derived when it is receivable, i.e. when the employee is legally entitled to receive the income and it can be obtained on demand.

Salary in Pakistan, includes, wages, any annuity, pension or gratuity, any fee, commission, allowances, perquisites, and profits in lieu of or in addition to salary or wages.[5] Salary is chargeable to tax either on 'due' basis or on 'receipt' basis, whichever matures earlier.

The employer is liable to deduct tax at source on the amount of salary payable at the average rate of tax prescribed for the financial year in the First Schedule in which the payments to employees are made.

Salary income in India includes, wages, any annuity or pension, any gratuity, any fees, commission, perquisites, profits in lieu of or in addition to any salary or wages, any advance of salary, and leave salary [Sec. 17 (1)].[6] In India, salary is chargeable to tax either on 'due' basis or the 'receipt' basis, whichever matures earlier.

Salaried Taxpayers in the Selected Countries

A comparison of salaried taxpayers and gross salary income in the selected countries is shown in Table 3.1.

As shown in the table, salaried taxpayers constituted a major part of the individual taxpayers and salary income was also the major constituent of the total income of individual taxpayers in most of these countries. The percentage of salaried taxpayers to the total individual taxpayers was very high in the developed countries. In the U.S., it was as high as 85.2 per cent of the total

TABLE 3.1. SALARIED TAXPAYERS AND GROSS SALARY INCOME IN THE SELECTED COUNTRIES

(amount in individual country currency)

Country	Income Year	Total Number of Individual Taxpayers	Salaried Taxpayers	Percentage of Salaried Taxpayers to Total Individual Taxpayers	Gross Total Income of Individual Taxpayers (in millions)	Gross Salary Income of Salaried Taxpayers (in millions)	Percentage of Gross Salary Income to Gross Total Income
U.K.	1997-98	27,900,000	20,700,000	74.1	469,700	331,700	70.6
U.S.	1997	122,421,991	104,404,985	85.2	4,969,950	3,613,918	72.7
Australia	1997-98	9,793,620	7,573,141	77.3	291,550	216,120	74.1
Malaysia	1997	1,459,134	1,033,838	70.8	71,728	35,464	49.4
Pakistan	1993-94	1,665,901	562,655	33.7	52,385*	19,321*	36.8
India	1996-97	9,049,398	1,620,983	17.9	864,233	118.801	13.7

Note: *These figures are for the year 1993-94 since the information for the income year 1997-98 was not available.

Source: Taxation Statistics of the Selected Countries as given in Table 2.12 (a) (b) (c) (d) (e).

individual taxpayers, followed by Australia where it was 77.3 per cent and the U.K. where it was 74.1 per cent. Among the developing countries, Malaysia had the highest percentage of salaried taxpayers, i.e. 70.8 per cent. In India, it was as low as 17.9 per cent whereas in Pakistan, it was 33.7 per cent. In all the countries selected for study, the employer had an obligation to deduct and pay tax on behalf of the employee. Therefore, the chances of salaried income going unreported were less in all these countries, including India and Pakistan. The reason for the low percentage of salaried taxpayers in India and Pakistan appears to be that a low percentage of population is in employment and low level of salary amount being paid to the employees as compared to the tax-free threshold limit for income tax. The gross salary income of salaried taxpayers as compared to the gross total income of individual taxpayers was also high in the developed countries. It was highest in Australia, where it was 74.1 per cent, followed by the U.S. where it was 72.7 per cent. Among the developing countries, the lowest percentage was in India, where it was 13.7 per cent. The reason for low taxable salary income in India may also be due to the fact that more concessions including a fixed standard deduction was allowed which reduced the tax base of salary income.

Taxability of Retirement Benefits

Retirement benefits are received in various forms such as pension, gratuity, provident fund or leave salary. Pension represents series of periodic money payments made to a person who retires from employment because of age, disability or the completion of an agreed span of service. Eligibility for and amounts of benefits are based on a variety of factors, including length of employment, age, earnings and in some cases past contributions. Pensions may be funded by making payments into a pension trust fund or by the purchase of annuities form insurance companies.[7] A gratuity is a gift of money given to the employee after retirement in recognition of long period of service, and is usually payable after some minimum years of service has been performed. On the other hand, lump sum retirement payment may also include employee's contribution besides employer's contribution.

In whatever forms these retirement benefits are provided, the concession in tax may be allowed in the following ways:

1. Exemption may be provided either fully or within limits at the time of contribution towards retirement benefits by the employer, employee or self-employed person, thus resulting in postponement of tax.
2. If lump sum payment received on retirement is also exempt partly or fully, then instead of postponement, there may be partial or complete exemption from tax. While any lump sum retirement payment if exempt is excluded from the gross salary to the extent it is exempt, on the other hand, contribution by the employee is either allowed as deduction from salary or as tax rebate to be deducted from the tax liability.

Considering the above factors, an analysis of the tax treatment of retirement benefits in the selected countries is made in this part. As there are number of retirement schemes provided for in the Income Tax Legislation of the selected countries, only a few such schemes have been taken for the purposes of analysis.

THE U.K.

Various retirement benefit schemes are provided in the U.K. to provide for future security of the taxpayer and these retirement benefit schemes are also used as a tax-planning device.

The two most popular retirement schemes are as follows:

1. Occupational Pension Schemes.
2. Personal Pension Schemes.

The Occupational Pension Scheme (OPS) is applicable to individuals who are employed. The employee can contribute up to 15 per cent of earnings and the maximum earnings on which the rate of 15 per cent is applicable, is also fixed. The amount is £91,800 per annum for the income year 2000-01.

Personal Pension Scheme (PPS) was introduced on July 1, 1988 to replace another scheme, i.e. retirement annuities. PPS is applicable to self-employed persons as well as employees. The maximum earning is also fixed as with OPS Scheme, and is £91,800 per annum for the income year 2000-01. The percentage of net relevant earnings[8] which can be contributed also varies depending upon the age of the taxpayer and is given in Table 3.2:

Tax treatment of both the schemes is same and is given below:

1. The employee's contributions within limits are exempt from tax and are allowed as deduction from the employee's income from employment.
2. The employer's contributions and in the case of unfunded schemes, benefits paid, are a deductible business expense.
3. The employer's contributions are not taxed as income of the employee.
4. Lump sum payment on retirement and death are exempt from income tax.
5. Pension when paid is fully taxable.

TABLE 3.2. PERSONAL PENSION MAXIMUM CONTRIBUTION LEVELS IN THE UK
(for the income year 2000-01)

Age at the start of the year	Percentage of Earnings
35 or less	17.5
36 to 45	20.0
46 to 50	25.0
51 to 55	30.0
56 to 60	35.0
61 to 74	40.0

Source: Alan Melville, p. 205.

Tax relief on pension scheme contributions may either be allowed in the year of payment or related back to an earlier year, if the taxpayer so decides. When the relief is taken in an earlier year, the tax liability of the earlier year is not disturbed. An amount representing the reduction in income tax liability for the previous year may be relieved:

(a) by repayment of tax previously paid.
(b) by set off against outstanding income tax liabilities, or
(c) by treating the amount repayable as a payment made on account for the year in which contributions were actually paid.[9]

Any eligible contribution to pension scheme which could not be availed of in any year in the U.K. may be carried forward for a maximum period of 6 years and applied to relieve contributions paid in future years, to the extent of excess of actual contributions in the future years over the specified percentage (17.5 per cent or higher).

Payments received by an employee on the death of the employee because of injury or disability, lump sum payments under approved superannuation schemes and statutory redundancy pay though considered emoluments are exempt from tax. Payments made to compensate an employee for loss of employment is exempt up to £ 30,000. Other termination payments which do not fall in any of the above categories are taxable as emoluments.

Social security benefits are given due weightage in the U.K. There the government provides retirement benefits to individuals. For this purpose, national insurance contributions (NIC's) are payable by the employers, employees and self-employed individuals. No tax relief is available for these contributions. Such contributions are collected by the Department of Social Security (DSS) and are paid into a National Insurance Fund. The fund is responsible to pay state retirement pension out of the contributions received and as well as the grant from the treasury.

THE U.S.

Various types of retirement benefits plans providing favourable tax treatment are available to employees and self-employed individuals in the U.S. These tax benefits are provided to stimulate savings accumulation for retirement as a supplement to the social security system. Tax reliefs are provided to the employee as well as the employer through deferral of taxes on contributions and earnings. Pension plan in the U.S. may be a qualified-pension plan or a nonqualified pension plan.

A qualified-pension plan is one which fulfils certain requirements including the following: (i) the plan must be formed and operated for the exclusive benefit of employees, (ii) it must not discriminate in favour of highly compensated employees and (iii) an employee's right to receive benefits from the employer's contribution must vest after a certain period or number of years of employment.

Under a qualified-pension plan, neither the employee's, nor the employer's contribution to the plan is treated as taxable income to the employee. The earnings on these contributions are not subject to tax until the employee makes a withdrawal from the pension plan, i.e. it becomes taxable when it is received by the taxpayer. On the other hand, in the case of a non-qualified exemption plan, neither the employee's contribution is exempt, nor the employer's contribution entitled to tax deduction. However, it become tax free at the time when lump sum payment is received. Thus, the two schemes are quite opposite to each other. While in the case of a qualified pension scheme, exemption from tax is granted gradually at the time of contribution by the employer and the employee. On the other side, in a non-qualified pension scheme, exemption is granted at a later stage when lump sum payment is received.

A qualified-pension plan may be either (i) a defined-contribution pension plan or (ii) a defined-benefit pension plan. In the case of first plan, retirement benefits are based on the total contributions (From both employee and employer) made to the plan along with the gains and losses (net of expenses) earned by the asset in the plan.

A defined-contribution plan may be either:

1. Money-purchase plan
2. Profit-sharing plan

In money-purchase plan, the company and the employee contribute a fixed percentage of the employee's salary to the pension plan. The contribution limit is the lesser of $30,000 or 25 per cent of the employee's taxable compensation for the income year 2000.

The profit-sharing plan does not require a fixed annual contribution. It must specify a formula for allocating the contribution among each of the plan's participant. The limit of this plan is $30,000 or 15 per cent of the employee's taxable compensation. Further, in both these plans, there is an overall ceiling on the amount of compensation eligible for calculating an employee's maximum contribution. The amount of ceiling is $170,000 in income year 2000.

In the case of the defined-benefit plan, the employer's contribution is so fixed as to provide a fixed retirement benefit plan. The retirement benefits are based on the number of years an employee has worked for the company, and the employee's annual salary. Under this plan, the annual normal retirement benefits for any employee may not exceed the lesser of $170,000 or 100 per cent of the employee's average compensation for the 3 consecutive years of highest compensation.

Thus, the defined-contribution plan and the defined-benefit plan are totally different. While the first plan is forward looking as it is based on current and future salary, the second plan is backward-looking, as it is based on only past salary.

Non-qualified pension plan have fewer restrictions and may be discriminatory in nature. In such case, certain restrictions are, however, placed on the outright transfer of the plan's benefit to the employee. As a result, the tax is imposed on the employee when the restrictions come to an end and the employer also gets deduction in the same year.

In the U.S., the social security is provided by the government as well as tax incentives are provided for contributions made towards future pension plans. Under the *Federal Insurance Contributions Act,* an employer is required to withhold social security taxes (including hospital insurance tax) from wages paid to an employee during the year. The combined tax rate is 7.65 per cent of wages for the income year, which consists of 6.2 per cent by way of old-age, survivors and disability insurance (OASDI) subject to an overall wage limit of $76,200 for 2000 income year) and 1.45 per cent component for hospital insurance contribution. The employer is also required to make matching contribution.

Self-employed persons are supposed to pay 15.3 per cent of tax on their self-employment income, which consists of a 12.4 per cent component for OASDI and a 2.9 per cent component for hospital insurance.

AUSTRALIA

Tax provisions relating to eligible contributions towards retirement benefits and retirement payments are extremely complicated and detailed. The government in Australia is committed to a retirement income policy so that people live a comfortable life after retirement. Since 1991, the government has made tremendous efforts in this direction. The government enacted the *Superannuation Guarantee (Administration) Act*, 1992 and introduced compulsory superannuation contributions effective from July 1, 1992. As a result of government's efforts, whereas 41 per cent of employees had superannuation coverage in 1988, after the introduction of compulsory superannuation, the percentage of employees who had superannuation coverage increased to 79 per cent by 1991, and further rose to 91 per cent by 1995.

In Australia, the Australian Prudential Regulation Authority (APRA) governs the operations of superannuation funds. According to APRA, the superannuation contribution in 1998-99 was AUD47.3 billion, an increase of 40 per cent over the previous year.

Contributions to a superannuation fund in Australia may be either tax deductible or may give rise to a tax rebate. A superannuation fund, which is basically a provident fund, may be a Complying Superannuation Fund (CSF) or a non-complying superannuation fund. A complying superannuation fund is a regulated superannuation fund, fulfilling certain requirements under the *Superannuation Industry (Supervision) Act,* 1993 (SISA). Besides superannuation funds, Retirement Savings Accounts (RSAs) which is simple, low cost and low risk savings product, is also popular and is operated in Australia by banks, building societies, life insurance companies and the prescribed financial institutions. RSA's in Australia get the same tax benefit as CSF.

Employer's contribution for the purpose of making provision for superannuation benefits for an eligible employee are deductible under Sec. 82AAC if the contributions are made to CSF or RSA's. Contribution to non-employing superannuation funds may also be deductible if the taxpayer making the contribution has reasonable grounds for believing that the fund is a complying fund. The employer's contribution to a superannuation fund or RSA is subject to an age-base limit of the employee for whom contributions are made. The deduction limit is (1) AUD10,000 for employees under 35 years of age, (2) AUD29,443 for employees aged above 35 and up to 49 years of age and, (3) the maximum limit is AUD73,019 for employees aged 50 years or above.

Employer's contribution to a non-complying superannuation fund may be deductible, but these contributions are treated as fringe benefits and become taxable in the hands of the employer.

The employee's contribution to CSF is also eligible for deduction provided the employees do not receive any employer's superannuation support. An employee receiving the employer's superannuation support is not allowed deduction for his contribution to the fund, but may be entitled to a tax rebate.

In Australia, employers who fail to provide a minimum level of support are liable to pay the superannuation guarantee charge equal to the amount of the shortfall plus an interest component and an administrative charge.

Retirement payments known as Eligible Terminal Payments (ETP) include payment from the superannuation fund, RSA's and miscellaneous payments. For tax purposes, ETP is divided into two components. In the case of ETP which relates to services up to June 30, 1983, 5 per cent of the amount is included in the assessable income and taxed at marginal rates. An ETP, which relates to service after June 30, 1983, is assessable in full at the maximum rate of tax of 20 per cent or 30 per cent for payments received under 55 years of age, depending on the source (whether taxed or untaxed) of payment. In the case of payments received at the age of 55 years or later, the tax rate on the first AUD93,731 of fully assessable amount is limited to nil or 15 per cent, with the tax year rate on the balance limited to 15 per cent or 30 per cent. Annuity and pension payments received by a person in each year are included in the person's assessable income for that year and taxed at marginal rates. However, the amount is reduced by the deductible amount in case of purchased annuities and pensions. Further, an annuity paid from a resident non-complying superannuation fund is exempt from tax. An annuity or pension recipient may be entitled to a rebate of tax in some cases.

In Australia, retirement benefits are taxable at the above specified rates only if they are within Reasonable Benefit Limits (RBL's). These RBL's are the maximum amount of retirement benefits that a person can receive over their lifetime at concessional rates of tax. Benefits taken in excess of RBL do not receive concessional treatment. The amount of RBL differs for lump sum payment and for pension. Every year, RBL's are indexed. For the income year

1998-99, the lump sum RBL was AUD471,088 and the pension RBL was AUD909,435. If a lump sum benefit is in excess of RBL, the excess will be taxed at the highest personal income tax rates, which is 47 per cent for the income year 1998-99. Any pension or annuity in excess of RBL will be subject to a reduced pension rebate.

MALAYSIA

Retirement gratuity and pension are exempt from tax if paid on account of retirement due to ill health, or if the retirement takes place on or after reaching the age of 55 or on reaching the compulsory age of retirement specified under any law. In the case of gratuity however, exemption is granted to individual who has had 10 years of continuous employment with the same employer or with companies in the same group. (Schedule 6, Sec. 25(1), Sec. 30.)

A lump sum payment in respect of a commuted pension in Malaysia is not income. Any pension or other periodical payment paid voluntarily to any person who has permanently ceased to exercise an employment or to his widow, child, relative or dependent by his former employer shall be taxable income. Annuity in general is assessable.

As regards the employee's contributions to an approved provident fund, if the contributions are obligatory and arise from a contract of employment or any provisions in the rules of the fund or scheme, such contributions are deductible up to RM5000 for the income year 1999. (Sec. 49(1).) Husband and wife can claim up to RM5000 each, unless the wife has no total income.

PAKISTAN

The tax treatment of gratuity depends upon the type of employment. Any death-cum-retirement gratuity received by the employees of the government, a local authority or a statutory corporation is totally exempt from tax. Similarly, gratuity received by employees covered by an approved gratuity under Sixth Schedule is also exempt. In case gratuity is approved by the Central Board of Revenue, the gratuity received up to PKR2,00,000 is exempt for the income year 1999-2000. In the case of other employees, gratuity is exempt to the extent of the lesser of the (i) 50 per cent of salary or (ii) PKR75,000. (Clause 27(i)(ii)(iii) of Second Schedule.) Gratuity is taxable as a separate block of income and is taxed at the average rate at which the employee was liable to be taxed during the preceding 3 years.

As regards pension, with effect from the assessment year 1992-93, pension is exempt without any age limit.

Annuity in general is taxable except in certain specific cases where exemption is provided under the *Income Tax Ordinance*, 1979.

In Pakistan, provident fund may be of the following types:

1. Statutory Provident Fund

2. Recognised Provident Fund
3. Unrecognised Provident Fund

The Statutory Provident Fund (SPF) is set up under the provisions of the *Provident Fund Act,* 1925 and is maintained by the government, semi-government institutions, railways, and recognised educational institutions.

Recognised Provident Fund (RPF) is one which is recognised by the commissioner of income tax in accordance with the rules contained in Part I of the Sixth Schedule of the ordinance. Unrecognised Provident Fund (UPF) is one which is not recognised.

In the case of SPF, the employer's contribution and interest thereon are exempt. The employee's contribution is fully deductible from the taxable salary income. Lump sum payment received is also exempt from tax.

As regards RPF, the employer's contribution is exempt up to 10 per cent of the salary. Interest credited is exempt if paid at the rate of 16 per cent per annum. Excess is, however, chargeable. The employee's contribution up to 20 per cent of salary is deductible, and lump sum payment received on retirement is also exempt from tax. The UPF is least beneficial. The employer's contribution to the UPF and interest thereon, are exempt but no deduction is allowed in respect of the employee's contribution, and it is therefore taxable. Lump sum payment received is taxable only to the extent of the employer's contribution and interest thereon.

INDIA

The tax treatment of gratuity depends on the nature of employment. Any death or retirement gratuity received by the government employee is wholly exempt. In the case of employees covered by the *Payment of Gratuity Act,* 1972, gratuity is exempt for the income year 1999-2000 to the extent of the least of the (i) 15 days' salary based on the salary last drawn for every completed year of service or the part thereof in excess of six months or (ii) Rs.350,000. In the case of any other employee, gratuity is exempt to the extent of the lesser of the (i) half month's salary for each completed year of service or (ii) Rs.350,000. The meaning of salary is different for the calculation of exempted gratuity in these cases.

Pension which also forms part of salary, if received monthly or is a periodical payment, is fully taxable both for the government as well as the non-government employees. Any commuted pension in the case of government employees is fully exempt and in the case of non-government employees is exempt to the extent of one-half of commuted value of such pension.

The tax treatment of employer and employee's contribution to different kind of provident fund in India is similar to Pakistan except that in the case of RPF, employer's contribution in India is exempt up to 12 per cent of salary and interest credited is exempt up to 12 per cent per annum for the income year 2000-01

Conclusion

In many developed countries including the U.S. and the U.K., the government also provide retirement benefits. Moreover, a fixed amount is contributed by employees, employers and self-employed individuals and is paid to the government in these countries. Besides, other retirement schemes are also run by the employer in these countries. The retirement benefits may be in the form of pension, contributory retirement funds or gratuity. Pension received monthly or in lump sum is taxable in the U.K. In Australia, rules regarding taxability of pension and annuity are very complicated. The tax rate depends whether pension is received within reasonable benefit limits (RBL) or not and also whether 50 per cent or more is received in the form of pension or annuity or not.

As regards the contributory superannuation benefits, all the selected countries provide tax relief up to a certain limit which is based on either a fixed percentage of salaries or wages or up to a fixed amount. In the U.K. and Australia, the limit is higher for aged individuals. While in Pakistan and India, maximum relief is provided to the government employees, in all other countries the tax relief is based upon the nature of fund or scheme, whether it is qualified or not. Thus, in all these countries, sufficient tax reliefs are provided at the time of contribution towards the retirement benefit scheme as well as at the time of receipt of lump sum payment on retirement.

TAXABILITY OF FRINGE BENEFITS

These are benefits that employees get from their job in addition to their salary. Employees are attracted to a job not only by the salary it carries, but also by the hidden benefits which go along with it. In fact, these hidden benefits commonly known as fringe benefits provide a large area for tax avoidance.[10] A generous attitude by the tax authorities in respect of the valuation of fringe benefits and the deductibility of mixed expenses, such as entertainment, travel and accommodation, which may relate to employment but have an element of personal consumption, results in discrimination in favour of people who enjoy a higher than average amount of fringe benefits or who can deduct a higher than average amount of mixed expenses.[11]

Fringe benefits may be provided in different forms, including the provision of free facilities, such as free accommodation, free servant, free meal, free education or it may be in the form of reimbursement by the employer of expenses incurred by the employee for personal use.

The concept of fringe benefit has changed over a period. While earlier, these benefits were provided by way of necessity, these are now also provided by way of luxury especially to high salary income earner. Since these benefits are provided in kind, these are converted into money so that they may be added in the salary. The proper valuation of fringe benefits is a complicated issue. To ensure equity and fairness of the tax system, it is necessary that these benefits are valued appropriately considering the overall socio-economic status of a country.

Fringe benefits may be valued either according to:

1. The cost to the employer;
2. The fair-market value of the benefit; or
3. The standard value fixed under the law.

The first two methods are commonly adopted by different countries. Though, the first method is easier to adopt, the second one is adopted to prevent the employer from giving wrong valuation. The third method may be adopted for some benefits for the purpose of administrative convenience. While the majority of the countries provide some tax-free fringe benefits to all the employees, it is important to see how other benefits are taxed in various countries. In this part, the provisions dealing with fringe benefits and their valuations in the selected countries are analysed.

THE U.K.

In the U.K., emoluments include benefits received in-kind. While some benefits in kind are assessable in all cases, some others are exempt in all cases, and there are some benefits which are taxable only in the case of higher paid employees.

Benefits taxable in all cases:

1. Non-cash vouchers
2. Cash Vouchers
3. Credit Cards
4. Discharge of employee's obligation
5. Free accommodation

Benefits tax-free to all employees:

1. Luncheon vouchers up to 15 pence per day.
2. Employer's contribution to approved pension scheme and retirement benefits scheme.
3. Staff entertaining (on social function exemption is up to £75 per head per year).
4. Free or subsidised meals in a staff canteen.
5. Provision of car parking space at or near the employee's place of work.
6. Removal expenses maximum up to £8,000, in connection with new employment or transfer to a new location.
7. Cost of work-related training courses for an employee.
8. The provision of workplace child care, sports and recreational facilities.
9. Non-cash long service awards maximum up to £20 per year of service.
10. Provision of a mobile phone.

Benefits Taxable in the Case of Higher-paid Employees (P11D Employees)

Higher-paid employees known as, P11D employees, are employees whose total emoluments, including the benefits-in-kind (valued as if the employees were a P11D employee) are at least £8500 per annum. If an employee works for more than one employer which is connected in some way, then the employee's emoluments from all connected employers are aggregated for the purpose of employee's classification. A full time working director who controls a material interest in the company (more than 5 per cent) is also a P11D employee even if his emoluments are less than £8500 per annum. The taxable benefit in the case of P11D employees include:

1. Assets loan for private use
2. Ancillary services connected with living accommodation
3. Car, van and fuel provided for private use
4. Beneficial loans
5. Medical insurance

For P11D employees, the general rule is that the employee is assessable on the benefits at the cost to the employer less any contribution made by the employee. Where an asset is loaned to the P11D employee, the cost to the employer is taken to be 20 per cent of the cost of the asset. Ancillary services connected with accommodation are restricted upto 10 per cent of the employee's net salary excluding the ancillary benefits if the accommodation is job related. The cost of providing a benefit is taken as the marginal cost incurred by the employer, i.e. the additional cost borne by the employer for providing the benefit.

Employees who are not P11D employees are known as the lower-paid employees (P9D employees). As a general rule, the lower-paid employees are taxed only on the benefits-in-kind that are convertible into money, i.e. they can be disposed of to a third party. In other words, the benefit is assessed at the second hand value rather than at the cost to the employer. Suppose a benefit costing £800 is provided to a lower-paid employee and its second hand value is £500, then the taxable value in the hands of the employee shall be £500.

THE U.S.

Fringe benefits form part of wages and salary in the U.S. In general, an employee is required to include the amount by which the fair market value of a fringe benefit exceeds the amount, if any, paid for the benefit. However, the U.S. law encourages certain types of fringe benefits to employees by allowing the employer to deduct the cost of the benefit and at the same time allowing employees to exclude the benefit from gross income. Certain fringe benefits such as cars, computers, entertainment, travel and other benefits may be excluded as working-condition fringe benefits. These benefits may, however, be included in the income to the extent the employee uses them for personal purposes. Fringe benefits in the form of payment of the employee's expenses by the employer, which are excluded from employee's income are:

1. Payments to qualified-pensions plan
2. Group-term life insurance
3. Health and accident insurance premiums
4. Meals and lodging provided by the employer

Any payment of life insurance premium paid by the employer is taxable in the hands of employees. Meals are exempt, if provided on the employer's business premises and if the provision of meals is for the convenience of the employer. Similarly, lodging provided by the employer is exempt if it is a condition of employment.

General fringe benefits exempt from tax include:

1. No-additional-cost services
2. Qualified employee discounts
3. Working-condition fringe benefits
4. Transportation fringe benefits
5. De minimis fringe benefits

No-additional-cost services and qualified employee discounts are exempt if available to employees on a non-discriminatory basis. The benefit must also be in the same line of business in which the employee works. An example is a free room to employees by a hotel employer or free air ticket by air authorities to employees. Working-condition fringe benefits means any property or services provided to an employee of the employer to the extent that if the employee paid for such property or services, such payment would be allowable deduction. Transportation fringe benefit means transportation in a commuter highway vehicle in connection with travel between the employee's residence and place of employment and any transit pass[12] subject to limitation of $65 per month in aggregate. Other fully exempt fringe benefits are uniforms, professional organisations dues and employer-provided free parking which is exempt up to $175 per month for the income year 2000. De minimis fringe benefits are those items that are too small to be accounted for. These include free coffee, and small Christmas gifts and are exempt.

In the U.S, there is another scheme, known as 'Cafeteria Plan', where the employee may choose to take the benefit either in cash or in kind. The benefit is fully taxable, if received in cash, and fully exempt, if received in kind. However, the scheme is applicable only when the benefits of the plan are available to all the employees on a non-discriminatory basis. If the benefit is provided to highly compensated employees only, then such benefit will be fully taxable. The scheme is designed to give benefit to those employees who cannot avail themselves of the benefit-in-kind. As in the case of single individuals, if they cannot get the benefit of child and dependant care, they can get cash in lieu of it.

AUSTRALIA

The Australian system is different from the system in most other parts of the world as salary in Australia does not include fringe benefits. Though, fringe benefits are received by the employees in Australia, they are not taxable in the hands of the employees. Fringe benefits in Australia are taxable in the hands of the employer under a separate Act known as, the *Fringe Benefits Tax Assessment Act,* 1986 (The FBTAA). The fringe benefits tax year runs from April 1, to the following March 31. The tax rate at which fringe benefit is taxable is also very high. For the year beginning April 1, 1998, this tax rate is 48.5 per cent.

The fringe benefits tax (FBT) was introduced in Australia on July 1, 1986 to improve the fairness of the tax system. It was designed to overcome the deficiencies in the income tax law, which allowed fringe benefits to be in effect a form of tax-free income. The FBT is payable on the gross-up value of the fringe benefits. Grossing-up rules were introduced on April 1, 1994, to ensure that salary income and fringe benefits to employees would receive a similar tax treatment.

Grossing-up Rules

Under the gross-up rules (Sec. 136AA), the aggregate fringe benefit amount is increased by:

$$\frac{1}{(1-\text{FBT rate})}$$

Based on the FBT rate applicable for the year ending March 31, 1999 of 48.5 per cent, the gross up rules effectively increase the amount against which the rate of FBT is applied for that year by 94.17 per cent. This is called the 'Fringe Benefits Taxable Amount'.

In order to ensure that employers are not subject to an increased tax liability under the gross up rules, an income tax deduction is allowed to employers for the amount of the FBT paid. Some tax-exempt employers, who are unable to claim an income tax deduction for payments of FBT, are able to claim a rebate instead. FBT payable in respect of some special benefits includes car benefit, car parking, interest-free loan, re-imbursement of non-business expenses, residential accommodation, discounted or free goods and other property provided to the employee. The provisions relating to the chargeability of various fringe benefits in Australia are truly vast and complicated.

MALAYSIA

Fringe benefits form part of employment income in Malaysia. Sec. 13(1) of the *Income Tax Act*, 1967 provides that all that flows from an employment, whether in cash or in kind is deemed income. The provisions of Sec. 13(1) are fairly widespread and are designed to provide a net within which to catch all tax avoidance devices initiated by the employer and the employee. The amount of benefits taxable in the hands of the employee is limited to the expenses incurred by the employer (cost to the employer) less any contribution by the employee and less what the employee incurs in the performance of the duties of his employment.

Benefits which are exempt from tax include:

1. the value of leave passages provided by an employer to the employee, his wife and children up to maximum of RM3000 for one overseas trip or up to a maximum of 3 local trips per year,
2. the value of any benefits arising from the provision of dental or medical treatment or a benefit for child care,
3. the benefits arising from the provision of recreational facilities,
4. lump sum payments made to employees on retirement (retirement gratuity),
5. withdrawals made by an employee from an approved pension or provident fund,
6. compensation for loss of employment.

Compensation for the loss of an employment is exempt (i) where the loss of an employment is due to ill health (ii) where the payment is in relation to a period of employment with the same employer or with companies in a group of companies under a common management. The exemption in this case is limited to RM4,000 per year multiplied by the number of completed years of service with that employer or that group of companies.

Various fringe benefits such as free meals, clothing, free domestic servant, and free accommodation are taxable. If clothing is required exclusively for employment purposes, it is tax-free. If the employer meets the charges for electricity, water and hire of appliances, the quantum of benefit taxable in the hands of the employee is the actual cost to the employer. Interest-free loan in general is taxable except where the loan is made from the free funds of the employer.

If travelling and entertainment allowances are received by the employee, such allowances are exempt to the extent that they are used for the business of the employer. The onus of proving the non-taxable content in such allowances rests on the recipient. If the travelling allowances include the cost of travelling from the residence of the employee to the employer's premises, that part shall be fully taxable. If travelling and entertainment expenses are reimbursed by the employer, the employee need not submit the documentary proof to back his claim for deductions.

PAKISTAN

Perquisites are taxable in general. For the assessment year 1998-99 and 1999-2000, if the salary including perquisites exceeded PKR300,000, then the perquisites were taxable separately at the special rate prescribed in the

Schedule, the rate being lower than the ordinary income tax rates. From the assessment year 2000-01, the perquisites are not taxable as a separate block of income but are taxable at the rates given in paragraph A of the Part 1 of the First Schedule. Perquisites which are exempt up to a certain limit include house rent allowance, rent-free accommodation, conveyance facility. Perquisites, which are exempt to the extent of actual expenditure incurred, includes free passage and free medical facilities.

House rent allowances in Pakistan are exempt up to 45 per cent of the minimum time scale and (if a minimum time scale is not given, then up to 45 per cent of the basic salary). Conveyance allowance is exempt to the extent of the greater of PKR3,600 or the actual expenditure. Entertainment allowance or entertainment expenses reimbursed are fully taxable. Any special allowance granted to meet the expenses wholly and necessarily incurred in the performance of the duties is exempt.

INDIA

Perquisites in India are taxable on a basis similar to that in the U.K. Perquisites may be divided into three categories:

1. Perquisites tax-free in all cases;
2. Perquisites taxable in all cases;
3. Perquisites taxable in the hands of specified employees only.

Perquisites Tax-free in All Cases

1. Payment/reimbursement of medical expenses incurred in a government hospital or for the treatment of prescribed diseases in an approved hospital. If treatment is taken from a private doctor, then it is exempt up to Rs.15,000 only.
2. If refreshment is provided during working hours outside the place of work, then the amount paid up to Rs.35 per day will not be treated as a perquisite, provided the amount is paid by the employer directly to the caterer, or the restaurant.
3. Goods manufactured by the employer, if sold by him to the employee at concessional rates.
4. Employer's contribution to staff group insurance scheme.
5. Premium paid by the employer on personal accident policy in respect of the employee.
6. Interest-free loan or loan to employees at concessional interest.
7. Leave travel concession, i.e. tickets or reimbursement of expenses incurred by the employee on himself, spouse, children or dependent parents or brother, sister on a ticket to undertake a journey to any place in India. Exemption is given in respect of a maximum of two journeys performed in a block of four calendar years.

Perquisites Taxable in All Cases

1. Value of rent-free accommodation provided to the employee;
2. Value of concession in respect of accommodation provided to the employee by his employer;
3. Value of any specified security allotted or transferred directly or indirectly, free of cost or at a concessional rate to an employee;
4. Amount paid by an employer in respect of any obligation of the employee and
5. Amount payable by an employer to effect an assurance on the life of the assessee or to effect a contract for an annuity.

Perquisites Taxable in the Hands of Specified Employees Only

There are some perquisites, which are taxable in the hands of specified employees.[13] These include: free car, free gas, electricity or water supply, free education, free transport, free domestic servant, free holiday home facility, free club facility, value of vehicle/furniture sold by the employer to its employees at concessional rates.

Conclusion

The taxable value of benefits-in-kind in many countries depend upon the type of employee, i.e. whether or not he is a higher income group employee. Many perquisites in the U.K., and India are taxable in the hands of the higher paid employees or directors only, whereas in Pakistan, some perquisites are taxable at a much higher value in case the salary income including perquisites and allowance exceed PKR 300, 000.

Meal and travelling expenses either directly incurred by the employer or reimbursed are exempt in the U.S., Australia and Malaysia only when incurred in connection with the employment. In the U.K. and India, subsidised lunches are exempt. In the U.K., even free lunch if provided in the staff canteen is exempt. Besides, in the U.K. luncheon vouchers are exempt up to 15 pence per day. In India, refreshment provided during working hours in office premises is exempt but if it is provided outside the place of work, it is exempt up to Rs.35 per day. Medical expenses are wholly exempt in Malaysia, and are exempt in Pakistan to the extent of actual expenses. In India, reimbursement of medical expenses are exempt up to Rs.15,000 while the expenses paid or reimbursed are fully exempt, if the treatment is taken in a government hospital. In the U.S., medical expenses are allowed as deduction not from the salary income, but from the total income in the form of itemized deduction, and are deductible only if they exceed 7.5 per cent of the adjusted gross income. Medical expenses, if reimbursed, are not deductible in the U.S.

In Australia, medical expenses are not deductible from salary income. However, a medical expenses rebate is allowed to an individual taxpayer if such expenses exceed AUD1250. Rebate is allowed to the extent of 20 per cent of the excess over AUD1250 (ITAA 36, Sec. 159P). Medical expenses paid directly by the taxpayer are not eligible for rebate, but if reimbursed, then they qualify for rebate. However, reimbursement will be treated as an expense fringe benefit and taxable in the hands of the employer.

Travelling expenses reimbursed by the employer are exempt to the extent they are used for the purposes of business or profession in all these countries. However, travelling expenses incurred in going from home to work place or vice versa are not deductible in general, except in India, where transport allowance is exempt up to Rs.800 per month.

Australia is different from all the other selected countries as benefit-in-kind are taxable in the hands of the employer and not the employee. For this purpose, the gross-up value of the benefit-in-kind is found out and a high tax rate of 48.5 per cent is charged to tax on the grossed up value of such benefit.

TAXABILITY OF CAR BENEFIT

Perquisites, commonly known as fringe benefits, are of various types and valued differently in different countries. As the amount of exemption and the condition subject to which exemption is granted, varies in all the selected countries, it is not feasible to compare all the perquisites.

The two most common perquisites, (i) car benefit and, (ii) living accommodation have been compared and analysed.

Car benefit is the most popular perquisite and generates the maximum revenue amongst all the taxable perquisites in most of the selected countries. In general, the private use of car benefit is taxable everywhere. The rules about how and to what extent the car benefit is taxable, differ in various countries. There are various ways of providing the car benefit. These are:

1. a car allowance is provided;
2. a free car is provided by the employer and the expenses of the car are also met by the employer;
3. a car is provided by the employer, but the expenses of car are met by the employee; or
4. the car is owned by the employee, but the expenses are met by the employer.

The provisions relating to the valuation of car benefit in the selected countries are examined below:

THE U.K.

Car benefit is taxable in the U.K. in the hands of specified employees who are either directors of a company or who earn a salary of £8,500 per annum or more. In the U.K., it is the availability of a motorcar for private use which produces a benefit and not the actual use to which the motor car is applied. During the income year 1997-98, the tax liability on the car benefit amounted to 53 per cent of tax liability on all benefits. Since April 6, 1994, the taxable benefit arising from the availability of a car for private use, or both for private and business use, has been governed by the list price of the vehicle.

The list price is taken to be:

(a) the manufacturer's list price including major accessories when the car was first registered, plus
(b) the cost of optional extras in excess of £100 (excluding telephones) fitted after the employee receives the car.

In the U.K., if car is provided and is used for private as well as for business purposes, then for the income year 1999-2000, the chargeable value is 35 per cent of the list price (or the market value). However,

(a) where the annual business mileage exceeds 2,500 miles, but does not exceed 17,999 miles, the taxable value is 25 per cent of the list price (or the market value).
(b) where the annual business mileage is 18,000 miles or more, the taxable value is 15 per cent of the list price (or the market value).

Cars which are 4 years old or more on the last date of the income tax year will be eligible for a further reduction of one quarter when calculating the tax benefit.

For valuing the car benefit, the maximum list price or the market price is limited to £80,000. If an employee makes a contribution towards the cost of acquiring a car or fitted accessories, then the contribution up to £5,000 may be deducted from the list price or the market value.

In addition to the car facility, if fuel benefit also arises, then such fuel benefit will also be taxable. Car fuel benefits in the U.K. are measured with reference to scale charges. Car fuel benefits in the U.K. are given in Table 3.3.

When applying the scale charges, no distinction is made between substantial and non-substantial use nor is the age of the car considered significant. When an employee uses his or her own motor car for business purposes and the employer pays a motor mileage allowance, such car mileage allowance paid to the employees in the U.K., is fully taxable, but the employee can submit an expense claim to obtain relief from income tax. However, to avoid the inclusion and exclusion both, if allowance is paid according to the Fixed Profit Car Scheme (FPCS), approved by the Inland Revenue, then neither the allowance will be taxable nor the employee be allowed to claim deduction in respect of expenses. The FPCS was introduced by the *Finance Act*, 1990. FPCS gives a tax-free mileage rate based on engine size and the

TABLE 3.3. CAR FUEL SCALE CHARGES IN THE U.K.

(for the income year 1999-2000)

Cylinder Capacity in Cubic Centimetres	Petrol Engines £	Diesel Engines £
Up to 1,400 cc	1,210	1,540
1401 to 2,000 cc	1,540	1,540
Over 2,000 cc	2,270	2,270

Source: Inland Revenue Statistics, 1999 (U.K.).

TABLE 3.4. AUTHORISED MILEAGE RATES IN THE U.K.

(for the income year 1999-2000)

Cylinder Capacity (cc)	Up to 4,000 miles	Over 4,000 miles
Up to 1,000 cc	28 P	17 P
1,001- 1,500 cc	35 P	20 P
1,501- 2,000 cc	45 P	25 P
2,001 cc and above	63 P	36 P

Source: Kenneth Tingley, *Daily Mail Income Tax Guide* 1999-2000 , p. 63.

number of business miles travelled. The authorised mileage rates for the income year 1999-2000 are given in Table 3.4.

Any excess over these rates paid by the employer is taxable, but shortfalls in the amount can be claimed by the employee as an allowable expense (under ICTA 1988, Sec. 198).

THE U.S.

Special valuation rules apply in the U.S. for determining the taxable value of car benefits. The value of personal use of an employer provided car can be computed by either of the two methods, viz., annual lease value tables or standard cents per mile rate prescribed by IRS. The annual lease value of an automobile is computed by first determining the fair market value (FMV) of the automobile on the first date it was made available to any employee for personal use. The employer's cost can be substituted for FMV if certain conditions are met. On the basis of FMV, the annual lease value that corresponds to the FMV as per the Annual Lease Value Table prepared by the IRS is determined. This annual lease value includes the FMV of maintenance and insurance for the automobile but does not include the cost of gasoline provided by the employer. The gasoline provided by the employer can be valued either at its FMV or at 5.5 cents per mile for all miles driven within the U.S., Canada or Mexico by the employee

The other method, viz., cent per mile method, is the simplest and can be used where the employee drives minimum 10,000 miles for the year including personal and business purposes. Personal miles are valued at 32.5 cents per mile for the income year 1999.

AUSTRALIA

Car benefit is the most common fringe benefit in Australia. During the fringe benefit tax year April 1, 1997 to March 31, 1998, 47.5 per cent of all fringe benefit tax paid was for car benefits. The car benefit, like any other fringe benefit is taxable in Australia, but in the hands of the employer as against employees in other countries. Car benefit is treated as a fringe benefit if it is provided in respect of the employment of the employee. Car benefit arises on any day where an employer's car is used on that day for private purposes by an employee or an associate of the employee; or is available for private use on that date by such a person. (Car kept in garage or near the place of residence of an employee.) The travel between home and workplace is generally regarded as private use, even if taking the car home is a condition of employment. In Australia, the existence of the car benefit is determined on a daily basis. The car benefit tax is calculated on the grossed-up taxable value. The grossing up is done by multiplying the benefit by 194.17 per cent.

Car benefit may be valued in Australia either by the *statutory formula* method or by the *operating-cost method.*

Statutory Formula Method

In this method, the value of the car benefit is found out by applying a statutory fraction(B) to a specially determined value of the car (A). The formula for calculating the car benefit value is

$$\frac{ABC}{D} - E$$

where A is the 'base value' of the car;

B is the 'statutory fraction';

C is the number of days during the year on which a car benefit was provided;

D is the number of days during the year; and

E is the amount of any 'recipient's payment'.

The base value of the car where the employer originally owned the car, is the cost price of car to the owner, when the owner first held it. The base value is reduced to two-thirds of the cost price if the car is 4 years old. In case the employer did not own the car when first holding it, the base value shall be the original leased value of the car at the earliest time when the employer held it. The base value of the car also includes the cost price of any subsequently fitted non-business accessory.

Statutory Fraction

The statutory fraction varies according to the number of kilometres travelled by the car during the year. The statutory fractions for the FBT year ending March 31, 1999 are given in Table 3.5.

TABLE 3.5. STATUTORY FRACTIONS IN RESPECT OF CAR VALUATION IN AUSTRALIA

(for the year ending March 1999)

Annualised Number of whole kilometres	Statutory Fraction
Less than 15,000	0.26
15,000 to 24,999	0.20
25,000 to 40,000	0.11
More than 40,000	0.07

Source: CCH, Australian Master Tax Guide, 1999, p. 1512.

Operating Cost Method

The taxable value of a car fringe benefit is based on the operating cost of the car. Employers using this method must ensure that various records are kept to show the total car expenses incurred during the relevant period and the proportions of business and non-business use of the car. The formula to determine the value of car benefit under the operating cost method is as follows:

$$C \times (100\% - BP) - R$$

where:

C is the operating cost of car during the holding period
BP is the business use percentage
R is the amount of any recipient's payment

Operating cost includes car expenses, registration, insurance cost, imputed interest cost, and depreciation/lease cost.

Business use percentage is the percentage of the total distance travelled by the car during the relevant period that relates to business use. Thus in Australia, while statutory fraction method is based on the cost of the car and the kilometre use of the car, the operating cost method is based on the car expenses and depreciation and also on the use of the car for personal purposes. The employer is free to choose any of the two methods whichever is beneficial to him. However, if an employer makes no express choice, then the statutory formula method applies.

MALAYSIA

The annual value of this benefit is taxable in the hands of all employees in Malaysia as against in the U.K., where this benefit is taxable in the hands of those employees who are either the director of a company or who earn salary beyond a prescribed amount (£8500 per annum presently). The value of this benefit is computed by reference to the actual cost divided by the average life span of the motorcar, which presently is 8 years. *Cost* means actual cost or market value of the car (rented/leased) including accessories but excludes financial charges, insurance premium and the road tax. However, the Inland Board of Revenue has notified the following table (Table 3.6) for valuation of benefits for the private use of the car and fuel provided by the employers.

In case the car is more than 5 years old, the value of the car benefits to be assessed will be equivalent to half the above value, but the value of the fuel will remain the same. If a driver is also provided to the taxpayer, the benefit of the driver will be charged to tax at RM300 per month. The value of the benefit is adjusted appropriately if the car is not provided throughout the year. In case the fuel is provided without a motorcar, the benefit to be assessed is equivalent to the actual value of the fuel provided.

TABLE 3.6. TAXABLE CAR BENEFIT IN MALAYSIA

(for the income year 1999)

Cost of Car RM	Annual Value of the Benefit RM	Fuel per annum RM
Up to 50,000	1,200	600
50,001 to 75,000	2,400	900
75,001 to 1,00,000	3,600	1,200
1,00,001 to 1,50,000	5,000	1,500
1,50,001 to 2,00,000	7,000	1,800
2,00,001 to 2,50,000	9,000	2,100
2,50,001 to 3,50,000	15,000	2,400
3,50,001 to 5,00,000	21,250	2,700
5,00,001 and above	25,000	3,000

Source: Income Tax Ruling, ITR 1997/2, Malaysia.

PAKISTAN

Perquisites form part of salary in Pakistan. Perquisites are valued and added to the salary for the calculation of taxable salary income. However, with effect from the assessment year 1997-98, the rules regarding the valuation of perquisites have changed. Perquisites in the case of those employees whose salary income inclusive of perquisites and allowances exceeded PKR300,000 became taxable in a different manner for corporate employees excluding the government employees. During the assessment year 1997-98 the perquisites were taxable in a discriminatory manner. The provisions were therefore changed with effect from the assessment year 1998-99 whereby all the salaried persons were taxed alike. From the assessment year 1998-99, the perquisites in the case of those employees whose salary income including allowances and perquisites exceeded PKR300,000 became taxable as a separate block of income at special rates prescribed for the taxation of perquisite. For such employees, the perquisites would be valued as per Rule 18B, i.e. a higher value is fixed for free accommodation and motor vehicle, whereas the value of any other perquisite, allowance or other benefit shall be taken to be the monetary value as certified by the employer.

With a view to rationalise taxation of perquisites, the First Schedule to the *Income Tax Ordinance*, 1979 has been amended. From the assessment year 2000-01, perquisites would not be taxable as a separate block of income and would be taxable at the rates given in paragraph of Part I of First Schedule.

Where the salary and perquisites do not exceed PKR300,000, the old rules of concessional valuation of perquisites shall continue. Thus, in the case of low paid employees, perquisites will not be valued at a higher value under Rule 18B.

Valuation of Car Benefit if the Salary Income Exceeds PKR300,000

The value of the car benefit in the case of employees whose salary including perquisites and allowances exceeds PKR300,000 shall be made as depicted in Table 3.7.

TABLE 3.7. VALUE OF CAR BENEFIT FOR EMPLOYEES WHOSE SALARY EXCEEDS PKR300,000

Nature of Benefit	Value to be Adopted for Addition to the Income	
i. Where the conveyance is used exclusively for private purposes.	i. The value shall be determined as follows:	
	Engine Capacity	Value of Car per annum (PKR)
	Less than 1000 cc	40,000
	1000 cc to less than 1500 cc	80,000
	1500 cc to less than 1800 cc	1,20,000
	1800 cc and over	2,00,000
ii. Where the conveyance is partly used for business and partly for official purposes.	ii. 50% of the value determined in clause (i).	
iii. Where the conveyance is used by more than one employee.	iii. The amount as determined in clause (i) divided by number of employees using the conveyance	

Source: Income Tax Rules, 1982 upto July 10, 2000 (Pakistan).

Valuation of Car Benefit in the Case of Low Paid Employees

Car benefit in Pakistan is valued at concessional rate in the case of those employees whose salary income including perquisites and allowances do not exceed PKR300,000. The valuation of the car perquisite in different circumstances is explained below:

Conveyance Used Exclusively for Private Purposes

Where the conveyance is provided by the employer for the use of the employee exclusively for private purposes, the amount spent by the employer on running and maintenance of the car (including depreciation) shall be the taxable value of the car benefit.

Conveyance Used Partly for Private and Partly for Business Purposes

Where the conveyance owned or hired by the employer is provided to the employee and is used partly for private and partly for business purposes and the running and maintenance expenses are also met by the employer, the taxable value of the car benefit as provided in Rule 13 shall be the lesser of the following.

(a) 50 per cent of expenses incurred by the employer, including hire or depreciation, or
(b) PKR3600 per annum.

If conveyance allowance is given to the employee only, then it will be exempt under Rule 10 to the extent of greater of the two:

(a) PKR3,600, or
(b) The actual expenditure

If conveyance allowance is given along with car facility in some form or the other, the allowance may be exempt up to a certain limit. The limit varies in different circumstances.

Where the conveyance is used by more than one person, the valuation of the car benefit shall be 50 per cent of the expenses incurred by the employer divided by the number of persons or PKR2,400 whichever is less. Where the conveyance is owned or hired by the employer and its running cost is borne by the employee, the amount by which the conveyance allowance paid by the employer exceeds PKR2,400 or 7.5 per cent of the basic salary (whichever is the higher) is considered as benefit to be included in the income. However, where both the conveyance is owned by the employee, and its running cost is also borne by the employee, the amount by which the conveyance allowance paid by the employer exceeds PKR3,600 or 10 per cent of the basic salary, whichever is higher, is considered as benefit for inclusion in the income.

Where the conveyance is owned by the employee but its running cost is borne by the employer, the amount by which the conveyance allowance paid by the employer exceeds PKR1,200 or 2.5 per cent of the basic salary (whichever is higher) is considered as benefit for inclusion in the income.[14]

INDIA

Car perquisite is taxable in India in the case of specified employees[15] only. Perquisites are valued in India on the basis of their value to the employee and not on the basis of the cost to the employer. In India, the valuation of car perquisite is done as follows:

Where the car is either owned or hired by the employer and the expenses of running and maintenance of the car are also met by the employer, and the car is used wholly for private purposes, then the taxability of the car benefit is the actual expenses plus normal depreciation/hire charges plus remuneration paid to the driver if any. If the car is used both for private as well as for official purposes, then a reasonable proportion of actual expenses plus normal depreciation/hire charges attributable to private use is taxable. If the determination on the above basis is difficult, Rs.600 per month where the horse power (HP) rating of the car does not exceed 16 or the cubic capacity (CC) of the engine does not exceed 1.88 litres and Rs.800 per month where the HP rating of the car exceeds 16 or the CC of the engine exceeds 1.88 litres. In case the driver is also provided, Rs.300 per month is added to the value of the car perquisites.

Where the car owned or hired by the employer is provided and the car is used for private purposes but the expenses of car are met by the employee, then the normal depreciation or hire charge is the value of perquisite. If the car is used both for private as well as for official purposes, then a reasonable proportion of normal depreciation or hire charges attributable to private use is taxable. If the determination on the above basis is difficult, Rs.200 p.m. where the HP rating of the car does not exceed 16 or the cc does not exceed 1.88 litres, and Rs.300 p.m. where the HP rating of the car exceeds 16 or the CC of the engine exceeds 1.88 litres. Car facility provided to any employee for journey by him from his residence to his office or from office to his residence is not treated as benefit.

However, when the car is owned by the employee and the car is used for private purposes and the expenses of running and maintenance are met by the employer, then actual expenses incurred by the employer are a taxable perquisite for all employees, i.e. specified and non-specified both. Where the car is used for both private and official purposes, a proportionate amount of expenses attributable to the private use is the taxable perquisite for both specified and non specified employees.

Conclusion

For the purpose of analysis, the car benefit provision in various countries are summarised in Table 3.8 as under.

As shown in the table, in the U.K., the car benefit is exempt in the hands of employees other than directors and having a salary of less than £8,500 per annum. In India, the car benefit is exempt in the hands of employees who are neither directors nor have substantial interest in the company and whose salary income is less than Rs.24,000 per annum (increased to Rs.50,000 p.a.). In Pakistan, a concessional valuation of the car benefit is done for employees having a salary income of less than PKR300,000. Except in Australia, the car benefit is taxed in the hands of employer by including the value of such benefit to the income of the employee at the rate applicable to such an employee. In Australia, the value of the car benefit is taxed in the hands of the employees at the maximum rate of tax 48.5 per cent for the income year 1998-99 and that too by grossing up the value of the car benefit with the tax payable thereon. The basis of valuation of the car benefit in the U.K., the U.S., Australia and Malaysia is the cost of car plus the fuel benefit provided, whereas in Pakistan and India, it is on the basis of the engine capacity of the car provided to the employee.

Thus, car benefit in most of these countries is based on either the cost of the car or the FMV of the car. The value of benefit in general is reduced if the car is 4 years old or more. In Table 3.9, the minimum and maximum taxable amount of car benefit has been found out on the basis of presumptive value of car.

The figure in Table 3.9 indicates that a very high value is charged in respect of car facility in the U.K., followed by Australia, Pakistan and Malaysia. The taxable value of the car is least in India. Thus, even in comparison to the developing country of Pakistan, the car benefit in India is undervalued.

TABLE 3.8. A SUMMARY OF PROVISIONS RELATING TO THE TAXABILITY OF CAR PERQUISITES

Particulars	U.K.	U.S.	Australia	Malaysia	Pakistan	India
Concession based on the amount of salary	Not taxable if salary is up to £8,500 p.a.	Nil	Nil	Nil	Concessional valuation for employee earning up to PKR3,00,000 p.a.	Not taxable if salary is up to Rs.24,000 p.a. Increased to Rs.50, 000 p.a. from income year 2001-02
Taxable in the hands of:	Employee	Employee	Employer	Employee	Employee	Employee
Basis of valuation	Cost of car and engine capacity	Fair market value	Cost of car or the operating cost of car	Cost of car	Engine capacity	Engine capacity
Concession given for old car	Taxable Benefit is reduced further by ¼, if car is 4 years old	n.a.	1/3 of cost price if car is more than 4 years old	50 per cent of cost of car if more than 5 years old	No Concession	No Concession
Valuation of car	Car cost limited to £80,000 and 15 per cent of car cost to be considered as perquisite if business mileage is 18,000 miles per annum or more: Fuel benefits fixed and linked to car cylinder capacity irrespective of fuel used for private use.	n.a.	Statutory fraction is gradually reduced for valuing car benefit as the total number of kilometres travelled by the car increases. Irrespective of kilometres travelled for private use.	Fixed sum, annual value of car benefit, which increases as the cost of car increases.	Fixed sum, which increases as the capacity of car engine increases.	Fixed sum per month. One for car engine capacity up to 1.88 ltrs the other beyond 1.88 ltrs.

TABLE 3.9. MINIMUM AND MAXIMUM TAXABLE CAR BENEFIT

(amount in Rs.)

Country	Car used for private and official purpose		Car used for private purpose	
	Minimum Value	Maximum Value	Minimum Value	Maximum Value
U.K.	159,700	408,900	189,700	508,900
U.S.*	90,560	90,560	181,125	181,125
Australia	60,000	200,000	60,000	200,000
Malaysia	10,350	27,600	20,700	55,200
Pakistan	20,000	100,000	40,000	200,000
India	7,200	9,600	Actual expenditure	Actual expenditure

Notes: Minimum taxable car benefit has been calculated presuming the cost of car to be Rs.300,000 and with engine capacity of up to 1400 CC, while maximum taxable benefit has been calculated presuming the cost of car to be Rs.1,000,000 and the engine capacity of above 2000CC. Further in all the cases, it has been presumed that the car has travelled 20,000 kilometres, i.e. 12,500 miles. The taxable value of car in the U.K. and Malaysia includes both car benefit and fuel benefit. The calculations are based on the car benefit provisions relating to the income year 1999-2000. However, in the case of India, these related to the income year 2000-2001.

* As cent per mile method.

Source: Author's Calculations.

TAXABILITY OF RENT-FREE ACCOMMODATION

Rent-free accommodation is another common perquisite though it is not as beneficial as car benefit from the revenue point of view. The mode of computation of the taxable value of the living accommodation in the selected countries is analysed below.

THE U.K.

In the U.K., the benefit of living accommodation constituted only 1 per cent of the total benefits as well as 1 per cent of the tax liability on total perquisites in the income year 1997-98. The benefit of living accommodation is an assessable benefit for all employees. The value of rent-free accommodation in the U.K. is the higher of the following:

1. the rateable value, i.e. gross annual value of the accommodation if the employer owns the accommodation
2. rent paid by the employer, where the employer does not own the property and the rent paid exceeds its rateable value.

Any contribution made by the employer is deducted from this value. In the U.K., the system of domestic rates was abolished in 1990. As such, the rateable value of the new properties is to be estimated.

Expensive Accommodation

Accommodation owned by the employer and costing more than £75,000 is regarded as 'expensive' and gives rise to an increase in the assessable benefit. This increase is calculated by applying an appropriate percentage to the amount by which the cost of accommodation exceeds £75,000. The appropriate percentage is the same as the official rate of interest used in beneficial loan calculations. The rate is altered from time to time. On March 6, 1999, it was 6.25 per cent per annum. Cost includes not only the expenditure laid out to acquire the accommodation, it also includes any further cost of improvements made to the property before the start of the year, less any capital contribution made by the employee.

If the property was acquired by the employer more than 6 years before it was made available to the employee, the purchase price of the property may be replaced by its market value on the date that it was first occupied by the employee.

The benefit of living accommodation in the U.K is not taxable in the following cases.

1. If it is necessary for the employee to reside in the accommodation for the proper performance of his duties as in the case of caretaker.
2. If it is necessary for the better performance of the employee's duties and it is customary to provide accommodation as in the case of clergyman.
3. Where there is a threat to the employee's safety and the accommodation is provided as part of social security arrangements.

THE U.S.

In the U.S., all non-cash benefits are included in employee's gross income except those, which are specifically excluded. The value of the benefits which are to be included in gross income is the cost incurred by the employer in providing the benefit. Accordingly, the fair market value of the rent-free accommodation is treated as the value to be included in the gross income of the employee. However, lodging facilities provided by educational or medical research institutions to its employees at the campus are excluded from the employee's gross income if an adequate rent is charged for the same. Lower of 5 per cent of the appraised value of the campus lodging or the average of the rentals paid by individuals other than students and employees of the educational institution during such calendar year for lodging which is comparable to the lodging provided to the employee is considered adequate rent and in case of inadequate rent, the difference is included in the employee's gross income as value of perquisites. The rental value of a dwelling furnished to a minister of the gospel is also not included in gross income. Rental allowance given to minister of the gospel to the extent used by him to rent or provide a home also does not form part of gross income.

AUSTRALIA

The housing fringe benefit as compared to the car benefit is relatively of little significance. During the FBT year 1997-98, the tax payable on housing benefit constituted only 3.9 per cent of the tax payable on all the fringe benefits. The grossed-up value of the housing fringe benefit is taxable in the hands of the employer.

A housing fringe benefit arises where an employer grants an employee a 'housing right', a right to occupy or use a unit of accommodation as the usual place of residence. The value of housing benefit depends upon whether the benefit is in a remote area or a non-remote area.

Value of Housing Benefit in Non-remote Area Accommodation

In case the accommodation is provided to the employee in non-remote area in Australia, the valuation of the benefit will be as follows:

If the accommodation is in a hotel, motel, hostel, guesthouse, caravan or mobile home, the taxable value of the benefit is either:

if the provider is not the employer, the market value of the accommodation less any rent paid, or

if the provider is the employer, 75 per cent of the amount that the public would pay less any rent paid.

For any other type of accommodation, the taxable value is 'statutory annual value' (SAV) of the right to occupy the accommodation. SAV is the market value of the right to occupy the accommodation for a year. This is reduced proportionately where the housing right does not exist for the whole year. Any rent paid by the employee is subtracted. In determining the market value of the right to occupy the accommodation, associated expenses of the occupant that might be paid by another person are disregarded.

Remote-area Accommodation

Concessional valuation rules apply in Australia where the accommodation is in a remote area.[16] An employer can choose between the discounted market-value method and the statutory amount method.

Discounted Market-value Method

In this case, the statutory annual value of the accommodation is reduced by 50 per cent.

Statutory Amount Method

In this case, a fixed amount, i.e. the statutory amount is the value of rent-free accommodation. For the year ending March 31, 1999, the amount is AUD26.68 per week for single person quarter and AUD106.98 per week for any other unit of accommodation.

MALAYSIA

In Malaysia, rent-free accommodation provided to the employee is a taxable benefit under Sec. 13(1)(a) of the *Income Tax Act*, 1967. The value of RFA is the lesser of the following:

1. the defined value, i.e. the rent payable for an accommodation, where the

accommodation is not affected by rent control or in any other case, the rateable value or the economic rent. Rateable value is the value determined for rating purposes. Economic rent means rent that can be obtained from letting those premises provided the lessor pays for the fire insurance, public rates, repairs and maintenance ignoring rent control regulations, or

2. 30 per cent of employee's gross incomes, i.e. the total of salary, leave pay, fee commission, bonus, gratuity, perquisites or allowances, as defined in Sec.13 (1)(a).

The above provisions apply to all employees other than directors but not service directors of controlled companies.[17] A director of a controlled company is charged with the full 'defined value' of the premises, which he occupies rent-free. No comparison is made between the 30 per cent of the salary and the defined value.

Where the accommodation in Malaysia is shared by two or more employees or where the employee is required to use part of the premises for the benefit of the employer's business such as entertaining clients, the defined value of the accommodation is either apportioned on a time basis or reduced to a reasonable amount and compared with 30 per cent of the gross income of the employee and the lower of the two is taxable.

Valuation of Accommodation in Specific Cases

The taxable value is to be limited to 3 per cent of the gross income from employment under Sec. 13 (1)(a) in case unfurnished accommodation is provided in a hotel, hostel or similar premises, or premises on a plantation or in a forest.

PAKISTAN

In Pakistan, with effect from the assessment year 1998-99, the RFA is valued at higher rate for high-income paid employees and at lesser rates for low-income paid employees.

Valuation of Rent-free Accommodation in the Case of Lower-paid Employees

The value of rent-free accommodation in the case of employees who earn salary including perquisites and allowances up to PKR300,000 for the income year 1997-98 is as follows (Rule 5)

Value of RFA = Annual Value minus 45 per cent of the Minimum Time Scale.

If no minimum time scale is provided, then the value shall be:

Value of RFA = Annual value minus 45 per cent of basic salary, subject to the maximum of 15 per cent of salary.

The annual value of accommodation shall be deemed to be the sum for which the property might reasonably be expected to be let from year to year. However, in case the property is let on rent, the annual value shall not be less than the rent payable by the tenant.

Valuation of Furnished Accommodation

Where the rent-free accommodation provided to the employee is furnished, the value of the unfurnished accommodation calculated under Rule 5 will be further increased by 10 per cent of salary (Rule 6).

If the accommodation is provided at a concessional rate, the value of the accommodation calculated under Rule 5 or Rule 6, shall be reduced by any amount paid by the employee to the employer (Rule 8).

Value of Rent-free Accommodation in the Case of Higher-paid Employee

Employees in Pakistan whose salary income including perquisites and allowances exceed PKR300,000 are subject to a higher valuation of rent-free accommodation under Rule 18B, as shown in Table 3.10.

Where the accommodation provided is furnished, the value shall be first calculated in accordance with the above rules, and a further value equal to 15 per cent of the said value shall be added. However, in case facilities of heating, cooling, security and domestic servants are also provided to the employee, such facilities shall be valued separately.

INDIA

Rent-free Accommodation (RFA) is a taxable perquisite in the hands of all employees whether specified or non-specified in India [Rule 3(a)]. For the purposes of valuation of the perquisite in respect of unfurnished accommodation, employees are divided into three categories:

1. Central and State Government employees.
2. Semi-Government employees.
3. Other employees.

Central and State Government employees includes Central and State

TABLE 3.10. VALUE OF RENT-FREE ACCOMMODATION IN PAKISTAN WHEN SALARY INCOME IS PKR300,000 OR MORE

Nature of Benefit	Value of Rent-free Accommodation	
Area of Accommodation	Areas falling within the limits of Metropolitan corporation, Municipal Corporation, Cantonment Board, or the Islamabad Capital Territory	Any other place
up to 250 sq. yards	PKR36,000	PKR24,000
up to 500 sq. yards	PKR96,000	PKR60,000
up to 1,000 sq. yards	PKR1,80,000	PKR96,000
up to 2,000 sq. yards	PKR3,36,000	PKR1,80,000
Above 2,000 sq. yards	PKR4,20,000	PKR2,40,000

Source: The *Income Tax Rules*, 1982 (Pakistan) upto July 10, 2000.

Government employees or government employees whose services have been lent to a public sector undertaking or a government body.

Semi-Government employees include mainly employees of the Reserve Bank of India or statutory corporations or registered societies, or companies in which all the shares are held by the Government or the Reserve Bank of India either singly or jointly.

Other employees covers employees who are neither government employees, nor semi-government employees.

The value of RFA in India is based on salary and Fair Rental Value (FRV) of the accommodation.

(Salary for this purpose include basic salary, dearness allowance, bonus, commission, fees, all other taxable allowances, income/ professional tax paid by the employer, and gas, water and electricity bills paid or reimbursed by the employer.)

(The FRV is the rent which a similar accommodation would realise in the same locality or the municipal valuation in respect of the accommodation, whichever is higher (Explanation 2 to Rule 3(a).) Where the accommodation is owned by the employer and the maintenance expenses of the garden, salary of the gardener, maintenance expenses of the swimming pool are borne by the employer, such expenses shall also be included in the FRV).

The valuation of rent-free unfurnished accommodation is given in Table 3.11.

In the case of both semi-government and other employees, if the FRV is less than 10 per cent of salary, then the FRV shall be the value of the perquisite. When, the accommodation provided to the employee is furnished, the valuation is made first as if the accommodation is unfurnished. The value so calculated is further increased by:

(a) 10 per cent per annum of the original cost of furniture, if furniture is owned by the employer.
(b) the actual hire charges payable (whether paid or not) if the furniture is hired by the employer.

TABLE 3.11. VALUE OF RENT-FREE ACCOMMODATION IN INDIA

Type of Employee	Location of Accommodation	Value of Perquisite
Government employees	Anywhere in India	As per rules framed by the Government for allotment of residences to its officers
Semi-Government employees	Anywhere in India	10% of salary or FRV of the accommodation, whichever is less
Other employees	(i) Delhi, Mumbai, Calcutta, Chennai	(i) If FRV is more than 10% but less than 60% of salary then value is 10% of salary. (ii) If FRV exceeds 60% of salary then value is FRV – 50% of salary.
	(ii) Place other than those mentioned above	(ii) If FRV exceeds 50% of salary, the value is FRV – 40% of salary.

Source: The Income Tax Rules, 1962 (India) as on June 1, 2001.

In all the cases, if any contribution is made by the employee towards the rent, then the amount of such contribution shall be subtracted from the value of the perquisite.

Conclusion

The basis of valuation of rent-free accommodation in the U.K., U.S., Australia is the FMV of the house. In Malaysia and India, both the FMV and salary are taken into consideration to find out the value of the RFA. In Pakistan, the value is high for employees whose salary exceeds PKR300,000 and the value is based on the area of the house and locality in which the accommodation is provided. Rules are complicated in India where employees are divided into three categories, and where the basis of valuation also differs depending upon the FMV, the amount of salary as well as the place where the accommodation is provided. Valuation of rent-free accomodation in case of the government employees at a concessional rate appears to be discriminatory as against the non-government employees.

DEDUCTIONS FROM SALARY INCOME

Unlike business income, deductions allowed from the salary income in general are not only less in number, but are relatively of lesser value. However, the base of taxable salary income of any country is affected by such deductions. Keeping in view this point, the provisions relating to deductions from salary income of the selected countries are compared and analysed in this part.

THE U.K.

In the U.K., the following expenses incurred by an employee are allowed to be deducted from income from employment for tax purposes:

(a) Contributions to an approved occupational pension scheme or premiums paid to secure a personal pension or retirement annuity subject to a statutory maximum limit.
(b) Subscription to relevant professional bodies.
(c) Donations made under a payroll-giving scheme.
(d) Travelling expenses necessarily incurred in the performance of the duties of employment. (However, travel between home and workplace is not permissible.)
(e) Other expenses incurred wholly, exclusively and necessarily in the performance of the duties of employment.

In general, entertaining expenses are not allowed except in the following two cases:

(a) The employer reimburses an employee for entertainments expenses incurred.

(b) The employer pays to the employee an allowance for entertainment purposes.

In both the cases, entertainment expenses must be incurred in the performance of the duty of employment.

Reimbursed Expenses

Where expenses relating to employment are reimbursed, the amount reimbursed will be added to the employee's emoluments, and expenses, if allowable, will be deducted from the employee's income for Schedule 'E' purposes.

THE U.S.

The provisions relating to the employee's expenses incurred in connection with the job are complicated. Expenses may be deducted as trade or business expenses (for AGI deduction) or as personal or itemized deduction (from AGI deduction), depending upon whether or not the expenses are reimbursed by the employer. Reimbursed expenses are treated in two ways:

1. Accountable plan
2. Non-accountable plan

In the accountable plan, an employee is required to give the employer adequate documents to support the expenditure being reimbursed as a valid business expense. Expenses incurred in relation to the job such as meals, lodging, travelling, if proved to be used in connection with the job are treated under the accountable plan. In the accountable plan, treatment of reimbursed expenses will differ depending upon how much of the actual expenses are reimbursed. The treatment under different circumstances is given below:

1. If the reimbursement equals the actual expenses, neither the reimbursement is included in the gross income, nor are the actual expenses allowed as deduction, thus producing no effect on the employee's income.
2. If reimbursement is greater than the actual expenses, and if the excess reimbursement is returned to the employer, then again neither will the reimbursement be added nor will the expenses be deducted. However, if the excess reimbursement is not returned to the employer, the excess will be included in the employee's gross income.
3. If the reimbursement is less than the actual expenses, then the reimbursement is included in the employee's income and the expenses reimbursed are deducted for adjusted gross income (for AGI deduction). Actual expenses in excess of the reimbursement are deductible as miscellaneous itemized deductions, subject to 2 per cent of the Adjusted Gross Income (AGI).

In the non-accountable plan, the employee must include the reimbursement in the gross income. No deductions for the AGI are allowed. The expense is deductible as a miscellaneous itemized deduction subject to 2 per cent of the adjusted gross income.

Unreimbursed employee's business expenses, investment expenses, i.e. expenses connected with the earning of the investment income such as publications and safe deposit box rentals, and other miscellaneous itemized deductions, such as fee for filing tax return, are all treated as miscellaneous itemized deductions and are subject to the 2 per cent AGI limit, and are deductible from the AGI.

Other itemized deductions such as charitable contributions, mortgage interest, are not subject to the 2 per cent AGI limit and are deductible from the AGI. Thus, provisions relating to employee's expenses in the U.S. are extremely complicated.

AUSTRALIA

In Australia, expenditure incurred by an employee in earning or producing assessable income are allowed subject to strict rules of substantiation in most of the cases. Expenditure must be related to employment and incurred as an express or implied condition of employment. Expenses generally allowed include tools, technical and trade books, journals, travel expenses, premium for sickness and accident insurance, and tax-related expenses.

Certain expenses which are not allowed in general include meal expenses, child care expenses, and occupational clothing. Travel expenses incidental to employment are deductible (ITAA 97, Sec. 8.1). These expenses cover not only transportation costs, but also, where relevant, the cost of meals and hotel expenses. The expenses of commuting between home and place of work are generally not deductible, except in exceptional circumstances, e.g. where the taxpayer is required to carry bulky equipment to work or where the home can be regarded as a base of operations.

Motor vehicle expenses incurred in the course of deriving assessable income are allowed as deduction. Car expenses are subject to substantiation rules. There are several methods of claiming car expense deductions, which can satisfy the substantiation rules. If the employee wishes to apportion car expenses between business use and private use, then he must use 'the log book method'. Under this method, claims must be supported by written evidence, logbook records and odometer records. Other methods which can be adopted, if detailed records are not kept, are 'one third of actual car expenses method', 'the 12 per cent of original value method and the 'cents per kilometre method'. The 'one third of actual car expenses method' and the 12 per cent of original value method can only be used, where the car travels for more than 5,000 km for business purposes. The 'cents per kilometre method' can only be used where the business use is 5,000 km or less.

Expenses Paid or Reimbursed by Employer

Expenses paid or reimbursed by the employer give rise to a fringe benefit which is taxable in the hands of the employer. Accordingly, the employee is neither liable to include the reimbursement in income, nor is he allowed to claim deduction in respect of the expenses incurred. Deduction may be allowed to the extent of the contribution made by the employee. But the employee is not entitled to a deduction for the contribution to the extent that the contribution is a payment for the private element of the benefit (ITAA 36 Sec. 51AJ).

MALAYSIA

In Malaysia, all expenses reasonably incurred for the appropriate performance of the duties of the office of employment qualify for deduction from salary income. However, the employee has to prove to the satisfaction of the Director General that the relevant expenses are incurred in the performance of his duties.

PAKISTAN

In Pakistan, salary income is computed according to provisions of Sec.16 of the *Income Tax Ordinance*, 1979. There are no direct deductions allowed from the salary income. However, there is indirect benefit allowed to salaried taxpayers. Taxpayers having more than 50 per cent of income chargeable under the head salary are not required to pay any tax if their total income does not exceed PKR50,000 as against PKR40,000 in the case of other taxpayers. As such, salaried taxpayers get an extra benefit of up to PKR 10,000. Salaried taxpayers having income above PKR50,000 where salary income constitutes more than 50 per cent of the total income get a rebate of PKR2,500 (PKR3,000 in case of working woman having more than 50 per cent of salary income) in tax as against PKR 2,000 allowed in other cases. This extra rebate of PKR500 in tax to the salaried taxpayers works out to be deduction of PKR10,000 in income at the lowest tax rate of 5 per cent chargeable on income up to PKR1,00,000. However, this amount or PKR 10,000 will get reduced in the case of the salaried taxpayer who has higher income. This rebate of PKR500 in tax as against PKR10,000 deduction in income appears to be more equitable as every salaried taxpayer irrespective of its income, gets the same benefit in tax.

The *Finance Ordinance*, 2000 has introduced another benefit for salaried taxpayers. From the income year 2000-01, the income tax liability on the income of salaried taxpayers whose salary income exceeds 50 per cent of total income, shall be reduced by 5 per cent to 80 per cent depending upon the income of such taxpayers.

The tax liability of full time teachers and researchers employed in non-profit education or research institution is further reduced by 50 per cent of the tax payable after the above reduction.

The benefit of tax rebates to salaried taxpayers in terms of income at different level of income is as shown in Table 3.12.

As shown in the table, there is no uniformity about the reduction in tax liability as well as deduction in income computed by applying maximum marginal rate to total tax rebate. The tax rebate is PKR12,250 on income of PKR700,000 as compared to tax rebate of PKR14,000 on income of PKR 500,000. Similarly, the amount of income deduction goes on increasing up to income of PKR500,000 but then comes down to PKR49,000 when income is PKR700,000 and again increases to PKR70,833 when income is PKR 1,000,000.

This benefit of reduction in tax liability for salaried taxpayers in Pakistan appears to be a substitute of direct deduction. However, this method of reduction in tax liability does not appear to be equitable as the reduction gets extended to income other than salary income as eligibility for claiming this benefit is of more than 50 per cent of salary income but reduction in tax liability is computed on total income which may include income other than salary.

INDIA

A fixed standard deduction is allowed from salary income irrespective of actual expenditure incurred in India.

The following deductions are allowed to be made from salary income in India:

1. Standard deduction
2. Entertainment allowance
3. Professional tax

Standard Deduction

In India, instead of actual expenses incurred in connection with employment, a fixed standard deduction is allowed. This deduction is allowed even if no expenditure has been incurred by the employee. The rate of standard deduction for the income year 2000-01 is as given in Table 3.13.

Entertainment Allowance

If any part of entertainment allowance is exempt, then it is allowed as deduction from the gross salary. The entertainment allowance is first fully included in the salary income and exemption, if any, is granted by way of deduction later on.

Professional Tax

Any professional tax levied by a State is allowed as deduction from the salary income.

TABLE 3.12. BENEFIT OF TAX REBATE TO SALARIED TAXPAYERS IN PAKISTAN

Total Income with more than 50 per cent income chargeable under the 'head salary'	Gross Tax Liability	Rebate including Basic Rebate of PKR2,000 Allowed to all Taxpayers	Net Income Tax Liability	Reduction in Tax Liability of Salaried Taxpayers	Total Extra Tax Rebate to Salaried Taxpayers Including Rebate of PKR500	Marginal Rate of Tax	Deduction of Income Worked Out on Extra Rebate by Applying Marginal Rate of Tax
60000	3000	2500	500	400	900	5	18000
80000	4000	2500	1500	1050	1550	5	31000
100000	5000	2500	2500	1500	2000	5	40000
150000	10000	2500	7500	3750	4250	10	42500
200000	15000	2500	12000	5000	5500	10	55000
300000	30000	2500	27500	8250	8750	15	58333
500000	70000	2500	67500	13500	14000	20	70000
700000	120000	2500	117500	11750	12250	25	49000
1000000	210000	2500	207500	20750	21250	30	70833
1500000	385000	2500	382500	19125	19625	35	56071

Source: Author's Calculations based on the *Income Tax Ordinance* upto July 10, 2000 (Pakistan)

TABLE 3.13 ALLOWABLE STANDARD DEDUCTION IN INDIA

(for the income year 2000-01)

Salary income before giving standard deduction but after giving deduction of entertainment allowance and professiona tax	Amount of standard deduction
Rs.100,000 or less	One-third of gross salary or Rs.25,000 per annum whichever is less.
More than Rs.100,000 but not more than Rs.500,000	Rs.20,000 per annum
More than Rs.500,000	Nil

Source: The *Income Tax Act* as on June 1, 2001 (India).

Conclusion

In a majority of the selected countries, including the U.K., the U.S., Australia and Malaysia, expenses incurred wholly and exclusively in connection with employment are deductible. However, such expense payment needs to be substantiated through proper written evidence and documents. Travelling expenses incurred from residence to work place or vice versa are not allowed in these countries. In Pakistan, no deduction is allowed from salary income as such. However, tax liability on salary income is reduced by 5 per cent to 80 per cent depending upon the income of such taxpayer whose salary income exceeds 50 per cent of the total income. In India, a fixed standard deduction is allowed irrespective of any actual expenditure incurred or otherwise

The employee's reimbursed expenses are taxable in all these countries to the extent these expenses relate to personal use, except medical expenses in some case. In the U.K., and Malaysia, reimbursed expenses are added to the salary first, and to the extent deduction is allowable, such expenses are deducted from the salary. However, in Australia, these expenses are taxable in the hands of the employer. In India and Pakistan, reimbursed expenses are added to the salary only when they are related to personal use.

The U.S. system regarding the reimbursed expense is complicated. Reimbursed expenses even if incurred in connection with the employment may not be allowed as deduction unless they are accounted for. Even if the expenses are accounted for, but if the reimbursement is less than the actual expenditure, then the extent to which the actual expenditure is more than the reimbursed expenses, it is allowed as an itemised deduction.

Thus, amongst all the selected countries, India is the only country which provides a fixed standard deduction up to a certain level of salary income, irrespective of actual expenditure incurred. Although it provides relief to the salaried employees who earn salary up to a certain limit, the base of taxable salary income in India gets reduced as a result of this deduction. The undervaluation of car benefit and a fixed standard deduction have affected the tax base of salary income in India.

NOTES

1. Alan Melville, *Taxation Finance Act: 2000* (Harlow, England: Pearson Education Ltd., 2001), p. 83.
2. Thomas R. Pope and John L. Kramer (eds.), *Prentice-Hall's Federal Taxation:* 1998 (Upper Saddle River, NJ: Prentice-Hall, 1998), pp. 3-13.
3. *CCH Australian Master Tax Guide* (Sydney, NSW: CCH Australia Limited), p. 330
4. The *Income Tax Act, 1967 (Act 53)* as on November 1, 1999.
5. The *Income Tax Ordinance, 1979,* upto July 10, 2000.
6. The *Income Tax Act,* 1961, as on June 1, 2001.
7. *Encyclopaedia Britannica.*
8. Net Relevant Earnings in the case of an employee are equal to the employee's earning from non-pensionable employment for that year, including benefits-in-kind, less allowable expanses and in the case of self-employed taxpayer are equal to his trading and business income, plus any income arising from furnished holiday lettings and less any loss reliefs claimed and set against trading income and trade charges paid in the year.
9. Kenneth Tingley, *Income Tax Guide* 1999-2000 (London: Orion Business Book, 1999), p. 31.
10. Veerinderjeet Singh and Teoh Boon Kee (eds.), *Malaysian Master Tax Guide* (Kuala Lumpur: CCH Asia PTE Limited, 2000), p. 150.
11. Ken Messere, *Tax Policy in OECD Countries: Choices and Conflicts* (Amsterdam: IBFD Publications, 1993), p. 229.
12. Transit pass means any pass, token, fare card, voucher or similar item entitling a person to transportation on mass transit facilities, or in transportation provided by any person in the business of transporting persons.
13. A specified employee is an employee who is either:
    (a) A director employee, including both full time and part-time director;
    (b) An employee who has substantial interest in the employer-company or business, i.e. he is a beneficial owner of equity shares carrying 20 per cent or more voting power; or
    (c) An employee whose cash salary exceeds Rs.24,000 per annum. (This limit has been increased to Rs.50,000 from the income year 2001-02.)
14. The *Income Tax Rules,* 1982, as on July 10, 2000.
15. For meaning, see note 13.
16. A remote area is one that is at least 40 km from a population centre of 14,000 or more and at least 100 km from a centre of 130,000 or more. If the area is in Zone A or Zone B, for income tax rebate purposes, it is remote, if it is at least 40 km from a population centre of 28,000 or more or at least 100 km from a centre of 130,000 or more.
17. A controlled company is one which has not more than 50 members, and is controlled in the manner described by Sec.139, by not more than five persons (Sec. 2).

CHAPTER 4

Depreciation Allowance

Like every other animate or inanimate object, business premises, machinery, plant and furniture, employed by a taxpayer in the course of his business or profession, have a limited effective life. The vigour, strength, capacity of every such object is gradually exhausted by the factors of use and time. These factors undoubtedly help a taxpayer to earn 'income' from business or profession, which is subjected to the levy of tax. Unless a provision is made for the proper recompense of such diminution in the vigour, strength and capacity of various assets used in business or profession, the apparent profits would not give a correct picture. Hence, the need for allowance for depreciation is borne out of the necessity for such recompense.

The deduction towards depreciation is therefore essential to arrive at the taxable income of the taxpayer. This reduces the tax liability in many cases to a considerable extent. While revenue expenditure incurred in earning the income is admissible as deduction in computing the taxable income, capital expenditure is generally not allowed as deduction. The logic is that the capital asset does not get exhausted or fully utilised during the year itself. Since it has a long life, the allowance of full expenditure as deduction would give a distorted picture of earnings in different years. However, it cannot be said that the capital asset used for earning the income does not get deteriorated or its value does not decrease due to wear and tear by use of such asset. As such, the object of providing for depreciation is to spread the expenditure incurred in an asset over its effective lifetime.

Determination of proper depreciation on fixed assets has always posed accounting problems. The problem does not relate as much to the concept of depreciation as to the application of the concept. Attempts have been made by professional accounting bodies and researchers to narrow down the differences on this vital subject by providing generally acceptable solutions. The *International Accounting Standard (IAS) 4 Depreciation Accounting*, defines the term 'depreciation' as 'the allocation of the depreciable amount of an asset over its estimated useful life. Depreciation for the accounting period is charged to income either directly or indirectly.'[1]

Depreciation is an allowance against income but not an actual expenditure incurred which can be measured precisely. It being essentially a notional expenditure, different countries have used depreciation allowance as part of their taxation policy to provide incentive to a particular industry, to the trade and industry as a whole, to give boost to economy or sometimes to promote and encourage the use of new technology by providing higher depreciation rates as also by providing special categories of depreciation like initial depreciation and additional depreciation. At the same time, depreciation allowance provisions have also been used to increase the tax collection by curtailing depreciation rate or withdrawing special categories of depreciation.

Different rates are prescribed for different types of assets depending upon the useful life of such assets as also to provide incentives for deployment of assets in certain socially desirable activities like checking of pollution etc. As per accounting rules, there are various methods of providing for depreciation such as straight-line method (SLM), diminishing or declining balance method (DBM), also called written down value (WDV) method, annuity method, and sinking fund method. However, for the purpose of tax laws, the first two methods, i.e. SLM and DBM are commonly used all over the world. In SLM, the rate of depreciation is lower than the rate in DBM method, but the depreciation is allowed at a fixed rate on the cost of the asset during its expected life. As such, the amount of depreciation for an asset is the same every year. In DBM, the rate of depreciation is higher than the rate for SLM, but depreciation is computed on the reducing balance of the cost of the asset after providing for depreciation for earlier years. Since the cost of the asset goes on reducing every year by the amount of depreciation, the depreciation allowance goes on decreasing. Accordingly, in DBM, the depreciation allowance is higher in the initial years and gets reduced in the later years.

A question arises as to why depreciation is allowed. Whether it is allowed:

1. due to the fact that the asset is used for the production purposes; or
2. due to wear and tear; or
3. to provide for the replacement of the asset; or
4. allowed as tax-incentive measure.

If it is allowed due to the first reason then it should be allowed as business deduction on a suitable basis, which may be the expected life of the asset. In that case, no special treatment need be given to the unabsorbed depreciation and the unabsorbed depreciation should become part of the business losses. If wear and tear is the cause, then depreciation should be less in earlier years and more in later years, as the deterioration increases with the passage of time and the use of asset.

If replacement of the asset is the main cause, then the depreciation reserve should be created to provide money for the replacement of the asset and if it is allowed as a tax incentive, then it can be allowed in a manner that provides the maximum benefit to the taxpayer. All the selected countries have made detailed provisions in their tax laws for depreciation allowance which are amended frequently to meet the changing needs of the economy and to promote industrial growth. This chapter provides a comparative review and evaluation of the methods of depreciation allowed for the computation of taxable income in the selected countries. The chapter is divided into two parts:

Part I. Depreciation Allowance: Plant and Machinery
Part II. Depreciation Allowance: Buildings

PART I: DEPRECIATION ALLOWANCE: PLANT AND MACHINERY

The provisions relating to depreciation allowance in respect of plant and machinery in the selected countries are analysed in three sections as given below:

1. Depreciation allowance provisions
2. Balancing adjustments
3. Carry forward of unabsorbed depreciation

DEPRECIATION ALLOWANCE PROVISIONS

The provisions relating to the methods of computation of initial allowance, annual allowance and rates of depreciation are examined in this section.

THE U.K.

In the U.K., depreciation on capital expenditure is termed as *capital allowance*. The provisions relating to capital allowance are contained in the *Capital Allowances Act*, 1990. The capital allowances on qualifying capital expenditure are deducted as a trading expense for a period of account during which a business is being carried on and there is a balance of qualifying expenditure.[2]

The provisions relating to capital allowances in the U.K. have been subject to frequent changes. One such change in the U.K. tax system which affected capital allowances was made by the *Finance Act*, 1994. Prior to April 6, 1994, the preceding year basis was adopted for finding out the taxable business income. Thus, the income of a business which ended on June 30, 1994, would be assessed for 1995-96. In the case of business commencing after April 5, 1994, the current year basis was adopted for the calculation of business income. Thus, the income of a business ending on June 1995 was to be assessed for the year 1995-96. The rules for calculating the basis period (income year) in the initial years were such that part of income could be taxed twice due to the overlapping periods. Special transitional rules apply to the year 1996-97. The change has affected the calculation of capital allowances also, as they are taxable on a basis similar to that of business income. Prior to April 6, 1994, capital allowances were not subtracted while calculating business profits. These allowances had to be given against those profits assessed to income tax. Capital allowances are now deductible from business profits in respect of business that commenced after April 5, 1994.

To be eligible for capital allowance, expenditure must be incurred in respect of scientific plant and machinery, industrial buildings, hotels, patents, know-how, research agricultural buildings and mineral extraction.

Any plant and machinery purchased wholly and exclusively for purposes of business qualifies for capital allowance. Prior to the *Finance Act*, 1994, plant and machinery were not defined in the legislation. As a result, many disputes arose which led to increase in the number of case laws. Schedule AAI of Sec. 117 of the *Finance Act*, 1984 prescribes a list of assets which are treated as buildings and another list of assets which, though part of a building, may qualify as plant.

In the case of *Yarmouth* vs. *France* (1887) 192BD 647,[3] a horse was held to be a plant. Though the case was not tax-based, and was related to the employer's liability, in order for the employee to receive compensation for injury caused by the horse in the course of his employment, the horse had to be a plant. In this case, Lindley L J, spelt out the characteristics of plant as follows:

(a) It must be an apparatus.
(b) It must be used by the claimant in carrying on the business.
(c) It must be kept for permanent use in the business.

In other cases, courts have generally applied the 'function versus setting' test. In *Dixon* vs. *Fitches Garage Ltd* (1975) STC 480, *and Cole Bros* vs. *Philips* (1982) STC 308, it was decided that, where the item performed a function in a business, it was more likely to be a plant, and where it was just part of the setting in which business was carried on, it would not be classified as plant.

Plant and machinery mainly include industrial equipment, tractors, motorcars, and computer software. Some of the items held to be plant and machinery in various decided cases include: a dry dock built for the repair and maintenance of ships, a swimming and padding pool, and movable office partitions.

Capital allowances in the U.K. are available in the year in which capital expenditure is incurred, even if the asset has not been brought into use in that period. The first year allowance (FYA) and the WDA, both are allowed in respect of plant and machinery. However, if the FYA is allowed in respect of the plant and the machinery in one year, the WDA is not allowed in respect of the same plant and machinery in the same year.

Methods of Computation of Depreciation:

While the FYA is calculated at a fixed rate in the first year in which the asset has been used, annual depreciation is calculated according to the DBM. These two types of depreciation are computed as shown below:

First Year Allowance

The FYA is allowed in respect of capital expenditure on plant and machinery (other than motor cars, ships and railway assets, and most of the leased assets). Though it was allowed in 1984 to the extent of 100 per cent to all types of business, it was phased out thereafter over a two-year period, withdrawn and re-introduced for a brief period of one year in 1992-93 to provide incentive to promote investment, and then again withdrawn. It was once again re-introduced in respect of capital expenditure incurred after July 2, 1997 only for small and medium-sized businesses. The FYA was allowed at the rate of 50 per cent for expenditure incurred between July 2, 1997 and July 1, 1998. The rate was further reduced to 40 per cent in respect of capital expenditure incurred during the period from July 2, 1998, to July 1, 2000. A business is a small and medium-sized business if it fulfils any two of the following three conditions:

Required Conditions	*Small Business*	*Medium Business*
1. Total assets	£1.4 million or less	£5.6 million or less
2. Turnover	£2.8 million or less	£11.2 million or less
3. Average number of employees	50 or less	250 or less

Thus, in the U.K, the FYA continues to be a tax-incentive device to promote investment. However, from July 2, 1997, it is available only to small and medium-sized business. It must be noted that in the U.K., more than 99 per cent of all business are covered under small and medium-sized business.[4]

Written-down Allowance

The annual written down allowance (WDA) in the U.K. is allowed at the rate of 25 per cent per annum on the WDV of the plant and machinery. Most items of the plant and machinery are pooled together. First, the WDV of all items in the pool on the first day of the year is calculated. After that, the purchase amount of the plant and machinery is added. Where any item is sold, or destroyed, then either the sale value or scrap value is deducted. However, the amount of sale value is restricted to the original cost of the item. The figure arrived at after adding purchases and subtracting the sale value is the WDV at the end of the year and the WDA is calculated at the rate of 25 per cent on such value. It is not, however, compulsory to claim the maximum allowance available for a period. Where in any year, profits are less and the taxpayer does not want to waste personal allowances, he may claim only part of the WDA. Any unclaimed WDA will be added to the WDV carried forward, thus increasing the allowances available in any future period. Items which are not pooled together include car and life-long assets. Cars used for business purposes and costing upto £12,000 are pooled together, but are kept in a separate pool from the general pool. Cars costing more than £12,000 are dealt with on an individual basis and the WDA on such cars is allowed upto a maximum of £3,000 per year. This restriction is not applicable in the case of taxis, short-term hire cars, and mobility allowance vehicles for the disabled. Since both the WDA and the FYA, are not allowed in the same year, the FYA in respect of new plant and machinery is calculated separately from the general pool in the year of acquisition, and the balance remaining after deducting the FYA is added to the remaining value of the WDV of the general pool at the end of the year. From the following year, the capital allowance is calculated just like any other item in the general pool.

Provision for De-pooling of Assets

The taxpayer in the U.K. has the option to charge capital allowance separately on the assets (excluding cars, ships), which have a short life, i.e. 4 years from the end of the period in which the expense was incurred. This will allow him to avail himself of the balancing allowance immediately in the year of sale. However, if the asset is not disposed of within four years of the end of the year in which it is acquired, it will become part of the general pool at its WDV, and will be chargeable along with the general pool assets.

Patent Rights and Know-how

Expenditure incurred for patent rights and know-how is eligible for the WDA in a manner similar to plant and machinery. Patent rights and know-how expenditure are pooled together and the WDA is allowed at the rate of 25 per cent per annum. The difference, however, is that no FYA is allowed in respect of patent rights and know-how and while the excess of the disposal value over the original cost of plant and machinery is charged to tax as capital gain, such excess in respect of patent rights and know-how is charged to tax as income from other sources under Schedule D, Case VI.

Expenditure on Scientific Research

Any capital expenditure on scientific research for the purpose of trading is eligible for 100 per cent capital allowance in the year in which the expense is incurred. Such expenditure excludes the cost of land and dwelling houses.

THE U.S.

In the U.S., provisions relating to depreciation, commonly known as *cost recovery*, have been subject to frequent changes. A deduction for depreciation may be claimed each year for property that is used in a trade or business, or held for the production of income. The method to be used for charging depreciation depends upon when the property is placed in service. An asset is placed in service, when it is set up and ready for its intended use for a business purpose. The term *Personal Property* is commonly used here which includes plants and machinery as well as furniture.

Methods of Computation of Depreciation

Depending upon the year in which the property is placed in service, depreciation deductions are computed by any one of the following three methods:

1. The Facts and Circumstances System (pre-1981)
2. Accelerated Cost Recovery System (ACRS)
3. Modified Accelerated Cost Recovery System (MACRS)

The Facts and Circumstances System (Pre-1981)

Prior to 1981, the methods used to claim depreciation were mainly *Facts and Circumstances and Asset Depreciation Range* (ADR).[5] Under these systems, taxpayers were required to depreciate an asset's net cost over its estimated useful life in the business. The methods commonly applied before 1981 were the straight-line, sum of the year's digits, or declining-balance methods. The taxpayers were free to estimate the useful life of the asset and it's a salvage value. However, under the ADR system, which was applicable for property placed in service after 1970, the specified classes for depreciable assets were prescribed along with the average life of assets in the class. Strict rules of record keeping were applicable to claim depreciation. Thus, variation in the estimated useful life of assets and a lot of record keeping made the provisions complicated and gave rise to several disputes.

Many changes pertaining to the computation of depreciation were made by the *Economic Recovery Act* of 1981. Later on, the *Tax Reform Act* of 1986, also made substantial revisions in the methods of providing depreciation. The major change was the reduction in the recovery period of the asset as compared to the economic useful life of the asset that allowed the taxpayer to claim depreciation at accelerated rates. The Internal Revenue Service (IRS) prescribed a list of assets according to the class life, and allotted a code number to each class of assets and also provided the recovery period of assets for each class that was lesser than the economic life of the asset.

Accelerated Cost Recovery System

In the U.S., the accelerated cost recovery system (ACRS) was introduced in 1981 to provide incentives, stimulate investment and standardise the depreciation system.[6] The controversial estimated life of assets system was done away with, and the IRS specifically prescribed the recovery period for each class of assets. The system of deducting salvage value was also withdrawn and for some assets the taxpayers were authorised to claim DBM in initial years and switch over to SLM in the later years when it provided more depreciation. The recovery period of assets was shortened, thus providing an overall benefit to the taxpayer.

The *Tax Reform Act* of 1986 reduced the individual tax rate from 50 per cent to 28 per cent, and the corporate tax rate from 46 per cent to 34 per cent. To compensate for the loss of tax revenue due to reduction in the tax rates and realising that the ACRS provided too great a tax benefit, the Congress made certain changes in the ACRS system and introduced the *Modified Accelerated Cost Recovery System* (MACRS). Though retaining many features of the ACRS, the most crucial change in the new system was increase in the recovery period with a view to reducing the speed at which depreciation was deductible. Since the MACRS applies in respect of assets purchased after December 31, 1986, it is examined in detail here.

Depreciation Deduction under MACRS

In the U.S., instead of FYA an annual deduction is allowed and instead of only one method, both the declining balance method (DBM) and the SLM method are allowed in such a manner that the taxpayer can use DBM in the initial years and may switchover to the SLM when this method starts providing more depreciation than the DBM. The taxpayer may use only the SLM or may use the SLM over longer recovery periods than normal recovery periods.

The MACRS is applicable in respect of assets placed in service after January 1, 1987. Recovery lives have been lengthened, and depreciation rates have been increased in respect of some assets. The MACRS is applied to tangible property used in a trade or business or held for the production of income. Tangible property may be either (1) personal property, or (2) real property.

Personal property is basically tangible property other than real property, such as plant and machinery, office furniture, and automobiles. Personal property here is different from personal use property. While personal property is meant for business purposes, personal-use property is meant for private purposes only.

Real property includes building, land improvements, and structures, but does not include land. The MACRS rules in the U.S. differ for personal property and for real property. Though the recovery period of assets under the MACRS has been increased in comparison to the ACRS, thus reducing the amount of allowable depreciation each year, depreciation is still allowed in the U.S. at higher rates as compared to the other selected countries under study.

Where the life of personal property is upto one year, the whole amount is allowed as depreciation in the year in which it is placed in service. In respect of personal property, in lieu of the first year depreciation, which was allowed prior to 1981, annual deduction is allowed up to a specified limit under Sec.179 *Expense Deduction*. The amount of deduction of up to $20,000 is allowed for the income year 2000, on an investment in tangible personal property. Husband and wife are considered one entity for claiming this deduction. Real property including buildings, residential property, and intangible assets such as patents, copyrights and goodwill, do not qualify for expense deduction. No deduction is allowed if the cost of property exceeds $220,000. The deduction limit is reduced by one dollar for each dollar of investment over $200,000. The deduction under Sec.179 cannot exceed the taxable income from the active conduct of trade or business. The taxable income here includes salary, wages, income from a business allotted to the taxpayer from a partnership, or small corporation in which the taxpayer actively participates. The effect of the taxable active trade or business income limit is to prevent the above deduction from creating business losses that offset income from investment income sources. The deduction, which could not be used because of the taxable income limit, can be carried forward and deducted from the future taxable income. If the taxpayer so desires, he may not use or carry forward part or the whole of the deduction. This applies especially when the taxpayer intends to invest continuously.

Personal property is divided into 3, 5, 7, 10, 15 and 20 year recovery periods. A 3-year property, including tractor units, and special tools, generally has an asset depreciation range (ADR), i.e. a useful life of less than four years. A 5-year property including automobiles, trucks, and computers has an ADR life of more than four years but less than 10 years. A 7-year property including office furniture, and equipment has an ADR life of 10 years or more, but less than 16 years. The 3, 5, 7 and 10-year personal properties are depreciated using the 200 per cent declining balance method (DBM) with an optional, automatic switch to the SLM. The 15 and 20-year personal properties are depreciated using the 150 per cent DBM. Under the DBM, the rate of depreciation is found out by dividing one by the number of years in the recovery period multiplied by either 200 per cent or 150 per cent, depending upon which DBM is allowed. In the case of 5-year property, the rate of depreciation will be one-fifth multiplied by 200 per cent, i.e. 40 per cent. This rate is applied each year to the adjusted basis of the property. (The *adjusted basis* is the balance amount left after deducting expense amount and depreciation for the previous years if any). However, for purposes of convenience, the IRS in the U.S. has prepared separate tables under different circumstances. The rates given in the following table are for the full year and are applied on the depreciable basis of the asset. (The *depreciable basis* is the asset's original basis for depreciation less any amount deducted under the Sec. 179 election to expense assets.) The tables have made the otherwise complicated depreciation system much easier to apply, and have helped in standardising the depreciation system and in reducing errors and disputes.

Another feature about the MACRS personal property is that the mid-year convention applies in the year of sale or disposal. It means that the half-year depreciation is allowed in the year when the asset is placed into service as well as in the year when the asset is sold or destroyed. However, if the aggregate basis of all the property placed in service during the last 3 months of the year exceeds 40 per cent of the cost of all personal property placed in service during the tax year, then a mid-quarter convention will be applicable. The IRS has prepared separate tables for all the four quarters. Thus, the taxpayer has just to find in which quarter the property is placed in service and the recovery period of the property. The depreciation rates under MACRS in respect of personal property are given in Table 4.1

It emerges from the table that in the U.S. a very high depreciation based on 200 per cent DBM can be claimed in the initial years and after some years when SLM provides more depreciation, then a switch over to SLM is allowed. In the case of a 10-year property, till the 6th year of life of the property, DBMs provide more depreciation and from 7th year onwards SLMs provide more depreciation, so the rates from the 7th year onwards are given according to the SLM.

To prevent the abuse of the depreciation deduction in the case of mixed-use property, the Congress enacted the listed property rules in 1984 and imposed restrictions on claims of depreciation on such assets. *Listed assets* are assets that are conducive to mixed business personal use. In the case of a listed property (where the property is used partly for business and partly for private purposes) including automobiles, computers, cellular telephones, the

MACRS can be used for that part which is used for business purposes. However, if the business use is 50 per cent or less, the taxpayer must use alternative depreciation system (ADS) (i.e. longer recovery period with straight line cost method)

Not only this, even if the business use percentage decreases below 50 per cent or less in the subsequent years, the excess of the MACRS depreciation allowed in the earlier years over depreciation allowable as per ADS is recaptured and shall be treated as ordinary income in the year when the business use percentage decreases to 50 per cent or less. In future also, the ADS system will be used, even if the business use percentage again increases to more than 50 per cent in the subsequent years.

In the U.S., depreciation deduction is restricted in respect of luxury automobiles even if such automobiles are used 100 per cent of the time for business. The MACRS depreciation for automobiles placed in service in 1997 is subject to $3,160 ceiling limitation for the first year, $5,000 for the second year, $3,050 for the third year and $1,775 for each succeeding year in the recovery period. In the years following the end of the depreciation period, depreciation upto $1,775 per year is allowed in the taxable years commencing

TABLE 4.1. MACRS DEPRECIATION FOR PERSONAL PROPERTY IN THE U.S.

(for the income year 1999, depreciation rates in %)

Recovery Year	3 years	5 years	7 years	10 years	15 years	20 years
1	33.33	20.00	14.29	10.00	5.00	3.750
2	44.45	32.00	24.49	18.00	9.50	7.219
3	14.81	19.20	17.49	14.40	8.55	6.677
4	7.41	11.52	12.49	11.52	7.70	6.177
5	11.52	8.93	9.22	6.93	5.713	
6	5.76	8.92	7.37	6.23	5.285	
7	8.93	6.55	5.90	4.888		
8	4.46	6.55	5.90	4.522		
9	6.56	5.91	4.462			
10	6.55	5.90	4.461			
11	3.28	5.91	4.462			
12	5.90	4.461				
13	5.91	4.462				
14	5.90	4.461				
15	5.91	4.462				
16	2.95	4.461				
17	4.462					
18	4.461					
19	4.462					
20	4.461					
21	2.231					

Note: Applicable Convention Mid-year, Applicable methods: 200 per cent or 150 per cent declining balance method switching to the straight-line method.

Source: Kevin E. Murphy, and Mark Higgins, *Concepts in Federal Taxation* (Cincinnati, Ohio South-Western College Publishing, 1999), p. 418

after the end of the recovery period until the business use portion of the automobile is fully depreciated.

MACRS Straight-line Election

In the case of personal property under MACRS, declining balance method (DBM) in the initial years and a switch over to SLM in later years is allowable, thus providing opportunity to claim the maximum depreciation in all the years. However, if the taxpayer so desires, he may instead use only the SLM method over the MACRS recovery period. As a result, lower depreciation will be claimed each year. This generally happens in the case of a taxpayer having low income or suffering a loss.

Alternative Depreciation System

Alternative depreciation system (ADS) requires the use of SLM over recovery periods longer than the MACRS recovery period. It can be used both for personal as well as for real property. It is opted for in case the taxpayer has low income or has suffered losses. It is also used to find out *the* alternative minimum tax (AMT).[7] In the U.S., the benefit of accelerated depreciation under the MACRS is not available to higher income groups. Where the adjusted gross income (AGI) of an individual or corporation exceeds the exemption limit (the limit is $40,000 for corporations and $33,750 for single individual taxpayer for the income year 1998), their income is recalculated after allowing depreciation under the ADR (lower depreciation) and after disallowing certain tax preferences. If the tax calculated on the basis of alternative minimum taxable income is more than the tax on regular income computed after making deduction under the MACRS, then excess tax is payable as AMT in addition to the regular tax liability.

Amortisation of Intangible Assets

Capital recovery of intangible assets such as patents, copyrights, and goodwill is known as amortisation. The cost of these assets is written off on a straight-line basis. However, these assets must be used for business purposes. In the case of acquired intangible assets, amortisation is deducted on a rateable basis over a 15-year period beginning with the month of acquisition. Internally created intangible assets have definite and limited lives and are therefore amortised over a defined period. Prior to 1993, goodwill was not amortised. But Sec. 197 enacted in 1993, allowed any goodwill that has been purchased to be written off.

Research and Experimental Expenditures

Research and experimental expenses, i.e. experimental and laboratory costs incidental to the development of a product may either be claimed as expense in the year in which the expenditure is incurred, or the cost may be deferred and amortised as a rateable deduction over a period of 60 months or more. A taxpayer must make an election to expense or defer and amortise the costs in the initial year in which the research and experimental expenditures are incurred. If no election is made, the costs must be capitalised.

AUSTRALIA

In Australia, capital expenditure on plants is treated separately from the capital expenditure on buildings and structural improvements .The term 'depreciation' is used in Australia in connection with depreciation on plants only and such deduction is allowed as business deduction to find out business income.

A deduction for depreciation is allowable on plants owned by a taxpayer and used by him during that year for the purpose of producing assessable income, and also on any plant owned by the taxpayer which has been installed ready for use for that purpose and held in reserve during that year. Thus, depreciation on plants in Australia is allowed even if it has not actually been used during that year but is installed ready for use during that year and held in reserve. The plant is treated as held in reserve, if its use is contingent on some future event occurring in the taxpayer's existing income-producing activities.[8]

In Australia, the ordinary meaning of the term 'plant' applies in general. Certain items, which are decided as plant in different cases, include: a dry dock, race horses, movable office partition and fixed site caravans. The Commissioner also provides a list of items which are plants along with details of their effective life. The main factor that determines whether an item of property is plant or not is its function. As decided in the famous case of *Yarmouth* vs. *France and J. Lyons & Co*, if the function is an apparatus or permanent means to produce the income, the item will be treated as plant and if the function is to provide setting or environment within which income producing activities are conducted it will not be treated as plant.

Items specifically included as plants [ITAA 97, Sec. 42-18, corresponding to ITAA 36, Sec. 54(21)] are articles, machinery, tools, race horses, plumbing fixtures and fittings including wall and floor tiling, mainly for the personal use of employees in the taxpayer's business.

Methods of Computation of Depreciation

In Australia, the system of computation of depreciation is different from both the U.K. and the U.S. The depreciation may be claimed either according to the diminishing value method (DVM) or according to the prime cost method.

Prime Cost Method

Under the prime cost method (PCM), a deduction equal to a percentage of the original cost of the plant is allowable in each income year over its effective life [ITAA 97, Sec. 42-165, corresponding to ITAA 36, Sec. 56(1)(6)].

Diminishing Value Method

Under the DVM, depreciation is calculated in the first year by applying a fixed percentage to the cost of the plant. In the second and following years, depreciation is calculated on the undeducted cost of the plant at the start of the income year [(ITAA 97, Sec. 42-160, corresponding to ITAA 36, Sec. 56(1)(9))].

The *undeducted cost* in Australia is equal to the cost of an item of plant less depreciation allowed or that would have been allowed, if plant had been used by the taxpayer for income-producing purposes from the beginning. The undeducted cost would be equal to the WDV where the plant is fully used for income-producing purposes from the beginning. However, if the plant is used only partly for business purposes, then the WDV is found out by deducting from the original cost, depreciation attributable to business use only. However, the following year's depreciation will be calculated on the undeducted cost (cost less depreciation attributable to the whole plant) and the depreciation so calculated will be deducted to the extent of business use from the opening WDV to find out the closing WDV. This process will continue in future also.

The taxpayer must decide which method is to be used for the income year in which a depreciation deduction is first allowable to the taxpayer for the item of plant [(ITAA 97, Sec. 42-120, corresponding to ITAA 36, Sec. 56(1)]. The taxpayer is free to choose one method for one item of plant and the other method for another item of plant. Similarly, he can make his choice on a year-by-year basis, i.e. one method for plant that is first depreciable in one year and another method for plant that becomes depreciable for the first time next year or later on. The choice made once will continue to apply for future years also.

Plants which are depreciated using the PCM can be switched to the DVM by allocating it to a depreciation pool (Plants may be pooled in Australia at the choice of the taxpayer. When pooled, only DVM is allowed). The taxpayer, however, cannot switch to the PCM by removing plant from a depreciation pool [ITAA 97, Sec. 42-370 (3)(c), corresponding to ITAA 36, Sec. 62 AAR(1)]. The total depreciation allowed for an item of plant cannot exceed its original cost in the taxpayer's hands.

In Australia, if the plant is used to produce an assessable income (or is installed ready for use for that purpose), for only part of the year, the depreciation deduction is calculated on a pro rata basis. Further, a 100 per cent deduction is available for plant costing AUD300 or less [ITAA97, Sec. 42-130, corresponding to ITAA 36, Sec. 55(2)] or where the effective life of the plant is under 3 years.

Rates of Depreciation

Rates of depreciation in Australia vary according to the effective life of a unit of plant. Since July 1, 1991, the taxpayers may make their own estimate of the effective life of a plant or adopt the effective life prescribed by the Commissioner. The annual depreciation rates for plants [(ITAA 97, Sec. 42-125(1), corresponding to ITAA 36, Sec. 55(5), 56(1)], are given in Table 4.2

As shown in the table 100 per cent depreciation is allowed in Australia in case the life of the asset is less than 3 years. The rates of depreciation under

TABLE 4.2 . ANNUAL DEPRECIATION RATES FOR PLANTS IN AUSTRALIA
(for the income year 1998-99)

Effective life in years	Prime Cost Method Rate (in %)	Diminishing Value Method Rate (in %)
Fewer than 3	100	100
3 to fewer than 5	40	60
5 to fewer than 20/3	27	40
20/3 to fewer than 10	20	30
10 to fewer than 13	17	25
13 to fewer than 30	13	20
30 or more	7	10

Source: CCH, 1999 *Austrilian Master Tax Guide*, p. 847

the prime cost method are approximately two third of the rates under the DVM. While in the U.S, depreciation under the SLM is found out by dividing the cost of the asset by the remaining life of the asset, in Australia, a fixed rate of depreciation is applicable on the original cost to find out depreciation as per the PCM.

In respect of items such as cars and motorcycles, art works, and plants related to employees' amenities, special rates of depreciation apply.

A taxpayer may elect a lower depreciation rate for any plant instead of the rate allowed under the Act. An election to use a lower depreciation rate must be made for the income year when the plant first becomes depreciable.

Car Depreciation Limit and Depreciation Rates

In Australia, there is a limit on the cost of the car for depreciation purposes. The car depreciation limit of the year in which it is acquired is not relevant, but the year in which the car is used, is. For cars used during the financial year 1998-99, the car depreciation limit was AUD55,134. The limit applies in case of both new and second hand cars. Annual depreciation rates of cars are given in Table 4.3 [(ITAA 97, Sec. 42-135, corresponding to ITAA 36, Sec. 55(6))].

TABLE 4.3. ANNUAL DEPRECIATION RATES OF CARS IN AUSTRALIA
(for the income year 1998-99)

Effective life in years	Prime Cost Method Rate (in %)	Diminishing Value Method. Rate (in %)
Fewer than 3	100	100
3 to fewer than 5	33	50
5 to fewer than 20/3	20	30
20/3 to fewer than 10	15	22.5
10 to fewer than 13	10	15
13 to fewer than 20	8	11.25
20 to fewer than 40	5	7.5
40 or more	3	3.75

Source: Same as Table 4.2

It is clear from Table 4.3 that in Australia, the depreciation on cars can be computed either according to the PCM or the DVM method as is applicable for other assets. However, the rates of depreciation on cars are lower than the rates applicable to other assets.

While the full cost of computer software was deductible in the year in which expenditure was incurred prior to May 11, 1998, software costs are subject to depreciation, if incurred after that date. The expenditure incurred in acquiring, developing or commissioning software will be amortised at 40 per cent per year on a prime cost basis.

Pooling Provisions of Depreciable Plants

In Australia, it is not compulsory to pool together plants entitled to the same rate of depreciation. If the taxpayer so desires, he may elect to pool the plants that are depreciable at the same depreciation rate. When plants are pooled, their WDV at the beginning of the year is aggregated and depreciation on the aggregated value is charged on the basis of the DVM. Only plants which are wholly used to produce assessable income (or installed ready for such use) and used for that purpose for the whole income year may be pooled. The depreciation in the year in which a plant is acquired will be calculated separately and the WDV of such plants will be added to the opening value of the relevant pool in the next year.

The taxpayer may remove any item of plant at any time and after removal, the plant must continue to be depreciated using the DVM.

If any plant from the pool is disposed of, then it may be treated in any one of the three ways:

1. The plant may be removed from the pool and the balancing charge or balancing deduction may be calculated in the normal way on the basis of the difference between the termination value and the WDV or the undeducted cost.
2. The termination value up to the original cost of the plant may be added to the assessable income and the WDV of the plant may remain in the depreciation pool.
3. The termination value up to the original cost of the plant may be offset against the cost or the WDV of replacement or other plant and the WDV of the plant may remain in the pool.

The taxpayer may choose the first method to take immediate benefit of balancing deduction if the termination value is less than the WDV He will prefer the third method if the termination value exceeds the WDV. Thus, the taxpayers in Australia are allowed to take maximum benefit by claiming the balancing deduction on individual asset sold as well as by delaying the balancing charge by adjusting the termination value up to the original cost against the cost of the new plant.

MALAYSIA

In Malaysia, tax incentives in the form of initial allowance, annual allowance and re-investment allowance are allowed to encourage investment in specified types of buildings and plant and machinery. Though capital allowances are also allowed in respect of qualifying agriculture and forest expenditure, the provisions relating only to capital allowances on qualifying plants and machinery and industrial buildings are analysed here.

Capital allowances on plant and machinery are given for a basis period, which in the case of trade and business, is the accounting period ending in the year preceding the relevant year of assessment. Where the accounting year ends on March 31, then for the year of assessment 1999, the basis period will be the year to March 31, 1998 (The year of assessment is 12 months period from January 1, to December 31.)

Initial as well as annual allowances are allowed in respect of the qualifying expenditure on plant and machinery. The Income Tax Act has not defined the term 'plant and machinery'. Thus, the ordinary meaning of plant and machinery applies. Many decided cases are also considered to find out whether a particular ítem is plant and machinery or not.

The capital allowance is given to a person who incurs qualifying plant expenditure and is the owner of the asset (Schedule 3, para 10 and 15). The expenditure on plant and machinery is deemed to be incurred on the day it is capable of being used for the purposes of the business. Where the expenditure is incurred for a business which is about to start, that expenditure shall be deemed to be incurred when the business commences.

Expenditure incurred on the installation of plant as well as on the alteration of an existing building or structure for installing plant and machinery will form part of the costs of the plant or machinery. In the case of a motor vehicle, other than that used for commercial purposes, a limit is fixed amounting to RM50,000 and thus, the qualifying expenditure on the car will not exceed RM50,000.

Methods of Computation of Depreciation

In Malaysia, similar to the U.K., both initial as well as annual allowances are allowed. While initial allowance is allowed at a fixed rate in the first year, the annual allowance is allowed according to the SLM method at the rates prescribed under the Income Tax Rules, which differ according to the nature of the industry in which the asset is used. The initial and annual allowances allowed in Malaysia are given below.

Initial Allowance

In Malaysia, a taxpayer is entitled to claim an initial allowance (IA) equal to 20 per cent of the qualifying expenditure incurred on plant and machinery for the purpose of business. The IA is a once for all allowance and is taken into account in computing annual allowances, balancing allowances and balancing charges.

Annual Allowance

Annual allowances on a qualifying plant and machinery are allowed at a fixed rate according to the SLM. Under this method, the standard rate is applied on the original cost each year. The amount of annual allowances each year is the same. Annual allowances are allowed based on the SLM on the purchase of plant and machinery, provided they were capable of being used during the basis period at the rates prescribed under the Income-tax (Qualifying Plant Annual Allowance) Rules 2000. The rates in general vary from 8 to 14 per cent except in some specified cases where even 20 per cent allowance is allowed.

Higher Allowances

An IA of 30 per cent is allowed on capital expenditure incurred on the plant and machinery in businesses involving construction works, road, structures and buildings. An IA of 60 per cent is allowed with effect from the year of assessment 1998 on capital expenditure incurred on the provision of plant and machinery in businesses involving the working of a tin ore or the extraction of timber from a forest or other prescribed activities.[9] An IA of 40 per cent and an annual allowance of 20 per cent of the qualifying plant expenditure incurred from January 1, 1997 is allowed to a public transport company providing buses that use natural gas for the business of public transportation and to a person providing natural gas refuelling equipment used at a natural gas refuelling outlet. Effective from the year of assessment 1996, an IA of 20 per cent and an annual allowance of 40 per cent are allowed on the qualifying plant expenditure incurred on the provision of computer and information technology equipment. With effect from the year of assessment 1999, an IA of 20 per cent and an annual allowance of 40 per cent are allowed on the capital expenditure incurred on the cost of provision of computer software or package. Capital allowances are not mandatory in Malaysia. These are granted only when claimed. As such, a taxpayer has a choice to limit his claim to one business or to certain types of assets only.

Re-investment Allowance

Companies which are resident in Malaysia and have been in operation for not less than 12 months and which embark on an approved project are entitled to a special incentive called, re-investment allowance (RA). An approved project means a project for manufacturing or processing undertaken by a company expanding, modernising or automating its existing business. With effect from the year of assessment 1997, the RA of 60 per cent is given on the qualifying expenditure incurred on a factory, plant, machinery or any other apparatus. The RA deduction is granted from the statutory income, i.e. after deducting capital allowances. However, the utilisation of RA for each assessment year is restricted to 70 per cent of the statutory income except in promoted areas of Malaysia. The unabsorbed RA is carried forward for setting off in future years.

PAKISTAN

In Pakistan, depreciation is allowed as deduction under clause (v) of Sec. 23(1) of the *Income Tax Ordinance*, 1979. The provisions relating to depreciation are given under the Third Schedule of the Ordinance.

In Pakistan, many of the provision relating to depreciation are common to plant and machinery as well as buildings. Such provisions, which are common and apply to buildings, are also included here.

Depreciation is allowed in Pakistan on building, machinery, plant and furniture. The term 'plant' includes ships, aircraft or vehicles registered in Pakistan and also books, scientific apparatus and surgical equipment. Furniture includes fittings. Depreciation is allowed only when the asset is owned by the assessee on the last day of the income year and the asset has been used for the purposes of business or profession.

Depreciation is allowed for a full year irrespective of the number of days the asset was used during the income year. Where the income year exceeds 12 months, depreciation shall be increased in the same proportion as the period exceeds 12 months. Where the income year is less than 12 months, the depreciation shall be allowed in full. But no depreciation is allowed if the asset is disposed of during the year. The resultant gain or loss is calculated with reference to each asset rather than the class or group of assets with effect from the assessment year 1991-92.

Methods of Computation of Depreciation

In Pakistan, the method of charging depreciation on plant and machinery and buildings is more or less same except that the rates vary and that in respect of plant and machinery, extra depreciation allowance and first year allowance can also be claimed in addition to initial depreciation in some cases. In both the cases, depreciation is charged on the WDV.

The basis of calculation of depreciation allowance in Pakistan is WDV of the assets. The WDV in the case of; (a) assets acquired in the income year means the actual cost to the assessee and; (b) in the case of assets acquired before the income year means the actual cost of acquisition less the aggregate of depreciation actually allowed (including unabsorbed depreciation). However, with effect from the assessment year 1992-93, the actual cost of the road transport vehicles (not plying for hire) shall not exceed PKR600,000. In computing the actual cost, the amount of any grant, subsidy or assistance shall be excluded.

In Pakistan, initial depreciation, normal depreciation and extra depreciation allowances can be claimed in respect of any asset in the same year. However, the aggregate of depreciation allowance allowed year after year shall not exceed the original cost of any asset.

Initial Depreciation

As provided under Rule 5 of the Third Schedule of the *Income Tax Ordinance*, 1979, initial depreciation was allowed on any building which was erected or any machinery or plant which was installed any time between

July 1,1976 and June 30, 2000 (both days inclusive) in the year of erection or installation or the year in which such building or machinery or plant is used by the assessee for the first time for the purpose of his business or profession or the year in which commercial production is commenced, whichever is later.[10]

Initial depreciation will not be available on any road transport vehicle not plying for hire or on any machinery, which has been previously used in Pakistan. The rate of initial depreciation in the case of machinery and plant is 25 per cent of the WDV. Any plant, machinery, equipment and industrial building to which additional depreciation allowance, re-investment allowance and industrial building allowance under Rules 5A, 5B and 5C respectively apply, the rate of initial depreciation in such cases is 20 per cent of the WDV. In addition to the initial depreciation allowance for the first year, an additional allowance of initial depreciation is allowed for the following year to an industrial undertaking, which is set up after June 30,1995 and manufactures engineering goods.

Normal Depreciation

Normal depreciation is allowed in Pakistan in respect of building, furniture, machinery and plant provided these are used for the purposes of business or profession during the income year. The rates of normal depreciation given in Rule 2 (1) of the Third Schedule are given in Table 4.4.

The rate of normal depreciation on plant in Pakistan as shown in the table is 10 per cent. Besides annual depreciation, initial depreciation at the rate of 25 per cent is also allowed.

Extra Depreciation Allowance

In addition to normal depreciation, an assessee is entitled to claim extra shift allowance equal to 50 per cent of normal depreciation on account of double shift working and equal to 100 per cent of normal depreciation on account of triple shift.

The extra shift allowance is to be calculated in proportion to the ratio which the number of days for which the concern worked in double or triple shift as the case may be, bears to the normal number of working days during the income year. Normal working days in a year for this purpose are taken at 300 days.

TABLE 4.4. RATE OF NORMAL DEPRECIATION IN PAKISTAN

(for the income year 1998-99)

Nature of Asset	Rate as % age of WDV
Building (in general)	5
Factory or workshops (excluding godowns and offices)	10
Residential quarters for labour	10
Furniture	10
Machinery and plant	10
Technical or professional books	20
Motor Vehicles	20

Source: The *Income Tax Ordinance* upto July 1999, paragraph 2(1) of Third Schedule. (Pakistan)

In Pakistan, besides normal depreciation and extra shift allowance, certain specified industries are also entitled to first year allowance (FYA). The provisions relating to FYA are given under Rule 5A.

First Year Allowance

In Pakistan, where any machinery, plant and equipment is installed by any industrial undertaking set up on or after November 21, 1997, and owned and managed by a company formed after the said date exclusively for operating the said industrial undertaking, further depreciation by way of FYA shall be allowed at the rates prescribed, in respect of the year of installation or the year in which such machinery, plant or equipment is used for the first time for the purposes of his business or profession or the year in which commercial production is commenced, whichever is the later. The FYA rates prescribed which are given in the table of Rule 5A of the Third Schedule differ for various types of industries. While the rate of FYA for some industries, including leather, textiles, footwear, electronics is 80 per cent of the WDV, the rate ranges from 40 per cent to 65 per cent of the WDV for other kinds of industries. The rate of FYA is 40 per cent of the WDV for service industry, infrastructure, social and agricultural sector, and 100 per cent of the WDV in respect of transport industry.

Re-investment Allowance

To encourage modernisation and expansion of plant and machinery in respect of expenditure incurred by an industrial undertaking after November 21, 1997, for the purposes of balancing, modernisation, replacement of plant and machinery already installed, re-investment allowance equal to 40 per cent of the WDV shall be allowed under rule 5B either in the year in which plant and machinery is first used or the year in which production is commenced, whichever is the later.

INDIA

In India, the law relating to depreciation allowance has been substantially altered by the *Taxations Laws (Amendment and Miscellaneous Provisions) Act,* 1986, with effect from April 1988. Prior to the assessment year 1988-89, three types of depreciation allowance, namely, normal depreciation allowance, extra depreciation allowance and initial depreciation allowance were allowed to the assessee in respect of building, machinery, plant and furniture. At that time, depreciation allowance for each asset had to be calculated separately, thus requiring lengthy calculations especially in those cases where the number of assets were many.[11] The procedure of computation of depreciation allowance was simplified with effect from the assessment year 1988-89 with the introduction of 'Block of assets' system. Under this system, all assets entitled to the same rate of depreciation are aggregated for the purposes of depreciation allowance.

Depreciation allowance is deductible from the income under the head

Income from business and profession under Sec. 32 of the Income Tax Act, 1961. Depreciation is allowed in respect of tangible and also intangible assets, if such assets are acquired after March 31, 1998. Tangible assets which qualify for depreciation allowance are 'building, machinery, plant or furniture'. Intangible assets eligible for depreciation allowance are 'know-how, patents, copyrights, trademarks, licenses, franchises'.

Depreciation is allowed in respect of the eligible asset in India provided the asset is owned by the assessee and is used for the purposes of business or profession during the relevant accounting year. The use of asset does not mean that asset should be used necessarily for manufacturing or production purposes. The user of the asset should be understood in a wide sense so as to embrace a passive as well as an active user. Thus, if an asset is kept ready for use, it will be treated as if it has been used. The assessee should be the owner, but in case the building is leased and the lessee has incurred further capital expenditure on the building, he will be allowed depreciation on the capital expenditure incurred by him.

Assets Put to Use for Less than 180 Days

Prior to the assessment year 1992-93, full depreciation used to be allowed, irrespective of the number of days for which an asset was used. Thus, even if an asset was purchased on the last day of the income year, full depreciation could be claimed for that year. However, with effect from the assessment year 1992-93, if any asset is acquired by the assessee during the previous year and it is put to use for the purposes of business or profession for a period of less than 180 days in that year, the deduction by way of depreciation shall be restricted to 50 per cent of the normal depreciation.

Methods of Computation of Depreciation

From the assessment year 1988-89, depreciation is allowed at the prescribed rate on the written down value (WDV) of a block of assets. The term 'block of assets' means a group of assets falling within a class of assets comprising:

1. tangible assets, being building, machinery, plant or furniture
2. intangible assets, being know-how, patents, copyrights, trademarks, licenses, franchises or any other business or commercial rights of similar nature in respect of which the same percentage of depreciation is prescribed.

Written Down Value of a Block of Assets

In India, the WDV is the basis of computation of depreciation allowance. The written down value under Sec. 43(6) means:[12]

1. in the case of assets acquired in the previous year, the actual cost to the assessee;
2. in the case of assets acquired before the previous year, the actual cost to the assessee less all depreciation actually allowed to him;

3. In case any asset of the block is sold during the year, the WDV of the block of asset shall be computed as follows:

Step 1: Find out the WDV value of the block of assets as on first day of the income year.
Step 2: Add the actual cost of any asset acquired during the previous year.
Step 3: From the figure so calculated, deduct the money payable in respect of the assets of the same block, which are sold or discarded or demolished or destroyed during the previous year together with the amount of scrap value, if any. The deduction cannot exceed the aggregate amount of step 1 and step 2.
Step 4: The resultant figure will be the WDV of the block at the end of the year. Depreciation will be charged on this value at the prescribed rates.

The term 'actual cost' means the actual cost to the assessee as reduced by the proportion of the cost thereof, if any has been met directly or indirectly by any other person or authority. Thus, any grant, or subsidy received from the government will reduce the cost. Expenses incurred in the acquisition and installation of the asset will form part of the cost of the asset.

Money payable in respect of any building, machinery, plant and furniture includes: (a) any insurance, salvage, or compensation money payable in respect thereof; (b) where the asset is sold, the price for which it is sold.

Rates of Depreciation

The rates of depreciation given in Appendix 1 to the Income Tax Rules in respect of some of the assets are given in Table 4.5.

The rates of depreciation as shown in the table are 25 per cent in respect of plant and machinery, which is much higher than 10 per cent rate applicable in Pakistan. However, in India, no initial depreciation is allowed, while in Pakistan, initial depreciation is allowed at the rate of 25 per cent. The rate of depreciation for patents and copyrights in India is 25 per cent only. The rate of depreciation in respect of some other plant and machinery is higher, such

TABLE 4.5. RATES OF DEPRECIATION IN INDIA

(for the income year 1999-2000)

Nature of Asset	Rate of Depreciation (%)
1 Residential building	5
2 Office buildings, factory, godowns	10
3 Hotel building	20
4 Furniture and fittings	10
5 Furniture and fittings used in hotel educational institutions, cinema houses	15
6 Plant and machinery (in general)	25
7 Patents, copyrights	25

Source: The Income Tax Rules, 1962 as on June 1, 2000 (India)

as in the case of buses, lorries, taxies used in the business of running on hire, the rate is 40 per cent, for computers it is 60 per cent, and in respect of air pollution control equipments, water pollution control equipment, energy saving devices, solid waste control equipments, the rate is 100 per cent and in the case of ships it is 10 per cent. Although, the rate of depreciation for furniture in general is 10 per cent, in some cases a higher rate of 15 per cent is allowed if the furniture is used in a hotel, an educational institution or a cinema house.

In India, depreciation is not allowed on cars manufactured outside India except in case of the business of running it on hire for tourists. Where an asset is used only partly for business purposes, depreciation allowance shall be restricted to a fair proportionate part thereof which the assessing officer may determine, having regard to the use of such building, machinery, plant or furniture for the purposes of business or profession.

Special Treatment in the Case of Power Units

In India, the depreciation in general is charged according to the reducing balance method. However, with effect from the assessment year 1998-99, an undertaking engaged in generation or generation and distribution of power can claim depreciation in respect of assets acquired after March 31,1999 either according to the SLM or according to the WDV. In the case of the straight-line method, depreciation is calculated at a specified percentage of the actual cost. (The specified percentage is given in Appendix 1A to the Income-tax Rules.) Under the WDV method, it is calculated at the prescribed rates applicable on the WDV of the block of assets at the end of the income year. The option must be exercised before the due date of furnishing of the return of income. The option once exercised shall be final and continue to apply in future years.

A summary of the relevant provisions of depreciation of all the selected countries is given in Table 4.6.

Conclusion

The method of providing depreciation in the selected countries differs in many respects. As shown in the table, the actual cost, i.e. historical cost is the basis of the computation of depreciation in all the selected countries. No country has enacted provisions for providing depreciation on the replacement cost basis. The reason why replacement cost basis is not adopted for allowing deduction on account of depreciation while computing income is to allow deduction of the actual expenditure incurred and not the expenditure one will incur in the future. As such, the historical cost basis therefore is in conformity with the basic concept of taxing the actual income and not the hypothetical income.

The methods commonly used for providing depreciation are the WDV or the SLM. The WDV method is adopted in all the selected countries except in Malaysia where the SLM is adopted. Taxpayers in the U.S. and Australia can make a choice between these two methods.

TABLE 4.6. A SUMMARY OF DEPRECIATION ALLOWANCE PROVISIONS RELATING TO PLANT AND MACHINERY IN SELECTED COUNTRIES

Sl. No.	Particulars	U.K.	U.S	Australia	Malaysia	Pakistan	India
1	Basis of cost	Actual cost	Actual cost	Actual cost	Actual cost	Actual cost	Actual cost
2	Method of providing depreciation	Written Down Value Method	WDV method with an option to switch over to SLM later on. SLM also allowed at the option of taxpayer.	Option to choose WDV or SLM individually for each item and each year.	Straight Line Method	Written Down Value Method	Written Down Value Method
3	Items included under plant and machinery	Industrial equipment, tractors, motorcars, computer software, movable office partitions.	Plant and machinery, office furniture, automobiles	Machinery, tools, fixtures, fittings.	Individual plant and machinery within its ordinary meaning	Shops, aircraft, vehicles, books, scientific apparatus and surgical equipments	All plants and machinery
4	Pooling of assets	Yes, except car costing more than UK £12000. Separate pool for car costing up to £12000 and used for business purpose.	Not Applicable	Pooling option allowed when declining value method used (i.e. DVM) However, in first year when plant is acquired, depreciation is computed individually.	Not Applicable	Not Applicable	Yes, Pooling is compulsory
6	Option to claim no depreciation or lower depreciation	Yes, can claim part of depreciation	Yes	Lower depreciation rate allowed But option has to be exercised in the income year when plant first becomes depreciable.	Claim is optional	Yes	No, with recent amendment claim of depreciation is now mandatory.

7	First year/initial allowance	40 percent (withdrawn from July 9, 2000).	No. However, annual deduction up to $20,000 for assets costing less than $2,00,000.	No, 100 percent deduction for plant costing AUD300 or less or where effective life of asset under three years.	20 per cent	Initial depreciation @25% of WDV. First year allowance 40% to 60% of WDV in respect of plant and machinery in specific industries.	Nil
8	Applicable convention	Depreciation is allowed for full year irrespective of number of days asset is used. No depreciation is allowed in the year of disposal.	Mid-year convention. Half-year depreciation is allowed in the year when asset is placed in service as well as in the year when asset is sold. However, if total value placed in the tax year in pool is more than 40 percent in last quarter then mid-quarter convention is applicable.	Pro-rata for number of days assets are in use both in the year of acquisition as well as in the year of disposal.	Depreciation for full year allowed irrespective of the number of days the assets were used.	Depreciation allowed for full year irrespective of the number of days assets were used. No depreciation if asset is disposed of during the year.	50 per cent of normal depreciation is allowed if the asset is put to use for less than 180 days. Otherwise full depreciation allowed.
9	Rate of depreciation	25 percent. For car, value is restricted to UK£12000. On Computer, rate is 100% if acquired after April 1, 2000.	Different rates for different types of assets based on the life of the asset ranging from 7.5 per cent to 66.66 per cent. For general machinery and office furniture, rate is 28.58 per cent. For motor vehicles, computers, rate is 40 per cent.	Different rates for different types of assets, based on the effective life. The general tate is 25% and 35% in case of DVM and 17% and 20% in case of PCM. On computer software 40 percent according to. Car value is restricted to AUD55,134	Rates vary from 8% to 14%. On computer software 40%.	Machinery and Plant: 10% Furniture: 10% Car: 20% Computers: 80%	Plant: 25% Furniture: 10% Car: 20% On computers: 60%

(contd.)

TABLE 4.6 (contd.)

Sl. No.	Particulars	U.K.	U.S.	Australia	Malaysia	Pakistan	India
10	Balancing adjustment	When all items in a pool in the case of pooled assets or any non-pooled asset, are disposed of, balancing charge/allowance is added or deducted from the trading profit.	On disposal of assets, gain on disposition to the extent of depreciation is recaptured as ordinary income. Balance is capital gain. Loss on disposition is ordinary loss.	Balancing deduction allowed in the year of disposal. However if any plant from pool is disposed of then at the option of the taxpayer either it may be removed from the pool and balancing charge/deduction computed in normal way or terminal value may be added to assessable income or adjusted against WDV of the replacement plant.	Balancing charge/deduction allowed in the year of sale. However balancing charge is taxable to the extent of depreciation allowed.	Balancing charge/deduction allowed in the year of sale to be added as business income or deducted as business deduction.	When all assets in a pool are disposed of, gain or loss is assessed as short-term capital gain or loss. If only some items of pool are disposed of, only short-term gain will be taxable, but loss will not be allowed.
11	Unabsorbed depreciation	If depreciation is not claimed at taxpayer's option, the WDV of future will increase. If claimed but not absorbed fully, it will become part of business loss.	Depreciation that could not be absorbed becomes part of business losses to be carried forward for maximum 15 years.	Depreciation that could not be absorbed becomes part of business losses to be carried forward, indefinitely.	If depreciation is not claimed, it can be claimed in future over longer periods. If claimed, but unabsorbed, it can be carried forward to be set-off against profits of the same business.	Unabsorbed depreciation could be carried forward indefinitely to be set off against business income in future.	Unabsorbed depreciation could be carried forward indefinitely to be set off against business income.

The FYA is allowed in the U.K. and Malaysia. In Pakistan, besides initial depreciation, a FYA at a rate ranging from 60 per cent to 80 per cent is also allowed in respect of some specific industries. In the U.S., instead of initial depreciation, an annual deduction ($20,000 for the income year 2000) can be claimed, thus providing more benefit to the taxpayer than the initial depreciation. No initial depreciation is provided in India. While the rate of depreciation in the U.S, and Australia are based on the life of plant and machinery, fixed rates are applied on the WDV of the asset in the U.K. In Malaysia, Pakistan and India, the rates of depreciation are based on the nature of the industry. In the U.S., the life of plant for charging depreciation is comparatively less than the expected life, thus allowing more depreciation. The rate of depreciation on plant and machinery is comparatively high, i.e. 25 per cent in the U.K. However, in the first year, a higher allowance of 40 per cent, called the FYA instead of annual allowance of 25 per cent is allowed. In the U.S., the rate of depreciation ranges from 7.50 per cent to nearly 66 per cent, and for the most common plant and machinery, it is approximately 28 per cent. In Pakistan, the rate is 10 per cent to 30 per cent of the WDV, while in Malaysia, the rate ranges from 8 to 14 per cent and in a few cases 16 per cent or even 20 per cent. In Pakistan, an initial depreciation of 20 to 25 per cent and in Malaysia, an initial allowance of 20 per cent can be claimed in addition to an annual allowance. Thus, in both the countries, depreciation in the first year of use of the asset shall be a minimum of 30 per cent. Depreciation on computers is allowed at the high rate of 40 per cent in the U.S, Australia and Malaysia, and at 60 per cent in India. Clearly, there is no uniformity in the rates of depreciation. However, rates are comparatively higher in the U.K. and the U.S.

Depreciation is allowed for a full year irrespective of the number of days the asset is used in the U.K, Malaysia and Pakistan. In Australia, depreciation is allowed pro-rata for the number of days the assets is in use. In the U.S., half-year depreciation is allowed in the year when the plant and machinery is purchased or sold. In India, 50 per cent of the normal depreciation is allowed if the asset is used for less than 180 days, and full depreciation is allowed if used for 180 days or more.

In respect of cars, in all the selected countries either a limit of amount is fixed on which depreciation is claimed such as £12,000 in the U.K, $15,000 in the U.S., AUD55,134 in Australia, or depreciation is allowed at lower rates, such as in Australia, Pakistan and India, where the rates of depreciation on cars are lesser than the rate of depreciation on other plants and machineries. This is to discourage investment in luxury assets and at the same time to not allow higher incentive for those assets which are not related to production.

Pooling of assets for the purpose of claiming depreciation is allowed in the U.K, Australia and India. It is compulsory in India and the U.K. The taxpayer in the U.K. has the option to charge depreciation separately on those assets which have a short life of less than 4 years. But pooling is optional in

Australia. In the U.K. and Australia, depreciation on plant and machinery purchased during the year is calculated separately from the pool and from next year, the WDV of such plant is added in the general pool. However, it is not so in India. Though 'pooling of assets' provisions are administratively convenient, these are not equity based as income/loss arising on the sale of assets does not get taxed in the year of occurrence.

Where any plant and machinery is used partly for business purposes and partly for private purpose, depreciation is allowed in all these countries in proportion to the business use. However, the manner in which the WDV on which depreciation is calculated, differs in these countries. While in Pakistan and India, the actual WDV is used for computing depreciation, in the U.K. and Australia, a notional WDV, i.e. WDV after charging full depreciation is used for computing depreciation. Thus, more depreciation can be claimed if the actual WDV is used for charging depreciation, as compared to the notional WDV. The difference in calculating depreciation in such cases will also affect the balancing charge and balancing deduction. The method adopted in the U.K. and Australia is equity-based and more rational as compared to India and Pakistan.

The maximum overall benefit to the taxpayer seems to have been provided in the U.S. where depreciation is allowed at accelerated rates along with the annual expense deduction. The maximum benefit in the first year appears to have been provided to the taxpayer in Malaysia and Pakistan as besides initial depreciation and normal depreciation, depreciation is provided for the full year irrespective of the number of days the asset is used. The taxpayers in the U.K. are also allowed a high first year allowance. However, the benefit of additional depreciation in the first year is not allowed to taxpayers in Australia and India. Thus, as compared to all other countries, the provisions in Australia appears to be equitable and the loss of revenue is likely to be minimum.

Balancing Adjustments

Balancing adjustments in the form of *balancing charge* (BC) or *balancing allowance* (BA) arise when any asset is disposed of or is scrapped or destroyed. The BC is usually the profit arising on the disposal of the asset, whereas the BA commonly refers to the loss arising on the disposal. The mode of computation of balancing adjustment is related to the system adopted by a country with respect to the computation of depreciation. Where depreciation is computed on individual assets, the profit or loss arising on the disposal of each asset can be computed. However, in countries where assets are pooled together, it is not possible to find out the profit or loss on the sale of a single asset. While in some countries, such profits are treated as business profits or losses, in the other selected countries these are treated as short-term capital losses or gains. The provisions relating to balancing adjustment of the selected countries are analysed below.

THE U.K.

In the U.K., the balancing adjustment may be required in the following cases:

1. when all the items in the pool are disposed of; or
2. when a non-pooled asset is disposed of; or
3. when a business ceases trading.

In the first case, if the disposal value exceeds the WDV of the plant and machinery, the excess is treated as BC, whereas the excess of WDV over the disposal value is treated as BA. Such allowance is not allowed in one year fully. It is rather allowed in the same way as an annual allowance, i.e. WDA is allowed.

If a non-pooled asset is disposed of, then the excess of disposal value over the WDV is treated as BC to the extent of depreciation allowed. The BA will be allowed to the extent the WDV exceeds the disposal value.

If a business ceases trading, the balancing adjustment will be calculated in the same manner as above. However, no WDAs or FYAs are given for the final chargeable period.

THE U.S.

Prior to 1962, any profit arising on the transfer of a depreciable property in the U.S., including plant and machinery was treated as long-term capital gain if it was disposed of after being held for more than one year. The loss if any on such asset was treated as an ordinary loss. However, with the introduction of Sec. 1245 in 1962, the benefits were reduced. The provisions of Sec. 1245 provided that any gain arising on the transfer of Sec. 1245 property which includes plant and machinery shall be treated as an ordinary income to the extent of depreciation already allowed. Losses, however, will continue to be allowed as an ordinary loss to the extent of the excess of WDV over the disposal value.

AUSTRALIA

Where the plant is used only for income-producing purposes in Australia, if the termination value, i.e. the sale price of the plant is less than the undeducted cost, the difference is deductible as the BA in the year of disposal [(ITAA 97, Sec. 42-195, corresponding to ITAA 36, Sec. 59(1)]. However, if the plant is only partly used for producing assessable income, the BA will be calculated as if the plant had been fully depreciable in the preceding years. However, the BA will be allowed only to the extent it is proportionate to business use, i.e. in the ratio of actual depreciation to notional depreciation.

Whether the plant in Australia is used only for business purposes or only partly for business purposes, the BC in both the situations is the excess of the termination value over the WDV. Since the WDV is calculated after deducting only the actual depreciation proportionate to business use, no adjustment is required at the time of calculating the BC. If the termination value is less than the WDV but more than the undeducted cost, no balancing adjustment applies because the gap between undeducted cost and WDV arises from the private use of the plant. Where the car is subject to car depreciation limit, the termination/sale value for finding out the balancing allowance/charge is found out by multiplying it by the ratio of the car depreciation limit to the actual original cost of the car as shown below:

$$\text{Sale Price} \times \frac{\text{Car depreciation limit}}{\text{Actual original cost of car}}$$

Thus, as the car value is reduced for claiming depreciation, the BC on the sale of car will also be reduced proportionately.

MALAYSIA

In Malaysia, the BC or the BA is computed in a manner in which the balancing adjustment of a non-pooled asset in the U.K. is computed. Thus, gain on the disposal in Malaysia is also treated as ordinary income maximum to the extent of the depreciation allowed. Loss, if any, is also treated as ordinary business loss.

When an asset is disposed of, its disposal value is the amount equal to the market value at the date of disposal. Where it is disposed of by sale, transfer or assignment, the value will be the sale price or the market value, whichever is greater. However, when a control sale or purchase is affected, the actual price at which an asset is transferred is ignored and no balancing adjustments are made. (Control sales mean sales where either the disposer or the acquirer has a control over the other person, i.e. acquirer or disposer).

However, the expenditure incurred in the demolition of building is added to the WDV for the purpose of calculating the balancing adjustments.

PAKISTAN

With effect from the assessment year 1991-92, if the sale proceeds of any asset which is disposed of, exceed the WDV, the excess shall be the income of that year and if the sale proceeds of any asset are less than the WDV, the deficit shall be an expenditure deductible from the profits and gains of the business or profession of that year. No depreciation is allowed in Pakistan in the income year in which any asset or class of assets is disposed of by an assessee. Where the asset is actually sold, sale proceeds mean, sale price or the fair market value, whichever is higher, and where the asset is discarded, demolished, destroyed or lost, the scrap value or the amount realized by the disposal thereof together with any insurance, compensation, or salvage money received or receivable in respect thereof and where the asset is compulsorily acquired under any law for the time being in force in Pakistan, the compensation paid thereof.

INDIA

Prior to the assessment year 1988-89, in the case of disposal of assets, a balancing allowance was allowed to the extent of the excess of the WDV of the asset over the sale value including scrap value together with any money received thereon. However, the BA was allowed only when the business in respect of which the asset was used, continued to be in existence. The BC was taxable as income prior to the assessment year 1988-89 to the extent of the excess of sale value including scrap value together with any money received over the WDV of the assets. The BC was taxable whether the business continued or not. With effect from the assessment year 1988-89, the system of charging depreciation in India has changed from depreciation on a single asset to the depreciation on a block of assets that are entitled to the same rate of depreciation. As a result, the gain or loss on a single asset could not be computed. Thus, the BA or the BC is no longer applicable. The gain or loss on the sale of assets is treated as follows:

1. Where only some of the assets in a block of assets are sold, the excess of the full value of the consideration received or accruing as a result of transfer of the asset over the aggregate of the following:

   (a) Written down value at the beginning of the income year,
   (b) The actual cost of any asset acquired during the income year, and
   (c) Expenses incurred in connection with the transfer shall be treated as short-term capital gain.

   On the other hand, if the consideration received is less than the aggregate of (a), (b) and (c) above, no loss shall arise.

2. Where the entire block of assets is sold or transferred, if the consideration received exceeds the aggregate of; (a), (b) and (c) shown in part (1) above, the excess will be a short-term capital gain. If the consideration received falls short of the aggregate of; (a), (b) and (c), the deficiency shall be treated as a short-term capital loss.

Thus, from the assessment year 1988-89 onwards, any profit or loss on an individual asset is not computed. Whatever profit arises on the sale of either some or all of the assets in a block of assets, the same is treated as a short-term capital gain. Loss may arise only when the entire block is sold, and the loss, if any, will also be treated as a short-term capital loss.

However, in the case of power units, excess of consideration received or accruing over the aggregate of; (a) WDV as at the beginning of the year and, (b) the cost of the assets acquired during the year shall be treated as a balancing charge of the income year in which the money payable becomes due. The deficiency, if any, will be allowed as terminal depreciation. In case the asset is sold or transferred in the same year in which the asset is first put to use, the loss will not be allowed as terminal depreciation, but will be treated as a short-term capital loss.

Conclusion

The provisions relating to balancing deduction/balancing charges arising at the time of disposal of plant and machinery are similar in one respect that loss on such disposal, i.e. balancing deduction is treated as business loss or deduction in all the countries except India. Such loss in India arises only when all the items in the pool are disposed of and is treated as short-term capital loss. Thus, the taxpayers in India cannot claim loss if any, on the sale of individual asset and as the loss is allowed only when all the assets in a block are disposed of, and as that loss is treated as short-term capital loss, such loss cannot be adjusted against any income except capital gains income. Depreciation in the year of disposal is allowed in the U.S. and Australia. However, the provisions in Australia are more equitable when assets are partly used for business purposes. In Australia, instead of the actual WDV calculated on the basis of proportionate use of assets for business purposes, the deduction is first computed on the basis of undeducted cost (i.e. WDV on the basis of full use of assets for business purpose) and the loss so arrived at, is then allowed in the ratio of the business use of the asset.

Any profit on the disposal of plant and machinery in the U.K., the U.S., Australia, and Malaysia are treated as assessable business income only to the extent of depreciation allowed. However, in Pakistan, the gain is treated as business income fully. In India, such gain is treated as short-term capital gain which may arise whether some or all of the assets in the pool are disposed of.

Balancing adjustment provisions in India are different even from the U.K. and Australia, where pooling of assets is allowed and even in the U.K., in such a situation the gain or loss is not treated as short-term capital gain or loss. Thus, while provisions in India are easy to administer, the provision in Australia and the U.K. are more equity-based.

CARRY FORWARD OF UNABSORBED DEPRECIATION

It is true that depreciation is an allowable business deduction. The basis of providing depreciation is that the capital expenditure incurred on plant, machinery, furniture and building is spread over the economic life of the asset. The whole of the capital expenditure incurred is not allowed as deduction in the year in which it is incurred because:

1. expenditure on capital asset being a capital expenditure is not allowed
2. the whole of the capital asset is not used for the production purposes in one year only

Thus, the depreciation is allowed only proportionately to the extent of the use of the asset for business purposes. There is no scientific way to find out exactly how much of that asset is actually used. Thus, depreciation is found out on the basis of the estimated economic life of the asset. The actual use in some years may be more or less than the depreciation actually claimed.

A question arises whether an option should be given to the taxpayer to claim depreciation or not. Should it be made compulsory to claim depreciation? It is important to find out how different countries deal with this aspect and how the unabsorbed depreciation is treated in different countries. The related provisions of the selected countries are compared below.

THE U.K.

In the U.K., the taxpayer has the option to claim lower depreciation or no depreciation so that the personal allowances are not wasted in a year in which profits are less or losses are suffered. As a result, the year in which lower depreciation or no depreciation is claimed, the WDV will also be reduced only to the extent of the depreciation claimed, and thus resulting in higher WDA next year. Unabsorbed depreciation representing disclaimed capital allowances are not lost permanently, since higher WDVs are carried forward allowing taxpayers to claim more depreciation in future. Thus, in such cases, not only higher depreciation can be claimed in future years but such depreciation can be claimed over a longer period.

THE U.S.

It is mandatory in the U.S. to claim depreciation thus leaving no scope for the taxpayer to use this as a tool to reduce or increase his taxable business income. Thus, depreciation has to be claimed by the taxpayer in the U.S. As a result of the depreciation claim, the taxable income in the U.S. may be reduced or in case of losses, the losses may be increased further. Thus, unclaimed depreciation indirectly becomes a part of business losses in the U.S. and is treated similarly. The net operating losses in the U.S. may be initially carried back for 3 years and offset against the taxable income of the preceding 3 years. If any loss still remains, it may then be carried forward for a period of 15 years.

AUSTRALIA

In Australia, depreciation is allowed as a special business deduction. Thus, in the year in which profits are not sufficient to absorb the whole depreciation or in case there are business losses, the unclaimed depreciation will become part of business losses. Such business losses including unclaimed depreciation can be carried forward to be set off against business income in future year without any time limit.

MALAYSIA

Similar to the U.K., in Malaysia also, the taxpayer has the option whether to claim depreciation or not. However, as the annual depreciation is allowed according to the SLM method, where depreciation is allowed at a fixed rate of percentage of the original cost, the benefit of the higher WDV in the following year resulting in higher depreciation is not available. However, the depreciation can help in reducing business income in future years and it can be claimed over longer periods. In Malaysia, depreciation is allowed to be set off in the current year only against the business income. Where the taxpayer claimed the depreciation allowance but where it could not allowed partly or fully due to lack of sufficient profit, such unabsorbed allowance is allowed to be carried forward in future years to be set off in the future only against the same business to which the unabsorbed depreciation relates.

PAKISTAN

Depreciation allowance of any income year is first deductible from the income chargeable under the head 'income from business or profession'. If it is not fully deductible under that head, it is deductible from income chargeable under other heads of income in the same income year. Depreciation still unabsorbed due to absence or inadequacy of profits or gains of that year can be carried forward to the subsequent assessment year or years. Unabsorbed depreciation can be carried forward for any number of years in future. However, in subsequent years, it will be deductible only after deducting current depreciation and brought forward business losses.[13]

INDIA

In a year in which income is insufficient to absorb the full depreciation, the total income is taken as nil, and the depreciation which could not be absorbed, is treated as unabsorbed depreciation, and in case there is business loss, the entire depreciation shall be treated as unabsorbed depreciation. The law relating to the setting off and carrying forward of depreciation was very liberal prior to the assessment year 1997-98. Till that time, the unabsorbed depreciation could be adjusted in the same year against business income first, and the balance unabsorbed depreciation could be adjusted against any other head of income. If still unabsorbed, it could be carried forward to the following year and could be adjusted against business income first, and the balance against any other income. This process of adjustment of unabsorbed depreciation could be carried over on for any number of years.

From the assessment year 1997-98 onwards, however, depreciation in the same year could be adjusted first against the business income and the balance, if any, against any other head of income. The balance still remaining unabsorbed could be carried forward for a maximum 8 assessment years and, when carried forward, it could be adjusted in subsequent years only against business income, provided the business or profession for which the allowance was originally computed, continued to be carried on by him. However, from the assessment year 2001-02, the condition of continuance of business has been withdrawn. The *Finance Act,* 2001, has amended the above provisions and has restored the provisions which were applicable prior to assessment year 1997-98. As such, unabsorbed depreciation of any year can be carried forward and adjusted against income of any subsequent years without any time limit.

Claiming of depreciation is mandatory in India from the income year 2001-02. Earlier, there was a controversy whether the taxpayer has a discretion to claim depreciation or not. The Supreme Court of India in a recent judgement in *Mahindra Mills Ltd* vs. *CIT* (2000) 243 ITR 56(SC) has held that depreciation is a concession though it is a legitimate charge on the taxable profits. As such, the taxpayer has a right to claim or not to claim depreciation. To overcome this, the *Finance Act,* 2001, has made the above amendment providing that the claim of depreciation under Sec. 32 shall apply whether or not the taxpayer has claimed deduction in respect of depreciation in computing the total income. Therefore, now in India, depreciation would be deemed to have been allowed even if the taxpayer has not claimed it. The claim of depreciation being an expense relating to the uses and wear and tear of the assets, should only be allowed in the year in which the asset is used and the taxpayer should not be given option to resort to tax planning through depreciation. As such, the new provisions in India are more equitable.

Conclusion

Any depreciation which was claimed but could not be allowed due to lack of sufficient profits or due to losses is treated as part of business loss in the U.K., the U.S. and Australia, and is allowed to be either carried back or forward according to the rules relating to the carrying forward of business losses. On the other hand, such unabsorbed depreciation in Malaysia, Pakistan and India, is usually allowed to be carried forward and set-off from business income in future without any time limit. However, in India the unabsorbed depreciation can again be adjusted from the business or any other income from the income year 2000-01. The business losses, on the other hand, in Pakistan and India could be carried forward only for a limited number of years. In Malaysia, the unabsorbed depreciation can be set off in future from the same business. Thus, on the cessation of a business, the right to adjust unabsorbed depreciation comes to an end in Malaysia

PART II. DEPRECIATION ALLOWANCE: BUILDINGS

Though plant and machinery are used to the maximum extent only in those undertakings where the production is carried on, the buildings are used by all types of business undertakings whether engaged in manufacturing, trading, consultancy or any type of work. There is difference in the cost also, as the cost of plant and machinery is usually much less than the cost of building. Thus, the difference in the depreciation rates of building by just 1 or 2 per cent may affect the taxable income considerably. In this part, the provisions relating to depreciation in respect of buildings of the selected countries are analysed under three parts as given below:

1. Depreciation allowance provisions
2. Balancing adjustments
3. Carry forward of unabsorbed depreciation

Depreciation Allowance Provisions

The depreciation allowance provisions relating to buildings of the selected countries, including the method of computation of depreciation, rate of depreciation and pooling provisions of the selected countries are examined below.

THE U.K.

In the U.K., depreciation allowance on buildings, known as, industrial building allowances (IBAs), are allowed in respect of capital expenditure on qualifying industrial buildings and certain hotels.

An industrial building includes:

1. Factories used for manufacturing purposes or for processing goods;
2. Ancillary buildings associated with such factories;
3. Staff welfare buildings (canteen etc.)
4. Sports pavilions for the welfare of employees.

IBA is allowed to a hotel which offers sleeping accommodation consisting wholly or mainly of letting bedrooms available to the general public and has at least 10 bedrooms, offers ancillary services of breakfast, evening meals, cleaning of rooms, and bed-making and is open for at least 4 months between April and October. Qualifying industrial buildings do not include dwelling houses, shops, showrooms and offices. IBA's are based on the qualifying expenditure of the person who first uses the building for industrial purposes. The qualifying expenditure is either the construction cost, if self constructed by the trader, or the price paid for the building, if bought unused from a builder or the lower of prices paid for the building and the original cost incurred by the building's first owner if bought unused from someone other than the builder. However, qualifying expenditure does not cover the cost of land but includes costs of land preparation.

Methods of Computation of Depreciation

In the U.K., initial allowance (IA) as well as annual allowance was allowed earlier. However, IA is no longer available.

Initial Allowance

In the U.K., the IA in respect of buildings has also been subject to frequent changes. Prior to March 1984, the IA was allowed at the rate of 75 per cent, and it was phased over the two-year period ending on March 31, 1986. It was again introduced for a brief period of one year in respect of the expenditure incurred between November 1, 1992 and October 31, 1993 at the rate of 20 per cent. The IA is not allowed in respect of capital expenditure incurred after October 31, 1993.

Written Down Allowance

Written Down Allowance (WDA) is allowed at the rate of 4 per cent of the qualifying expenditure (2 per cent if the expenditure was incurred before November 6, 1992) on SLM basis as against the DBM for plant and machinery. However, it is necessary that the building has been brought into use during that period. Pooling provisions do not apply to industrial buildings. Therefore the allowance on each building is calculated separately. The WDA is available in relation to an industrial building so long as it is in use at the end of the chargeable period. But it is not allowed in the year of sale or disposal. The WDA is given in proportion to the length of the chargeable period for which the allowances are claimed. The WDA in relation to an industrial building may not be disclaimed as may be done in relation to plant and machinery as the WDA in relation to an industrial building is fixed at 4 cent on a straight line basis since the building has a tax life of 25 years. The WDA is not allowed if at the end of the chargeable period the building is used for non-industrial purposes. However, a notional WDA is still calculated for such a chargeable period and deducted from the WDA of the building in the usual way. However, a notional WDA is not available to the trader. Where the FYA is available, both the FYA and the WDA can be claimed in the same chargeable period as against plant and machinery where both FYA and WDA cannot be claimed in the same year. However, total allowances can never exceed the qualifying expenditure. As such, where the FYA is allowed, the WDA will cease earlier than the tax life of 25 years of the industrial building. The WDA is not allowed on shops, showrooms and offices, except those falling in enterprises zones subject to the fulfilment of certain conditions.

In the U.K., agricultural building allowances (ABA's) are also allowed in relation to the capital expenditure incurred on the construction of farm-houses, farm buildings, fences, and drawing works. However, only one third of the expenditure on a farmhouse is eligible for ABA's. The cost of land is not included. The WDA is calculated at 4 per cent per annum on SLM basis.

THE U.S.

In the U.S., buildings are divided into two parts; (1) residential real property and, (2) non-residential real property.

Method of Computation of Depreciation

Real property may be residential-rental real property which has a 27.5 year recovery period and non-residential real property with a recovery period of 39 years. (Residential rental real property is property from which at least 80 per cent of the gross rental income is rental income from dwelling units). In the case of real property, the Sec.179 election to expense deduction is not allowed. Only the SLM is used for calculating depreciation of real property. Instead of a mid-year convention in the case of real property, a mid-month convention is allowed in the year of acquisition and in the year of disposition. Thus, if a real property is purchased on November 4, 1998, and the income/fiscal year ends on December 31, then only one and half month's depreciation will be allowed.

Taxpayers in the U.S. may also use alternative depreciation system (ADS) in respect of real property also and in such a case, depreciation will be charged according to the SLM over periods longer than the MACRS recovery period.

AUSTRALIA

In Australia, depreciation on building is called *'Capital Allowance'*. A taxpayer is allowed to claim deduction for capital expenditure incurred in constructing capital works including buildings and structural improvements. Capital works deductions are available on the cost of construction of buildings or extensions, alternations or improvements to buildings and includes factories, offices, shops, blocks of flats, rental home units, hotels, motels and research and development buildings. Structural improvements include sealed roads, driveways, car parks, airport runways, bridges and pipelines. For claiming capital allowance, the capital works must actually be used in a deductible way in the income year in which the deduction is claimed. (Capital works are used in a deductible way if used for the purpose of producing assessable income or carrying on research and developmental activities.) Capital works are used for a particular purpose if they are maintained ready for use for that purpose, provided that they are not used for any other purpose and the intended use has not been abandoned. Capital works deductions are also available for the cost of constructing capital works that are environment protection earthworks or their extensions or improvements.

The construction expenditure is determined on the basis of the actual cost incurred in the construction of a building and includes the architect's fees and costs associated with building approvals, but does not include the cost of acquiring land and the cost of demolishing existing structure, levelling and filling. When a taxpayer buys from a builder, the builder's profit element is excluded.

Methods of Computation of Depreciation

The rate of capital allowance for non-residential building is 4 per cent of the construction expenditure. For residential buildings, the rate is 2.5 per cent of the construction expenditure. However, for residential buildings used as short-term traveller accommodation, the rate is 4 per cent of construction expenditure. As such, the life of the building is estimated either 25 years or 40 years. Capital works deductions are allowed after the construction of the capital works has been completed and is calculated separately for each capital works project. Even in the case of extension of an existing building, the extension is treated separately from the existing building. Capital works deduction is allowed to the owner only. The owner of capital works is generally entitled to claim the deduction for particular capital works. A subsequent owner can also claim capital works deduction based on the original construction expenditure. The actual purchase price is not relevant. Capital works deduction is calculated proportionately for the number of days in the income year the capital works are used.

MALAYSIA

In Malaysia, capital allowances are allowed in respect of the qualifying expenditure on eligible industrial buildings that are used for specified purposes. The term *industrial building* as given under paragraphs 63 to 66 of Schedule 3, includes building used as a factory, a dock, a wharf jetty, warehouse, building used for research and training or for approved industrial training or for approved service projects. The term also includes canteens, rest rooms, recreation rooms for the welfare of workers and living accommodation for workers and child care facilities. But dwelling houses, retail shops, showrooms, hotels and offices are not considered as industrial buildings and as such no capital allowance is allowed on such buildings.

Where only part of a building or structure is an industrial building, and the cost of that part which is not industrial building is 10 per cent or less of the total cost, the whole of the building will qualify for the allowance. Where the non-industrial part exceeds 10 per cent, the costs have to be split and only the industrial part will be eligible for the allowance.

Methods of Computation of Depreciation

In Malaysia, initial as well as annual allowance, both are allowed, in respect of buildings in the first year and in subsequent years, only annual allowance can be claimed.

Initial Allowance

Where in the basis period for a year of assessment, a person has incurred qualifying expenditure on the construction of a building which is used for business purposes, an initial allowance equal to 10 per cent of that expenditure shall be allowed to him. However, the initial allowance is allowed only on the construction of a building and not on the purchase of a building. The qualifying building expenditure includes cost of preparing, cutting, tunnelling or levelling land in connection with the construction of the building, cost of construction, cost of demolishing the existing building, cost of installing fittings, cost of any additions or alterations to an existing building and legal charges and stamp duties to the extent these are related to the building or the structure. But it does not include expenses incurred in acquiring the land and legal charges and stamp duty connected with the title. The expenditure incurred for allowances must be incurred by either a taxpayer who occupies the building for the purpose of his trade or by a taxpayer from whom a person carrying on a qualifying trade is a direct lessee. Capital expenditure incurred on the purchase of a building which is used at any time after its purchase as an industrial building also qualifies for capital allowance.

Annual Allowance

In Malaysia, an annual allowance, equal to one-fiftieth, i.e. 2 per cent of the qualifying building expenditure using the SLM is allowed to a person who has incurred such expenditure on the construction of the building, provided at the end of the basis period for a year of assessment, he was the owner of the building and it was in use as an industrial building for the purposes of his business.

In the case of purchase of an industrial building, the annual allowance will be the qualifying cost divided by the number of completed years of assessment from the date of purchase upto and including the 50th year of assessment after the building was constructed. Thus, if the building is purchased after 10 years of construction of the building, the rate of the annual allowance shall be 1/40 instead of 1/50.

No allowance is granted if the building is owned for less than 2 years. In such a case, allowances already allowed are withdrawn.

Higher Building Allowance

A higher initial allowance of 40 per cent will be allowed on the construction of a new building for the accommodation of the employees other than the directors, administrative or clerical staff of the business. In lieu of both initial and annual allowances, an allowance equal to 10 per cent of the qualifying expenditure will be granted for 10 years in the case of purchase or construction of the building in the following cases:

1. Where a person carries on a manufacturing, hotel or tourism business or an approved service project and the building is to be used for the accommodation of employees, excluding directors;
2. The building is used for the purpose of child care facilities;
3. The building is a school or an educational institution approved by the Minister of Education or the building is used for purposes of industrial, technical or vocational training approved by the Minister; or
4. The building is a warehouse used solely for storage of goods for export or for storage of imported goods for further processing and re-export.

Thus, where normally full allowances are allowed within 50 years, allowances in the above cases may be claimed within 10 years.

PAKISTAN

In Pakistan, depreciation provisions in respect of buildings are similar to that of plant and machinery with the exception that the first year allowance (FYA) which is allowed on plant and machinery in certain industries, extra depreciation allowance and re-investment allowance are not allowed in respect of buildings. The term *building* means only superstructure and does not include site or land.

Unlike the depreciation system in the U.K., the U.S., Australia and Malaysia, where depreciation on building is computed according to the SLM, depreciation on buildings in Pakistan is computed on the basis of the WDV method.

In respect of buildings in Pakistan, initial depreciation, normal depreciation and the industrial building allowance (IBA) are allowed.

Initial depreciation

Initial depreciation is allowed in respect of any building erected between July 1, 1976 and June 30, 2000. It is allowed at the rate of 10 per cent for ordinary building and at the rate of 25 per cent in the case of residential buildings for industrial labour and building used by an educational institution on a basis similar to that of Malaysia.

Besides initial depreciation, normal depreciation is allowed on the WDV in respect of buildings in Pakistan.

Industrial Building Allowance

Industrial sheds or structures created by an industrial undertaking in respect of which Rule 5A is applicable, shall be allowed under Rule 5C, an industrial building allowance equal to 20 per cent of the WDV in respect of the year of erection of such structures.

The rate of depreciation as shown in Table 4.4 is 5 per cent in respect of building in general, and is 10 per cent for both residential quarters for labour and for factory or workshops. While depreciation for the full year is allowed in the year of acquisition of asset, no depreciation is allowed in the year of disposition.

INDIA

The procedure for calculating depreciation on buildings in India is akin to Pakistan, but is quite different from other countries. The term *building* has not been defined under the Act. Building means superstructure only and does not include the cost of land. Building, however, includes roads, bridges, culverts, wells and tube-wells. No initial allowance is allowed in respect of buildings in India. Only normal depreciation is allowed on the WDV of the building. Just like plant and machinery, buildings entitled to the same rate of depreciation are pooled together for claiming depreciation.

If the building is put to use for less than 180 days in the year in which it is acquired, in such a case 50 per cent of depreciation is allowed.

The rate of depreciation as shown in Table 4.5 varies from 5 per cent to 20 per cent. While the lowest rate of 5 per cent is applicable in the case of residential buildings, the rate of 10 per cent is applicable to office buildings, factories and godowns and the higher rate of 20 per cent is applicable in the case of hotel buildings.

BALANCING ADJUSTMENTS

Provisions relating to the balancing adjustment of buildings also vary in different countries, thus affecting the taxable income. In this part, the balancing adjustment provisions of the selected countries are analysed.

THE U.K.

In the U.K., buildings are not pooled for depreciation purposes. The WDA is allowed in the year of sale and the balancing adjustment is calculated as in the case of non-pooled plant and machinery, if the building is wholly used for industrial purposes. However, if it is only partly used for industrial purposes, the building is written down by notional WDAs during a period of non-industrial use. If the building is then sold (within it's tax life) the balancing adjustment made on the sale depends upon whether the building is sold for more or less than its original cost and is calculated as follows:

1. If the building is sold for more than the original cost, the balancing charge made on the sale is restricted to the actual allowances given to date (i.e. excluding the notional WDAs)
2. It the building is sold for less than the original cost, the required balancing adjustment is calculated as follow:

   'Net cost' = original cost – sale proceeds

   $$\text{'Adjusted net cost'} = \text{net cost} \times \frac{\text{period of industrial use}}{\text{period of total use}}$$

   Balancing adjustment = adjusted net cost – actual allowances given
3. The second hand buyer's WDAs are based on the lower of the residue expenditure and the second-hand price paid.

THE U.S.

If a real property (land and building) is disposed of in the U.S. after 1986, any gain arising on such disposal if the property is transferred after it was held over for more than one year will be treated as long-term capital gain and as ordinary gain, if sold before the expiry of one year. However, the long term capital gain is treated as ordinary income to the extent of excess of accelerated depreciation over the depreciation as per SLM basis. The loss, will be treated as ordinary loss, whether the real property is sold after holding for more than one year or less than one year.

AUSTRALIA

The balancing deduction is allowed in the year in which the building is destroyed or demolished. The amount of the balancing deduction is the undeducted construction expenditure of the capital works at the time of destruction or demolition less salvage/insurance recoveries. The balancing deduction is reduced to the extent the taxpayer or another person did not use the capital works for the purposes of generating assessable income. However, if the amount received on destruction/demolition exceed the undeducted expenditure, no amount is assessed.

MALAYSIA

In the case of Malaysia, the balancing adjustment in respect of building is calculated in a manner similar to that of plant and machinery.

PAKISTAN AND INDIA

The balancing deduction/balancing charge provisions in respect of buildings in Pakistan and India are similar to that of plant and machinery. These provisions are analysed in Part I.

Conclusion

Any profit or gain on the disposal of buildings used for business purposes is treated as business profit or loss in all these countries except India. In Australia, if the amount received on destruction/demolition exceed the undeducted expenditure, the excess is not taxable. However, in the U.S., the profit is treated as business profit only to the extent of depreciation charged in excess of depreciation according to the SLM in respect of buildings acquired before 1986, and the gain is treated as capital gain if the building is acquired after 1986. In Pakistan and India, where the SLM is used the rates are also high, i.e. 10 per cent. The rates are much less, i.e. around 2.5 per cent to 4 per cent in the developed countries. The position of India is different from all other countries, as pooling of buildings for depreciation purposes is allowed only in India and it is only in India that gain or loss is treated as short-term capital gain or loss (except in the U.S. after 1987). This shows that due to a higher rate of depreciation and that too on the WDV, taxpayers in India can take the benefit of a higher claim of depreciation. The benefit of adjustment of loss on sale of building in India will be restricted. Such loss in India can be adjusted only against the capital gain. Similar to the provisions of plant and machinery, the balancing deduction provisions are not equitable in India, where the building is used only partly for business purposes.

Carry Forward of Unabsorbed Depreciation

The provisions of carry forward of unabsorbed depreciation in respect of buildings are similar to that of plant and machinery and these are discussed in Part I of this chapter.

A summary of the relevant provisions of depreciation in respect of buildings of the selected countries is given in Table 4.7.

TABLE 4.7. A SUMMARY OF DEPRECIATION ALLOWANCE PROVISIONS RELATING TO BUILDINGS

	Particulars	U.K.	U.S.	Australia	Malaysia	Pakistan	India
1	Basis of cost	Actual construction cost of the building, excluding land cost.	Actual construction cost including cost of land improvement, excludes land cost.	Actual cost incurred in construction but excluding cost of acquiring land, levelling and filling.	Actual construction cost including land development, excluding expenses incurred in acquiring land.	Actual cost of superstructure does not include land cost.	Actual cost incurred in construction or purchase price paid excluding land cost.
2	Method of providing depreciation	SLM	SLM	SLM	SLM	WDV	WDV
3	Rate of depreciation/ Recovery period	4 per cent per annum /Recovery period 25 years.	Residential property 3.636% Recovery period 27.5 years. Non-residential 2.564%. Recovery period 39 years.	Non residential building including short term residential traveller accommodation 4%. Recovery period 25 years. Residential Building and Structure Improvement 2.5%. Recovery period 40 years.	2 per cent per annum/Recovery period 50 years	Factory building excluding godowns and offices 10%, General building 5%.	Residential building-5%, Office building, Factory, godown 10% Hotel building 20%.
4	Items included in building	Industrial building and certain hotels but excluding dwelling houses, shops, showrooms and offices.	All real property used in trade or business or held for production of income.	Factory, shops, offices, hotels.	Industrial buildings used as factory, dock, warehouse, but does not include dwelling houses, retail shops, showrooms, hotels and offices.	All buildings used for business purposes. No depreciation allowed on building rented out and where income is not assessed as business income.	All buildings used for business purposes. No depreciation allowed on building rented out. 25 per cent of rental income is allowed as deduction for repairs.

5	Pooling of assets	Not applicable; individual asset basis.	Not applicable; individual asset basis.	Not applicable; individual asset basis.	Not applicable; individual asset basis.	Not applicable; individual asset basis.	Buildings carrying same rate of depreciation are pooled together.
6	Option to claim no depreciation or lower claim	No disclaimer possible as building has a tax life of 25 years.	Fixed life of 27.5 years or 39 years.	Fixed life of 25 years and 40 years.	Fixed life of 50 years.	No fixed life. Depreciation to be deducted when used for business.	No fixed life. Depreciation to be deducted when used for business.
7	First year/Initial Allowance	Not allowed.	Not allowed.	Not allowed.	10 per cent on construction of building, not on purchase of building.	10 per cent	Not allowed.
8	Applicable convention	Allowance is given proportionate to the length of the period for which it is claimed.	Mid month convention allowed in the year of acquisition and year of disposal/sale	Proportionately for the number of days the building was used.	Building be in use for business purposes at the end of the basis period.	Building be owned and in use for the purpose of business or profession on the last day of the year for full year depreciation.	If put to use for less than 180 days, 50 per cent of normal depreciation allowed, otherwise normal depreciation is allowed.
9	Balancing adjustments	Balancing charge or balancing allowance occurs in the year of sale/disposal.	On disposal of real property to the extent the excess depreciation of earlier years is recaptured, is treated as ordinary income and balance is taxed @ 25 per cent as capital gain. Loss on disposition is ordinary loss.	Balancing deduction is allowed if building is demolished or destroyed to the extent of undeducted construction expenditure. But if salvage value is more, no income is assessable.	Balancing charges/ balance allowances occur in the year of sale. Balancing charge is restricted to total of capital allowances granted on the asset in question.	Balancing charge/ allowance is income or expenditure of business.	When block is exhausted deficit/ gain is treated as short-term capital loss/gain.

Conclusion

The methods of providing depreciation on building differ in many respects among the selected countries. Table 4.7 shows that, while the actual cost is the basis for computing depreciation, the cost of land is excluded in all these countries. The rationale for excluding land cost is that land does not get depreciated. In Australia, even the cost of levelling and filling of land is excluded whereas in the U.S. and Malaysia, it is specifically included in building costs. The SLM is used for charging depreciation in the U.K., the U.S., Australia and Malaysia, whereas the WDV method is applicable in Pakistan and India. The useful life estimated for allowing depreciation on building in the U.K. and Australia is 25 years, in the U.S., it is 27.5 years for residential buildings and 39 years for non-residential buildings. In Malaysia, the useful life of the building is taken at 50 years, while in Pakistan and India, it works out to be 29 years. Thus, there is large variation in the expected life of buildings in these countries. As regards buildings eligible for claiming depreciation allowance, there is a great variation. While in the U.S., all real property used in trade or held for production of income are eligible, in India and Pakistan, all buildings used for business purposes only are eligible. Buildings used for earning rental income are not eligible, though deduction of a fixed percentage on account of maintenance is allowed against rental income in these countries but this maintenance allowance does not reduce the WDV of building. In Australia, only factory, shop, office and hotel buildings are eligible, whereas in the U.K., industrial buildings and certain hotels are eligible but shops, showrooms, offices and dwelling houses are not eligible. In Malaysia, even hotel buildings are not eligible. Not allowing depreciation on shops, offices, showrooms despite the same being used in business in the U.K. and Malaysia does not seem to be equitable. In this regard, provisions in the U.S. appear to be more equitable where all real property used in business are eligible for depreciation.

The rate of depreciation on buildings in the U.K. is 4 per cent, and in the U.S. approximately 3.6 per cent, in Australia 4 per cent, and in Malaysia 2 per cent. The rate of depreciation on buildings is 10 per cent both in Pakistan and India. Considering the fact that Pakistan allows even initial depreciation for office, godown and factory, the benefit to the taxpayer appears to be maximum in Pakistan. Besides Pakistan, FYA equivalent to 10 per cent is also allowed in Malaysia.

Pooling provisions are not applicable in respect of depreciation on building in any country except India. Full year depreciation irrespective of the number of days the building was used or put to use is allowed in the U.K., Malaysia and Pakistan. On the other hand, depreciation in Australia is provided on the basis of the number of days the building is used. In the U.S., mid-month convention is applicable in the case of buildings. In India, 50 per cent of normal depreciation is allowed if it is used for less than 180 days.

Thus, the method of computation of depreciation in respect of buildings in Pakistan and India are different from all other countries in two ways; that first, a higher rate is allowed and second that depreciation is allowed on the

WDV of the building in these two countries. This tax-incentive in the form of high depreciation will help taxpayers, but will result in the loss of revenue to the government. The provisions are not equitable as the effective life of the asset turns out to be much more than the life for which depreciation is allowed. The pooling provision of India is against the general trend in all other countries. However, the benefit of higher depreciation may not be available in India in case of corporate taxpayers due to the application of minimum alternate tax.

It, therefore, emerges that though the depreciation provisions of India are easy to administer, these are not equitable. While the benefit in India, appears to be more to the taxpayer in the initial years, the benefit seems to be the least in the later years, especially in the case of loss. The provisions of the U.K., U.S., Australia and Malaysia are more or less the same, as the same amount of depreciation at lower rates is provided over longer recovery periods as compared to Pakistan and India.

NOTES

1. International Accounting Standard (IAS) 4, Depreciation Accounting—International Accounting Standards Committee, 1976 paragraph 2.
2. Kath Nightingale, *Taxation, Theory and Practice* (Harlow, England: Pearson Education Ltd., 2000), pp. 108-34.
3. Nightingale, op. cit., p. 111.
4. Alan Melville, *Taxation: Finance Act,* 2000 (London: Pitman, 2001), p. 151.
5. Kevin E. Murphy and Mark Higgins, *Concepts in Federal Taxation* (Cincinnati, Ohio: South-Western College Publishing, 1999), p. 407.
6. Thomas R. Pope and John L. Kramer (eds.), *Prentice-Hall's Federal Taxation:* 1998, *Individuals* (Upper Saddle River, N.J.: Prentice Hall, 1997), pp. 10-15.
7. For details, see Chapter 7.
8. *CCH Australian Master Tax Guide* (Sydney: CCH Australia Ltd., 1999), pp. 833-66
9. Veerinderjeet Singh and Teoh Boon Kee (eds.), *Malaysian Master Tax Guide* (Singapore: CCH Asia PTE Ltd., 2000), pp. 371-9.
10. *The Income Tax Ordinance*, 1979 as on July 10, 2000.
11. N.A. Palkhivala and B.A. Palkhivala, *The Law and Practice of Income Tax,* Vol. I (Bombay: N.M. Tripathi Private Ltd., 1990), p. 495.
12. The *Income Tax Act,* 1961 as on June 1, 2000.
13. Ikramul Haq, *Practical Handbook of Income Tax* (Lahore: Lahore Law Publications, 1999), p. 185.

CHAPTER 5

Capital Gains Taxation

Taxation of business gain or income has been an accepted fact, but the taxation of capital gains has been a controversial issue. The controversy revolves around the issue, whether capital gains is income or not? Income tax is a tax on income and is not meant to be a tax on anything else.[1] The ordinary accounting and commercial concepts of income are based upon the distinction between items of capital and revenue nature. While revenue receipts are considered as income, capital receipts are excluded from its scope. However, according to the net accretion principle, '*Income*' is defined as the net accretion to economic power between two periods of time, or what accrues to an individual over a period as measured by the amount of his spending plus net accretion to his wealth. This definition of income takes into account (a) cash income (b) imputed income (c) accrued income and (d) appreciation in the value of assets which continue to be held, i.e. capital gains. Capital losses should be set-off against capital gains and net capital losses should be treated as a reduction in income (economic power) of an individual. Thus, according to the net accretion principle, capital gain is income and should be taxed. The arguments against the taxation of capital gain is that it is not an income according to accounting and commercial concepts and that capital gains are unexpected and unsought for and as such can not form part of taxable income. The capital gain results from inflation and is illusory in real terms and therefore do not represent a real increase in the taxpayer's spending power. Another argument against taxing capital gain is that it discourages the transfer of assets and thereby it restricts the mobility of capital. The arguments for taxing capital gains are based on equity and efficiency consideration. As capital gains represent the net accretion to spending power, like any other income, equity requires that these be taxed like any other income.

Despite the above controversy, many countries have introduced capital gains tax provisions. While the U.S. was the first amongst the selected countries to introduce capital gains tax in 1921, it was introduced in Australia in 1985. The controversy on capital gains tax is not limited to whether or not it should be taxed, it also extends to whether capital gains be given a favourable treatment or not and, whether capital gains tax be levied on unrealised capital gains or on realised capital gains.

There is uniformity on the issue of realised and unrealised capital gains. In all the countries, capital gains tax is levied on realised gains only. Those who are in favour of preferential treatment say that the reduction in the tax rate will increase the tax revenue, because taxpayers owning appreciated assets will be encouraged to sell the same. Also, this will encourage capital formation which will lead to the creation of more jobs. On the other hand, some other people find the preferential treatment benefiting only the high-income taxpayers.[2]

In spite of the controversy surrounding the chargeability of capital gains, many countries have levied tax on capital gains. The issue therefore is how capital gains tax is computed in different countries. Certain issues relating to the taxation of capital gains are given below:

1. Whether capital gains income is taxable on an accrual basis or on the receipt basis?
2. Whether or not indexation provisions are applicable to reduce the impact of inflation on capital gain?
3. Whether the market-value substitution provision is applicable in respect of assets acquired long ago. (Indexation normally takes into account 15 or 20 years period during which the asset was held prior to the acquisition. The market-value substitution helps in reducing the impact of even those years for which indexation provisions are not applicable.)
4. Whether annual exemption is available or not?
5. Is any tax avoidance measure taken to prevent the taxpayer from converting the gain into a loss or from increasing the capital losses?

The first part of this chapter examines in detail as to how capital gains income is computed in the selected countries and how the above issues are tackled in these countries.

The provisions relating to the taxation of capital gains in the selected countries are analysed under the following heads:

1. Computation of capital gains
2. Capital loss adjustments
3. Rate of tax on capital gains
4. Capital gains tax reliefs
5. Capital gains and tax revenue

Computation of Capital Gains

The provisions relating to the computation of capital gains in the selected countries, including the concept of capital asset, cost of acquisition and disposal value are given below. Whether the indexation allowance and the market-value substitution applies in these countries is also examined.

THE U.K.

Capital gains tax (CGT) was introduced in the U.K., by the *Finance Act*, 1965, with a view to achieving a greater degree of equity in the British tax system. In his budget speech of that year, James Callaghan said, 'Yield is not my main purpose . . . the failure to tax capital gains is . . . the greatest blot on our system of direct taxation. This new tax will provide a background to equity and fair play'.[3] The provisions relating to capital gains tax are contained in the *Taxation of Chargeable Gains Act,* 1992 (TCGA 1992). Since its inception, many changes have been incorporated in it, removing the deficiencies and adjusting to the changed circumstances to make the provisions more equitable.

A liability to CGT in the U.K. may arise when a chargeable person makes a chargeable disposal of a 'chargeable asset'. The term 'chargeable person' includes, an individual resident and an ordinarily resident in the U.K., partners of a partnership firm, trustees and personal representatives. Companies do not pay CGT. They, however, pay corporation tax on their capital gains.

Capital Assets

All forms of property are regarded as chargeable assets for CGT purposes, whether situated in the U.K., or not, except for those assets which are specifically exempt.from CGT (Sec. 21 TCGA, 1992). The assets which are exempt from CGT include: the principle private residence, chattels (tangible moving property) sold for £6,000 or less, motor cars, wasting chattels (tangible moving property with a life of 50 years or less), National Savings Certificates, foreign currency acquired for personal use, winnings from lottery, betting, compensation for personal injury, gilt-edged securities and qualifying corporate bonds.

Chargeable Disposals

A chargeable disposal occurs if there is:

1. sale of all or a part of a chargeable asset;
2. gift of all or a part of a chargeable asset; or
3. loss or destruction of all or a part of a chargeable asset.

Disposals exempt from tax

The following disposals are exempt in the U.K.:

1. gifts to charities, art galleries, museums
2. transfer of assets on the death of the taxpayer
3. transfer of assets as security for a mortgage or loan
4. transfer between husband and wife

Chargeable gain, i.e. capital gain in the U.K. is computed by deducting from the net disposal value (i.e. disposal value less the incidental cost of disposal) the following:

1. the acquisition cost of the asset;
2. the incidental cost of acquisition;
3. the enhancement expenditure.

Disposal Value

The disposal value in case of the sale of an asset is the sale proceeds. However, the disposal value is taken to be the market value in the following cases:

1. transfer between connected persons;[4]
2. transfer by way of a gift; or
3. where the consideration cannot be valued.

Cost of Acquisition of the Asset

The cost of acquisition is the price at which the asset is acquired. However, if the asset is acquired by way of gift or from a connected person, the market value on the date of acquisition shall be taken as the cost of acquisition.

Indexation

With a view to charging to tax only real capital gains and not the gains arising out of inflationary impact, an indexation allowance (IA) was introduced by the *Finance Act*, 1982.[5] The IA is applicable to each item of allowable expenditure (i.e. cost of acquisition, incidental cost of acquisition and enhancement expenditure). The IA is calculated using monthly figures taken from the retail price index (RPI). The IA of an expenditure is computed by multiplying the amount of that expenditure by an indexation factor, computed as follows (rounded to three decimal places).

The formula for computing the Indexation Allowance is as follows:

$$\text{Expenditure} \times \frac{\text{RPI for the month of disposal} - \text{RPI for the month of expenditure}}{\text{RPI for the month of expenditure}}$$

Where more than two items of expenditure have been incurred in relation to an asset in different months, separate calculations must be prepared for each item. The IA cannot be used to convert an indexed gain into an indexed loss or to increase an unindexed loss.

Taper Relief

In the U.K., the indexation allowance has now been replaced by taper relief in respect of capital gains arising from the disposal of capital assets which took place after April 5, 1998. Taper relief is calculated separately in respect of gain on each asset and the amount of relief depends upon whether the asset disposed of is a business asset or a non-business asset and the number of completed years for the which asset is held after April 5, 1998. The relief is applied before the annual exemption but, after deducting the current year loss and any brought forward loss. The amount of taper relief available for business and non-business assets is given in Table 5.1.

Taper relief as shown in the table is higher in respect of capital gains arising from the transfer of business assets as compared to gains on non-business assets. No relief is provided if a business asset is disposed of within a year, or if a non-business asset is disposed of within 3 years of its acquisition. The amount of relief, however, gradually increases for both types of assets as

TABLE 5.1. TAPER RELIEF IN THE U.K IN RESPECT OF CHARGEABLE ASSETS

Number of completed years after 5.4.98	Business Assets Percentage of gain Chargeable	Non-Business Assets Percentage of gain Chargeable
0	100.0	100.0
1	87.5	100.0
2	75.0	100.0
3	50.0	95.0
4	25.0	90.0
5	25.0	85.0
6	25.0	80.0
7	25.0	75.0
8	25.0	70.0
9	25.0	65.0
10 or more	25.0	60.0

Source: Alan Melville, op. cit., p. 259

the number of completed years after April 5, 1998, for which the asset was held prior to its disposal increases. The maximum relief is 75 per cent in respect of business assets and 40 per cent in respect of non-business assets.

Market-value Substitution

In respect of assets acquired before March 31, 1982, the market value of the assets as on March 31, 1982, is substituted for its original cost. However, if the re-basing results in a higher gain, then the calculation based on the original cost is applied. The IA for the assets acquired before March 31, 1982 is based on the change in RPI between March 1982 and the month of disposal. In both the cases, whether the calculation is done on the original cost or on the basis of the market value as on March 31, 1982, the IA is calculated with reference to the greater of the original cost and the market value on March 31, 1982, i.e. the same IA is given in both the cases. If the re-basing calculation gives a loss and the original calculation also gives a loss, the allowable loss is the smaller of these two losses. If one gives a gain and another gives a loss, then there is no chargeable gain and no allowable loss.

Tax Treatment of Chargeable Gains in Special Circumstances: Chargeable Gain on the Disposal of Chattels and Wasting Assets

In the U.K., no capital gain or loss arises on the disposal of a chattel (a tangible moving property) for £6,000 or less (Sec. 262). Disposal proceeds means gross disposal proceeds before deducting the incidental costs of disposal. If the gross disposal value exceeds £6,000, the chargeable gain shall be restricted to five-thirds of the amount by which the proceeds exceed £6,000 marginally. No loss is allowed if a chattel is disposed of for less than £6,000. However, if a chattel is acquired for more than £6,000 but is sold for less than £6,000, then the loss will be allowed presuming the disposal proceeds to be £6,000. Thus, the loss to the extent that the disposal price is less than £6000 will not be allowed. Where a part of a chattel is sold for less than £6,000, the gain on the disposal will be exempt only if the combined value of the part disposed of and the part remaining is less than £6,000. Wasting chattels (i.e. tangible moving property with an expected useful life of 50 years or less) are exempt from tax, except depreciable assets used in business. Where a depreciable asset, i.e. plant and machinery is sold, the gain will be computed in the ordinary manner. The loss, however, will be reduced by the amount of capital allowances, i.e. depreciation available.

Chargeable Gain in the Case of Partial Destruction of or Damage to Assets

In the U.K., any compensation received or any amount received under an insurance policy for the loss or destruction of a chargeable asset is treated as a chargeable disposal. However, if the assets are not completely destroyed and the money received is used to restore the assets, the gain may be deferred and will become taxable on the future disposal of the assets (Sec. 23(1), TCGA, 1992).

The gain will be deferred in the following circumstances:

1. the capital sum is wholly applied in restoring the asset;
2. at least 95 per cent of the capital sum is used to restore the asset; or
3. the capital sum is not greater than five per cent of the assets value.

Where only part of the capital sum is used in the restoration of the asset, the part not spent on the restoration of the asset shall be treated as a part disposal.

If the Asset is Completely Lost or Destroyed

If the entire asset is lost or destroyed, it is treated as deemed disposal which may give rise to a chargeable gain or loss. Where any compensation is received, the date of disposal is the date when the capital sum is received. If no compensation is received, the capital gain may be rolled over if the compensation is used to buy a replacement asset within 12 months. The cost of the replacement asset will be reduced by the amount of gain exempted from tax. If only a part of the money received is spent on the purchase of the replacement asset, the amount not used for the replacement will give rise to a chargeable gain. The balance of the gain will be deferred and will be reduced from the cost of the replacement asset.

THE U.S.

Capital gains receive preferential tax treatment in the U.S. The preferences and limitations applicable to capital gains have varied throughout the years depending upon the economic and political climate in the U.S. Prior to 1987, an individual taxpayer was allowed a deduction of 60 per cent from the net long-term capital gain (NLTCG). Thus, only 40 per cent of NLTCG was taxable. During this period, ordinary income tax rates were applicable on capital gains and the top marginal tax rate was 50 per cent. In a way the maximum marginal rate on a long-term capital gain was only 20 per cent (40% x 50%). Thus, capital gains taxation provided a great relief to high-income taxpayers. Although, the former President George Bush wanted the preferential capital gain treatment in the form of 60 per cent deduction to be continued, the Congress did not support it and the deduction was withdrawn from 1987 onwards. The tax rates were reduced by the *Tax Reform Act*, 1986, but were again increased in 1990 and the maximum individual tax rate was raised to 31 per cent. However, the maximum tax rate of 28 per cent on the net capital gain was allowed to individual taxpayers in respect of capital gains recognised after 1990. In 1993, while the tax on capital gains for individuals remained 28 per cent, the maximum marginal rate was increased from 31 per cent to 39.6 per cent. Another attempt to provide a deduction of 50 per cent of the net capital gain was vetoed by President Bill Clinton in 1996. However, exclusion up to 50 per cent of the gain realised on the disposal of qualified small business stock held for more than 5 years was allowed.

Prior to 1997, the tax rate of 28 per cent on capital gains did not provide any tax relief to those individuals whose income was taxable at a rate lower than 28 per cent. The *Taxpayer Relief Act*, 1997 lowered the rate on long-term capital gains realised after May 6, 1997 to 20 per cent (10 per cent for taxpayers whose ordinary income was taxable at the rate of 15 per cent). As a result of this change in the rate of tax on capital gain, the low income group will also enjoy tax benefit on long-term capital gain.

The terms commonly used in the U.S. with regard to capital gains are, *Realised and Recognised Gain or Loss*. Realised gain or loss represents the difference between the amount realised on the disposal of property and the adjusted basis of property when a sale or exchange occurs. The entire realised gain may not be taxable, and the loss may not be deductible. The gains or losses may not be recognised as they are either exempt or deferred or are disallowed. The amount of gains or losses that are taxable and are actually reported in the tax return are called the recognised gain or losses.

Capital Assets

Sec. 1221 of the *Internal Revenue Code*, 1986 provides a list of properties that are not capital assets. These are:

1. an inventory;
2. accounts or notes receivable;
3. real or depreciable property used in a trade or business;
4. a copyright, literary, musical or artistic composition, letter or memorandum, or similar property held by the person creating the property or held by a person who received the property as a gift from its creator;
5. certain U.S. Government publications.

Disposal Value

The disposal value commonly known as amount realised is the gross sales price less all the selling expenses. The gross sales price is the price agreed upon by the seller and the buyer. Depending upon different circumstances, the gross sale price may include the amount received by the seller from the buyer in the form of:

1. cash;
2. fair market value of property received;
3. fair market value of services received;
4. amount of the seller's expenses paid by the buyer; or
5. amount of seller's debt assumed by the buyer.

Less:

1. amounts given by the seller to the buyer;
2. amount of the buyer's expenses paid by the seller; or
3. amount of the buyer's debt assumed by the seller.

Cost of Acquisition

The cost of acquisition called as *adjusted basis* of the property is the initial basis of the property and includes capital additions and excludes capital recoveries, i.e. depreciation. The basis of property in the case of an acquired property is its cost. Cost is the amount paid for the property in cash or the fair market value (FMV) of another property given in the exchange.

Basis of Property Received as a Gift

The basis of property received as a gift is generally the same as the donor's basis. To prevent a taxpayer from shifting unrealised losses to another taxpayer by making gifts of property, the rules are so designed that losses are minimised. In case the FMV is equal to or greater than the donor's basis, the donee's basis is treated as the same as the donor's basis for all purposes, i.e. to find out the gain or loss. However, if the FMV is less than the donor's basis, the donee has a dual basis for the property, one basis for gain and another for loss. If the donee later transfers the property at a loss, the donee's basis is the property's FMV at the time of gift (basis for loss). If the donee transfers the property at a gain, the donee's basis is the same as the donor's basis (basis for gain).

Property Received from a Decedent

The basis of property received from a decedent is generally the FMV of the property on the date of the descendant's death or the FMV of the property on an alternate valuation date. The alternate date is generally 6 months after the date of death. An executor may elect to use the alternate valuation date to reduce the estate taxes owed by the estate. However, this will also reduce the basis of property included in the estate in the hands of the heirs who inherit the property.

Property Converted from Personal Use to Business Use

If a personal use asset in the U.S. is converted to business use, the basis for computing depreciation is the lower of the FMV or the adjusted basis of the property at the time the asset is converted to business use. If a personal-use asset is transferred to business use when its FMV is less than its adjusted basis, and if the property is sold at a loss (at a price which is less than the FMV on the date of conversion, less depreciation before sale), the basis for determining the loss is its FMV. However, if such property is sold at a gain (at a price which exceeds the FMV on the date of conversion, less depreciation before sale) the basis for determining the gain is the adjusted basis at the time of conversion. Thus, the ultimate objective is to discourage persons from converting assets to business use to claim more depreciation or later to transfer them to claim losses.

Short-term or Long-term Capital Gain

In the U.S., capital gain is classified into three different categories depending upon the period of holding of the asset for the purpose of taxation. A long-term capital gain takes place if an asset is transferred after it was held for 18 months or more prior to its transfer. (12 months if transferred before May 6, 1997). A short-term capital gain arises if an asset was held for less than 12 months prior to its transfer. A mid-term capital gain arises if the asset was held for more than 12 months but less than 18 months prior to its transfer. The holding period is determined differently under different circumstances.

Holding Period

The holding period is the length of time an asset is held before it is disposed of. While determining the holding period the day of acquisition is excluded but the disposal date is included. In the case of a property received as a gift, if the donor's basis is used to find out the gain or loss, the period during which an asset was held by the donor will be added to the donee's holding period. If donee's basis is the FMV of the property on the date of the gift, the donee's holding period starts on the date of the gift. The holding period of the property received from a descendent is always a long-term. Thus, the period during which the property is held by the descendent or his heir is not relevant. In the case of non-taxable exchanges, the holding period of the property received includes the holding period of the property transferred.

AUSTRALIA

The capital gains tax (CGT) was introduced in Australia, in 1985, and is applicable in respect of assets acquired after September 19, 1985. In spite of that, the rise in capital gains by 570 per cent from 1988-89 to 1997-98 is remarkable. During the income year 1997-98, AUD3.9 billion was capital gains tax payable by individuals, companies and funds on the net capital gains totalling AUD17.2 billion. Out of AUD3.9 billion, the share of capital gains tax payable by individuals was more than 1.5 billion which amounted to 37.5 per cent of the total tax capital gains.

The provisions relating to capital gains tax are given in the *Income Tax Assessment Act*, 1997. Assets acquired by a taxpayer before September 20,

1985 are known as 'Pre-CGT Assets' and assets acquired after the said date are called 'Post-CGT Assets'.

In Australia, the net capital gain is added to the assessable income and is taxable just like any other income. A capital loss cannot be deducted from a taxpayer's assessable income, though it can reduce a capital gain in the current income year or a later income year.

The provisions relating to CGT in Australia are detailed and complicated. Capital gain or loss arises if a CGT event happens [ITAA 97 Sec. 102-20 corresponding to Sec. 160z(1)]. Different sections prescribe different CGT events. More than 35 such events are prescribed under the *Income Tax Assessment Act*, 1997. Some of these CGT events are:

1. Disposal of a CGT asset.
2. Use and enjoyment of a CGT asset before title passes.
3. Loss or destruction of a CGT asset.
4. Cancellation, surrender, abandonment, forfeiture of a CGT asset.
5. End of option to acquire shares.
6. Creating contractual or other rights.
7. Granting an option.
8. Creating a trust over a CGT asset.
9. Granting a lease.
10. Shifts in share values.
11. Forfeiture of a deposit.
12. CGT assets start becoming trading stock.

While in most cases capital gain is the excess of capital proceeds over the cost basis, in the case of option to acquire shares, it is the excess of capital proceeds from granting option over expenditure in granting it. Thus, the cost base may be determined differently under different circumstances. The time when a CGT event happens depends upon the nature of the CGT event and that time is also prescribed under each section explaining a CGT event. Most CGT events involve a CGT asset. The CGT assets include land and buildings, shares, units in a unit trust, collectables and personal-use assets.

A capital gain arises if a taxpayer receives amounts from the CGT event, which exceed the taxpayer's cost associated with that event. The taxpayer's total costs associated with a CGT event are usually calculated in two different ways. For finding out capital gain, these costs are called the 'cost base' of the CGT asset. For finding out a capital loss these costs are called the reduced cost base (RCB) of the asset. The important difference in the two costs is that the cost base is indexed for inflation in working out a capital gain, but not in working out a capital loss. To find out a capital gain, the cost base for the CGT asset is subtracted from the capital proceeds (sale proceeds). If the capital proceeds exceed the cost base, the difference is a capital gain. If there is no capital gain, then the capital proceeds from the CGT event are subtracted from the RCB of the asset. If the RCB exceeds the capital proceeds, the difference is a capital loss. If the capital proceeds are less than the cost base but more than the RCB, there is neither a capital gain nor a capital loss.

Capital Assets

A capital assets known as, the capital gains tax asset (CGT asset) is any kind of property or legal or equitable right that is not property (ITAA 97, Sec. 108-5). CGT assets include, (1) part of or an interest in property or a legal or equitable right that is not property; (2) goodwill or an interest in it; (3) an interest in a partnership asset' and (4) an interest in partnership that is not an interest in a partnership asset.

Disposal Value

The full value of the consideration received known as capital proceeds in Australia from a CGT event is generally the sum of the money received or receivable and the market value worked out as at the time of the event of any other property received or receivable as a result of the CGT event happening [(ITAA 97, Sec.116-20 corresponding to ITAA 36, Sec. 160ZDW)]. In some cases, the market value is substituted for capital proceeds. This happens in cases where (a) the taxpayer does not receive any capital proceeds from a CGT event; (b) if some or all of these proceeds cannot be valued; (c) if the capital proceeds are more or less than the market value of the asset; (d) the parties to the CGT event are not dealing with each other at arm's length; or (e) if the CGT event is the redemption, release, abandonment, surrender, forfeiture or cancellation of the asset. The capital proceeds are increased, if the buyer acquires the CGT assets subject to liability to the extent of the amount of the liability assumed.

COST OF ACQUISITION

The cost base of a CGT asset is indexed for inflation if the taxpayer owns it for 12 months or more. The cost base of a CGT asset has five elements (ITAA 97, Sec. 25). These elements (except the third element) can be indexed if the relevant CGT asset is held for 12 months or more. The five elements of cost base are:

1. *Acquisition cost*: It is the element of the money paid or required to be paid in respect of acquiring a CGT asset and the market value of any other property given or required to be given in respect of acquiring the CGT asset.
2. *Incidental cost:* It is the incidental cost incurred in acquiring a CGT asset or in relation to a CGT event. It includes remuneration for the services of a lawyer, surveyor, agent, stamp duty, cost of the transfer, cost of advertising and cost relating to the making of any valuation.
3. *Non-capital costs*: These include interest on money borrowed to acquire an asset, cost of maintaining, repairing and insuring an asset, rates and land tax, interest on money borrowed to refinance the money borrowed to acquire an asset and interest on any money borrowed to finance capital expenditure incurred to increase an asset's value. The cost of obtaining a loan is not part of the cost base of the asset acquired because it is a cost

which relates to the borrowing not the asset financed by the borrowing. There is no third element for collectables or personal-use assets. It is not indexed for inflation.

4. *Enhancement cost*: It includes capital expenditure incurred to increase the value of the CGT asset.
5. *Title costs*: These include capital expenditure incurred to establish, preserve or defend the title to the asset.

The RCB is important in finding out if there is a capital loss from a CGT event. The RCB has all the elements of the cost base except the third one. The elements of RCB are not indexed. Expenditure is not included in any element of the RCB if it is deductible or if non-assessable recoupment is receivable in respect of expenditure.

Indexation

The cost base of a CGT asset is indexed if it was acquired by the taxpayer for 12 months or more. The elements of the cost base (except the third element dealing with non-capital cost) are indexed. [(ITAA 97, Sec. 960-275)]. Generally expenditure is indexed from the time when it is incurred even if some or all of the expenditure is not actually paid until a later time. However, if there is an acquisition that did not result from a CGT event, the first element of the cost base of the CGT asset is indexed from the time when the expenditure was made. The indexation period ends in the quarter in which the relevant CGT event happens to the asset (the asset is disposed of). The indexation factor for expenditure included in any one of the cost base elements (except the third element) is generally worked out by applying the following formula:

$$\frac{\text{The index number for the quarter of the year in which the CGT event happened to the asset}}{\text{The index number for the quarter in which the expenditure was incurred}}$$

An indexation factor must be rounded to three decimal places, before being applied against an element of an asset's cost base.

MALAYSIA

In Malaysia, the capital gains tax was introduced at a very late stage and that too for a different purpose and had a very narrow scope. With an object to cut down speculation in land, a tax, called land speculation tax was levied with effect from December, 1973. The rate of tax was 50 per cent and was levied on any gain arising from the disposal of land and buildings only where the disposal took place within two years from the date of acquisition and the consideration was in excess of RM.200,000. However, to make the provisions equitable a new Act called, the *Real Property Gain Tax Act*, 1976 (RPGT)was introduced to replace the *Land Speculation Tax Act*, 1974.[6] The present provisions relating to capital gains tax are contained in the RPGT *Act*, 1976. This Act is deemed to have come into force from November 7, 1975. Since its inception, frequent changes have been made in the rate structure of the real property gains tax provisions. The highest tax rate has been reduced from 50 per cent prior to 1977 to 30 per cent from 1995. In Malaysia, prior to 1984, capital gains tax was leviable only in respect of land and building. Many taxpayers with a view to avoiding tax at the time of increase in the market value of their property, instead of selling the real property, formed a company and sold the shares of that company. In this way, the taxpayer was able to avoid tax at that time because shares were not part of chargeable assets at that time. To prevent the avoidance of tax through the sale of shares of real property companies, the *Share (land based company) Transfer Tax Act,* 1984 was introduced. Under this Act, a tax of 2 per cent on the gross value of every disposal or aggregate disposals within a period of 12 months of shares of the value of RM one million or more in a land-based company not listed on the stock exchange was imposed. However, the Act failed to achieve the desired results. As a consequence, the *Share (land based company) Transfer Tax Act,* 1984 was repealed and paragraph 34A, Schedule 2, was incorporated in the RPGT *Act,* 1976. Thus, with effect from October 21, 1988 gains from the disposal of shares in companies owning real properties were also brought within the scope of the RPGT Act, 1976.

In Malaysia, real property gains tax is charged in respect of chargeable gain accruing on the disposal of any chargeable asset. Chargeable assets include real property and shares in real property companies. Real property means any land situated in Malaysia and any interest, option or other right in or over such land. The definition of land is fairly extensive and includes buildings, structures, standing timber, crops and land covered by water. Every person whether resident or non-resident in Malaysia shall be chargeable in respect of a chargeable gain accruing to him in that year on the disposal of a chargeable asset. A person includes partnership, individuals, companies, a Hindu joint family, executors, trustees.[7] A chargeable gain, i.e. capital gain, arises if the disposal price exceeds the acquisition price and a loss arises if it is less than the acquisition price.

Cost of Acquisition

The cost of asset, known as the acquisition price is amount of money or money's worth given by the owner for the acquisition of the asset plus any incidental costs. However it excludes:

1. any compensation or similar receipts for any damage, injury, destruction, depreciation of the asset;
2. receipts under an insurance policy for any damage or destruction of the asset; and
3. deposits forfeited, if any, in respect of that asset [(Schedule 2, Section 4(1)].

Market-value Substitution

In Malaysia, if a chargeable asset which is disposed of, was acquired by the disposer prior to January 1, 1970, then the market value of the asset as on

January 1, 1970 will be substituted for the consideration and therefore the incidental costs and expenses which relate to the period prior to January 1, 1970, will not qualify for deduction. The market value will also be substituted for the purchase price where the asset was not acquired at an arm's length.

Disposal Value

The disposal price of an asset is the amount or value of the consideration in money or money's worth for the disposal of the asset less the following:

1. all expenses wholly and exclusively incurred in enhancing or preserving the value of the asset such as alterations, improvement;
2. all expenses incurred in establishing, preserving or defending his title to the asset; and
3. all incidental expenses relating to the disposal of the asset;

In case a chargeable asset is exchanged for another asset (whether chargeable or not), the market value of the asset received by the disposer shall be taken as the consideration for the disposal. If the market value is not ascertainable, the Director General may take the market value of the assets disposed of as the consideration for the disposal

Capital Gains on the Disposal of Shares in Real Property Companies

After October 21, 1988, capital gains tax is also chargeable in respect of gains on the disposal of shares in a real property company in addition to gain on the disposal of land and buildings. An acquisition of shares in a real property company shall be deemed to be an acquisition of a chargeable asset and will be liable to real property gains tax on the disposal notwithstanding the fact that at the time of the disposal of the shares, the company has ceased to be a real property company (Para (1)). A 'real property company' (RPC) is a controlled company which owns real property or shares or both, the defined value of which is not less than 75 per cent of the value of its total tangible assets. The value of total tangible assets means the aggregate of the defined value of real property or shares or both and the value of other tangible assets.

[The term 'defined value' means the value of real property or the acquisition price of shares as determined by the formula given under Schedule 2, Section 34A(3).]

PAKISTAN

The basis of chargeability of capital gains in Pakistan is given under Sec. 27 of *Income Tax Ordinance,* 1979 which provides that any profits and gains arising from the transfer of a capital asset shall be chargeable under the head 'capital gains'. It shall be deemed to be the income of the income year in which the transfer took place. Capital gain in Pakistan is taxable in the income year in which the effective transfer of title is conveyed and registered, irrespective of the fact whether the capital asset has been delivered or not. In Pakistan, every person whether resident or non-resident is liable to capital gains tax. The term *person* includes an individual, a firm, a company, an association of person, Hindu undivided family (HUF), a local authority and every other artificial juridicial person.

To find out the scope of capital gains in Pakistan, it is necessary to look at the meaning of 'capital asset' and 'transfer of capital asset'.

Capital Assets

The term 'capital asset', as defined in Sec. 2(12), means property of any kind held by an assessee whether or not connected with his business or profession. However, the following assets are excluded from the definition of capital assets:

(a) any stock-in-trade (not being stock and shares), consumable stores or raw materials held for the purpose of his business or profession;
(b) personal effects, including wearing apparel, jewellery and furniture held for personal use by the assessee or any member of the family dependent on him; and
(c) any land from which the income derived by the assessee is agricultural income.

The following capital assets although they fall in the definition provided in Sec. 2(12)] are held outside the ambit of chargeability under 'capital gains' by virtue of Sec. 27(2)(a):

1. Any asset or class of assets in respect of which the assessee is entitled to an allowance for depreciation under the Third Schedule.
2. Any immovable property, i.e. land and/or building.

Besides the assets which are excluded from the category of capital assets, all other assets are included in the category of capital assets. Thus, every other asset, whether movable or immovable, tangible or intangible or whether incorporeal and freehold is a capital asset and gain on such assets is chargeable under the head 'Income from capital gains'. The category of capital assets include: (a) tenancy rights or leasehold rights; (b) industrial licences and import/export licences acquired for a consideration; (c) share of a partner in a firm or association of persons; (d) right to subscribe for shares; (e) mining rights; (f) licence to manufacture certain products or render certain services; (g) foreign currency; (h) the contractual right of a purchaser to obtain title to an immovable property; (i) all precious metals, gems, stones, antique pieces and jewellery which is not held by the assessee for his personal use (including even gold and silver coins, art collections); and (j) goodwill purchased. In Pakistan, self-generated goodwill is not treated as a capital asset.

Transfer of Capital Asset

Transfer in relation to a capital asset includes sale, disposition, exchange, relinquishment of an asset and extinguishment of any rights therein, but does not include:

1. any transfer by reason of compulsory acquisition of any capital asset under any law for the time being in force;
2. any transfer of a capital asset under a gift, bequest or will or an irrevocable trust;
3. any distribution of assets of a company to its shareholders on its liquidation; and
4. any distribution of capital assets on the dissolution of a firm or an association of persons or the partition of a Hindu undivided family.

The computation of capital gains as mentioned under Sec. 28 provides: 'in computing the income under the head "capital gains", the cost of acquisition of the capital asset and any expenditure incurred wholly and exclusively in connection with the transfer thereof shall be deducted'.

The above provision relating to the computation of capital gains seems to be incomplete as it does not mention from which amount the cost of acquisition of the capital asset and expenditure shall be deducted. In the repealed Act of 1922, Sec. 12B, which is replaced by Sec. 28, it is clearly mentioned that deductions are to be made from 'the full value of consideration'. The same provision exist in the *Indian Income-Tax Act* presently. Therefore, the full value of consideration is taken to be the amount from which deductions are to be made.

Cost of Acquisition

In general, the value for which the capital asset is acquired is the cost of acquisition of the asset. Expenses of a capital nature necessary for acquiring the asset are includible in the cost of acquisition (Sec. 29). In many cases, the fair market value (FMV) of the asset is taken to be the cost of acquisition (Sec. 29(1). These include cases where the transfer is not treated as transfer. In all such cases the FMV of the assets as on the date on which it became the property of the assessee shall be deemed to be the cost of acquisition.

Transfer between Connected Persons

To prevent the avoidance of tax in those cases where arrangements are made between the assessee and the purchaser to reduce the full value of consideration, the Deputy Commissioner of Income Tax has been authorised to direct that, where the capital asset has been transferred by a person directly or indirectly connected with him, the FMV of the capital asset on the date of transfer shall be deemed to be the consideration received by the assessee for its transfer. The FMV is either the price which the capital asset would ordinarily fetch on sale in the open market on the relevant date, and where the price referred to is not ascertainable, such price as may be determined by the Deputy Commissioner of Income Tax after obtaining the approval of the Inspecting Additional Commissioner. However, this provision will not apply where the object of transfer is not the avoidance or reduction of the tax liability.

INDIA

Capital gains tax was introduced in India in the beginning of the year 1947-48 to prevent further inflationary rise in prices in the aftermath of the Second World War. Mr. Liaqat Ali Khan, the then Finance Minister, following the U.S. model, levied capital gain tax on a graduated basis. The twin objectives sought to be achieved were to check the inflation and to ensure equitable distribution of wealth. The capital gains tax provisions since then have undergone many changes. The jewellery, which was earlier excluded, has been included in the capital assets from the assessment year 1973-74. The conversion of capital assets into stock in trade is also treated as transfer with effect from the assessment year 1985-86. The indexation of the cost of acquisition and improvement started from the assessment year 1993-94.

Capital gain in India arises from the transfer of a capital asset and is chargeable to tax in the previous year in which the transfer took place [Sec. 45(1)]. In India, every person is liable to capital gains tax. The term 'person' includes, an individual, a firm, a company, an association of person, or a Hindu undivided family (HUF).

Capital Assets

Capital asset as provided under Sec. 2(14) means property of any kind held by an assessee whether or not connected with his business or profession, excluding;

1. any stock in trade, consumable stores or raw material held for the purposes of business or profession;
2. personal effects, that is to say, movable property (including wearing apparel and furniture but excluding jewellery) held for the personal use of the assessee or any member of his family dependent upon him.
3. agricultural land in India situated in an area having a population of less than 10,000 people or situated beyond a distance of 8 kilometres from the local limits of a municipality or a cantonment board;
4. specified government securities.

In India, capital gain or loss may be either short-term or long-term capital gain or loss, depending upon whether the asset transferred is short term or long term. A short-term capital gain (STCG) arises on the transfer of a short-term capital asset and a long-term capital gain (LTCG) arises on the transfer of a long-term capital asset.

A short-term capital asset is an asset held by an assessee for not more than 36 months immediately prior to the date of its transfer. However, the following assets are treated as short-term, if held, for not more than 12 months:

1. shares in a company.
2. securities listed in a recognised stock exchange.
3. units of the Unit Trust of India or a Mutual Fund, specified under Sec. 10(23D).

A long-term capital asset means a capital asset which is not a short-term capital asset.

Capital gain arises only when a capital asset is transferred. The term transfer is most crucial because the liability to capital gain tax depends upon whether a transfer is treated as transfer or not.

Transfer of Capital Assets

In India, transfer in relation to a capital asset includes sale, exchange, or relinquishment of the asset or the extinguishing of any rights therein or the compulsory acquisition thereof under any law, or the conversion of capital asset into stock in trade [Sec. 2 (47)].

Although the sale, exchange or relinquishment of the asset or the extinguishment of any rights therein are treated as transfer almost everywhere, compulsory acquisition of an asset by the government or a specified authority is exempt in Malaysia and Pakistan. The conversion of a capital asset into stock-in-trade is treated as transfer in India with effect from the assessment year 1985-86. Though it is not actually transfer, still for the purpose of capital gain it is treated as transfer and the FMV on the date of conversion is taken as the full value of the consideration. But this capital gain is chargeable in the year in which such stock-in-trade is sold and not in the year in which conversion was effected.

Though the sale, exchange and compulsory acquisition are all treated as transfers, in the following circumstances in India, a transfer is not treated as transfer and thus, no capital gain arises:

1. distribution of assets in kind by a company to its shareholders on liquidation;
2. any distribution of capital assets in kind by a Hindu undivided family (HUF) to its members at the time of total or partial partition;
3. any transfer of capital assets under a gift, will or an irrevocable trust;
4. any transfer of capital assets by a company to its wholly owned Indian subsidiary company; or by a wholly owned subsidiary company to its Indian holding company;
5. any transfer of shares in an Indian company held by a foreign company to another foreign company as a result of amalgamation between the two foreign companies if at least 75 per cent of the shareholders of the

amalgamating foreign company continue to remain shareholders of the amalgamated foreign company;

6. any transfer in a de-merger of a capital asset by the de-merged company to the resulting Indian company;
7. any transfer or issue of shares by the resulting company to the shareholders of the de-merged company if the transfer or issue is made in consideration of the de-merger of the undertaking;
8. any transfer of shares by a shareholder in a scheme of amalgamation;
9. any transfer of capital assets by a non-resident of certain foreign currency convertible bonds of shares as mentioned in Sec. 115AC(1) held by him to another non-resident where the transfer is made outside India;.
10. any transfer of agricultural land in India effected before March 1, 1970.
11. any transfer of capital assets due to the conversion of a sole proprietorship or a firm into a company where the transferor receive consideration in shares of the newly formed company, and all the assets and liabilities relating to the business immediately before the succession becomes the assets and liabilities of the company and sole proprictor, or all the partners become the shareholders in the new company and the aggregate of the shareholding in the company of the sole proprietor or of the partners of the firm is not less than 50 per cent of the total voting power in the company and their shareholding continues for a period of five years from the date of succession;
12. any transfer by way of the conversion of bonds or debentures (or debenture stock or deposit certificates) of a company into shares or debentures of that company.

Capital gain in India is found out by deducting from the full value of the consideration the following:

1. cost of acquisition;
2. cost of improvement; and
3. expenses incurred wholly and exclusively in connection with the transfer.

Disposal Value

The full value of consideration commonly known as the disposal price is the sales price without any deduction whatsoever. It may include money or any property received in consideration for the transfer of an asset.

Cost of Acquisition

In India, the cost of acquisition of an asset is the value or the price paid for acquiring the asset. Expenses of a capital nature for completing or acquiring the title to the property are a part of the cost of acquisition. Interest on the money borrowed to purchase asset is also part of the cost of asset. In case the assessee acquired the asset on or before April 1, 1981, he has the option to choose either the actual cost or the FMV on April 1, 1981 as the cost of acquisition. If any advance money or other money is received by the taxpayer and is forfeited, the cost of acquisition shall be reduced by such amount.

Cost of Acquisition: Special Cases

In the following cases, the cost of acquisition is taken at the cost at which the previous owner acquired the property:

1. distribution of assets on the total or partial partition of a Hindu undivided family (HUF);
2. any transfer under a gift or a will or an irrevocable trust;
3. any transfer by succession, inheritance or devolution; or
4. any distribution of assets on the liquidation of a company;
5. any transfer by a wholly-owned subsidiary company to its Indian holding company or by a company to its wholly-owned Indian subsidiary company; or
6. any transfer in a scheme of amalgamation.

In the above cases, the period for which the asset was held by the previous owner is included to ascertain the holding period.

In case of the conversion of debentures, debenture stock or deposit certificates of a company into shares or debentures of that company, the cost of acquisition shall be that part of the cost of debentures, debenture stock or deposit certificates which has been appropriated towards the shares or debentures. To find out whether the asset is a short-term or a long-term capital asset, the period of holding shall be determined from the date of allotment of shares and the indexation will start from the date of conversion of debentures into shares [Sec. 49(2A)].

In case of bonus shares, if original and bonus are both acquired prior to April, 1981, then the cost of bonus shares shall be FMV on April 1, 1981. If bonus shares are allotted after April, 1981 then the value of bonus shares is taken to be nil.

In case of right share, the cost of right share is the amount actually paid by the taxpayer for acquiring the asset. If the right is renounced in favour of another person, the cost of acquisition to such person shall be the purchase price paid to the renouncee of rights entitlement plus the amount paid to the company which has allotted the right shares.

In case of depreciable assets, any gain or loss on transfer is a short-term capital gain or loss. The indexation provisions do not apply to the cost of the acquisition of such assets. The cost of the acquisition of depreciable assets is the aggregate of the following:

1. The written down value of a block of assets at the beginning of the previous year; and
2. The actual cost of any asset falling within that block of asset purchased during that year.

As the cost of the acquisition of depreciable assets relates to a block of assets, gain or loss on an individual asset is not found out. If only some of the assets in a block are sold, the excess of sales consideration if any, over the cost of acquisition computed in the manner stated above for the block of assets and expenditure on transfer shall be treated as short-term capital gain with no further depreciation on the block of assets. If the sales consideration is less than the cost of acquisition and expenditure on transfer, the balance is considered as the written down value of the block of assets on which depreciation as per applicable rate continues to be provided. However, if all the assets in a block are sold, the excess shall be a short-term capital gain and the shortfall shall be treated as a short-term capital loss.

The cost of acquisition of some specific self-generated assets (self-generated asset is an asset which does not cost anything to the assessee in terms of money in its creation or acquisition) is taken as nil. These are: (a) goodwill of a business, (b) tenancy rights, route permits and loom hours, and (c) right to manufacture, produce or process any article. No capital gain or loss shall arise in India on the transfer of self-generated assets other than these assets. When these assets are purchased, the cost of acquisition shall be the price paid for acquiring these assets.

Cost of Improvement

The cost of improvement includes all expenses of a capital nature incurred in making any additions to the capital asset on or after April 1, 1981 by the assessee or the previous owner (in those cases where the cost to the previous owner is taken as the cost of acquisition).

Instead of the actual cost and the cost of improvement, the indexed cost of acquisition and the indexed cost of improvement are deducted from the full value of consideration in case the asset transferred is a long-term capital asset. The manner of computation of the indexed cost of acquisition and the indexed cost of improvement are given below.

The Indexed Cost of Acquisition

The 'indexed cost of acquisition' is the amount which bears to the cost of acquisition the same proportion as the cost of inflation index (CII) for the year in which the asset is transferred bears to the CII for the first year in which the asset was held by assessee or for the year 1981-82, whichever is later.

(The year 1981-82 is the base year for indexation, thus the CII for the year 1981-82 will be taken in those cases where the asset was acquired by the taxpayer or the previous owner either in the year 1981-82 or in years prior to 1981-82) The formula for the indexed cost of acquisition is:

$$\text{Cost of acquisition} \times \frac{\text{CII for the year in which the asset is transferred}}{\text{CII for the first year in which the asset was held by the assessee or for the year 1981-82, whichever is later.}}$$

The Indexed Cost of Improvement

The 'indexed cost of improvement' is the amount which bears to the cost of improvement the same proportion as the CII for the year in which the asset is transferred bears to the CII for the year in which the improvement to the asset took place. Thus the formula for indexed cost of improvement is

$$\text{Cost of improvement} \times \frac{\text{CII for the year in which the asset is transferred}}{\text{CII for the year in which the improvement took place}}$$

Thus, in the case of the transfer of a long-term capital asset the cost of acquisition and the cost of improvement both are indexed to provide the taxpayer some relief from the effects of inflation.

Specific Provisions Relating to Computation of Capital Gains in Certain Cases

Insurance Claim

Prior to the income year 1999-2000, any damage or destruction of a capital asset due to flood, fire or natural calamity was not treated as transfer. However, Sec. 45(IA) inserted by the *Finance Act*, 1999, provides that where any money or other asset is received from an insurance company on account of damage or destruction of a capital asset as a result of flood, fire or other natural calamity, riot or civil disturbance, or action by an enemy, then profits or gains arising from the receipt of such money shall be taxable as capital gain in the income year in which such money or other asset was received, and the value of any money or the FMV of the assets on the date of such receipt shall be deemed to be the full value of the consideration.

Conversion of Capital Assets into Stock-in-trade

With effect from the assessment year 1985-86, the conversion of a capital asset into stock-in-trade is treated as transfer. For purposes of the computation of capital gain, the FMV of the asset on the date of conversion shall be treated as its disposal value and the capital gain will be taxable not in the year of conversion, but in the year in which the converted asset is ultimately sold (Sec. 45(2).

Compulsory Acquisition of Assets

Where any capital asset is acquired by way of compulsory acquisition under any law, any capital gain from such acquisition is not taxable in the year in which the capital asset is transferred, but it is taxable in the first year in which the initial compensation (or part thereof) is received. Enhanced compensation, if any, is also taxable in the year in which it is received. The cost of acquisition and the cost of improvement in the case of enhanced compensation shall be taken as nil. Such capital gain shall be long-term or short-term depending upon the original capital gain [(Sec. 45(5)].

Money or Other Assets Received by Shareholders at the Time of Liquidation of the Company

While any distribution of assets in kind by a company on liquidation is not treated as transfer, on the other hand, money or other assets received by the shareholder at the time of liquidation of the company is taxable under the head, 'capital gain'. To find out the capital gain, the full value of consideration shall be the amount of money received or the fair market value of other assets received in excess of the deemed dividend received by the shareholder at the time of liquidation (Sec. 46).

Transfer of Shares in Lieu of the of Shares of the Amalgamating Company

While the transfer of shares by the shareholder in a scheme of amalgamation is not treated as transfer, the shares received in lieu of that transfer in the amalgamated company if sold will be treated as transfer. The period of holding in such cases shall be determined from the date of the acquisition of shares in the amalgamating company and the indexation will start from the date of allotment of shares in the amalgamated company [Sec. 47(vii)].

Purchase by a Company of its Own Shares or Securities

With effect from the income year 1999-2000, any consideration received by a shareholder from any company on purchase of its own shares or other specified securities including the employee's stock option is chargeable to tax on the difference between the cost of acquisition and the value of the consideration received by the shareholder as capital gains (Sec. 46A).

A summary of methods of computation of capital gains tax provisions are given in Table 5.2

Conclusion

The levy of capital gains tax is on transfer of capital assets. The base of capital gains tax is very narrow in Malaysia where capital assets include only real property and share in real property companies. The base is also limited in Pakistan, where jewellery, depreciable assets and land and buildings are not regarded as capital assets. It is interesting to note that Pakistan has excluded land and building from the purview of capital gains tax, whereas Malaysia levies capital gains tax only on land and buildings (including shares in real estate companies)

In the U.K., tangible moving properties with life of 50 years or less are excluded from the category of capital assets, while in Pakistan and India, agricultural land is excluded from the definition of capital assets. In Pakistan, all agriculture lands are excluded, whereas in India, agricultural lands away from urban areas only, are excluded.

In the U.S and India, capital gain is classified as a short-term capital gain (STCG) and a long-term capital gain (LTCG). There is no such classification in other selected countries. But these countries provide beneficial treatment to assets held for longer periods prior to disposal either in the form of lower tax rates or by allowing annual exemption. Indexation allowance which helps in mitigating the effects of inflation on capital gains is applicable in the U.K, Australia and India. However in the U.K, the indexation allowance has

TABLE 5.2. A SUMMARY OF CAPITAL GAINS TAX PROVISIONS

Particulars	U.K.	U.S.	Australia	Malaysia	Pakistan	India
Year of introduction	1965	1921	1985	1975	1947	1947
Taxable under which Act	Taxation of Chargeable Gains Act 1992.	Internal Revenue Code.	The Income Tax Assessment Act, 1997.	The Real Property Gains Tax Act, 1976.	The Income Tax Ordinance, 1979.	Income Tax Act, 1961.
Assets which are not capital assets.	Cars, tangible moving property with life of 50 years or less, foreign currency held for personal use, and certain specified government securities and bonds.	Inventory, accounts or notes receivable, real or depreciable property used in a business, copyright, literary, musical or artistic composition and certain U.S. Government publications.	Cars, motor cycles, collectables, costing AUD500 or less, personal use assets costing AUD10,000 or less, main residence.	All other assets except real property or shares in real property companies.	Stock in trade consumable stores, raw materials for business purposes, personal use assets, agricultural land, depreciable asset and any immovable property.	Stock in trade, consumable stores, raw material for business use, agricultural land in specific areas, personal use assets, specific government bonds.
Difference in short-term and long-term capital gain.	No difference. However the amount of taper relief increases as the life of the asset increases.	Yes, STCG if held for less than 12 months, LTCG if held for more than 18 months, and mid-term capital gain if held for more than 12 months, but less than 18 months prior to transfer.	No difference. However indexation is done if asset was acquired for 12 months or more.	No, difference, however tax rates are reduced gradually according to the life of the asset.	No difference, however gains from the transfer of assets held for more than 12 months are given some exemption.	Yes, gain on assets held for more than three years are LTCG.

(contd.)

TABLE 5.2. (contd.)

Particulars	U.K.	U.S.	Australia	Malaysia	Pakistan	India
Year of introduction	1965	1921	1985	1975	1947	1947
Indexation.	Indexation allowed, but cannot convert gain into loss or it cannot increase loss.	No indexation.	Yes, allowed in case of assets held for 12 months or more prior to transfer.	No indexation.	No indexation.	Yes, can convert gain into loss.
Market-value substitution for old assets	In respect of assets acquired prior to March 31, 1982, the taxpayer may opt for FMV as on March 31, 1981 as the cost of acquisition.	No market value substitution.	No market value substitution.	Yes, in respect of assets acquired prior to January 1, 1970, the market-value as on January 1, 1970 shall be taken as the cost of acquisition.	No market-value substitution.	Yes, in respect of assets acquired prior to April 1, 1981. The taxpayer has an option of FMV as on April 1, 1981 as the cost of acquisition.
Chargeability of short term capital gain	All gains are treated as ordinary income.	S.TC.G is treated as ordinary income.	All gains are treated as ordinary income.	All gains are treated as ordinary income.	All gains are treated as ordinary income.	Short-term capital gains are treated as ordinary income.
Annual exemptions	Annual exemption of £7,100 for income year 1999-2000 is allowed from capital gain after adjusting current loss.	No, annual exemption.	No annual exemption.	Yes, annual exemption is RM 5000 or ten per cent of gain whichever is higher.	Yes, annual exemption is Rs. 5000 or 60% of capital gain, whichever is higher.	No annual exemption. Yes, can convert gain into loss.

been replaced by taper relief which provides more relief to assets held for longer time prior to disposal, but is not related directly to inflation.

In the U.K, Malaysia and India, the market-value substitution rule in place of cost of acquisition is applicable in respect of old assets purchased prior to a fixed period. This helps in reducing capital gains in respect of old assets which were purchased at a very nominal price and fetch a very high value in the year of disposal. Besides this, annual exemption from capital gains is also allowed in the U.K, Malaysia and Pakistan.

Capital gains income is likely to provide the maximum revenue in the U.S. as exemptions are least there. Further, the U.S. also does not provide for any annual exemption, indexation benefit and market-value substitution benefit. On the other hand, capital gains tax is not likely to provide sufficient revenue in the U.K., Malaysia and Pakistan. While in the U.K., a large number of exemptions in addition to annual exemption, indexation benefit and market value substitution are provided, in the other two countries, the base otherwise is very narrow.

CAPITAL LOSS ADJUSTMENTS

The provisions relating to capital loss adjustments are very important especially to find out whether loss can be set off from the same or from other income too. And if it could not be fully set off during the current year, whether it can be carried forward or not, and if yes, then in future how it is allowed to be adjusted. Further, whether the loss adjustment provisions of individual taxpayers are different from that of corporate taxpayers.

In this part, the capital loss adjustment provisions of the selected countries are analysed.

In all the selected countries, the capital losses are allowed to be set off against the capital gains income first, and the remaining loss can be carried forward to be adjusted against capital gains in future.

THE U.K.

In the U.K., no distinction is made between the long-term and short-term capital gain or loss. The net capital loss arises where the total capital loss exceeds the total capital gain in a particular income year. Capital losses are first adjusted against capital gain and in case capital losses exceed the capital gains, the net capital loss will arise. The amount of annual exemption in that year will be lost. The net capital loss may however be carried forward without any time limit and may be set off against the capital gains of the future years. However, in the succeeding years the deduction from capital gains will be allowed according to the following priority:

1. capital losses of the same year.
2. unrelieved losses brought forward without wasting the annual exemption.
3. the annual exemption.

Thus, while current losses are to be off set fully to the extent of capital gains, the past losses are offset only to the extent the gains are in excess of the annual exemption to prevent annual exemption from being wasted. The remaining unabsorbed losses can be further carried forward without any time limit and adjusted against capital gains in future. Business losses can be adjusted against capital gains in the current year. In such cases, business losses will be adjusted in priority over capital losses brought forward from an earlier year. The capital loss of one spouse cannot be adjusted against the capital gain of the other spouse. Capital losses cannot be carried back like business losses. Capital losses which occur in the year of death cannot be carried forward. However, such losses can be carried back and set off against the net gains of the previous three years.

THE U.S.

The first step in computing net capital gain in the U.S. is to adjust short-term capital loss against short-term capital gain and long-term capital loss against long-term capital gain. Mid-term capital gains and losses, collectible gains and losses, and gains from the sale of qualified small business stock are adjusted along with long-term gains or losses. The result may be either a net short-term capital gain or loss or a net long-term gain or loss. Thereafter, the net short-term capital loss (NSTCL), if any, will be adjusted against the net long-term capital gain (NLTCG) and the net long-term capital loss (NLTCL), if any, will be adjusted against the net short-term capital gain (NSTCG) or vice versa. If the net NSTCL is in excess of NLTCG, it is treated as an ordinary loss and is deducted up to $3,000 in any one year against ordinary income and the balance capital loss is carried forward for an indefinite number of years.

If the NLTCL is in excess of the NSTCG, the excess is NLTCL and is deductible up to $3,000 per year against ordinary income. If one has both NSTCL and NLTCL, the NSTCL is offset against ordinary income first and the balance remaining out of $3,000 deduction is used to offset NLTCL.

AUSTRALIA

Similar to the provisions of the capital gains tax in the U.K., no distinction is made between short-term and long-term capital gain or loss in Australia also. A net capital loss is the excess of capital losses over the capital gains for the income year. A net capital loss is not deductible from a taxpayer's assessable income. However, it can be adjusted against capital gains made by the taxpayer in the succeeding years. Net capital losses are offset against capital gains in the order in which they are incurred.

MALAYSIA

An allowable loss from the disposal of a chargeable asset arises to the extent the disposal price is less than the acquisition price, Sec. 6 (Schedule 4). In

Malaysia, an allowable loss is not directly deducted from the chargeable gain. Rather adjustment is made from the tax liability on the capital gain. In case there is an allowable loss, then the tax relief is calculated by multiplying the loss with the tax rates applicable on the chargeable asset depending upon the number of years for which the asset was held. The tax relief so calculated is deducted from the tax liability on the chargeable gain. In case it is not fully deductible, the balance will be carried forward and deducted from the next year's tax liability. If still unabsorbed it can be carried over until the whole tax relief has been allowed under Schedule 4 [paragraph 7, part 4(a)(b)].

PAKISTAN

Where an assessee sustains a loss in any assessment year under the head 'capital gains', such loss shall be carried forward to the following assessment year and set off against the capital gains chargeable for that assessment year under the said head, and if it cannot be set-off in this manner, the amount of the loss not so set-off shall be carried forward to the following assessment year and so on, but no loss shall be carried forward for more than 6 assessment years immediately succeeding the assessment year for which the loss was first computed (Sec. 37).

In Pakistan, capital loss can be carried forward only to the extent it exceeds PKR5,000. No loss shall be carried forward if it is less than PKR5,000. Where the capital loss is carried forward it can be adjusted only against capital gain in future and no other income.

INDIA

In India, although the method of computation of LTCG and STCG and tax rates applicable on LTCG and STCG are different but for adjustment of capital losses there is no difference between long-term capital loss (LTCL) and short-term capital loss (STCL). First STCL is adjusted against STCG and LTCL is adjusted against LTCG and the remaining STCL can further be set off against LTCG and the remaining LTCL can be set off against STCG if any. After making these adjustments, the balance of either STCL or LTCL cannot be adjusted against income under any other head of income in the same year. On the other hand, losses under any other head of income can be set off against capital gains in the same year.

Any capital loss, whether LTCL or SCTL which has not been set off against capital gain in the same year can be carried forward to be set off against capital gain in subsequent years. However, capital loss incurred in any year can be carried forward up to a maximum of 8 assessment years from the end of the assessment year in which the capital loss was incurred.

Thus, in India the tax treatment of LTCG and STCG is different. While the indexed cost of acquisition and improvement is taken to find out only LTCG or LTCL, there can be cases in India where gain is converted into a loss or the loss is increased due to indexation. This is in contrast to the provisions in the U.K. and Australia, where indexation can be applied to reduce the capital gains, but cannot be used to convert the capital gains into losses or to increase the losses. LTCG are taxable at flat rate of 20 per cent in the case of individuals, firms, and companies.

The provisions relating to capital loss adjustments are given in Table 5.3

Conclusion

As regards the setting off and carrying forward of capital loss in all the selected countries, capital loss in the current year can be adjusted against capital gain only except in the U.S. where first STCL can be adjusted against ordinary income to the extent of $3,000 and if there is no STCL or the STCL is less than $3,000, the LTCL too can be adjusted to the extent of $3,000 or the remaining balance. In Malaysia, the capital loss is not deducted directly from the capital gain. First the relief on the loss is calculated by applying the tax rates and such relief is deducted from the capital gain tax.

In all the selected countries other than Pakistan and India, capital loss can be carried forward to be set off in future against capital gain without any time limit, while in India, it can be carried forward for a maximum of 8 years. In Pakistan, the loss can be carried forward for a maximum of 6 years and only when it exceeds PKR5,000 and can be carried forward to the extent it exceeds PKR5,000.

Thus, capital losses in majority of these countries are adjusted during the current year against capital loss only. It is only in the U.S. that capital losses can be adjusted within certain limits against ordinary income. This will provide relief to medium taxpayers who take the risk of loss and invest in capital assets. Another major difference in the U.S. is that while the capital loss of individuals cannot be carried back, it can be carried forward indefinitely. The capital loss of corporate taxpayer can be carried back as well as carried forward up to 5 years.

RATE OF TAX ON CAPITAL GAINS

One of the ways adopted by many countries to give preferential treatment to capital gain is to charge tax at lower rates. The tax rates applicable on capital gains in respect of individual and corporate taxpayers in the selected countries are examined below:

THE U.K.

The CGT liability for a tax year is based upon the chargeable disposals made during the year. If total gains exceed total losses, the losses are subtracted from the gains to give the net gains for the year. The net gains for the year are reduced by an annual exemption and the remainder is capital gains. The annual exemption for individuals for the income year 1999-2000 is £7,100. It is available to both husband and wife separately. But there is no annual exemption for companies. In the case of individual taxpayers if the net gains

TABLE 5.3. A SUMMARY OF PROVISIONS RELATING TO CAPITAL LOSS ADJUSTMENTS

Particulars	U.K.	U.S.	Australia	Malaysia	Pakistan	India
Capital loss adjustment	Capital loss can be adjusted against capital gain in the current year before deducting annual exemption. However, brought forward loss is allowed without wasting annual exemption. The remaining loss is carried forward and adjusted against future capital gain.	STCL is adjusted against LTCG and LTCL is adjusted against STCG, the net STCL is deductible against ordinary income up to £ 3000, net LTCL can also be adjusted against ordinary income after adjusting net STCL. Balance loss is carried forward for an indefinite period.	Capital loss can be adjusted against capital gain in the current year. The remaining loss if any, is carried forward to be adjusted against future capital gain.	Loss is treated differently. Just as tax on gain is computed by applying the prescribed rates, similarly, relief on loss is computed by applying the tax rates and the relief so calculated shall be deducted from tax on capital gain. If unabsorbed, the balance shall be carried forward and deducted from the next year tax liability until the whole relief has been allowed.	Capital loss can be carried forward to the extent it exceeds Rs. 5,000 and can be adjusted against capital gain maximum upto 6 assessment years. No loss shall be carried forward if it is less than Rs. 5,000.	STCL is adjusted first against STCG and then against LTCG. Similarly, LTCL is adjusted first against LTCG and then against STCG. Balance of loss whether net STCL or net LTCL may be carried forward to be adjusted against capital gain in future, up to a maximum of 8 assessment years.

are less than the annual exemption in any year, the capital gains liable to tax for that year are nil and the balance annual exemption is lost.

Though capital gains are taxable in the U.K. under a separate Act, the *Taxation of Chargeable Gains Act*, 1992, the tax rates applicable on capital gains are the same which are applicable on ordinary income. In case of individuals, the amount of CGT payable for a tax year is equal to the amount of extra income tax which the taxpayer would be liable to pay if the capital gains assessment for that year were regarded as the extra taxable income. Tax rates applicable on ordinary income for the year 1999-2000 are such that the lower rate band of 10 per cent is applicable on incomes up to £1,500, basic rate band of 23 per cent is applicable on incomes above £1,500 but not exceeding £28,000 and higher tax rate band of 40 per cent is applicable on incomes exceeding £28,000.

However, capital gains income which is taxable like savings income in the U.K., is taxable at the lower rate of 10 per cent if the total income including the capital gain does not exceed £1,500, and is taxable at the rate of 20 per cent if the total income including capital income exceeds £1,500 but does not exceed £28,000. The capital gain income is taxable at the higher rate tax band of 40 per cent if the income exceeds £28,000.

Capital gains income in the case of a company is taxable at the rates applicable on companies. The rates for the income year 1999-2000 for small companies are 20 per cent and for large companies 30 per cent.

THE U.S.

In the U.S., net STCGs of both corporate and individual taxpayers are treated as ordinary income. Only net LTCGs of individuals are charged to tax at different rates. Tax treatment of short-term and long-term capital gains (LTCGs) and losses is given in Table 5.4.

As shown in Table 5.4, net short-term capital gains in the U.S are taxable like ordinary income. Although LTCG's are taxable at preferential rates, the tax rates vary for different types of LTCG's. Net mid-term capital gains, net collectible gains and gains on qualified small business stock are all taxed at 28 per cent. A tax rate of 25 per cent is levied on the unrecaptured Sec. 1250 gain. All other LTCG's of individual taxpayers are taxable at the rate of 20 per cent. A lower rate of 10 per cent is charged if the taxpayer's ordinary income is taxable at the lowest 15 per cent marginal rate. LTCG of a company is taxable as an ordinary taxable income.

AUSTRALIA

A net capital gain is added to the assessable income of an income year in Australia. The net capital gain is found out by deducting capital losses from the income year. The net capital gain so computed is further reduced by unabsorbed net capital losses carried forward from earlier income years. Thus, capital gains in Australia are taxable at the rates applicable to ordinary

TABLE 5.4. TAX TREATMENT OF SHORT-TERM AND LONG-TERM CAPITAL GAINS AND LOSSES IN THE U.S.

(for the income year 1999)

Capital Gain/Loss	Individual Tax Payers	Corporate Tax Payers
1. Short-term capital gain	Ordinary income	Ordinary income
2. Adjusted net capital gain[1]	Taxed at 20% (10% for 15% marginal rate taxpayers)	Ordinary income
3. Unrecaptured Section 1250 gain [2]	Taxed at 25%	Not applicable
4. Net mid-term capital gain.	Taxed at 28%	Ordinary income
5. Net collectables gain.[3]	Taxed at 28%	Not applicable
6. Gain on qualified small business stock[4]	Taxed at 28% (50 % of the gain is excluded)	Not applicable
7. Short-term capital loss	Deductible from ordinary income up to $3000 per year.	No current deduction: may carry back 3 years and forward 5 years to offset capital gains.
8. Long-term capital loss.	Deductible from ordinary income up to $3000 per year. Any short-term losses are applied against the $3000 limit before long-term losses are deducted.	No current deduction: may carry back 3 years and forward 5 years as a short-term capital loss to offset capital gains.

Notes: 1. *Adjusted net capital gain* is the net long-term capital gain excluding gains taxable at 28 per cent and 25 per cent and after deducting short-term capital losses and long-term capital loss carry over from previous years.

2. *Unrecaptured Sec. 1250 gain* is a long-term capital gain on real property to the extent the gain is not recaptured on account of the depreciation charged earlier.

3. *Net Collectable Gain* - Gains arising from the sale of collectibles that are held for more than 18 months in excess of losses. Collectibles include works of art, rugs, antiques, metals, gems, stamps, coins and alcoholic beverages.

4. *Gain on qualified small business stock* - Qualified small business stock issued after August 1, 1993 by a corporation that did not have gross assets in excess of $50 million and acquired at its original price directly from the corporation or through its underwriter. The corporation must be an active corporation, and must use at least 80 per cent of the assets in the active conduct of a trade or business during the five-year holding period.

Source: Kelvin E. Murphy and Mark Higgins, *Concepts in Federal Taxation* (Cincinnati, Ohio: South Western College Publishing, 1999), p. 471

taxable income. However, there is a provision for averaging for individuals to provide them relief from high income tax being paid at a progressive rate. Averaging is achieved by working out the amount of tax that would be payable if only 20 per cent of the capital gains component was included in the taxable income and multiplying that amount by five. The resulting amount is the tax payable on the net capital gain. This averaging does not provide any benefit, if the capital gains component does not cause the taxpayer's taxable income to cross a marginal tax threshold (maximum tax rate threshold).

MALAYSIA

Any gain from the disposal of a chargeable asset in Malaysia is exempt up to RM5,000 or 10 per cent of the profits whichever is higher. Although in Malaysia, there is no difference between STCG and LTCG, yet the tax rates are so designed that high tax rates are charged if assets are disposed of within a short period. Tax rates get reduced according to the life of the asset. The tax rates applicable in the case of individuals and companies on real property gain are given in Table 5.5.

As shown in Table 5.5, the maximum rate of tax of 30 per cent in Malaysia is charged in case the assets are sold within 2 years of their acquisition. The rates are reduced gradually as the number of years for which the asset is held increases. In the case of an individual taxpayer, the minimum rate of 5 per cent is charged if the assets are sold in the 5th year after acquisition, while the minimum rate of 5 per cent in the case of company is charged if the assets are sold in the 5th year or 6th year of acquisition. No tax is levied in Malaysia if the assets are sold after the 6th year of acquisition in the case of individuals. However, tax at the rate of 5 per cent will continue to be levied in the case of companies even if assets are disposed of in the 6th year after acquisition or thereafter. Tax rate for individuals who are not citizens or permanent residents is 30 per cent where a chargeable asset is disposed in the 5th year after acquisition and 5 per cent if disposed of in the 6th year after acquisition or thereafter.

TABLE 5.5. RATES OF TAX ON GAINS ARISING FROM THE DISPOSAL OF CHARGEABLE ASSETS IN MALAYSIA

(for the income year 1999)

The period for which assets were held prior to disposal	Individual (in %age)	Companies (in %age)
Where the asset is disposed of within two years of acquisition.	30	30
If disposed of in the third year after acquisition	20	20
If disposed of in the fourth year after acquisition	15	15
If disposed of in the fifth year after acquisition	5	5
If disposed of in the sixth year after acquisition or thereafter.	nil	5

Source: CCH, 2000 *Malaysian Master Tax Guide*, p. 710

PAKISTAN

In Pakistan, capital gains are taxable at the ordinary tax rates, which in the case of an individual taxpayer ranges from a minimum of 5 per cent if the taxable income is up to PKR100,000 to a maximum of 35 per cent if the taxable income exceeds PKR1,000,000. On the other hand, a flat rate of 33 per cent is applicable in the case of a public company and 43 per cent in the case of a private company.

Though no difference exists in Pakistan between STCG and LTCG, indirectly capital gains arising from the transfer of a capital asset after 1 year of its acquisition are either taxable at preferential rates in the case of a company taxpayer or are exempt up to a certain limit in the case of an individual taxpayer.

In Pakistan, capital gain forms part of the total income. Where the total income includes capital gain and the capital gain arises from the transfer of a capital asset held for not more than 12 months from the date of its acquisition, then the total income including the capital gain is taxable at ordinary tax rates applicable to individual or company taxpayer [Para A(4)(a) of First Schedule]. Where the total income includes capital gain and such gain has arisen as a result of the transfer of an asset after the expiry of one year from the date of its acquisition by him, then in the case of a company and a firm the tax on the total income excluding capital gain shall be payable at the normal tax rates, while the capital gain will be taxable at the rate of 25 per cent [Para A(4)(b)(i) of First Schedule].

In the case of an individual taxpayer if the total income includes capital gain and such gain arises from the transfer of an asset after the expiry of 12 months from the date of its acquisition, then tax at ordinary rates will be payable on the total income excluding capital gain, plus the amount of capital gain as reduced by:

(a) an amount equal to 60 per cent of the capital gain or
(b) PKR5000, whichever is greater

Thus, if capital gain arises from the transfer of a capital asset after the expiry of 12 months, a minimum tax relief of 60 per cent is allowed. If the capital gain in such a case is up to PKR5000, the entire amount shall be exempt and if it exceeds PKR5,000, only 40 per cent will be taxable [Para A(4)(b)(ii) of First Schedule].

INDIA

In India, STCGs are treated just like ordinary income and are taxable at the ordinary tax rates applicable to an individual or other assessees. LTCGs in India are taxable at preferential rates. Though LTCG forms part of the total income in India for purposes of computation of the total income, however, tax on LTCG is computed separately. For the income year 1999-2000, the tax rate applicable on LTCG for an individual firm, company and other assessee is 20 per cent. However, at the option of the taxpayer, LTCG arising from the sale of listed securities can be taxed at the rate of 10 per cent without the benefit of indexation. A surcharge of 10 per cent of the tax (reduced to 2 per cent for the income year 2001-02) is also levied. Rebate under Sec. 88 in respect of long-term savings is not allowed from tax on LTCG. Tax on income other than LTCG and tax on LTCG are aggregated to find out the total tax liability.

The provisions relating to the rate of tax on capital gain in the selected countries are given in Table 5.6

Conclusion

The capital gain in the U.K. and Australia, is treated as an ordinary income and taxable at the rates applicable to such income. In Malaysia, tax rates for capital gains are different from the tax rates applicable on ordinary income. The tax rates here are the highest for the disposal made in the 2nd year after acquisition and lowest for the disposal made in the 5th year after acquisition. In Pakistan, capital gains arising from the transfer of assets if disposed of after they have been held for more than 12 months are taxable in the case of companies at a flat rate of 25 per cent, and in the case of individual taxpayers as ordinary income but after allowing deduction of the higher of the two, i.e. (1) PKR5,000 or (2) 60 per cent of capital gain. In the U.S. and India, STCG are treated as ordinary income. However, LTCGs gets preferential treatment in these two countries.

In the U.S., LTCGs of individual taxpayers are taxable at a rate ranging from 10 per cent to 28 per cent, depending upon the income level of the individual taxpayer and the nature of the capital asset, while LTCGs of companies are taxable at the rates applicable to companies. In India, LTCGs are taxable at a flat rate of 20 per cent for both individuals as well as corporate taxpayers.

Thus, LTCGs get preferential treatment in tax rates in the U.S., Malaysia, Pakistan and India. However, the manner of giving concession differs. The U.K., otherwise provide other concessions including annual exemption. Hence, Australia is the only country where only indexation allowance benefit is given and no concession is given in tax rates.

Capital Gains Tax Reliefs

Various reliefs are provided from capital gains tax either in the form of exemption from tax or in the form of deferment of capital gains tax. Such reliefs provided in the selected countries are examined here.

THE U.K.

Many reliefs in the U.K. tax laws relating to capital gains tax are provided with a view to encouraging taxpayers to either utilise the whole or part of the consideration received on disposal or to invest the whole or part of the

TABLE 5.6. RATES OF TAX ON LONG TERM CAPITAL GAINS

Particulars	U.K.	U.S.	Australia	Malaysia	Pakistan	India
Individual taxpayer	Capital gain is taxable at the rates applicable on ordinary income. However, just like savings income, such income is considered top slice income and taxable either at 20 per cent or 40 per cent tax rate depending upon the total income including capital gains.	LTCG are taxable at 20 per cent. However a lower rate of 10 per cent is applicable if ordinary income is chargeable at the lowest 15 per cent rate. Mid-term capital gain and gain on qualified small business stock are taxable at 28 per cent whereas unrecaptured gain is charged at 25 per cent.	Capital gains are taxable at ordinary tax rates applicable to individuals ranging from 20 per cent to 47 per cent at different levels of income.	Rate of tax on capital gain for individual taxpayers is 5 per cent if sold in the fifth year after acquisition and gradually increases to 15 per cent, 20 per cent and 30 per cent if sold in the 4th year, 3rd year, 2nd year after acquisition respectively. No tax if sold, in the 6th year after acquisition or thereafter.	After deducting annual exemption, the gains are taxed at the rates applicable on ordinary income ranging from 5 per cent to 35 per cent.	Long term capital gains are taxable at preferential tax rate of 20 per cent.
Corporate taxpayer	Capital gains are a part of companies total income and are taxable either at 20 per cent or 30 per cent	LTCGs are taxable at different rates ranging from 15 per cent to 35 per cent.	Capital gains are taxable at a flat rate of 36 per cent	Same as above. A minimum rate of 5 per cent confinues to be charged even if the assets are sold in the 6th year of onwards.	Tax is charged at lower rate of 25 per cent without any deduction.	Same as above.

capital gains arising on the disposal of the capital asset, in acquiring specified assets within a specified time. Relief may be provided either by way of complete exemption from CGT or in the form of deferrement of gain until further disposal. The main reliefs from the CGT provided to the taxpayer in the U.K are given below:

Roll-over Relief on Replacement of Business Assets

Capital gains arising from the disposal of specified assets used for the purpose of a business may be 'rolled over', i.e. deferred, and offset against the cost of acquiring a replacement asset. The cost of the replacement asset in such a case is reduced by the amount of capital gain rolled over. The gain so exempt will be taxable in future when the replacement asset is sold. Exemption is allowed on the following conditions:

1. both old and replacement assets fall within a restricted list, which includes land and building used for business purposes, fixed plant and machinery, ships, aircraft, goodwill and milk and potato quotas.
2. both the assets, the one which is disposed of and the replacement asset must be used for trade purposes throughout the period of ownership.
3. the asset must be replaced within 12 months before or 36 months after the disposal of the old asset. In the case of a depreciable asset, the gain deferred will become taxable even before the disposal of the new asset, if the replacement asset ceases to be used for the purposes of trade or after the expiry of 10 years from the purchase of the replacement asset, whichever is earlier.
4. if the whole of the sale proceeds of old assets are used to acquire the new asset, the whole gain will be rolled over.
5. if only a part of the proceeds are used to acquire the new asset, the amount chargeable shall be the lower of the amount of money retained and not used in the purchase of replacement asset; or the whole of the capital gain arising out of the disposal of the original asset.

Hold-over Relief

Any gain arising on the gift of business assets is taxable in the U.K. in the hands of the transferor. However, the gain arising on a gift of business assets may be held over or deferred until the transferee disposes of the asset received as a gift. The gifts qualifying for the relief as per Sec.165 must be made of any of the following assets:

(a) assets used in a business carried on by the transferor;
(b) agricultural property;
(c) shares or securities in unlisted trading companies; or
(d) shares or securities in listed trading companies where the transferor retains a substantial interest.

Any gain arising from the transfer of the above assets is exempt fully if either no consideration is received or the consideration received is less than the allowable expenditure (allowable expenditure includes the cost of acquisition, incidental cost of acquisition and enhancement expenditure). The gain will be taxable to the extent the consideration received exceeds the allowable expenditure. However, the cost of asset in the hands of transferee will be reduced to the extent the gain is exempt.

Where the asset was used for non-business purposes prior to its transfer, the part of gain related to the non-business use shall not be exempt. Where retirement relief and gift relief both are allowed, the retirement relief is given first and the balance can be claimed as hold-over relief.

Retirement Relief

Any capital gain arising on the disposal of business assets by a sole trader, on the disposal of a partnership share or on the disposal of shares in a personal company (A company is an individual's personal company if the individual is a full time working officer or an employee owning at least five per cent of the voting shares.) is exempt if the taxpayer is at least 50 years old (55 years for disposal between March 19, 1991 and November 28, 1995) or has retired on the grounds of ill-health if the taxpayer is below the age of 50 years (Sec. 163(1). The amount of retirement relief available for the income year 1998-99 is as follows:

(a) 100 per cent of the gains up to £250,000 plus
(b) 50 per cent of the gains between £250,000 and £1,000,000

To claim relief, it is necessary that there must be a material disposal of business assets and the business must have been owned by the taxpayer for at least 10 years. The limits of £2,50,000 and £1,000,000 are scaled down proportionately if the taxpayer has a qualifying period of at least one year but less than 10 years. The relief is mandatory. No claim for relief is required except when the relief is claimed on account of ill health. Retirement relief is available only on the disposal of specified business assets (chargeable business assets). If the relief is given on the sale of shares in an individual's personal company, and the company holds both chargeable business assets as well as non-business assets, then relief on the gain will be allowed as follows:

$$\text{Chargeable gain} \times \frac{\text{Chargeable business assets}}{\text{Total chargeable assets}}$$

Although the limit of retirement claim is fixed, relief may be available in respect of separate disposals of qualifying assets. The retirement relief is given after the indexation allowance but before providing taper relief.

With effect from April 6, 1999, the retirement relief is being phased out as shown in Table 5.7.

As shown in the table, the retirement relief available in respect of capital gains on the disposal of business assets has been reduced gradually from

TABLE 5.7. PHASING OUT OF RETIREMENT RELIEF IN THE U.K.

Income Year	Lower Limit £	Upper Limit £
1998-99	250,000	1,000,000
1999-00	200,000	800,000
2000-01	150,000	600,000
2001-02	100,000	400,000
2002-03	50,000	200,000
2003-04	Nil	nil

Source: Kath Nightingale, *Taxation: Theory and Practice* (London: Pitman, 2000), p. 380.

1999-2000 income year onwards. Also, the retirement relief will not be available from 2003-04 income year.

Re-investment Relief

Chargeable gain arising on the disposal of any asset may be held over if the gain is reinvested in the ordinary shares of a listed trading company carrying on a qualifying trade. Certain activities excluded from qualifying trade are: commodity dealing, banking, insurance, financial or leasing services, legal and accounting services, farming, and property development. To claim relief, the reinvestment must be made either one year before and 3 years after the date of disposal. The amount of relief is the lower of the following:

1. the amount of capital gain reinvested; or
2. the amount of chargeable gain.

This relief is different from the rollover relief. While the rollover relief is available on the basis of proceeds that are invested, the reinvestment relief is based on the amount of capital gain reinvested.

Deferred Relief

Any capital gain arising from the disposal of any asset may be exempt if the taxpayer invests it in any of the following two schemes within a period starting 12 months before and ending 36 months after the date of disposal. These are:

1. Enterprise investment linked scheme.
2. Venture capital trust shares.

The relief is available on a subscription for shares and cannot be obtained where shares are acquired from another shareholder. The exemption is linked to the smallest of the following:

(a) the gain arising on the disposal;
(b) the cost of acquiring eligible shares; or
(c) any lower amount which the claimant may specify.

In the enterprise investment linked scheme (EIS), the relief is available on that part of the capital gain which is invested in shares issued by a company to which the EIS scheme applied. However, the maximum amount which can be invested is limited to £150,000. In the venture capital trust share scheme also, the relief is available on that part of the capital gain which is invested in shares issued by a venture capital trust. In both the cases, the amount must be invested by way of original subscription.

Deferral of Gain on the Transfer of a Business to a Limited Company

Any chargeable gain arising from the transfer of a business to a limited company may be deferred if the following conditions are satisfied:

1. the business is transferred as a going concern.
2. all the assets of the business except cash balance is transferred to the company.
3. the consideration for the transfer is wholly or partly in exchange for shares in the company above.

The relief is automatic and no claim is required. The part of the gain that is held over is calculated as follows:

$$\text{Chargeable gain} \times \frac{\text{Value of the shares received}}{\text{Total consideration received}}$$

The deferred gain will however be taxable in the year in which the transferor disposes of the shares received in exchange for the transfer.

Principal Private Residence

A principal private residence (PPR) is an exempted asset in the U.K. And any capital gain or loss on the sale of it is not taxable [Sec. 223(1)]. It is however necessary that the taxpayer actually resides in the PPR for at least part of the period during which it is owned by him. If a taxpayer has to live in a different accommodation due to job requirement, the condition of actual stay may be relaxed. Further, the last 36 months of ownership are treated as a period of residence whether or not he actually stays in it during that period.

If a property has been occupied as a PPR for only a part of the period of ownership, only a part of the gain realised on its disposal will be exempt. If a taxpayer owns and lives in two or more properties, the taxpayer may elect any property to be regarded as PPR within 2 years of the date.

A married couple may have only one PPR between them, even though they are taxed independently.

THE U.S.

To encourage taxpayers to utilise the capital gains in re-acquiring assets similar to those which are disposed of, exemptions from capital gain is provided subject to the fulfilment of certain conditions. In fact, the gain is not recognised until the capital asset which is reacquired is sold finally or ultimately. The exemptions from capital gains tax (CGT) provided in the U.S. are as follows:

1. Like-kind exchanges.
2. Involuntary conversion.
3. Sale of a personal residence.
4. Exemption from gain of a principal residence.

Like-kind Exchanges

As provided under Sec. 1031, if a property held for productive use in a trade or business or for investment is exchanged for property of like kind which is to be held either for productive use in a trade or business or for investment, then no gain or loss is recognised. Wherever a like-kind exchange takes place, non-recognition of gain or loss is mandatory. A like-kind exchange will be eligible for exemption only when a direct exchange occurs. If there is no direct exchange, exemption may still be granted if the property to be received in exchange is identified within 45 days after the date of transfer of the property relinquished in the exchange. In such a case, the replacement property must be received within the earlier of two periods, i.e. 180 days after the date the taxpayer has transferred the property or the due date of filing return for the year in which the transfer of property occurs.

In the like-kind exchange property, the words *like-kind* have reference to the nature or character of the property and not to its quality. Thus, the exchange of building for a land qualifies as 'like kind' exchange. However, if real property is exchanged for personal property, it will not be treated as 'like-kind'. An exchange of inventory or securities does not qualify as a 'like-kind' exchange. In the case of a like-kind exchange, the gain will be taxable to the extent the basis of property received is less than the fair market value (FMV) of the property transferred. Where property is exchanged partly for like-kind property and partly for money or non-like-kind property, the gain is recognised to the extent of money or non-like-kind property received. (Money or non-like-kind property is known as boot).

The basis of like-kind property received in the U.S. is computed by subtracting the unrecognised gain from its FMV or by adding the unrecognised loss to its FMV.

The holding period of a like-kind property received includes the holding period of the property exchanged. Thus, the period for which the transferred asset was held by the taxpayer is included in the period for which the asset acquired is held prior to its disposal to find out whether the gain or loss, if any is short-term or long-term.

Involuntary Conversions

In the U.S., if a taxpayer realises a gain due to the involuntary conversion of property, such gain may be deferred if a qualifying property is acquired within 2 years after the close of the tax year in which the involuntary conversion occurred (Sec. 1033). The gain is deferred to the extent the cost of property acquired is more than or equal to the amount received from the involuntary conversion. *Qualifying property* is property similar to or related in service or use to the property that is to be converted. It is different from the like-kind exchange because if a building is exchanged for land, both being real property, the exchange is exempt. But if a building is destroyed and against it a new land is purchased, then the capital gain on such conversion will be taxable.

Sec. 1033 is applicable where a property is compulsorily or involuntarily converted into money or another property against the taxpayer's will. An involuntary conversion may arise due to theft, seizure, requisition, condemnation or destruction of the property. The gain will be taxable to the extent the amount realised from the conversion exceeds the cost of the replacement property.

Provisions relating to Sec. 1033 apply in the U.S. only to gains and not to losses. The taxpayer has the right to choose whether or not to apply Sec. 1033 in the case of gain. Thus, the deferral of gain is done at the choice of the taxpayer. But if there is a direct conversion, then non-recognition of the gain is compulsory. As the gain on involuntary conversion is deferred, it becomes taxable at the time the replacement property is sold. As a result, the basis of the replacement property will be the cost of the property less the deferred gain. Another advantage to the taxpayer is that the period of holding of the replacement property includes the holding period of the converted property.

Deferment of Capital Gains on Sale of Principal Residence

Prior to May 7, 1997, any gain recognised on the sale of the principal residence of the taxpayer could be deferred if a new principal residence was acquired or built within two years before and ending 2 years after the sale of the old residence (Sec. 1034). The gain was deferred fully if the cost of the new residence was more than the adjusted sale price of the old residence (the adjusted sale price is the amount realised, reduced by the fixing-up expenses). (Fixing-up expenses are expenses incurred to assist in the sale of the old residence including repairs and the cost of painting). The gain to the extent of the excess of the adjusted sale price over the cost of acquiring the new residence was taxable. The new residence was required to be used as the taxpayer's personal residence during the two-year replacement period. (If the gain on the sale of the principal residence was deferred, the taxpayer would not be entitled to defer the gain again on the sale of the residence within two years from the date of sale.) The old principal residence must have been occupied for the taxpayer's residence prior to sale but it was not necessary for the taxpayer to occupy the old residence on the date of sale. The basis of new residence was the cost of acquiring a new residence less the unrecognised gain on the sale of the old residence. The holding period of the old residence used to be added to the holding period of the new residence.

Exemptions in Respect of Gain on the Sale of Principal Residence

An individual taxpayer who was 55 years old or more, before the sale was entitled under Sec. 121 to exclude gain on the sale of the principal residence up to $125,000 once in a life time if the sale took place before May 7, 1997. (The limit was $62,500 for married taxpayers filing separate returns). However, the *Taxpayer Relief Act,* 1997 replaces the deferral of gain provision (Sec. 1034) and the $125,000 exclusion (Sec. 121) with an election to exclude up to $500,000 ($250,000 in case of married taxpayers filing separate returns) of capital gains on the sale or exchange of a principal residence [amended Sec. 121(b)(3)]. Thus as a result of this new provision any individual taxpayer whether aged 55 years or less on the date of the sale of the residence, can claim exemption up to $500,000 if the returns are filed jointly. However, the taxpayer must have owned and occupied the property as the principal residence for at least 2 of the previous 5 years before the sale or exchange. The exemption is available only for one sale or exchange every 2 years. This change under Sec. 121(b)(3) with increased exemption to all individual taxpayers without any age restriction along with the right to claim exemption once in every 2 years may give boost to housing construction industry as well as lead to more frequent purchase and sale of residential houses.

Business Assets and Depreciation Recapture

During the early and mid-1930's business property was classified as a capital asset. Due to depression in the U.S. economy, many business properties depreciated in value and could be sold only at a loss. However, due to the limited deductibility of capital losses, taxpayers preferred to retain business assets and claimed depreciation for them instead of selling them.

The *Revenue Act,* 1938 added business property to the list of properties not considered to be capital assets. Thus, from1938 to 1948, gains/losses on the sale of business assets were treated as ordinary gains/losses. In those circumstances, taxpayers with appreciated business properties were reluctant to sell the asset because they were supposed to pay tax at a high rate on the sale of assets. Though real property and depreciable assets were excluded from the term capital asset, yet to encourage the mobility of business assets, Sec. 1231 was introduced in 1942 which allowed taxpayers to treat net gains from the sale of business property as capital gains and net losses as ordinary losses. Sec. 1231 provides the maximum benefit to the taxpayer where there are capital gains or losses from the sale of business assets. In the case of gain, the taxpayer gets the benefit of preferential tax treatment and in case of loss, he gets the maximum benefit of loss deduction. A Sec. 1231 Property is a real property or depreciable property used in a trade or business that is held for more than one year.

Recapture Provisions under Section 1245

The Congress on realising that taxpayers claiming depreciation were getting double benefit of depreciation deduction and in case of sale, the benefit of preferential rates, enacted Sec. 1245 in 1962. As a result, a gain from the disposition of Sec. 1245 Property (A Sec. 1245 Property is certain property subject to depreciation and includes depreciable personal property, and intangible assets subject to amortisation. Business and structural components are generally not Sec. 1245 Property.) is treated as ordinary income to the extent of the total amount of depreciation allowed since January 1, 1962. The gain recaptured as ordinary income cannot exceed the amount of the realised gain.

Recapture Provisions under Section 1250

Sec. 1250 was enacted in the U.S., in 1964 in order to extend the 'recapture' concept to include most depreciable real property. Whereas under Sec. 1245, recapture is based upon the total amount of the depreciation allowed, Sec. 1250 applies solely to additional depreciation or excess depreciation. Additional depreciation is the excess of the actual amount of accelerated depreciation over the amount of depreciation that would be deductible under the straight-line method. (A Sec. 1250 property is any depreciable real property other than Sec.1245 property except a non-residential real property placed in service after 1980 and before 1987 under ACRS rules.)

Sec. 1250 has the effect of converting a portion of Sec. 1231 gain into ordinary income when real property is sold or exchanged. Sec. 1250 does not apply to assets sold or exchanged at a loss. Ordinary income as a result of Sec. 1250 cannot exceed the realised gain.

AUSTRALIA

In Australia, though indexation of the cost base is done which ultimately reduces the capital gain, still many exemptions in respect of capital gains are provided either by way of concession for personal requirements or by way of promoting the reinvestment of capital gains. CGT exemptions are given below:

Car and Motor Cycles

Capital gains arising from the transfer or sale of a car, a motorcycle or a similar vehicle are exempt from tax. (A car is a motor vehicle designed to carry a load of less than one tonne and less than nine passengers including the driver.)

Collectables

Capital gains on the transfer of collectables costing AUD500 or less are exempt. A collectable is an artwork, an item of jewellery, an antique, a coin, a medallion, a rare folio, a rare manuscript, a rare book, a postage stamp that is used or kept mainly for personal use or enjoyments. (ITAA 97, Sec.108-10). Capital losses from collectables can only be used to offset capital gains from collectables.

Personal-use Assets

Any capital gain from the sale of a personal-use asset or part of the asset is exempt if it was acquired for AUD10,000 or less. A personal-use asset is a CGT asset other than a collectables that is used or kept mainly for the personal use or enjoyment of the taxpayer. A taxpayer cannot make a capital loss from a personal-use asset.

Damages Received for any Wrong, Injury or Illness

Any gain or loss arising from compensation or damages received for any wrong, injury or illness suffered by a taxpayer is exempt. Winnings or losses from gambling, or a game or a competition with prizes are also exempt.

Main Residence Exemption

In the case of an individual taxpayer, any gain from the transfer of the main residence is exempt provided it was used as the taxpayer's main residence throughout the ownership period and the interest did not pass to the taxpayer as a beneficiary in or as the transfer of the estate of a deceased person. However, a capital gain or loss may arise if the dwelling was also used for income producing purposes. Even after the taxpayer's main residence stops being his/her main residence, it may still be treated as his/her main residence for a maximum period of 6 years, if the dwelling is used for income producing purposes while the taxpayer is absent. If the dwelling is not used for income producing purposes during the taxpayer's absence, it can be treated as the taxpayer's main residence indefinitely. Only a part exemption applies if the dwelling was partly used for income producing purposes at the time it stopped being the taxpayer's actual main residence.

If during a year, a dwelling is the taxpayer's main residence and another dwelling is the main residence of the taxpayer's spouse, only one of the dwellings can be treated as the main residence of both the taxpayer and the spouse for the period. Alternatively, both dwellings can be treated as main residences for the period. If this happens, the exemption is split.

Small Business Retirement Exemption

In the case of a small business, the capital gain arising from the disposal of an active asset[8] may be exempt to the extent the taxpayer elects to treat the capital gain as a retirement benefit, i.e. is an eligible termination payment (ETP) that is taken into consideration while finding out the taxpayer's reasonable benefit limit (RBL). Small business is one where the net value of the business and related businesses and entities is not more than AUD 5,000,000.

An individual carrying on business as a sole trader or partner, private companies and trusts, are all eligible to claim this exemption. The exemption is available only in respect of actual consideration. (i.e. the market value substitution rule does not apply). Further, the taxpayer must have a roll-over asset[9] and must satisfy the asset value test[10] in respect of an income year and the roll-over asset must have been an active asset for more than half the period it was owned by the taxpayer.

There is a lifetime maximum retirement exemption limit of AUD500,000. A taxpayer under 55 years of age can claim exemption only if an amount equal to ETP is immediately rolled over into a complying superannuation fund.

Goodwill Exemption

Capital gains arising in relation to the goodwill of a business may be exempt to the extent of 50 per cent provided the net value of the business and related business is less than the exemption threshold. The net value of business is the amount by which the sum of the market value of the assets including goodwill of the business exceeds the sum of its liabilities. The business exemption threshold for 1998-99 is AUD2,248,000.

Besides the exemptions from capital gains tax as given above, under different circumstances, capital gain may be deferred or rolled over subject to the fulfilment of certain conditions.

Deferment of Capital Gains Tax

In Australia, capital gains tax may be postponed under certain circumstances. Similar to the roll-over provisions applicable in the U.K and the U.S, deferment in Australia also applies in case new assets are acquired or if an individual converts his assets into the shares of a company. The cases where capital gain arising from a CGT event in Australia may be deferred includes the following.

Replacement of Business Assets of an Individual by Shares in the Company

In Australia any capital gain arising on the transfer of CGT assets by an individual to a company may be exempt if the taxpayer opts for roll-over provided the individual receives consideration in the form of non-redeemable shares in the transferee company. (ITAA 97 Sec. 122-15; corresponding to ITAA 36, Sec. 160 ZZN). The market value of the share received by the taxpayer must be substantially the same as the market value of the asset or assets disposed of, reduced by any liabilities assumed by the company in respect of the asset or assets. The exemption is allowed only when the taxpayer owns all the shares in the company just after the CGT event. The exemption is not available for some CGT assets including collectables, personal use assets, or an asset that becomes the trading stock of the company just after the CGT event. Whenever the capital gain is deferred in the above circumstances, the first element of the cost base of each share in the company is the asset's cost base at the time when the taxpayer transferred it minus any liability the company assumes in respect of it.

Replacement Asset Roll-overs

Capital gains arising from the transfer of a CGT asset in Australia may be deferred if a replacement asset or assets are acquired. A replacement asset roll-over may be available in various circumstances including; (1) replacement of a small business asset by a different small business asset; (2) involuntary disposal of asset, (3) exchange of shares in a company for shares in the same company; (4) exchange of units in a unit trust for units in the same unit trust; (5) renewal or extension of a statutory licence. Though there are many more replacement asset roll-over cases, besides the above mentioned case, the first two cases are taken up for comparison purposes. These are as follows:

Small Business Asset Roll-overs

Capital gain arising from the transfer of an active asset by a taxpayer operating a small business, i.e. having a net asset value not exceeding AUD5 million may be deferred if such assets are replaced with other active assets provided; (1) the asset is a roll-over asset of the taxpayer for an income year; (2) for assets other than a share or unit, the asset is either an active asset immediately before the disposal or the asset was an active asset for more than half of the time it was owned by the taxpayer; (3) if the asset is one in respect of which exemption has been claimed earlier, the asset was acquired more than 5 years before the disposal. That means the asset should not be sold before the expiry of 5 years from the date of acquisition and (4) the taxpayer must give in writing his option to claim roll-over relief.

Although shares do not qualify as roll-over assets in general, still they may qualify as a roll-over asset if the company is a resident private company and the taxpayer is the controlling individual of the company at the time of disposal. (Controlling individual is one who has the right to exercise or control the exercise of at least 50 per cent of the power of the company.)

In Australia, a replacement asset may be two or more than two and in case the replacement assets exceed more than one, the net roll-over amount, i.e. deferred capital gain will be apportioned over the replacement assets in a specified manner depending upon whether the replacement asset is goodwill, non-goodwill, shares or units or a mix of any of these.

Where roll-over assets are disposed of in an income year and capital gain arises on such disposal, it may be deferred only when the taxpayer nominates over one or more 'approved assets' as replacement assets in respect of the net roll-over amount (capital gain ITAA 36, Sec. 160ZZPT). The nomination is restricted to approved assets acquired in the period beginning one year before and ending two years after the last disposal by the taxpayer of a roll-over asset in the relevant income year. The nomination must be made within two years of the last disposal of any roll-over asset in the income year to which the roll-over amount relates. There are restrictions on the type of asset to be nominated. A taxpayer cannot nominate an asset for which a capital gain is ignored, e.g. trading stock or an asset used solely to produce exempt income or a roll-over asset that is taken to be disposed of and immediately reacquired by the taxpayer.

Involuntary Disposal of Asset

In Australia, if an asset owned by the taxpayer is compulsorily acquired by an Australian Government agency; or an asset, or part of an asset, owned by the taxpayer is lost or destroyed or if the lease granted by the Australian Government agency expires and is not renewed, in all such cases capital gain may be deferred if a replacement asset or assets are acquired within the time limit (ITAA 97, Sec. 124-70, corresponding to ITAA 36, Sec, 160ZZK; 160ZZL). The exemption is available only if the taxpayer receives money or another asset (or both) as compensation for the CGT event happening or under an insurance policy against the risk of loss or destruction of the asset. The exemption is available if:

1. either the taxpayer acquires another asset or if the part of the original asset is lost or destroyed, incurs expenditure of a capital nature in repairing or restoring it;
2. some of that expenditure is incurred either one year before or one year after the end of the income year in which the CGT event happens;
3. the asset was used for business purposes at the time of CGT event and the new asset is used in a business for a reasonable time after the taxpayer acquired it, and
4. if the original asset was not used in a business, the exemption is available if the new asset is used for a purpose similar to that for which it was originally used before the CGT event happened.

Same Asset Roll-over

Capital gain or loss from a CGT event may be ignored if the taxpayer transfers the asset to another taxpayer. To some extent this provision is similar to the cases in India where transfer is not treated as transfer. Such gain on the transfer of a CGT event may be deferred and taxable in the hands of the transferee when he disposes of the asset received from the taxpayer. A same asset roll-over may be available if:

(a) a CGT event happens to an asset in connection with the breakdown of the taxpayer's marriage;
(b) an asset is transferred between companies in the same wholly owned group; or
(c) the trust deed of a complying fund is amended or replaced.

MALAYSIA

In Malaysia, there are cases where the disposal price is deemed to be the acquisition price and therefore no capital gain arises (Schedule 2 Sec. 3). These cases are:

1. the transfer of assets of a deceased person under his will;
2. the transfer of assets between spouses;

3. the transfer of assets owned by an individual, or his wife or by an individual jointly with his wife or with a connected person to a company controlled by the individual, by his wife or by the individual jointly with his wife or with a connected person for a consideration consisting substantially of shares in the company and the balance of a money payment;
4. an acquisition from or disposal to a nominee or trustee resident in Malaysia by an individual or his wife or by both being absolutely entitled as against the nominee or trustee;
5. conveyance or transfer by way of security;
6. gift made to a government, a state government a local authority, or a charity that is exempt from Malaysian income-tax;
7. the disposal of an asset as a result of a compulsory acquisition under any law;
8. the disposal of an asset by a person to an Islamic bank under a scheme where that person is financed by such a bank in accordance with the syriah principle.

Besides the above cases, where a gift is made between husband and wife, parent and child or between grandparent and grandchild, and the gift is made within 5 years after the date of acquisition of the asset by the donor, no capital gain will arise in the hands of the donor. The cost of the asset to the donee shall be the donor's acquisition price (cost to the donor) plus all the permitted expenses. Where the asset is acquired as a gift on death, instead of the acquisition price, the market value on the date of transfer of ownership of the asset shall be the cost to the recipient.

Transfer of Assets between Companies in the Same Group

In Malaysia, where assets are transferred between companies in the same group to bring about greater efficiency in operation, or between companies in any scheme of reorganisation, reconstruction or amalgamation, or by a liquidator under a scheme of reorganisation, reconstruction or amalgamation, the disposal will not give rise to a gain or loss and therefore no capital gains tax will accrue to the transferor company or the liquidator.

In case there is a transfer of assets between the companies in the same group and the transferee company takes up the assets in its trading stock, at a value which exceeds the acquisition price of the transferor company, the excess will be treated as a taxable gain to the transferee company.

Exemption for Capital Gains in Respect of Private Residence

In Malaysia also, as in the case of U.K, the U.S and Australia, any capital gain arising from the disposal of the private residence by an individual who is a citizen of Malaysia or an individual who is not a citizen but is a permanent resident of Malaysia is exempt from tax.

A private residence is a building or part of a building in Malaysia owned by an individual and occupied or certified for occupation as a place of residence.

An individual is entitled to claim exemption in respect of capital gains tax arising on the disposal of a private residence only in respect of one such residence. However, the individual must elect in writing to the Director General that the exemption shall apply to a particular private residence. A private residence in Malaysia which is owned and occupied by an individual or his wife or by them jointly, will be deemed to be occupied by the individual. Where only part of a building is occupied as a private residence, then at the time of disposal, the exemption will be apportioned in accordance with the area occupied as the private residence.

PAKISTAN

Capital gains arising from the sale of specific assets in Pakistan are exempt from tax. The specific exemption from capital gains are given below:

1. Any distribution received by an assessee from the National Investment (Unit) Trust or a mutual fund established by the Investment Corporation of Pakistan out of the capital gains of the said trust or fund on which tax has already been paid (Clause 112 Schedule II, Part I)
2. Any capital gain arising from the sale of moderaba certificates or any instrument of redeemable capital as defined in the Companies Ordinance, 1984 (XLVII of 1984), listed on any stock exchange in Pakistan or shares of a public company (as defined in the First Schedule) and the Pakistan Telecommunications Corporation Vouchers issued by the Government of Pakistan (Clause 116).
3. Any capital gain arising from the sale of shares of moderaba certificates or a public company (as defined in the First Schedule), derived by any foreign institutional investor duly approved by the Federal Government (Clause 116A).
4. Any capital gain arising from the sale of shares of industrial units of public sector corporations by the Privatisation Commission (Clause 116B).
5. Capital gain arising from the sale of shares of a public company (as defined in the First Schedule) set up in any special industrial zone referred to in Clause (126C) derived by an assessee for a period of five years from the date of commencement of its commercial production (Clause 116C).
6. Capital gain derived by an assessee from an industrial undertaking set up in an area declared by the Federal Government to be a 'zone' within the meaning of the *Export Processing Zones Authority Ordinance*, 1980 (VI of 1980) (Clause 117).
7. Any capital gain derived by an individual from the transfer of his membership rights or share of a stock exchange in Pakistan to a company at any time between July 1, 1988 and June 30, 1999 and between July 1, 2000 and June 30, 2001 (Clause 117A).
8. Any share of income received by an assessee out of capital gains on which tax has been paid by the firm of which he is a partner (Clause 118).
9. Any capital gain derived by an assessee from the sale of shares representing foreign equity in such company and on such conditions as the Federal

Government may by notification in the official gazette specify (Clause 126B(ii)).

Provided that the exemption under this clause shall not be available to an assessee from the sale of shares representing foreign equity in such companies which do not qualify for exemption under sub-clause (1).

INDIA

The following exemptions from capital gains tax are provided in India with a view to encouraging the assessee to buy either similar assets or invest in specified securities.

Capital Gains on the Transfer of Residential House

In case of an individual or HUF any long-term capital gain (LTCG) from the transfer of a residential house shall be exempt to the extent such capital gain is invested in the purchase of another residential house within 1 year before or 2 year after the date of transfer or in constructing a residential house within a period of 3 years after the date of transfer (Sec. 54).

Capital Gains or Transfer of Land
Used for Agricultural Purposes

Any capital gain arising to an individual from the transfer of any agricultural land being used by an individual or his parents for at least 2 years before the transfer, for agricultural purposes, shall be exempt to the extent the capital gain is invested in buying another agricultural land within 2 years from the transfer (Sec. 54B)

Capital Gains on Compulsory Acquisition of
Land and Building

Any capital gain arising to an industrial undertaking from the compulsory acquisition under any law of any land and building shall be exempt to the extent such a capital gain is invested in the purchase or construction of another land and building within 3 years from the date of compulsory acquisition (Sec. 54D).

In all the three cases if the new asset so acquired is transferred within a period of 3 years from the date of its purchase or construction, the cost of the new asset will be reduced by the amount of the capital gain exempted earlier. Thus in such cases, the capital gain which was granted exemption earlier will be taxable on the transfer of the new asset within 3 years.

Investment of Net Sales Consideration in Specified Assets

Any LTCG, arising to any assessee from the transfer of any capital assets on or after 1.10.96 was exempt up to the income year 1999-2000 if the entire net sales consideration was invested within a period of 6 months after the date of such transfer in the specified bonds/debentures/shares of specified institutions/public companies or units of any mutual fund referred to in Sec. 10(23D). The gain was exempt proportionately if only part of the con-sideration was invested in the specified securities (Sec. 54EA).

Investment of Capital Gain in Specified Assets

Prior to the income year 1999-2000, any LTCG, arising to any assessee from the transfer of any capital asset on or after 1.10.96 was exempt to the extent such a capital gain was invested within a period of 6 months from the date of such transfer in a specified asset provided such a specified asset was not transferred or converted into money within a period of 7 years from the date of its acquisition (Sec. 54EB).

If the specified assets were transferred or converted into money within a period of 3 years (Sec. 54EA) and 7 years (Sec. 54EB) from the date of their acquisition the amount of the gain which was exempt earlier was deemed to be the LTCG of the previous year in which such specified securities were transferred or converted into money. The above provisions stand withdrawn from 1.4.2000.

Investment of Capital Gain in Shares of Companies

From the income year 2001-02, one more avenue for claiming exemption of capital gains tax has been added by the *Finance Act*, 2001. Any capital gain arising from the transfer of long-term capital asset shall be exempt if the same is invested in acquiring shares of eligible issue of capital of a company (Sec. 54ED). The *Finance Act*, 2000, has inserted Sec. 54EC applicable from the income year 2000-01. It provides that any capital gain arising from the transfer of any long-term capital asset by an assessee (whether individual, firm, company or other person) shall be exempt to the extent the capital gain is invested within 6 months from the date of transfer in acquiring any bond redeemable after 3 years issued by the National Bank for Agricultural and Rural Development (NABARD) or by the National Highways Authority of India. Such bonds should not be transferred or converted into money before the expiry of 3 years from the date of their acquisition (Sec. 54EC). From the income year 2001-02, bonds issued by Rural Electrification Corporation have also been included as eligible investment for claiming exemption.

Capital Gains on the Transfer of Asset other than a Residential House

In the case of an individual or HUF, any LTCG arising from the transfer of any capital assets other than a residential house property shall be exempt if the net sales consideration is invested in the purchase of a residential house within 1 year before or 2 years after the date of the transfer of the asset or in the construction of a residential house within 3 years after the date of such transfer. The gain will be exempt proportionately if only a part of the net sales consideration is invested (Sec. 54F). The above exemption will be available if the assessee does not own more than one house on the date of the transfer.

If the new house is transferred within a period of 3 years of its purchase or construction, the capital gain earlier exempt shall be taxable as the LTCG in the previous year in which the new asset is transferred. If the individual or HUF, purchase or construct one more residential house (other than the new house) within the time specified, the capital gain exempt under Sec. 54F shall be treated as the LTCG of the year in which the second house is purchased or constructed (Sec. 54F).

Capital Gain on Transfer of Assets in Case of Shifting of Industrial Undertakings from Urban Areas

Any long-term or short-term capital gain arising to any industrial undertaking from the transfer of assets being land, building, plant and machinery effected in the process of shifting from an urban area to any other area shall be exempt to the extent such capital gain is invested for purchasing or constructing a new plant or machinery, or building, or incurring expenses on shifting of the old undertaking or other specified expenses within one year before or 3 years after the date of its transfer. If the new asset is transferred within a period of 3 years of its purchase or construction, the capital gain exempt earlier under Sec. 54G shall be deducted from the cost of acquisition of the new asset. Thus, the gain earlier exempt will be taxable on the sale of the new asset (Sec. 54G).

In all the above cases except Sec. 54EA, 54EB and 54EC, if either the amount of the capital gain or the full value of consideration is not utilised by the assessee in acquiring the specified asset before the date of furnishing the return of income, it should be deposited by him in any branch of a public sector bank in accordance with the Capital Gains Accounts Scheme 1988.

A brief review of capital gains tax reliefs are given in Table 5.8

Conclusion

The base of capital gains tax has been narrowed down further on account of several reliefs and exemptions from capital gains tax in all the selected countries. In the developed countries like the U.K, the U.S. and Australia, gains are normally deferred in case either the sales proceeds or the capital gains are invested in mainly business assets, or replacements assets, and in case of loss or destruction of assets or compulsory acquisition of assets, the money received is invested in restoring the damaged assets or in acquiring the replacement assets. In the U.K., the gain is also deferred if it is invested in specified investment schemes. In the U.S., while the gains on the disposal of business assets are treated as capital gains, the losses on such disposal are treated as ordinary loss, thus providing the maximum benefit to the taxpayer, as he will pay preferential tax on such capital gains and will be able to claim loss adjustment from any income in the current year. However, the gain is treated as ordinary gain to the extent of the depreciation claimed. While in the developed countries, the gain is usually deferred and becomes taxable on the disposal of the asset later on, in India, gains are normally exempt if invested in buying the specified asset except when the new asset is sold

TABLE 5.8. A SUMMARY OF PROVISIONS RELATING TO CAPITAL GAINS TAX RELIEFS

Particulars	U.K.	U.S.	Australia	Malaysia	Pakistan	India
Capital gain reliefs; (a) Deferment	Gain is deferred on replacement of business assets, on gift of specified assets until the transferee disposes of the asset or the gain is invested in the ordinary share of a listed trading company carrying on a qualifying trade, or the gain is invested in specified investment schemes. In case of partial loss or destruction of asset, the gain is deferred if 95% of the sum is invested in restoring the asset, and in case of complete loss or destruction, money received is invested in buying replacement assets within 12 months.	Gain is deferred if property used for business or investment purposes is exchanged for property of like kind to be used for the same purpose or if an involuntary conversion takes place due to theft, seizure, condemnation or destruction of property and a qualifying property is purchased.	Gain is deferred if an individual receives non-redeemable shares in a company in lieu of transfer of business assets to a company, or if a taxpayer running a small business disposes of active assets and replaces them with other active assets or in the case of loss, destruction or compulsory acquisition of asset by the government agency, the taxpayer acquires another asset or incurs expenditure of a capital nature in repairing or restoring it.	Gain is deferred in cases gift is made between husband and wife, parent and child or between grandparent and grandchild or if a gift is made to government, state government. Gain is exempt in the case of transfer of assets of a deceased person under his will, or if there is transfer of assets between spouses, or if there is compulsory acquisition under any law, or if a gift is made to the government state government.	No incentive is provided in the form of deferment of capital gain in Pakistan. Capital gains arising from the disposal of specific assets including moderba certificates, shares of a public company set up in a special industrial zone and from the sale of shares representing foreign equity in such a company are exempt.	Gain is deferred if capital gain on the transfer of a residential house is invested in a new house or if on transfer of agricultural land a new agricultural land is acquired within two years or if on compulsory acquisition of land and building forming part of an industrial undertaking, a new land or building is acquired within three years or if on transfer of any asset, the amount is invested in acquiring specified assets or bonds within a specified period. In all the above cases, if the new asset is sold after the expiry of three years, from the date of transfer, the gain on the transfer will be exempt.
(b) Exemption	Gain up to a fixed limit is exempt on the disposal of business assets by an individual who is 50 years old or has retired due to ill health.		Gain may be exempt, if the taxpayer opts to treat the capital gain arising from the disposal of active asset of a small business as retirement benefit. Gain is exempt in case of sale of personal use asset upto AUD10,000.			

before the expiry of 3 years. In Malaysia and Pakistan, capital gain on the compulsory acquisition of an asset is exempt. In Pakistan, capital gain on the disposal of many specified shares is also exempt.

To sum up, it has been found that all these countries provide concession in tax on capital gains arising from the transfer of assets held for more than one year. More incentives are provided in respect of gains on business assets. However, personal-use assets are not treated as capital assets up to a certain fixed limit in the U.K. and Australia. So far as residential property is concerned, gain on the transfer of only such residential property is exempt in the hands of either the husband or wife, in the case of married taxpayers in all these countries without any condition of re-investment in new-residential property. In India, exemption is given only when a new residential house is purchased.

CAPITAL GAINS AND TAX REVENUE

Capital gains tax provisions in most of these countries are very detailed and many tax reliefs are provided. Several reliefs and exemptions have affected tax revenue. The statistics available in respect of some of these countries reveals that capital gains tax revenue is negligible in all these countries.

The share of capital gains income of individual taxpayers in the total income and the share of capital gains tax in the total tax of the selected countries is given in Table 5.9.

As shown in Table 5.9, capital gains income constitute a very small part of total income in all these countries. It forms only around 1 per cent in the U.K., and Australia, 3 per cent in India and 5 per cent in the U.S. As compared to this ratio, the ratio of CGT to total tax is higher in all these countries, i.e. around 2 per cent in the U.K. and Australia, around 4 per cent in India and maximum in the U.S., i.e. 11 per cent. The ratio of CGT to the total tax in the U.S. appears to be high because capital gains do not get any other concession except for preferential tax rates.

The share of capital gains income of corporate taxpayers in the total income and the share of capital gain tax in the total tax of the selected countries is given in Table 5.10.

As shown in the table, ratio of capital gains income to total income in the case of corporate taxpayer as compared to the ratio in the case of individual taxpayer is much higher in all the three developed countries. However, the ratio is much less in India, the only developing country for which statistical data is available. The ratio is 18 per cent in the U.S., followed by 7 per cent in the U.K., 4 per cent in Australia and is the lowest, i.e. 1.45 per cent in India. The ratio of CGT to total tax is higher in the case of corporate taxpayers of the developed countries. The ratio is again highest in the U.S., i.e. 25 per cent, 5 per cent in Australia and 4.88 per cent in the U.K., and is around 1.36 per cent in India. One obvious reason for this is that in the U.K., U.S., and Australia, company tax rates are applicable on LTCG, whereas the rates on LTCG of companies in India is a flat rate of 20 per cent, which is

TABLE 5.9. CAPITAL GAINS INCOME AS PERCENTAGE OF TOTAL INCOME AND CAPITAL GAINS TAX AS PERCENTAGE OF TOTAL TAX OF INDIVIDUAL TAXPAYERS

(amount is in millions)

Particulars	U.K. £ (1997-98)	U.S. $ (1997)	Australia AUD (1997-98)	Malaysia RM	Pakistan PKR	India Rs. (1996-97)
Capital Gains	5470 (1.15)[1]	244027 (5.62)	4656 (1.63)	n.a.[2]	n.a.	26023 (3.01)
Total Income	475170	4342703	284953	n.a.	n.a.	864233
Capital Gains Tax	1664 (2.05)[3]	68328 (11.37)	1570 (2.30)	n.a.	n.a.	4951 (4.48)
Total Tax	81164	601059	68390	n.a.	n.a.	110548

Notes: 1. Figures in brackets show percentage of capital gains to total income.
2. n.a. means not available.
3. Figures in brackets show percentage of capital gains tax to total tax.

Sources: 1. *Inland Revenue Statistics, 1999,U.K.*
2. *IRS, Statistics of Income Bulletin*, Winter 1998-99,U.S.
3. *Taxation Statistics*, 1997-98, Australia.
4. *Taxation Statistics*, 1998, Malaysia.
5. *All India Income Tax Statistics*, Assessment year 1997-98, India.

much less than the corporate tax rate in India.

In terms of equity it is difficult to judge as to which country provides more equitable basis. Each country has its own priorities. However, one point is clear that in all the three developed countries, instead of exemptions, gains are deferred till the new asset which is purchased is sold again. While in the U.K., U.S., Australia, no concession in tax rate on capital gain is provided to company taxpayers, in India, the companies also enjoy tax rate concession similar to individuals. In the U.S., to prevent taxpayers from showing losses,

TABLE 5.10. CAPITAL GAINS INCOME AS PERCENTAGE OF TOTAL INCOME AND CAPITAL GAINS TAX AS A PERCENTAGE OF TOTAL TAX OF CORPORATE TAXPAYERS

(amount is in millions)

Particulars	U.K. £ (1997-98)	U.S. $ (1997)	Australia AUD (1997-98)	Malaysia RM	Pakistan PKR	India Rs. (1996-97)
Capital Gains	9100 (7.19)[1]	171035 (18.68)	4010 (4.02)	n.a.[2]	n.a.	12244 (1.45)
Total Income	126550	915397	99737	n.a.	n.a.	844514
Capital Gains Tax	1847 (4.88)[3]	59862 (25.00)	1056 (5.00)	n.a.	n.a.	3713 (1.36)
Total Tax	37856	239394	21082	n.a.	n.a.	270035

Notes: 1. Figures in brackets show percentage of capital gains to total income.
2. n.a. means not available.
3. Figures in brackets show percentage of capital gains tax to total tax.

Source: Same as for Table 5.9.

special tax avoidance provisions are included in the case of gift of assets or conversion of personal-use assets to business use. In Malaysia and India, conversion of capital asset into stock-in-trade is treated as transfer of assets.

As far as administrative convenience is concerned, the U.S. law is easier to administer. The provisions in the U.K., Australia and India are vast and complicated.

After analysing the taxation of capital gains in selected countries, one reaches a conclusion that all countries have not accepted the argument that capital gain is an income like any other income. All these countries treat the capital gain differently from the other income. Capital gains is not considered as ordinary income. That is why all the countries have provided various reliefs in one way or the other. After going through the provisions and capital gain tax collection in these countries for levying capital gains tax, the real objective appears not so much to raise revenue as to plug the possible leakage in tax collection and also to use the capital gains tax provisions as social welfare measures and as an incentive to give direction and growth to the economy.

NOTES

1. *London County Council* vs *Attorney General* (1990) 4TC 265 (H.L.).
2. Thomas R. Pope and John. L. Kramer, *Prentice-Hall Federal Taxation 1998: Individuals* (Upper Saddle River, N.J.: Prentice-Hall, 1997), p. V-33.
3. Kath Nightingale, *Taxation: Theory and Practice* (London: Pitman, 2000), p. 269.
4. Connected persons include an individual's spouse, relatives (i.e. brothers, sisters, ancestors and direct descendents) and their spouses, business partners and their spouses and relatives.
5. Alan Melville, *Taxation Finance Act,* 2000 (Harlow, England: Pearson Education Ltd., 2001), p. 257.
6. Veerinderjeet Singh and Teoh Boon Kee (eds.), *Malaysian Master Tax Guide* (Singapore: CCH Asia PTE Ltd., 2000), p. 693.
7. Richard Thornton, *MLJ Tax Handbook* (Kuala Lumpur: Malaysian Law Journal, 1998), p. 111.
8. Active assets: An 'active asset' is an asset such as plant and machinery owned by the taxpayer and used in the course of carrying on a business. Active assets do not include shares in companies or interest in trust.
9. Roll-over assets: A roll-over asset is an asset of a business carried on by a taxpayer excluding share in a company or unit in a unit trust and such an asset was disposed of in the income year and the asset value test is satisfied at the disposal test time.
10. Asset value test: The asset value test means that the sum of the following should not exceed AUD five million.
    (a) the net value of the assets of a taxpayer;
    (b) the net value of the assets of entities connected with the taxpayer;
    (c) the associate's share of the net value of the partnership assets.

CHAPTER 6

Tax Reliefs and Tax Incentives

Relief from tax in one form or the other is provided in many countries in order to achieve various social and economic objectives. Many of the reliefs are provided to taxpayers on the basis of income, age, gender and health. Others are allowed in order to promote a particular activity in a backward or a remote area, or to encourage foreign investment, or for any other specified purpose. Different terms are used in different parts of the world for such tax reliefs. These terms are 'tax expenditure', 'tax preference', 'tax break', 'tax incentives', 'tax reliefs' 'tax rebates', or 'tax credits'.

Tax relief is a fiscal advantage conferred on a group of taxpayers or in respect of a particular activity, by reducing the tax liability rather than the payment of a cash subsidy. The first report of the United States Secretary of the Treasury on tax expenditures defined tax expenditure as 'the major respects in which the current income tax base deviates from widely accepted definitions of income and standards of business accounting and from the generally accepted structures of an income tax'.[1]

According to McLure, the rationale for tax incentives is not clearly defined and may include industrialisation, technology transfer, provision of jobs and development of economically backward regions.[2] Each incentive is meant to provide some benefit or promote some activity. Investment incentives encourage the use of capital-intensive methods of production, whereas, employment incentives encourage the use of labour-intensive technology. Incentives provided to achieve one objective might however distort other objectives. Incentives to encourage industrialisation may also encourage migration to cities, thus aggravating urban problem.

According to tax incentives undermine the equity of the tax system as they primarily benefit wealthy investors. Further, the loss of revenues inherent in the provision of tax incentives implies that tax rates must be higher than otherwise. Besides having an adverse effect on non-preferred sectors, high tax rates cause a problem that is not adequately recognised. They accentuate the need to use 'creative accounting' to shift income (from non-preferred activities) to jurisdictions where tax-rates are lower and to shift deductions into jurisdictions offering the incentives.

It is indeed true that the provision of a large numbers of tax incentives complicate the tax system as many conditions are required to be fulfilled to avail of these incentives, and consequently, tax rates to the desired extent have to be increased to compensate for the loss of revenue involved. Reduction in tax rates and the elimination or substantial reduction in tax incentives, were in fact the two major tax reforms proposed by many authors, policy-makers and tax reform committees during the eighties and the nineties.

The legal provisions relating to tax incentives in the selected countries are analysed in this chapter. (Exempted incomes are outside the preview of this chapter.)

The chapter has been divided into three sections:

1. Social-welfare incentives
2. Investment incentives
3. Business incentives

SOCIAL-WELFARE INCENTIVES

These incentives take the form of either a tax-free threshold or personal allowance, spouse allowance, dependent allowance or are by way of a higher allowance or rebates to aged and disabled persons. The social-welfare incentives in the selected countries are examined below.

THE U.K.

In the U.K., various allowances are allowed to the taxpayer based on his personal needs and circumstances. While some allowances are deducted from the statutory total income, other allowances are tax reducers, i.e. deducted from the tax liability. The amount of these allowances are adjusted for inflation every year. The social-welfare incentives provided in the UK are as follows:

Personal Allowance

All resident individuals and some non-resident individuals are entitled to a personal allowance. In the U.K., there is no minimum exemption or tax-free threshold. This personal allowance is in fact a substitute for the tax-free threshold. The amount of personal allowance for the income year 2000-01 is £4,385 for taxpayers who are below 65 years of age, £5,790 for taxpayers between 65 and 74 years of age and £6,050 for taxpayers over 75 years of age.[3] The amount of the increased allowance available to older taxpayers is reduced if the total income exceeds £17,000 by one-half of the excess. This process of reduction continues until the personal allowance is reduced to the level of £4,385. This means even individuals who are earning high income and are above 65 years of age will receive the minimum basic exemption of £4,385 in any case. Husband and wife are entitled to receive the allowance separately. The allowance is given in full in the income year in which a taxpayer is born or dies and is available to adults and children.

Married Couple Allowance

In the U.K., Married Couple Allowance (MCA) was allowed to all the married couples up to the income year 1999-2000. However, from the income year 2000-01, it is available to a married couple who live together for at least a part of the tax year so long as at least one of the spouses was born before April 6, 1935. Thus, this allowance is now allowed to older couples, or to couples at least one of the spouses of which is older.

This allowance is deducted from the tax liability at the rate of 10 per cent of the allowance. For the income year 2000-01, the allowance is £5,185, unless the older spouse is aged 75 or more at any time during the year, in which case the allowance rises to £5,255. This allowance, like personal allowance, is reduced if the statutory total income of the husband exceeds £17,000 by one half of the excess. However, the allowance is never reduced to less than a specified minimum amount which is £2,000.

Children's Tax Credit

In the U.K., till the income year 1999-2000, an additional personal allowance (APA) to the extent of £1,970 was allowed to certain taxpayers who had a qualifying child resident with them for at least part of the income year. The allowance was intended primarily to help single-parent families. The *Finance Act*, 1999, however, has abolished this allowance and has introduced a new allowance, known as children's tax credit (CTC). This allowance is available from April 6, 2001 and it allows credit to the taxpayers who have one or more children under the age of 16 living with them. The credit is allowed at the rate of 10 per cent of the amount which is £4420 for income year 2001-02.

The tax credit will be allowed to the partner with the higher income, if a child is living with a couple, whether married or unmarried. In case, neither partner is a higher tax rate taxpayer, the couple can make a choice to share it equally or to allocate the whole credit to either of them. However, both the CTC and the MCA (for older taxpayers) cannot be claimed. A taxpayer, who is entitled to claim both, the MCA and the CTC, may elect to claim either of the two, whichever is more beneficial to him.

Widow's Bereavement Allowance

Widow's Bereavement Allowance (WBA) was allowed to the widow in the year in which the husband died, provided they were living together at the time of death and were not separated. The amount of WBA is £2,000 for the year 2000-01, to be deducted from tax liability at 10 per cent of the allowance. This allowance has been abolished from the income year 2001-02.

Blind Person's Allowance

An individual who at any time is registered as blind in a register maintained by a local authority may obtain a Blind Person's Allowance (BPA) of £1,400 for the income year 2000-01. It is deductible from the taxable income.

The allowances are given in full in the income year in which the taxpayer is first registered as a blind person. If both husband and wife are registered blind persons, they can each claim the allowance. If a husband or a wife who is granted the BPA cannot make full use of it, then the unused part can be transferred to the other spouse, even if that spouse is not a registered blind person.

Private Medical Insurance

Any premium paid on private medical insurance on policy taken before July 2, 1997 for persons aged 60 or over were deductible.

Maintenance Payments

The payer of maintenance payments made to the child under 21 years or ex-spouse is entitled to claim for tax relief at 10 per cent of the amount paid or £1,970, for the 1999-2000, whichever is lower, provided the payment is made under a court order. Thus, it is allowed by way of rebate from the tax liability.

Incentive for Vocational Training

Any payments in the form of course fees and examination fees paid by an individual for his or her vocational training is allowed as deduction, if the trainee is 30 years or over and the training is full time, and for more than four weeks, but less than a year.

Gift Aid Scheme

As an inducement to charity, a Gift Aid Scheme is available in the U.K. This scheme encourages individuals to make lump sum donations to charity and obtain tax relief. To qualify, the donation must be in money and should not be subject to any condition leading to repayment. The sum paid must not be less than £250. No upper limit is placed on the maximum sum which an individual may contribute under the scheme.

Deed of Covenant

An individual is entitled to deduct and retain income tax at the basic rate (23 per cent for income year 1999-2000) on payment made under a deed of covenant.[4] The charity can obtain repayment of the tax deducted from the Inland Revenue Board. A taxpayer liable to tax at the higher rate of 40 per cent can obtain further relief by offset against income otherwise chargeable at higher rate. The company can also claim the advantage of making payment under the deed of covenant.

Gift Aid Scheme and Deed of Covenant have undergone a radical change from April 6, 2000. The new Gift Aid Scheme applies to any charitable donation, large or small, whether one off or made regularly according to the terms of the deed of covenant. The gift is treated as if it was made net of basic rate of income tax (22 per cent for income year 2000-01) and the charity can then recover the amount of tax which is deemed to have been deducted at source. The donor is required to pay income tax equal to at least the amount of tax deemed to have been deducted from the gift.

THE U.S

Many social-welfare incentives are provided in the U.S. which take care of the basic requirements and other special circumstances of individuals who are by far the largest single group of taxpaying entity there.

Social-welfare incentives in the U.S. are provided in the form of deductions as well as rebates. Deductions allowed from the adjusted gross income[5] (AGI) are of two types. These are:

A. Personal and dependency exemptions.
B. Standard deductions and itemized deductions.

Besides this, some incentives are also provided in the form of tax credits.

Personal and Dependency Exemptions

These exemptions are provided to enable taxpayers to fulfil their basic requirements as well as to give some relief to those who look after either dependent child or relative.

Personal Exemption

Though there is no tax-free threshold or basic exemption for the individual taxpayer, each individual taxpayer is allowed a personal exemption of $2,750 for the income year 1999. This exemption is deducted from the AGI to arrive at the taxable income.

Exemption for Spouse

A married taxpayer is entitled to claim exemption for spouse also. The amount is same as is for the personal exemption, i.e. $2,750 for the income year 1999. To claim exemption for spouse, the individual must be married at the close of the tax year, or if any spouse dies, at the date of death. The taxpayer and the spouse need not live together. Persons legally divorced or separated under a decree are considered single and not married. If the spouse had any gross income, the taxpayer can claim his or her exemption only if he or she files a joint return. However, even if an individual file a separate return, he or she may claim exemption for spouse provided the spouse had no gross income and was not a dependent of another taxpayer. This exemption is also deducted from the AGI.

Exemption for Dependants

Besides the above two exemptions, an individual is allowed a further exemption of $2,750 for each dependent. It is deducted from the AGI. To qualify as a dependent, a person must meet the following five tests:

1. The person must be either a relative or a full time member of taxpayer's household.
2. The person must be a citizen or resident of the U.S. or a resident of Canada or Mexico.

TABLE 6.1. THRESHOLD AMOUNT FOR PHASING OUT PERSONAL AND DEPENDENCY EXEMPTIONS

(for the income year 1999)

Filing Status	Base Amount
Single taxpayer	$ 126,600
Married taxpayers filing returns jointly and surviving spouse	$ 189,950
Head of household	$ 158,300
Married taxpayers filing returns separately	$ 94,975

Source: CCH, 2000, *U.S. Master Tax Guide*, p. 99.

3. The person must not file a joint return with another person.
4. The person must receive one-half of his or her support from the taxpayer.
5. The person must have less than $2,750 in 1999 in gross income for the year unless he or she is taxpayer's child and is either under age 19 or a full time student under the age of 24.

In the case of divorced parents, the parent normally having the custody of the child is entitled to claim the exemption.

The benefit of personal exemption, exemption for spouse and exemption for dependants are adjusted for inflation every year and are phased out for taxpayers whose AGI level exceeds a fixed amount. The reduction starts when the AGI exceeds the following base amounts, which depends on the individual's filing status. The amount at which phasing out of exemptions begin is given in Table 6.1.

For married individuals filing returns jointly in 1999, the personal and depending exemption is reduced by 2 per cent for each $2,500 or a fraction thereof by which the AGI exceeds the base amount. For married individuals filing returns separately, the exemption is reduced by 2 per cent for each $1,250 or fraction thereof by which AGI exceeds the base amount. Thus, the personal and dependency exemption are not available when the AGI reaches a certain level.

Standard Deduction and Itemized Deductions

While personal expenses are not allowed as deduction in general, certain specified personal expenses, losses and contributions including medical expenses, charitable contributions, investment interest, casualty and theft losses and miscellaneous deductions are allowed as deductions within limits by way of *itemized deductions*. To claim it, one has to keep necessary records to give proof of the genuineness of the expenditure or loss or contribution. With a view to avoid this record keeping, the Congress in the U.S. has allowed deduction of a fixed amount known as *standard deduction*. The individual taxpayer can claim the higher of the two, i.e. itemized deduction or standard deduction.

Standard Deduction

The amount of the standard deduction is based on the filing status of the taxpayer, i.e. whether single[6] or married filing returns separately or married

TABLE 6.2. AMOUNT OF STANDARD DEDUCTION ALLOWED TO DIFFERENT CATEGORIES OF TAXPAYERS

Filing Status	Standard Deduction (Income Year 1999)
Single taxpayers	$4300
Married taxpayers filing returns jointly and surviving spouses	$7200
Married taxpayers filing returns separately	$3600
Head of household	$6350

Source: Same as given in Table 6.1, p. 97.

filing returns jointly or surviving spouse or head of the household[7] and is adjusted for inflation every year. The amount of standard deduction for the income year 1999 is given in Table 6.2.

Taxpayers who are either blind or who have attained the age of 65 years by the end of the income year are allowed *additional standard deductions*. The additional amount for married individuals (whether filing jointly or separately) and surviving spouses is $850 in the income year 1999. Thus, married taxpayers can claim four additional standard deduction amounts if both of them are over 65 years and blind.

Although an individual can claim higher of the two deductions, i.e. itemized deduction or standard deduction, in the case of a married taxpayer filing return separately, if one spouse itemises, the other must also itemize, or else he will not be entitled to claim standard deduction.

Itemized Deductions

Itemized deductions are allowed from the adjusted gross income (AGI) in lieu of the standard deduction. Various itemized deductions allowed are given below:

Medical Expenses

Medical expenses paid by the taxpayer for himself, his or her spouse or the dependent are deductible to the extent they exceed 7.5 per cent of the taxpayer's AGI. The purpose of fixing this limit seems to be that time and paper work spent in checking small medical bills is saved. Small income taxpayers whose medical expenses are less can make use of standard deduction. The higher income earners who itemize their expenses are disallowed medical expenses upto 7.5 per cent of the AGI. Transport and meal expenses essential to qualified medical cases are also part of medical expenses, but meal expenses are deductible to the extent of 50 per cent. $50 per individual is fixed for lodging of the patient or nurse, parent or spouse. Medical insurance premium and contribution to medical savings account also qualify for the deduction.

Certain Taxes

Certain specified taxes are allowed as deduction from gross income if directly connected with trade or business and these taxes are allowed as itemized deductions if incurred for personal use. The few taxes that are allowed as itemized deductions are given below:

(a) State, local or foreign real property tax.
(b) State or local personal property tax if based on value.
(c) State, local and foreign income, war profits and excess profits taxes.

Charitable Contribution

An individual in the U.S. is allowed itemized deduction for any charitable contribution made to a qualified organisation upto a maximum of 50 per cent of the taxpayer's AGI. The deduction is allowed in the year in which contributions are made, irrespective of the taxpayer's method of accounting.

If a person donates a property instead of cash, in such a case its value depends upon whether it is capital gain property[8] or ordinary income property.[9] A capital gain property is valued at the fair market value (FMV) on the date of contribution. However, to prevent the misuse of charitable contribution provisions, in case a capital gain property is donated to a private non-operating foundation, or in case such property is donated to a charity but the charity uses the property unrelated to its charitable function, in both the cases the amount of the contribution deduction must be equal to the property's FMV minus the LTCG, that would be recognised if the property were sold at its FMV.

If ordinary income property is contributed to a charitable organisation, the deduction is equal to the property's FMV minus the amount of gain that would be recognised if the property were sold at its FMV.

The overall limit of 50 per cent will be reduced to 30 per cent of the AGI for contribution of cash or ordinary income property to private non-operating foundations and capital gain property to public charities. Contributions in excess of deductible ceiling for any income year can be carried forward for a period of 5 years.

Interest

The deductibility of interest income in the U.S. depends upon its nature. If any interest is paid to earn business or trading income, it is fully deductible from the gross income, i.e. it is a deduction for AGI. Investment interest is deductible to the extent of the taxpayer's net investment income (excess of investment income over investment expense). This restriction is imposed to prevent the taxpayer from avoiding the tax by investing in assets, which are appreciative in value, but do not provide any income or provide negligible income.

Although personal interest is not deductible since 1990 onwards, interest expenses incurred to purchase, construct or improve a qualified residence is allowable as discussed later on in this chapter under the head investment-related incentives.

Casualty and Theft Losses

Casualty and theft losses include losses that arise due to fire, storm, shipwreck theft or other casualty. According to the Internal Revenue Service (IRS), a deductible casualty loss is one that has occurred in an identifiable event that was sudden, unexpected or unusual. Casualty and theft losses incurred during the course of business are deductible from the gross income (for AGI deduction), while such losses of a personal nature are deductible by way of itemized deduction (from AGI deduction). Casualty losses on personal use property are reduced by $100 for each separate casualty and then the total amount of all net casualty losses for such property are reduced by 10 per cent of the taxpayer's AGI for the year. Thus, these losses form part of the itemized deduction and deductible only when the total of all net casualty losses exceed 10 per cent of the AGI.

The amount of loss sustained in a casualty is the amount by which the property's FMV is reduced as a result of the casualty. If business or investment property is fully destroyed in a casualty, the loss will be the taxpayer's adjusted basis in the property, even if it is greater than the property's FMV. But if a personal-use property is totally destroyed, the amount of the loss is limited to the lesser of the reduction in the property's FMV or the property's adjusted basis.

Miscellaneous Itemized Deductions

Besides the above specified itemized deductions, there are other miscellaneous expenses, which are allowed as itemized deductions subject to some limits. These are as follows:

(a) Employment-related expenses of employees such as unreimbursed expenditure for travel and transport, union dues, subscriptions to trade journals, and dues to professional organisations.
(b) Investment-related expenditures such as rental fees for safe-deposit boxes and bank service charge if these are incurred for non-business purpose.
(c) Cost of tax advice such as the tax return preparation fees and appraisal fees incurred in determining the amount of a casualty loss related to personal use.

The above expenses are deductible as itemized deduction subject to 2 per cent of the AGI limitation, i.e. these are allowed to the extent they exceed 2 per cent of the AGI.

The total amount of itemized deductions is further reduced for high income taxpayers' by the lesser of 3 per cent of the AGI over the threshold amount which was $126,600 for the income year 1999 ($63,300 for married people filing separate returns) or 80 per cent of the total itemized deductions other than medical expenses, investment interest, casualty losses and wagering losses.

Thus, while taxpayers are entitled to various itemized deductions only when expenses, contributions or losses exceed a certain fixed percentage of the AGI, the total amount of these deductions are reduced to a fixed limit and therefore high income earner cannot take undue advantage in case they incur more expenses or pay a higher contribution for charitable purposes.

Tax Credits

Many other incentives in the U.S. are provided in the form of tax credits, i.e. by way of deduction from the tax liability. While incentives in the form of deductions from total income are more beneficial for the high income taxpayer's point of view, the incentives in the form of tax credits are equally beneficial to higher and lower taxpayers both. Personal tax credits are provided in the U.S as a social welfare measure to provide tax relief to low income earners or elderly taxpayers or to those taxpayers who incur expenses on the maintenance of child and dependants. Business tax credits are provided to encourage research activities or to encourage employment in distressed urban and rural areas. Tax credits may be refundable (i.e. excess of tax credit over tax liability may be refunded to the taxpayer) or non-refundable (i.e. tax credit is allowed only to the extent of tax liability). However, some non-refundable tax credits are allowed to be carried over upto a limited time and adjusted in the earlier or future year's tax liability. Most of the tax credits except the *earned income credit* are non-refundable. Personal tax credits allowed in the U.S. are as under:

Child and Dependent Care Credit

The child and dependent care credit is allowed to taxpayers who incur qualifying child or dependent care expenses (expenses incurred for house keeping, nursing and baby sitting) due to their being engaged in employment. The credit is designed to encourage taxpayers who work and have children to provide them with adequate care while they are at work. The credit is available if the taxpayer incurs qualifying expenditure[10] for the care of the following individuals.

(a) A dependent under the age of 13 years;
(b) Any person including the taxpayer's spouse who is physically or mentally incapable of caring for himself or herself;
(c) Certain dependent children of divorced parents.

The credit is equal to 30 per cent of employment-related expenses (for the income year 1999) for taxpayers with AGI of $10,000 or less. The maximum amount of eligible employment-related expenses is $2,400 for one qualifying child or dependent and $4,800 for two or more dependants. The expenses are limited to the extent of earned income.[11] In the case of married taxpayers, expenses are limited to the earned income of the lower earning spouse. The credit is reduced by one percentage point for each $2,000 of AGI or fraction thereof over $10,000. The credit is not reduced below 20 per cent and is 20 per cent if the AGI is $28,000.

Thus, not only the expenses eligible for rebate are upto a certain fixed amount, the percentage of benefit is also reduced as the AGI exceeds $10,000.

Adoption Credit

Individual taxpayers can claim a credit of $5,000 for the income year 1999 ($6,000 in the case of child with special needs) for qualifying adoption expenses[12] incurred for each eligible child[13] The credit is phased out rateably for taxpayers with a modified adjusted gross income over $75,000 and is reduced to zero if that exceeds $115,000.

Credit for the Elderly or the Disabled

This credit is allowed to taxpayers or their spouse who are 65 years old or more or those taxpayers who are below 65 years of age but are totally or permanently disabled. For the income year 1999, the credit is allowed to the extent of 15 per cent of an initial amount of $5,000($7,500 for married individuals filling jointly). The credit is reduced for those taxpayers whose AGI exceeds certain limit (reduced to zero if the AGI exceeds $17,500 for individual taxpayers and $25,000 for married taxpayers filing joint return). Credit is also reduced if any non-taxable social security or pension is received.

Child Tax Credit

With effect from the income year 1998, taxpayers are allowed child tax credit in respect of a child, dependent step child, or eligible foster child who is below 17 years of age and is a U.S. citizen. The amount of credit is $500 for the income year 1999. The amount is reduced gradually when the AGI exceeds $110,000 for married taxpayers filing jointly and $55,000 for married taxpayers filing returns separately and $75,000 for single taxpayers.

Higher Education Tax Credits

Individual taxpayers who incur expenses for higher education can elect to claim one of two tax credits: the Hope Scholarship Tax Credit (HSTC) or the Lifetime Learning Tax Credit. Started in 1998, these credits are allowed in respect of tuition and related fees incurred by students pursuing college or graduate degrees or vocational training. The maximum amount of eligible Hope Scholarship Tax Credit is $1,500 per student for each of the first two years of post secondary education. The Lifetime Learning Tax Credit allowance is equal to 20 per cent of qualified higher education expenses (maximum up to $5,000 expenses). The maximum amount of such credit cannot exceed $1,000 irrespective of the amount of qualified expenses. Married taxpayers must file a joint return to claim either of the credit. Like other credits, these credits are also phased out if the modified AGI reaches a certain level, and are reduced to zero if it exceeds a certain limit.

Earned Income Credit

This credit is allowed to an individual with qualifying children and to certain individuals without children if either the individual or his spouse is at least 25 but not more than 64 years of age and whose modified AGI (AGI including tax-free interest, non-taxable pension, annuity and 75 per cent of brought forward business loss) or earned income, the higher of the two does not exceed certain limit. Maximum credit allowed for the income year 1999 is $347 for an individual without a qualifying child, $2,312 with one qualifying child and $3,816 with more than one qualifying child. This credit is refundable. No credit is allowed if his investment exceeds $2,350 (investment income includes, dividends, taxable and tax-free interest, net rental income and capital gain net income).

Thus, all these tax credits in the U.S. are gradually reduced as the AGI of the taxpayer exceeds a certain fixed limit.

AUSTRALIA

Social-welfare incentives provided under the income tax law of Australia are as follows:

Personal Exemption/Tax-free Threshold

In a manner similar to the U.S. tax system, incentives in Australia are provided by way of deductions and tax rebates. In Australia, a tax free threshold of AUD 6,000 for the income year 2000-01 is allowed to all individual taxpayers. Besides this, many personal rebates are allowed which provide tax reliefs to individual taxpayers. These include dependent rebates, sole parent rebate, medical expenses rebate, and low income rebate. As the provisions relating to tax rebates are vast and these rebates are allowed subject to various conditions, only some aspects of tax rebates have been covered under this chapter. Although some of these rebates including child rebate, sole parent rebate and spouse rebate with dependent child are not allowed during the income year 2000-01, these are, however, required to be calculated as these are considered for calculating the value of some other rebates. All these rebates except a few are non-refundable, i.e. are allowed maximum only to the extent of tax payable and the unused rebate cannot be carried forward. Refundable rebates include private health insurance offset and franking rebate for franked dividends. Personal rebates admissible in Australia are examined below:

Dependant Rebate

A resident taxpayer in Australia may be entitled to a dependent rebate if he contributes to the maintenance of one or more resident dependents. Dependent includes a dependent spouse,[14] a child housekeeper, invalid relative,[15] parents[16] of the taxpayer, or the taxpayer's spouse. Child housekeeper means a child of the taxpayer (including an adopted child, step-child or ex-nuptial child) who is wholly engaged in keeping house for the taxpayer, i.e. who is engaged in caring for a child of the taxpayer below 16 years or an invalid relative of the taxpayer or a spouse of the taxpayer who is in receipt of a disability support pension.

The spouse and child housekeeper rebates are allowed up to a maximum of AUD1,365 each.[17] However, a child housekeeper rebate may go upto AUD1,637 in case a taxpayer qualifies for a notional child or student rebate.

The maximum amount of invalid relative rebate is AUD614 and the maximum parent or parent-in-law rebate is AUD1,227. All these rebates are reduced by AUD1 for every complete AUD4 by which the separate net income of the dependent exceeds AUD282. The spouse and child housekeeper rebate is not allowed if the *separate net income*[18] of these dependents exceeds AUD5,741 and no invalid relative or parent or parent-in-law rebate is allowed if the separate income of these dependents exceed AUD2,737 and AUD5,189 respectively.

From the income year 2000-01, a taxpayer is not entitled to a spouse rebate for any period in the year during which the taxpayer or the taxpayer's spouse is eligible for the Family Tax Benefit (FTB), Part B (discussed later) in relation to a dependent child or student.

Housekeeper Rebate

The amount of housekeeper rebate and the conditions for the grant of this rebate are the same except that instead of child housekeeper, a taxpayer engages a housekeeper (an outsider) who is wholly engaged in keeping house for the taxpayer in Australia and in caring for a child under 16 or an invalid relative or a spouse of the taxpayer.

Medical Expenses Rebate

A resident taxpayer in Australia is entitled to claim medical expenses rebate in respect of medical expenses paid for himself/herself or a resident dependent. The rebate is allowed if the medical expenses exceed AUD1,250. The amount of rebate is 20 per cent of the excess over AUD1,250. The rebate is not allowed if medical expenses are reimbursed by a government or public authority or a society, association or fund. However, medical expenses reimbursement by the employer will qualify for the rebate though it will also be taxable as expense payment fringe benefit.

Private Health Insurance Offset

An individual taxpayer is entitled to claim a rebate equal to 30 per cent of the cost of private health insurance premium, provided the benefit is not claimed in the form of direct payment or reduced health insurance premiums under the *Private Health Insurance Incentives Act*, 1998. This is a refundable tax rebate.

Low Income Rebate

Low income rebate is available to taxpayers whose taxable income in the income year is less than AUD24,450. The amount of rebate for the income year 2000-01 is AUD150, reduced by 4 cents for every AUD1 by which the taxpayer's taxable income exceeds AUD20,700.

Sole Parent Rebate

Prior to the income year 2000-01, a sole parent rebate could be claimed by a taxpayer who looked after a dependent child under 16 or a student including brother or sister of the taxpayer. Instead of this rebate, a sole parent is now entitled to FTB Part B. The rebate, however, is notionally allowed only for the purpose of calculating the zone and overseas forces rebates and for determining the entitlement to the medicare levy family income threshold. The maximum sole parent rebate for the income year 2000-01 is AUD1,282.

Pensioner Rebate

A taxpayer who receives certain taxable Australian social security or service pensions and benefits, including old age pension, sole parent pension, disability support pension, widow's pension, bereavement allowance and education entry payment, is allowed a pensioner rebate of AUD1,358 for the income year 1999-2000. The rebate is reduced by 12.5 cents of each AUD1 of taxable income over the threshold of AUD12,190 and is not allowed if the taxable income exceeds AUD23,054.

Beneficiary Rebate

Taxpayers whose assessable income includes certain benefits are entitled to a beneficiary rebate. The benefits include: new start allowance, sickness allowance, mature age allowance, widow allowance, taxable parenting payment, farm household support, commonwealth education or training payments. The rebate is calculated on the basis of the following formula:

Lowest marginal tax rate × (taxpayer's benefit amount – AUD6000).
(The lowest marginal tax rate is 17 per cent for the income year 2000-01.)

Taxpayer's benefit amount is the actual amount of rebatable benefit (i.e. the benefits, allowances in respect of which the beneficiary rebate is payable) received by the taxpayer during the income year.

Where a taxpayer is entitled to both the beneficiary rebate and the pensioner rebate, only one of the two rebates, i.e. the higher of the two rebates will be allowed.

Low Income Aged Person's Rebate

The low income aged person's rebate is basically meant for those individuals who are low income self-funded retirees, and can be claimed by an individual who is of pensionable age for at least one day in the income year and is not entitled to a pensioner or beneficiary rebate and has a taxable income below the relevant pensioner rebate cut-out threshold. The amount of rebate is same as for pensioner rebate, i.e. AUD1,358.

Family Tax Assistance

In Australia, families with low income and dependent children were provided family assistance in the form of either a higher tax-free threshold or direct payment. The scheme is known as family tax assistance. Family Tax Assistance (FTA) was introduced for the first time in 1996 and became effective on Jan. 1, 1997. The FTA provides tax relief to low and middle income families with dependent children in the form of increased tax-free threshold. The FTA provides two benefits. The first, Part A benefit is provided to families with at least one dependent child and family income of less than AUD70,000. (The amount increases by AUD3,000 for each dependent child after the first) Part A benefit increases the tax-free threshold (AUD5,400 for 1998-99) for one member of a couple or for a sole parent by AUD1,000 for each dependent child. Therefore with one dependent child, the exemption limit will be AUD6,400 with two dependent child, it will be AUD7,400 and so on.

Part B benefit provides benefit in addition to Part A benefit to families with one primary breadwinner and at least one dependent child under five year. In such case the tax-free threshold is further increased by AUD2,500.

A low income earner who cannot take full advantage of the increased threshold may get the Family Tax Payment (FTP) as an alternative to FTA. These families may receive fortnightly payments from the Department of Social Security equal in value to the tax savings from FTA. Thus, both these schemes are very useful to families with low income specially those families who have dependent children under age five and have only one prime breadwinner.

With effect from July 1, 1999, the scheme has been modified. Now three forms of family assistance, administered by the Family Assistance Office, are available to taxpayers, namely Family Tax Benefit (FTB) Part A; Family Tax Benefit (FTB) Part B, and Child Care Benefit (CCB). The eligibility conditions and the amount of payment of family assistance are set out in the *A New System (Family Assistance) Act,* 1999. Taxpayers receive family assistance as direct fortnightly payments from the Family Assistance Office or as reduced child care fees. A taxpayer has to pass an income test to claim family assistance. Family assistance payments are exempt from income tax.

Gifts

In Australia, every person is entitled to a deduction from the assessable income for individual gifts of AUD2 or more made during the year to nominated funds endorsed by the commissioner or specifically listed by name in their regulations as eligible to receive deductible gifts. A transfer of property constitutes a gift if the property is transferred voluntarily and no advantage of a material character is received by the taxpayer in return.

MALAYSIA

Many incentives and tax rebates are provided in Malaysia. These are given below:

Personal Allowance/Tax-free Threshold

Malaysia offers a large number of tax reliefs and tax preferences. This is evident from the fact that the *Income Tax Act*, 1967, of Malaysia provides for both tax-free threshold of RM2,500 and personal relief of RM5,000. Personal releifs which are deductible from the assessable income to find out the total income are as follows:

Personal Relief

A resident individual taxpayer is entitled to a personal relief of RM5,000 in a basis year. Though this amount includes RM4,000 for the individual and another RM1,000 for dependent relatives, yet the full allowance of RM5,000 is allowed even if a taxpayer does not have any dependent relatives. If the income of a wife is assessed separately, she can also claim a personal relief of RM5000.

Wife Relief

Instead of spouse relief, wife relief is allowed in Malaysia. An individual taxpayer whose wife is not assessed separately or is not working, is entitled to claim a wife relief of RM3,000 in a basis year. In addition, a further relief of RM 2,500 is allowed for the wife if she is a disabled person. Full wife relief is allowed to the husband in the year in which the wife ceases to live together with the husband or both cease to be husband and wife. If the alimony payments are made under the court order, the husband can claim relief of an amount not exceeding RM3,000 per year.

Child Relief

An individual resident taxpayer can claim child relief, if he pays wholly or in part for the maintenance of the child. The child relief is allowed separately for each child. The relief can be claimed for any number of children. The amount of child relief may differ under different circumstances as shown below:

The Type of Child	*Amount of Relief*
a. For an unmarried child below 18 years	RM800
b. For a child studying full time in a college or university in Malaysia	RM3,200
c. For a child studying full time in a college or university outside Malaysia	RM800
d. For a disabled child	RM5,000

Medical Expenses

A taxpayer can claim relief of medical expenses upto RM5,000 incurred for himself, his wife or child in respect of serious diseases only. A deduction of RM3,000 is allowed for the medical or educational insurance in respect of himself, spouse or child. This relief of RM3,000 is allowed to women taxpayers also for the medical or educational insurance of her husband, child. Other reliefs allowed in Malaysia are for the wife of the taxpayer, not for the husband of the taxpayer.[19]

Education Expenses

Tax relief upto RM2,000 is allowed to an individual taxpayer on account of fees paid for any course of study in Malaysia at a recognised institute for the purpose of acquiring technical, vocational or industrial skills.

Tax Rebates

The following rebates are allowed to a resident individual from the tax liability.

(a) A rebate of RM110 to an individual who has been allowed personal relief under section 46(a) for that year of assessment, where his chargeable income does not exceed RM10,000.
(b) A rebate of RM60 in the case of an individual who has been allowed a wife allowance and an allowance for maintenance payments for the year of assessment, where his chargeable income for that year of assessment does not exceed RM10,000.
(c) A rebate is allowed for any zakat, fitrah or any other Islamic religious dues, payment of which is obligatory, and which is evidenced by a receipt issued by an appropriate religious authority.
(d) A rebate of RM400 in respect of purchase of a personal computer provided the computer is not used for the purposes of his business and the rebate has not been granted to the spouse.

The above rebates are non-refundable. Excess of rebate over tax liability cannot be carried forward to be set off in future years.

Further a rebate of an amount equivalent to 2 per cent prorated per annum on the outstanding balance of the loan given by a person to a small business is allowed. This rebate is non- refundable, but can be carried forward to be set off in future years.

Gifts

In Malaysia, a deduction is allowed from taxpayers' income for any gifts of money to the government, state government, local authority or any institution or organisation approved by the Director General. Gifts in kind to public institutions however, do not qualify for deduction. Gifts of money upto RM20,000 made by the individual taxpayer to public libraries and libraries of schools and institutions of higher learning are also deductible. Gifts of money made to the Ministry of Culture, Arts and Tourism for the sponsorship of cultural performances including orchestra, theatre and other performances are also deductible. With effect from the income year 1998, gifts of money or contributions in kind made by an individual taxpayer for the provision of facilities in public places for the benefit of disabled persons are also deductible. Gifts of money or the cost or value of any gift upto RM 20,000 made by an individual taxpayer for medical equipment for approved health care facilities is deductible. Gifts in the form of manuscripts or painting to the government are eligible for deduction at the amount equal to the value as may be determined by the Department of Museums and Antiquities or the National Archives. The deduction on account of the gift can only be set off if there is statutory income and any balance unallowed can be carried forward.

PAKISTAN

In Pakistan, like other countries, certain incentives related to social welfare are allowed to individual taxpayers.

Personal Allowance

An individual taxpayer in Pakistan is not entitled to any tax-free threshold or personal exemption. However, no income tax is payable in case the total income of taxpayer does not exceed PKR 40,000. The exemption limit is PKR50,000 in case salary income constitutes more than 50 per cent of the total income.

Taxpayers having more income than the above amount are liable to pay tax on the total income but are entitled to tax rebate of PKR2,000. The tax rebate is PKR2,500 in case the salary income constitutes more than 50 per cent of total income.

Extra Relief to Women Taxpayers

Women are entitled to a higher tax credit of PKR3,000 as against PKR2,500 in case their salary income constitute more than 50 per cent of the total income.

Tax Rebate to Elders

Taxpayers with 65 years of age or above having income upto PKR200,000 are entitled to a special tax rebate of an amount equal to 50 per cent of tax payable. The rebate is in addition to other rebates.

Tax Rebate for Education of Dependent Children

In Pakistan, to promote education, a taxpayer is entitled to a rebate of 5 per cent of the expenditure incurred on the education of his dependent children subject to the condition that the expense does not exceed PKR30,000 and the receipt of such expense bears the National Tax Number (NTN) of the educational institution.

Medical Expenditure by Individuals

A resident individual taxpayer is entitled to deduction of personal expenditure on medical services. The only condition to be fulfilled for claiming this deduction is that receipt in respect of such expenditure bearing name, NTN and the complete address of the medical practitioner is to be furnished along with the return of total income.

Deduction for Donations

In Pakistan, a taxpayer is entitled to an allowance in respect of any amount paid as donation to any approved educational institution, hospital, any relevant fund and any other institution or fund which is established for religious or charitable purposes and is approved by the Central Board of Revenue and such other institutions, societies, boards, trusts or funds as are specified in the *Income Tax Ordinance*, 1979. However, donation to private religious institutions or funds which do not ensure benefit to the public are not eligible for deduction. The donation has to be paid only by a crossed cheque drawn on a bank. Donation in kind of such articles or goods as may be prescribed are also eligible for deduction. The aggregate amount of donation eligible for deduction is limited to 15 per cent of the total income in the case of companies and 30 per cent of the total income in the case of any other taxpayer. However, the ceiling is not applicable if the donation is made to the Quaid-e-Azam Memorial Fund or to a specified institution, museum, library or monument.

INDIA

Prior to 1965, the tax reliefs in India were provided by way of rebates and concessional rates of tax. The *Finance Act*, 1965, introduced for the first time the scheme of allowing deductions from gross total income. Beginning with just a few sections, the chapter 'Deduction from gross total income' has grown in size and has made the law a complicated one especially due to the introduction of more deductions and the imposition of several conditions to be satisfied to claim any deduction. Deductions for a social cause are given below:

Personal Allowance/Tax-free Threshold

The social-welfare incentives allowed to individual taxpayers in India are limited. A tax-free threshold of Rs.50,000 in the income year 2000-01 is available to individual taxpayer.

The wife and husband cannot file a joint return and in case the spouse has taxable income, she has to file her return separately and will be entitled for tax-free threshold of Rs.50,000. Accordingly, no spouse and dependent allowance are provided. Income, other than the income that arises on account of any manual work done by a minor child or from activity involving application of his skill, talent or specialised knowledge and experience, of minor children below 18 years of age has to be clubbed with that of parents having higher income. In case of clubbing of the income of a minor child, a deduction to the extent of such income not exceeding Rs.1,500 in respect of each minor child is allowed.

Children Education Allowance

A children education allowance to the extent of Rs.1,200 p.a. per child for 2 children, paid by the employer to its employee is exempt from tax.

Allowance for Medical Treatment of Handicapped Dependent

A fixed deduction of Rs.40,000 irrespective of the amount incurred is allowed from the gross total income of a resident individual taxpayer for the medical treatment, training and rehabilitation of a handicapped dependent (Sec. 80 DD). Besides, a resident taxpayer can claim a deduction of Rs.40,000 irrespective of actual expenditure incurred on the medical treatment of certain specified diseases or ailments for himself or dependent relatives. (Sec. 80 DDB) The deduction is Rs.60,000 in case the taxpayer or the dependent relative is of the age of 65 years or more.

Incentive to Senior Citizens

A resident taxpayer who is of the age of 65 years or more at any time during the income year is entitled to a tax rebate from the amount of tax on his total income. The tax rebate is an amount equal to 100 per cent of such tax or Rs.15,000 whichever is less. This tax rebate is non-refundable and also cannot be carried forward. (Sec. 88B)

Incentive to Women

In India, from the income year 2000-01, the resident women taxpayers are entitled to a tax rebate from the amount of tax on their total income. The amount of the tax rebate is an amount equal to 100 per cent of such tax or Rs.5,000, whichever is less. (Sec. 88C) The resident women taxpayers of the age of 65 years or more are not eligible for this rebate as they become eligible for senior citizens rebate of Rs.15,000 as stated above.

Incentive for Medical Insurance Premium

The taxpayer is eligible for deduction in respect of medical insurance premium paid during the tax year to keep in effect an insurance on the health of the taxpayer or the spouse or dependent parents or dependent children. The amount of deduction is limited to Rs.10,000 (Sec. 80D). However, the limit is Rs.15,000 in case the mediclaim insurance premium is paid to keep in force the insurance in relation to the taxpayer or the spouse or dependent parents who are at least of 65 years of age at any time during the income year.

Incentive for Contribution to Pension Fund

An individual taxpayer in India is entitled to a deduction of Rs.10,000 of the amount paid under an annuity plan to any insurer for receiving pension. (Sec. 80CCC) However, the amount received by the taxpayer as pension will be taxable in the hands of the taxpayer in the year of the receipt. As such, this incentive is a postponement of tax.

Incentive for Repayment of Loan for Higher Studies

An individual taxpayer is entitled to a deduction of up to Rs.40,000 on the repayment of loan including interest being a loan from any financial institution or an approved charitable institution for the purpose of pursuing his higher education (Sec. 80E).

Incentives for Promoting Social and Economic Welfare

Incentive by way of deduction from business income is allowed for expenditure incurred on eligible projects or schemes for promoting social and economic welfare or upliftment of the public. These include drinking water projects, dwelling units for economically weaker sections, promotion of sports, pollution control, etc. A company taxpayer can directly incur expenditure on an eligible project after approval of the scheme from the National Committee constituted by the government. A taxpayer other than company can claim deduction by way of contribution to institution or association or local authority engaged in such project or scheme. There is no ceiling fixed on the amount eligible for deduction. As such, any amount incurred or paid for eligible projects or schemes is eligible for deduction as business expenditure (Sec. 35AC).

Incentive for Family Planning Expenditure

In India, to control population and promote family planning, incentive is allowed to company taxpayers only by way of allowing deduction of expenditure incurred by it for the purpose of promoting family planning among its employees. Such expenditure if capital is allowed one-fifth in each year over a period of 5 years [Sec. 36(1)(ix)].

Deduction for Donations

Incentive is provided to taxpayers in India by way of deduction in respect of donations to specified government funds, institutions, organisations (Sec. 80G). The specified funds include 'Prime Minister's National Relief Fund' 'National Defence Fund'. Donation to non-specified funds or institutions including donation to notified temple, mosque, gurudwara, church and donation to the government or any approved authority for family planning, are restricted in the first stage to 10 per cent of the adjusted gross total income.[20] After reducing the donation of non-specified funds to the limit prescribed, either 50 per cent or of 100 per cent of the donation (depending upon the nature of donations and the deductible percentage specified for that donation) is allowed to be made from the gross total income.

Analysis of Social-welfare Incentives

Analysis of the income tax provisions relating to social-welfare incentives reveal that developed countries provide more social reliefs. To find out the impact of these reliefs on tax revenues, the statistical data on social reliefs which were provided in these countries during the income year 1997-98 were collected. Though data in different countries are given in different forms, and in different currency value, an attempt has been made to present the data in a comparable form. In some countries, tax reliefs are given by way of tax rebates, in other countries, reliefs are given by way of deduction from the gross income. These deductions were converted into tax reliefs on the basis of average rate of income tax. Further, tax liability is also given in these countries in different forms. The tax liability therefore, has been calculated by adding all tax credits, tax rebates and tax-free threshold, if deducted earlier. Various social-welfare reliefs provided in these countries are given in Table 6.3.

TABLE 6.3. SOCIAL INCENTIVES IN THE SELECTED COUNTRIES
(for the income year 1997-98[1], amount in millions)

Social Tax Reliefs	U.K. (£)	U.S. ($)	Australia (AUD)	Malaysia (RM)	Pakistan (PKR)	India (Rs.)
Personal Allowance/ Tax-free Threshold	29,300	352,169[2]	12,139[3]	1,260[4]	n.a.	51,943[5]
Spouse Allowance	2,750	IPA[6]	422	176	n.a.	IPA
Age-related Allowance	1,050	2,800	n.a.	n.a.	n.a.	n.a.
Single Parent Allowance	210	n.a.	298	n.a.	n.a.	n.a.
Children/Dependent Allowance	n.a.	IPA	ISA[7]	207	n.a.	n.a.
Life Insurance/Medical Insurance Relief	130	IPA	307	338[8]	n.a.	4,376[9]
Other Reliefs	12,215	9,262	1,701	18	n.a.[10]	7,678
Total Reliefs	45,745	364,231	14,867	1,999		63,997

Notes:

1. The year covers the income year of the selected countries, i.e. calendar year 1997 in the case of the U.S. and Malaysia, income year April 6, 1997 to April 5, 1998 for the U.K., income year July 1, 1997 to June 1, 1998 for Australia and income year April 1, 1996 to March 31, 1997 for India.
2. The table includes relief on account of personal exemption, itemized deductions and standard deductions, computed on the basis of average rate of tax which was 21 per cent for individuals.
3. It includes relief on account of tax-free threshold of AUD11,629 millions and family tax assistance of AUD510 millions, on the basis of 23 per cent average rate of tax.
4. It includes relief on account of tax-free threshold of RM415 millions and personal dependent relief of RM845 millions.
5. It includes only tax-free threshold.
6. IPA means included in personal allowance.
7. ISA means included in spouse allowance.
8. It also includes provident and pension fund contribution.
9. It also includes contribution towards provident fund, government securities and other savings.
10. n.a.: Not available.

Sources: (a) *Inland Revenue Statistics*, 1998-99 (U.K.).
(b) *IRS, Statistics of Income Bulletin*, Fall 1999 Publication (U.S.).
(c) *Taxation Statistics*, 1997-98 (Australia).
(d) *Taxation Statistics* 1998 (Malaysia).
(e) *All India Income Tax Statistics*, Assessment Year 1997-98.

As shown in Table 6.3, personal allowance and tax-free threshold constitute the major part of social-welfare incentives in all these countries. These reliefs form 96.69 per cent of all social incentives in the U.S., followed by Australia 81.65 per cent, India 81.16 per cent and the U.K. 64.05 per cent. Other reliefs do not affect tax revenue much except in the U.K.

TABLE 6.4. SOCIAL TAX RELIEFS AS PERCENTAGE OF TOTAL TAX RELIEFS
(for the income year 1997-98, amount in millions)

Country	Currency	Social Reliefs	Total Tax Reliefs	Social Tax Reliefs as % of Total Tax Reliefs
U.K.	£	45,745	52,810	86.62
U.S.	$	364,231	379,451	95.99
Australia	AUD	14,867	34,421	43.19
Malaysia	RM	1,999	n.a.	n.av.
Pakistan	PKR	n.av.	n.a.	n.av.
India	RS.	63,997	113,377	56.45

Source: Same as in Table 6.3.

Social Reliefs as percentage of Total Tax Relief

The share of social reliefs in the total tax relief is given in Table 6.4

It emerges from Table 6.4 that the U.S. provides social incentives in abundance, where these form 95.98 per cent of total tax reliefs, followed by 86.62 per cent in the U.K., 56.45 per cent in India. The least is in Australia, i.e. 43.19 per cent.

Conclusion

Social-welfare incentives are provided in different forms based on the social structure and economic growth in each country.

One common incentive allowed in all the countries is the provision for a tax-free threshold or personal exemption. Income tax is a tax on income, which means that tax is to be levied on what one has earned during the year. Income earned during the year is computed by deducting all expenses incurred to earn that income. While computing income only those expenses which have been incurred to earn that income are allowed. The expenses incurred by the individual taxpayer on himself are not allowed to be deducted. Keeping this in view, exemption is allowed in all these countries to all individual taxpayers either by way of a tax-free threshold, or by way of personal exemption or by giving tax rebate. Each country has fixed its own limit taking into account its social structure, its standard of living, and the minimum basic requirements of a person. In this respect, the U.S. provides highest exemption, i.e. a personal exemption of $ 2,800 each for self, spouse as well as for dependent children plus a standard deduction of $3,600 each for self and spouse. Clearly, the U.S. takes into consideration not only the personal basic requirements of the individual taxpayer but also the basic requirement of his family and also certain other personal expenses incurred by the taxpayer on medical, interest, charity, taxes, casualty, tax advice etc. The U.S. also gives option to the taxpayer to file returns individually or jointly with the spouse. As such, the benefit of these allowances will be greater in case the spouse does not have any income. However, if the spouse has income and opts to file the return separately, the benefit of these allowances will be restricted. (Some tax credits are allowed only to married couples when they file joint returns).

In Australia, relief from tax is allowed for self, spouse and the children. In the U.K., instead of a tax-free threshold, a personal allowance is allowed. Allowance for spouse in the U.K. has been withdrawn from the income year 1999-2000. However, allowance for children is allowed by way of tax rebate.

In contrast, no such allowance is admissible in Pakistan and India for spouse and children. One possible explanation for this can be that the threshold/personal exemption in Pakistan and India includes exemption for spouse and children also. However, this interpretation gets rebutted as the spouse can also claim the personal/threshold exemption in case the spouse has taxable income. As such, the benefit of this exemption gets doubled if the spouse has an independent income in Pakistan and India. In Malaysia, both tax-free threshold and personal exemption are allowed simultaneously, though the aggregate amount of both these exemptions is still very low. Besides in Malaysia, a husband is eligible for wife allowance and child allowance. This allowance is per wife and can be claimed for more than one wife. Evidently in Malaysia, despite being a developing country, consideration of family has been taken into account while allowing threshold/ personal exemption to individual taxpayers. It is only in Pakistan and India that no such consideration appears to have been taken into account while fixing threshold/personal exemption. Absence of such consideration may not be equitable but is certainly administratively convenient for these countries with large population. From the point of view of revenue also it may not be beneficial to have a separate allowance for spouse and children.

All these countries except Malaysia provide extra incentives to persons who are 65 or more. The maximum benefit on account of age is allowed in the U.K. where additional personal allowance and married couple allowance both are allowed. In the U.S., U.K., and Australia, the extra incentive provided to aged persons is withdrawn beyond a particular income. However, in India, rebate up to a certain limit is allowed to all senior citizens irrespective of their total income.

Another incentive available in the selected countries is relief in respect of the medical expenses and medical insurance premium incurred by the taxpayer on self, spouse and dependent. Unlike personal allowance, medical allowance for meeting medical expenses cannot be a fixed allowance. Hence, deduction on account of medical expenses is based on actual expenditure. In the U.S., deduction of medical expenses including medical insurance premium incurred in excess of 7.5 per cent of AGI can be claimed as itemized deduction, which means that petty expenses can be claimed as part of standard deduction. In Malaysia, the relief of medical expenses is allowed for serious diseases, whereas in Pakistan, full amount of expenditure incurred on medical services is eligible for relief. In India, no direct deduction of medical expense is allowed as tax relief. However, medical insurance premium paid is allowed as deduction from the total income. In the U.K. though no tax relief is provided for medical expenses, the taxpayer has to make payment towards National Insurance Contribution (NIC), which takes care of medical treatment of the U.K. residents.

To promote charity and social welfare, any amount paid as donation, and gift to charitable organisations are eligible for tax reliefs in all these countries. The amount of relief on account of donation or gift differs. This incentive shows a recognition of the role of charitable organisations in all the countries under study.

To promote education, tax incentive is allowed for expenditure incurred on education. In India, although no direct deduction is allowed, deduction is allowed in respect of the repayment of loan taken for higher studies. On the other hand, no such rebate is available in the U.K., the U.S., and Australia, except payment of fees for vocational training in the U.K. and a higher education tax credit in the U.S.

Another interesting tax relief allowed in Pakistan and India only, is additional tax rebate to women taxpayers. No other country provides any special incentive to women taxpayers. The additional tax rebate in Pakistan is PKR500, whereas in India it is Rs.5,000. These are tax rebates and are deducted from the tax liability. Allowing higher incentive to all women taxpayers in these countries does not appear to be equitable. Women, being a part of the family, additional rebate to a family having both man and women as income earners does not appear to be equitable as compared to a family with only a single male income earner.

All countries have made provisions for social incentives considering their individual social structure and requirement of the society. In fact, various social welfare incentives allowed in these countries show the state of the society in each country under study and the concern of the government to promote the welfare of the society by providing tax relief to the taxpayer. However, the incentives provided for the needs of the family are more in developed countries as compared to the developing countries.

Investment Incentives

Many incentives are provided to encourage taxpayers to invest their money for specified purposes or fund. Through them, taxpayers are attracted to invest their money in either buying life insurance policy, or contributing towards the retirement benefits, or in acquiring property, capital asset, specified bonds or securities. Though retirement benefits[21] (contribution to provident fund, pension) and dividend imputation credit[22] are investment incentives, these are not discussed here.

The investment incentives of the selected countries are analysed below:

THE U.K

The major investment incentives provided in the U.K., are as under:

Enterprise Investment Scheme

The Enterprise Investment Scheme (EIS), was introduced in 1994 to encourage investment in industry and has replaced the business expansion scheme. In this scheme, a tax relief is provided to taxpayers who subscribe for newly issued shares in certain qualifying companies.[23] A minimum of £500 and a maximum of £1,50,000 can be invested in each tax year. Relief is allowed at the rate of 20 per cent of the amount invested and is reduced from the amount of tax due on the taxpayer's taxable income. The taxpayer has to retain shares for a minimum period of 3 years. For shares acquired before April 6, 2000, the minimum holding period is 5 years. Dividend income from such shares are taxable but capital gains arising on the sale of such shares are exempt.

Venture Capital Trusts

Similar to EIS, there is Venture Capital Trusts (VCT)[24] Investment Scheme. A taxpayer can obtain tax relief in respect of an investment in newly issued shares of VCT. The relief is equal to 20 per cent of the amount invested subject to a limit of £1,00,000 per year. Dividends received on the first of £1,00,000 of VCT shares acquired each year are exempt from income tax unlike the dividends received from investment in shares under EIS, which are taxable. Capital gains arising on the disposal of shares are also exempt. The minimum holding period required has been reduced from 5 years to 3 years for shares acquired after April 6, 2000.

Personal Equity Plans

A tax-efficient means of investing in stocks and shares used to be provided by Personal Equity Plans (PEP) till April 5, 1999. Under this plan, funds invested in PEP were managed by a plan manager who used to invest the funds in qualifying investments, being listed, ordinary or preference shares of companies incorporated in the U.K. or elsewhere in the European Union. Dividend and interest paid on PEP investments and capital gains on the disposal of investment in PEP were exempt from tax.

Tax Exempt Special Savings Account

Tax Exempt Special Savings Accounts (TESSA) Scheme was in operation in the U.K. till April 6, 1999. Under this scheme, banks and building societies were able to offer tax exempt accounts to encourage savings. Interest received on a TESSA is exempt from income tax provided no capital is withdrawn during the tax-exempt period of 5 years. Upto £9,000 in total may be invested in a TESSA but not more than £3,000 could be invested in the first year and no more than £1,800 per year in the subsequent 4 years. This scheme has been replaced by a new scheme called Individual Savings Accounts (ISA) from April 6, 1999. However, taxpayers who held TESSA's on April 5, 1999 could continue to pay money into their TESSA's and would retain tax exempt status for the remaining period of 5 year.

Individual Savings Accounts

A new scheme called, the Individual Savings Account (ISA) has been introduced from April 6, 1999, to replace the PEP and the TESSA which includes three components, i.e. cash deposits, stocks, and shares and life insurances products. An ISA which includes a stocks and shares component plus either or both of the other two components is called, the maxi-ISA. An ISA, which includes only one component is called mini-ISA. A taxpayer may put money into either a single maxi-ISA, or upto three mini-ISA's, one for each component. In the first two years of the scheme, no more than £7,000 may be invested in each year. Interest, dividend, bonus and capital gains arising on ISA investments are exempt from tax. Withdrawals may be made from ISA at any time without loss of tax relief. The scheme is guaranteed to run for 10 years and will be reviewed after 7 years to decide changes if any to be made after the 10 year period. ISA's are run by banks, building societies, insurance, companies and some high street stores and super markets.

National Savings Certificates

In the U.K., interest arising on National Savings Certificate (NSA) is exempt from tax. This exemption is more beneficial to higher rate taxpayers as compared to those taxpayers who are chargeable at lower rate or are not chargeable to tax.

Life Assurance

Tax relief on premiums paid on life assurance policies are limited to only those policies made before March 13, 1984. No relief is allowed on policies issued after that date. On policies issued till March 13, 1984, the relief reduced the cost of premium by 12.5 per cent.

Interest Payment

In the U.K., incentive is provided to the taxpayer by giving tax relief for any interest paid. This relief is provided on interest paid which satisfies prescribed conditions. The interest paid wholly and exclusively for business purposes is generally treated as an allowable business expense and is deducted from business profits. However, interest paid on certain loans other than wholly and exclusively for business purposes are treated as a charge on income. The eligible interest payments include a loan to buy equipment, a loan to purchase an interest in partnership, a loan to buy shares in an employee-controlled company, a loan to purchase ordinary shares in a close company and a loan to pay inheritances tax.

Mortgage Interest Relief

In the U.K., the mortgage interest relief (MIR) is given for the interest paid on loans for the purchase of a property, caravan or a houseboat which will be the only or the main residence of the borrower and on loans to purchase a life annuity where the annuitant is aged 65 or more. Relief was available upto April 6, 1988, for loans taken for the improvement of property and for the purchase of house for a dependent relative or divorced or separated spouse.

To be eligible for the MIR, the property must be in the United Kingdom or the Republic of Ireland. A limitation has been placed on the maximum amount of interest paid by an individual in the year ending on April 5, 2000 which can qualify for relief. This limitation is imposed by restricting relief to interest on loans of £30,000 and this is the maximum amount incorporating all qualifying loans attributable to residences.

However, despite the system of independent taxation, a husband and wife living together cannot each obtain the benefit of £30,000 limit. This limit applies to the aggregate amount of qualifying loans made to a husband and his wife. The relief is computed at the rate of 10 per cent on the eligible gross interest.

Relief on mortgage interest repayments has been withdrawn from April 6, 2000.

THE U.S.

Qualified Residence Interest

In sharp contrast to the U.K., only few incentives are provided to encourage investments in the U.S. These are as follows:

In the U.S., a taxpayer may generally deduct interest paid or accrued within the income year on indebtedness. The interest must pertain to the debt of the taxpayer and must result from a debtor—creditor relationship. However, personal interest is not deductible except interest paid for qualified residence[25] and interest on qualified educational loans. Qualified residence interest is interest paid or accrued during the tax year on acquisition indebtedness[26] or home equity indebtedness[27] with regard to any qualified residence. Married taxpayers who file separate returns are treated as one taxpayer with each entitled to take into account one residence unless both give consent in writing to having only one taxpayer take into account both residences. Interest paid or accrued on a limited amount of indebtedness is desirable. The limit for acquisition indebtedness is $1,000,000 and for home equity indebtedness is $100,000. In case of married individuals these amounts are halved in case they file returns separately. There is no limitation of $1,000,000 on acquisition indebtedness incurred on or before October 13, 1987. However, the amount of such debt reduces the amount of $1,000,000 limitation available for new acquisition in debtedness for improvements. Thus, taxpayers are entitled to deduct interest paid on loans upto $100,000 raised against residence even though the same may have been used for personal purposes.

Tax Exempt Interest on Municipal Bonds

In the U.S., interest on bonds issued by school districts, port authorities, road commissions, counties, fire districts, municipalities are exempt from tax. Taxpayers can also purchase and eventually redeem Series EE bonds tax free, if they use the proceeds to pay certain college expenses for themselves, or a spouse or dependants. The exclusion of interest on municipal bonds is considered to be one of the few remaining tax shelters.

AUSTRALIA

In Australia, various investment-related incentives are available to the taxpayer which are as under:

Income from Pooled Development Fund

Dividend received from Pooled Development Fund (PDF) and income from the sale of PDF shares are exempt from tax in Australia. Capital gain realisation by a PDF on a qualifying small-medium enterprises (SMEs)[28] investment is also exempt to the extent it is contributed to a complying superannuation fund. (PDFs are eligible investment companies registered under the *Pooled Development Fund Act*, 1992 to provide equity capital for eligible activities to a resident Australian company with total assets not exceeding AUD50,000,000). PDFs are taxed in the same way as other companies except that they are taxed at concessional rate on SME income component at 15 per cent and on the unregulated investment component at 25 per cent. The objective of this 2-tier rate structure is to encourage PDFs invest their uncommitted funds in SMEs in preference to holding interest-bearing investment for long periods. As such, a taxpayer in Australia gets incentive by making investment in Pooled Development Fund shares as PDF itself is taxed at a concessional rate and the dividend received by the taxpayer including income from the sale of PDS shares is exempt from tax.

Dividend Income

In Australia, the individual shareholders who receive dividends from a company are entitled to a rebate on tax paid by the company on its income. As a result, the dividend paid to shareholders becomes effectively tax free to a varying extent.

Interest on Infrastructure Borrowings

Interest on infrastructure borrowings for certificates issued before February 14, 1997 is exempt from tax in Australia, upto 15 years if the prospectus was issued after December 16, 1994 and upto 10 years if the same was issued prior to December 16, 1994. Where the borrowing was made in response to a prospectus issued prior to December 16, 1994, the interest on such borrowing was not deductible to the borrower. In case of borrowing made in response to a prospectus issued after December 16, 1994, the lender has the option of including the interest income and receiving a tax rebate at the rate of 34 per cent for the income year 2000-01.

MALAYSIA

In Malaysia, various investment related incentives and deductions are available. The major investment-related incentives available are as under:

Deduction for Life Insurance Premium and Contribution to Pension and Provident Fund

Deduction in respect of premiums on life insurance policies, payment to approved pension and provident fund and contribution to statutory widows and orphans pension scheme are allowed to residents. The husband and wife are entitled to a deduction of upto RM5,000 each. However, if the wife has no income of her own, the total deduction allowed is RM5,000. In addition, a deduction of RM3,000 from the income year 2000 (RM2,000 upto the income year 1999) is allowed for premium paid for any insurance on education or medical benefit in respect of the taxpayer, his wife or child.

Dividend Income

Any tax paid by the company in Malaysia is imputed to its shareholders. Dividend income received by a shareholder is grossed up at the tax rate applicable to the company and credit is allowed to the shareholder of the dividend thus grossed up. As such, dividend income is virtually tax-free in the hands of the shareholders. Moreover, in case the tax liability of the shareholders is less than the credit of the tax allowed on dividend income, the shareholder can claim refund also. Dividends received from co-operative societies by its members are also exempt from tax.

Interest Income

All individuals are exempt from tax arising from various sources of interest income. The sources of interest income that are exempt include savings deposits, fixed deposits and investment accounts. Deposits within certain banks are exempt without any limit, whereas with certain banks and financial institutions, the exemption is of interest on deposit upto RM100,000 only. Interest on deposits exceeding RM100,000 is subject to withholding tax at the rate of 5 per cent. The 5 per cent withholding tax is the final tax and individuals are not taxed again on this interest income. In Malaysia, interest received from any savings certificates issued by the government is exempt. Interest earned by individuals on bonds issued by public companies which are listed on the Kuala Lumpur Stock Exchange is tax exempt. Interest on bonds other than convertible loan stock issued by companies which are rated by the rating agency are also exempt from January 1, 1993. Interest from savings bonds issued by the Central Bank of Malaysia are also exempt.

PAKISTAN

Premium paid for Life Insurance

In Pakistan, an individual taxpayer is entitled to an allowance for premium paid on the insurance policy of the taxpayer himself or of the spouse of the taxpayer or for any deferred annuity on the life of the taxpayer or his spouse. The premium paid for life insurance policy during an income year should not exceed 10 per cent of the capital sum assured.

Allowance for Investment in Defence Savings and NIT Certificates

A taxpayer (not being a company) is also entitled to an allowance in respect of any sum invested by him in the purchase of Defence Savings Certificates. Unit certificates issued by the National Investment (unit) Trust of Pakistan and the specified government securities, certificates of Mutual Funds, Modarba certificates, any debenture or debenture stock issued by Public company approved by the Central Board of Revenue (CBR) and any stocks and shares of such a Pakistan industrial public company as may be approved by the CBR.

Allowance for Contribution to Provident Fund

A taxpayer in Pakistan is entitled to an allowance as investment rebate for any sum deducted from the salary by the government or any contribution not exceeding 20 per cent of salary in the income year to any approved provident fund.

Investment in the Share Capital

A taxpayer is also eligible to claim deduction of such portion of his total income as is invested by him in the income year on the acquisition of the shares of a Pakistani company that is an investment company or a holding company or an industrial public company which is owned and controlled directly or indirectly by the Federal Government and is approved by the CBR for this purpose.

Amount paid for Retirement Annuity

A resident individual is allowed deduction from his total income in respect of any sum paid by him in the income year for obtaining a retirement annuity with the State Life Insurance Corporation of Pakistan or the Pakistan Post Office Life Insurance Department. This benefit is available to those taxpayers having salary income from an employment that is not pensionable or which does not provide any other retirement benefit and taxpayers having profit or gains from any business or profession.

The total amount of allowance under all the above five categories cannot exceed one-third of the total income of the taxpayer or PKR50,000 whichever is less. These allowances are not to be deducted from the total income. Investment rebate is allowed at the average rebate of tax in the following manner:

Rebate = Gross Tax/Total income x Amount of investment made.

Retirement Annuity for Professionals

In addition to the above allowances for contribution to retirement annuity, an additional allowance is allowed to professionals who are resident individuals deriving income from the exercise of a profession. The deduction allowed is 5 per cent of income from such profession subject to a maximum of PKR10,000.

Allowance for Books

In Pakistan, every assessee is eligible to an allowance in respect of any amount expended for the purchase of books of religious or professional or technical nature or of scientific or general knowledge. The only requirement is to furnish purchase receipt containing National Tax Number of the bookseller. There is no ceiling on the amount of the allowance and the scope and nature of books is very wide and includes books on almost all subjects.

Contribution to Benevolent Fund and Group Insurance

A taxpayer is entitled to deduct any sum paid to a benevolent fund in order to make provision for his spouse or children or any person dependent on him for any premium paid to an approved group insurance scheme. There is no ceiling on the amount of contribution.

Interest on Deposits

Interest on deposits on postal savings, banks or National Savings or Deposit certificate under the National Savings Scheme are exempt. Similarly, income derived by a taxpayer from an investment in monthly savings account scheme of the Directorate of National Savings is exempt to the extent it does not exceed PKR1,000. Interest derived from foreign currency accounts held by authorised banks in Pakistan is also exempt. Interest on deposits with any banking company or any financial institutions, interest on bonds, debentures issued by a banking company or any local authority and dividend income are taxable at concessional rate of 10 per cent only.

INDIA

Deduction in respect of certain specified payments and investments are allowed under Sec. 88. These include:

Premium paid for Life Insurance

A taxpayer is entitled to an allowance on the premium paid for insurance policy taken on the life of the taxpayer or the spouse or any child of such individual. The rebate allowed is at the rate of 20 per cent on the amount of premium paid. This is a tax rebate and is deducted from the tax liability. The maximum amount on which rebate can be claimed is Rs.60,000 along with the other investments in public provident fund, national savings certificates etc as stated hereinafter. This is a non-refundable rebate and is restricted to the extent of the tax liability.

Contribution to Provident Fund and Investment in National Savings Certificates

A taxpayer is entitled to a tax rebate at the rate of 20 per cent of the amount contributed to a recognized provident fund, public provident fund and the amount invested in purchasing National Savings Certificates out of his income during the income year. The maximum amount which can be invested is Rs.60,000 along with the premium paid for life insurance if any. The rebate is allowed from the tax liability. However, this is a non-refundable rebate.

Tax Rebate on purchase of Residential House Property

An individual taxpayer is eligible for a tax rebate at the rate of 20 per cent on payment made by way of instalments or on repayments of the amount borrowed for the purchase or construction of a residential house property. The deduction is allowed at the rate of 20 per cent of the amount which cannot exceed Rs.20,000. This amount of Rs.20,000 shall be included for claiming rebate for life insurance premium and contribution to public provident fund, and investment in national savings certificates. The aggregate amount eligible for deduction shall be Rs.60,000.

Tax Rebate for Subscription to Equity Shares or Debentures

A taxpayer is eligible for claiming tax rebate at the rate of 20 per cent of the amount paid as subscription to equity shares or debentures of any eligible issue of capital[29] or subscribing to any units of mutual fund which in turn subscribe in the eligible issue of capital of any company. The maximum amount on which rebate can be claimed is Rs.80,000 including tax rebate for life insurance premium, contribution to provident fund, investment in NSC, and payment for construction or purchase of house, etc. As there is a separate ceiling of Rs.60,000 for these deductions, the net additional amount on which this rebate can be claimed comes to Rs.20,000 only.

Deduction for Interest paid for Housing Loan

To promote housing and encourage investment in housing, an individual taxpayer in India is entitled to claim deduction upto Rs.30,000 for the interest paid on amount borrowed for the purpose of construction or acquisition of a house which is self-occupied by the taxpayer. Higher deduction upto Rs.100,000 is allowed if the amount is borrowed after April 1, 2001 and the house is acquired or constructed before March 31, 2003.

Exemption of Interest Income

In India, interest income from certain government securities and specified bonds are exempt from tax. The *Income Tax Act*, 1961 provides that any income by way of interest, premium on redemption or other payment of such securities, bonds, savings certificates, issued by the Central Government and deposits as notified by the government shall be tax exempt [Sec. 10(15)]. Besides, interest on many government securities, specified bonds, interest on deposits under the notified scheme, interest on deposits with a bank and on deposits with specified institutions are deductible upto Rs.9,000. In addition, a sum of Rs.3,000 is also exempt on account of interest income from government securities (Sec. 80 L).

Conclusion

Evidently, investment-related incentives allowed in the selected countries are fewer than social-welfare incentives. In developing countries, these incentives seems to have been provided by way of social security to individual taxpayer at the time of old age. All three developing countries, Malaysia, Pakistan and India provide tax relief to taxpayers for contribution to life insurance premium, provident funds etc., though the amount of tax relief differs in these countries. Interest on certain deposits with the government and other specified securities are exempt in the selected countries. In Malaysia and Pakistan, by and large all interest received from banks and financial institutions are exempt.

The U.K. provides the largest investment-related incentives by way of enterprise investment scheme and venture capital trusts, besides individual savings accounts. The incentives provided in these schemes are substantial and are meant to promote investment in certain qualifying companies. Allowing incentive on the basis of investment itself does not seem equitable. Though it may be desirable from the point of social security in developing countries and for the growth of economy or capitalisation, it benefits those taxpayers who have spare money to invest more. From the view point of the ability-to-pay principle, those who can save, have more ability and should pay more tax rather than getting higher tax relief.

BUSINESS INCENTIVES

The role of industrial growth in the economic prosperity of a country cannot be underestimated. Considering this, many tax reliefs are provided in some countries for promoting certain industries or for promoting exports. These are analysed below

THE U.K.

No direct tax incentive is provided to any business because of its nature, or location except that capital allowance upto a maximum of 100 per cent is available for the cost of constructing buildings, including commercial buildings in an enterprise zone. The other business-related indirect incentives are in the form of exemptions given for subscribing to shares under the Enterprises Investment Scheme, Venture Capital Trust, Personal Equity Plans, Tax Exempt Savings Account and Individual Savings Account. These incentives allowed to taxpayers are basically to mobilise investments for business as discussed earlier under the head, 'Investment Incentives'.

THE U.S.

In the U.S., various tax credits are provided to increase employment, encourage energy conservation and research and experimental activities and also to encourage certain socially desired activities. The business-related tax credits are non-refundable as these can only be used to offset a taxpayer's tax liability. The tax credits commonly available to businesses are grouped into a special credit category called 'the general business credit'. The general business credit is the sum of the following tax credits:

Investment Credit

The investment credit is composed of the rehabilitation credit, the energy credit and the reforestation credit.

(a) *Rehabilitation Credit.* A credit for expenditure for the rehabilitation of older industrial and commercial buildings and certified historic structures[30] is allowed. The credit is 10 per cent for structures that were originally placed in service before 1936 and 20 per cent for certified historic structures. The credit is allowed only for trade or business property and property held for investment that is depreciable. Residential property other than certified historic structures are not eligible for this benefit. The basis of the property for depreciation is, however, reduced by the full amount of the credit taken.

(b) *Energy Credit.* To encourage energy conservation measures, credits are allowed to businesses that invest in energy conserving properties such as solar and geothermal property. The business energy credit is 10 per cent of the basis of energy property placed in service during the year. For claiming the credit, the construction, reconstruction or erection of the property must be completed by the taxpayer and its original use must commence with the taxpayer.

(c) *Reforestation Credit.* Reforestation credit is allowed at the rate of 10 per cent of the amortizable basis of qualified timber property acquired during the tax year. Amortizable basis is the portion of the basis of qualified timber property attributable to reforestation expenditure that does not exceed $10,000 ($5,000 for married individuals filing returns separately).

Work Opportunity Credit

The work opportunity credit is intended to reduce unemployment for individuals who are usually economically disadvantaged. The credit is 35 per cent of the first $6,000 of qualified wages paid to each employee hired from one or more of the economically disadvantaged groups.

Increased Research Credit

To encourage research and experimental expenditure, the tax law in the U.S., provides two options to the taxpayer. The first option is to deduct research and experimental expenditure immediately or amortise it over a period of 60 months or more. The second option is to avail of a tax credit for the qualified research expenses. Upto July 1, 1995, the credit was allowed at the rate of 20 per cent of qualified research expenses incurred in a tax year in excess of the base amount[31] plus 20 per cent of basic research payments made to a qualified organisation. From July 1, 1996, a new alternative way for computing the research credit has been allowed. The new alternative way employs a three-tiered credit regime with reduced credit rates and fixed base percentages to benefit taxpayers whose base amount is very high because of higher sales.

Low Income Housing Credit

Low income housing credit is allowed to the owner of a qualified low income housing project[32] that is constructed, rehabilitated or acquired. The tax credit is available on a per unit basis for the low income units and can be claimed over a 10-year-period that begins with the tax year in which the project is placed in service or at the taxpayer's election, in the next tax year. The applicable credit rates are the appropriate percentages issued by the IRS for the month in which the building is placed in service.

Disabled Access Credit

A disabled access credit is allowed to eligible small business[33] for expenditure incurred to make business accessible to disabled individuals. The amount of the credit is 50 per cent of the amount of eligible access expenditure[34] for a year that exceeds $250 but that does not exceed $10,250.

Renewable Sources Electricity Production Credit

Credit is allowed for the domestic production of electricity from qualified energy resources such as wind energy facilities. The credit is 1.7 cents per kilowatt-hour of electricity produced during the 10-year-period after the facility is placed in service. The credit is adjusted for inflation annually.

Empowerment Zone Employment Credit

To provide economic revitalisation of distressed urban and rural areas, credit is allowed to employers at the rate of 20 per cent on the first $15,000 of wages paid per employee including training and educational costs paid to full and part-time employees who are residents of an empowerment zone,[35] provided that the employer's trade or business and the principal place of abode are within the empowerment zone. The employer's deduction for wages is, however, reduced by the amount of the credit.

Besides the above, there are other tax credits allowed in the U.S. such as:

(a) the alcohol fuel credit
(b) the enhanced oil recovery credit
(c) the Indian employment credit
(d) the employer social security credit
(e) the orphan drug credit
(f) the welfare to work credit

The components of the general business credit arising in a single year are deemed used in the same order in which they are listed above. The general business credits are combined for the purpose of computing an overall dollar limitation on their use because these credits are not refundable. The general business credit cannot exceed the net income tax minus the greater of the 75 per cent of the tentative minimum tax or 25 per cent of the net regular tax liability above $25,000. Unused general business credits are carried back to 3 years. Any remaining unused credits are then carried forward for 15 years. The entire amount of unused credit is first carried to the earliest year.

Thus, tax incentives are being used in in the U.S. to promote economy and at the same time to achieve certain socially desired activities.

AUSTRALIA

In Australia, very few incentives are available which are business-related. These are as follows:

Income from Sale of Mining Rights

Income from sale, transfer or assignment by a genuine prospector of rights to mine for gold and certain prescribed metals and minerals in Australia are exempt from tax. The exemption applies to assessments for the year 1997-98 and later income years. To be eligible to claim this exemption, the recipient must have acquired the rights before 29 August, 1996. This exemption does not extend to consideration received for plant or mine development work and the royalty income arising indirectly from the sale of a mining right.

Income from an Australian Film

Tax concessions are granted to taxpayers for investing in Australian films. A special deduction for capital expenditure incurred in acquiring an interest in the initial copyright of a new Australian film is allowed to a resident of Australia who becomes the first owner or one of the first owners of the copyright in the film. Further exemption is also allowed for the net earnings from the film up to a fixed percentage of capital investment.

Concession for Primary Producers

In Australia, special tax concession is available to taxpayers engaged in primary production business. This concession is available only to taxpayers to carry on a primary production business, but not to a shareholder in a primary production company or to a person employed in such company.

Concessions available to taxpayers engaged in primary production include special deduction for capital expenditure. Any capital expenditure incurred in establishing horticulture plants can be written off at accelerated annual write-off rate. Capital expenditure incurred in establishing grapevines for use in primary production is deductible at the rate of 25 per cent over a period of 4 years. Capital expenditure on the construction, acquisition or installation of plant or a structural development for the purpose of conserving or conveying water for use in carrying on primary production business is allowed to be deducted over 3 years, i.e. one third every year.

Another incentive allowed to primary producers is *drought investment allowance* to prepare for future droughts by investing in *drought mitigation property* such as fodder storage facility, water storage facility, water transfer facility and minimum tillage equipment. A taxpayer who incurs capital expenditure of at least AUD5,000 on a new item of drought mitigation property qualifies for a deduction of 10 per cent of expenditure with a limit of AUD5,000 in relation to deductions.

Expenditure incurred on land care is deducted outright in the year the expenditure is incurred. Low-income taxpayers are entitled to claim tax offset instead of claiming outright expenditure in a year because of low income.

Income Averaging

Primary producers in Australia are allowed another tax relief, i.e. *income averaging* to ensure that primary producers with fluctuating incomes pay no more tax over a number of years than those on comparable but steady incomes. This is achieved by making averaging adjustment. When the average income is less than the taxable income, the adjustment takes the form of tax offset which reduces tax. When the average income is greater than the taxable income, the adjustment is made by increasing the tax payable. The average income is calculated over a 5 year period. However, for the first averaging calculation, a minimum period of 2 years is required in which the basic taxable income of the second year must not be less than of the first year.

Farm Management Deposit

Farm Management Deposit (FMD) is an arrangement allowing primary producers to shift income from good to bad years in order to deal with adverse economic events and seasonal fluctuations. The arrangement allows primary producers to claim deductions for the FMD's made in the year of deposit and to include the amounts withdrawn in the assessable income in the repayment year. The minimum deposit allowed is AUD1,000 and the total of all deposits cannot exceed AUD3,00,000. The minimum withdrawal allowed is AUD1,000 with a condition that the deposit cannot be repaid within 12 months except when the owner dies or becomes bankrupt or ceases to be a primary producer.

Research and Development Expenditure

Companies which spend money on research and expenditure (R & D) are entitled to the following tax concessions:

1. 125 per cent deduction is allowed for wages, salaries, other labour costs and expenditure incurred on Research and Development (R & D) if the aggregate R & D expenditure for the year is more than AUD20,000. Higher deduction at the rate of 125 per cent is not allowed if the aggregate expenditure is AUD20,000 or less.
2. 100 per cent deduction is allowed for expenditure incurred in acquiring rights to the existing core technology.
3. Expenditure on R & D plant incurred after August 20, 1996 is allowed at 125 per cent, deductible in 3 years at the rate of 41.67 per cent.

Rebate for Residents of Isolated Areas

In Australia, rebate of tax is allowed to individuals who are residents of specified remote areas. Those areas comprise two zones; Zone A and Zone B. While the first Zone comprises those areas where the factor of isolation, uncongenial climate and high cost of living are more pronounced, Zone B comprises the less badly affected areas. The rebate for Zone A residents is accordingly higher than the rebate for Zone B. A special category of zone allowances is available to taxpayers residing in particularly isolated areas, called special areas in both the zones.

To be eligible for the zone rebate, a taxpayer must have either resided in a zone area for at least 183 days in the income year or the taxpayer has actually been in a zone area for more than half the income year. The zone rebate is made up of a basic amount plus a percentage of the relevant rebate amount. (The relevant rebate amount is the sum of the rebates to which the taxpayer is entitled during the income year for a dependent or housekeeper as well as any rebate to which the taxpayer would have been entitled if rebates were still allowed for dependent children and students, i.e. notional dependent rebates and sole parent rebate if it were still available.) The zone rebates for the income year 2000-01 are as under:

Resident of special areas in Zone A or special areas in Zone B	=	AUD1,173 + 50 per cent of the relevant rebate amount
Resident of ordinary Zone A	=	AUD338 + 50 per cent of the relevant rebate amount
Resident of ordinary Zone B	=	AUD57 + 20 per cent of the relevant rebate amount

The zone rebate is in addition to the dependant's rebates and the housekeeper rebate. However, the sum of all rebates cannot exceed the amount of tax otherwise payable.

MALAYSIA

To promote the establishment of industrial, agricultural and other commercial enterprises and for the promotion of exports in Malaysia, many reliefs, incentives and tax rebates are provided. Malaysia has a special Act called the *Promotion of Investments and Development Act*, 1986, which provides a large number of reliefs to the taxpayers engaging themselves in various specified activities. The business-related incentives available in Malaysia are as under:

Income from Sea Transport Business

Income arising from the business of transporting passengers and cargo by sea on board Malaysian ships is exempt from tax from the income year 1999. The exemption has been extended to income from the letting of Malaysian ships on voyages on time charter basis to encourage local shipping industry. Dividend declared out of exempt income is also not taxable in the hands of the shareholders.

Income of Tour Operators

Income of tour operators who are resident in Malaysia and are approved and registered with the Ministry of Culture, Arts and Tourism, arising from the business of operating group inclusive tours is exempt from tax if the tour operators bring in at least 500 foreign tourists. This exemption is available upto the income year 2000-01.

Exemption to Construction Companies

The income of a company resident in Malaysia which is derived from a construction project carried on outside Malaysia is exempt from tax to the extent of 70 per cent.

Exemption to Offshore Companies

Offshore companies carrying on business outside from Labuan[36] enjoy special tax incentives. Offshore companies involved in real estate management, and investment business are exempt from tax, whereas those engaged in trading companies have a choice of paying income tax at the fixed rate of 3 per cent or pay a lump sum of RM20,000 for each year. The offshore trading company has also the option to pay an annual administrative fee of RM 20,000 in lieu of income tax. Tax exemptions are also available in Labuan in respect of professional services income, income from construction projects, dividends, royalties and interest. All these incentives are intended to promote Labuan as an international offshore financial centre.

Exemption of Overseas Income

Income remitted by Malaysian companies investing overseas are exempt from income tax except business income from banking, insurance, sea and transport businesses.

Exemption to Research Companies

Approved research companies and institutions which are established to undertake research and development for a particular industry, enjoy a tax exemption for a period of 5 years. Dividends distributed by such a company are also exempt in the hands of its shareholders. In Malaysia, cash contribution to an approved research institute or for any payment for the use of services of an approved institute, is eligible for double deduction.

Income from Repair and Maintenance of Luxury Boats and Yachts

Income from repair and maintenance activity in relation to luxury boats and yachts in Langakawi, an island of Malaysia has been granted exemption for a period of five years to make it a popular centre for the repair and maintenance of luxury boats and yachts for the tourists who visit this island.

Income from Sports, Culture and Arts

To promote organisers of sports, culture and arts activities, 50 per cent exemption of income tax is allowed to organisers of car and motorcycle racing events, sports, cultural and art shows, exhibition and festivals involving foreign participation at the National Sports Complex, National Theatre, National Art Gallery. Income of non-residents performing in these events and drivers of cars and motorcycles in races held in Malaysia is exempt from income tax.

Incentives for Employment of Disabled Persons

In Malaysia, a taxpayer who employs a physically or mentally disabled person is eligible for double deduction in respect of remuneration paid to such a person if the said remuneration is incurred wholly and exclusively in the production of income. A company is also eligible for double deduction of expenses incurred in training of any handicapped person who is not an employee of the company.

Double Deduction of Insurance Premiums for Import/Export

A taxpayer who incurs insurance premium on the cargo imported into Malaysia is entitled to double deduction in respect of such premiums if the risks are insured with a company incorporated in Malaysia. The expenses are eligible for double deduction in respect of insurance premiums paid to local insurance companies for the insurance of exported cargo and for payments in respect of export credit insurance obtained from Malaysia Export Credit Insurance Berhod.

Freight Charges

Manufacturers in Malaysia are entitled to double deduction of freight charges incurred on the shipment of manufactured goods from Sabah and Sarawak to Peninsular Malaysia if they use the ports in Peninsular Malaysia.

Pioneer Status

All companies participating in a promoted activity[37] or producing a promoted product are eligible to pioneer status whereby an exemption is given from income tax for a period of 5 years. Tax holiday of the qualifying company starts from the day of production. The exemption until November 1, 1999 was 100 per cent of profits. However, from November 1, 1999, only 70 per cent of the statutory income from the pioneer business for each of the 5 years is exempt from tax. The balance of the statutory income is taxable at the normal corporate tax rate. Projects eligible for pioneer status located in promoted areas[38] are eligible for 85 per cent deduction of the statutory income. Small-scale manufacturing companies[39] are also eligible for pioneer status. The dividends.paid by a pioneer company out of its exempt income are exempt in the hands of the recipient shareholders.

Incentives to Banks

To encourage and develop the banking industry in Malaysia, a tax rebate is given to commercial banks and financial institutions which provide loans to small business under the public loan scheme. The tax rebate allowed is 2 per cent of the amount worked out by dividing the loan amount by the interest rate. It is to be noted that this is a tax rebate and as such, the amount is deducted from the income tax liability, and not from the income.

Incentives to Insurance and Shipping Industries

In Malaysia, resident companies carrying on sea transport business are exempt from tax. Income of insurance companies from inward reinsurance business, inward life reinsurance business and from insuring offshore risks are taxed at a concessional rate of 5 per cent instead of the normal rate of 28 per cent.

Incentives to Operational Headquarters

Income of multinational companies derived from the provision of qualified services[40] to the operational headquarters' offices or related companies outside Malaysia are taxed at a concessional rate of 10 per cent.

Incentives to Service Projects

In Malaysia, income tax incentives are available to approved service projects in relation to transportation, communications, utilities or any other sectors as may be approved, considering the large capital investment and long gestation period, imports substitution, generation of employment opportunity, etc. The deduction allowed is 70 per cent of the statutory income for a period of 5 years. However, for companies in Sabah, Sarawak and designated Eastern Corridor of Peninsular Malaysia, the deduction allowed is 85 per cent of the statutory income. For companies of national and strategic importance, the exemption for approved services project is 100 per cent of the statutory income for a period of 10 years.

A company undertaking approved services project, instead of claiming exemption of income can opt for investment allowance which is 60 per cent of the capital expenditure for 5 years. For companies in Sabah, Sarawak and the designated Eastern Corridor of Peninsular Malaysia, the investment allowance rate is 80 per cent of the capital expenditure and for companies of national and strategic importance, the rate of investment allowance is 100 per cent for a period of 5 years only. However, the investment allowance is restricted to 70 per cent, 85 per cent and 100 per cent of the statutory income respectively for all the three classes of companies stated above.

Incentive for Multimedia Super Corridor

To develop state of the art information-based industries, Multimedia Super Corridor (MSC) is a region crafted to enable mutual enrichment of companies and countries using leading technology in a borderless world. Companies setting up new business in a MSC-designated cyber city are eligible to receive a 5 year exemption from tax on their statutory income and they can renew the exemption for a second 5 year term on the basis of its performance in transferring technology or knowledge to Malaysia. Alternatively, these companies can claim 100 per cent Investment Tax Allowance on investments made in the MSC.

Training Incentives

Manufacturing companies, non-manufacturing companies and companies carrying on hotel or tour operating business are entitled to double deduction in respect of fees incurred on the training of their employees.

Income from Royalty for use of Artistic Work, Musical Composition

Income of RM6,000 derived by a resident individual taxpayer from royalty or payment in respect of publication or use of any artistic work and royalty in respect of recording discs or tapes is exempt from income tax. Similarly, income of RM12,000 in an income year derived by a resident individual taxpayer as payment in respect of any musical composition or in respect of any translation of books or literary work at the request of any agency of the Ministry of Education or the Attorney General's chambers is exempt from income tax. Income from royalty in respect of publication or use of any literary work or any original painting is exempt upto RM20,000.

Investment Tax Allowance

Investment tax allowance is allowed to activities in manufacturing, agriculture, tourist and other industrial and commercial undertakings and is available to companies carrying on promoted activities or carrying on production of promoted products which are of national and strategic importance to Malaysia and which are located in promoted areas. The allowance is admissible at the rate of 60 per cent of the capital expenditure incurred on industrial buildings, and plant and machinery directly used for the purposes of promoted activities or for the production of promoted products, but it is restricted to a maximum of 70 per cent of the statutory business income. Investment Tax Allowance from November 1, 1991 is not granted to a company, which has previously benefited directly or indirectly from pioneer status or investment tax allowance in respect of a similar related activity or product.

Industrial Adjustment Allowance

Industrial Adjustment Allowance (IAA) means any activity proposed to be undertaken by a particular sector in the manufacturing industry to restructure by way of reorganisation, reconstruction or amalgamation within that particular sector with a view to strengthening the basis for industrial self-sufficiency, improving industrial technology, increasing productivity, and enhancing the efficient use of natural resources and the efficient management of manpower. Presently, the Government of Malaysia accepted in principle six sub-sectors for industrial adjustment which are bar and road rolling, veneer and plywood saw milling, motor car assembly, oil palm refining and fractionation and ship building.

The IAA is a new incentive which came into effect from the income year 1991, and is available to a manufacturing company which undertakes an approved industrial adjustment programme. To be eligible for this allowance, a company must be one that has been granted pioneer status or is eligible for investment tax allowance. The allowance is admissible in respect of capital expenditure other than capital expenditure on which investment tax allowance has been granted after the pioneer tax holiday or the investment tax allowance relief period has ended. The allowance is admissible at a certain percentage not exceeding 100 per cent of the capital expenditure incurred on a factory or any plant or machinery used in Malaysia in connection with and for the purposes of the manufactured product.

Infrastructure Allowance

The infrastructure[41] allowance is allowed to a resident company which has incurred capital expenditure on infrastructure in respect of business in a promoted area. It is given at the rate of 100 per cent of the capital expenditure incurred on infrastructure.

Investment Allowance

Malaysian resident companies which have been in operation for not less than 12 months and which embark on an approved project[42] are eligible for an investment allowance. The allowance is admissible at the rate of 60 per cent on capital expenditure incurred on factory, plant, machinery or any other apparatus used for the purpose of the project. The investment allowance is deducted from statutory income and is restricted to 70 per cent of it. Any unabsorbed investment allowance is carried forward for set off in future years until it is fully utilised.

Incentives for Export

Incentives are allowed to a manufacturing company or a company engaged in agriculture for increased exports to encourage the promotion of exports. The relief is given at the rate of 10 per cent of the value of increased export of manufacturing products where the products exported have at least 30 per cent value addition whereas the rate is 15 per cent if the value addition is at least 50 per cent. For increased export of agricultural produce, the rate is 10 per cent. However, export of certain products such as tin, ingots, tin ore, natural rubber, crude palm oil, copra, logs, petroleum oil, gases, etc., are not eligible for this allowance. The allowance is restricted to 70 per cent of the statutory income. However, no unutilised allowance is allowed to be carried forward.

Exemption for Export Promotion

For promotion of export in Malaysia, double deduction is allowed in respect of expenses incurred for the promotion of exports which includes overseas advertising, free samples, export market research and expenses attributable to participation in trade fairs.

The entire service sector in Malaysia is also eligible for double deduction on expenses incurred in the promotion of the export of services, research and development and training. The double deduction for expenditure incurred on local advertising of Malaysia in branded products is also allowed in case at least 20 per cent of the total sale of the Malaysian brand name goods in the relevant year of assessment are exported and the Malaysian company itself is the registered proprietor of the Malaysian brand name used in the advertisement.

PAKISTAN

One of the several objectives of the taxation system in Pakistan, i.e. to promote specific economic activities, is achieved through a variety of tax concessions and exemptions, rebates and credits.

The most distinguishing feature of the exemption is the agricultural income, which is totally tax-exempt. The business-related deductions allowed in Pakistan are as under:

Incentive for Newly Established Industrial Undertakings

The newly established industrial undertakings that commenced commercial production any time between July 1, 1995 and June 30, 1998 are eligible for claiming exemption from tax payable on such profits and gains as are derived from the manufacture or process of goods or materials, ship building, generation, transmission, distribution or supply of electrical energy or hydraulic power. The deduction allowed is equal to 10 per cent of the capital employed in the said undertakings.

Income from Running of Computer Training Institution

Any profits and gains derived by taxpayer from running a computer training institution or computer training scheme which is recognised by the Board of Education or University and is set up between July 1, 1997 and June 1, 2005, is exempt for a period of 5 years beginning from the month in which such institution is set up. Income from the running of an education institution set up between July 1, 1997 and June 30, 2000 is also exempt for a period of 5 years.

Income from Transport Business

Any income derived by a taxpayer from the plying of any vehicle registered in the territory of Azad Jammu and Kashmir other than the income arising from the operation of such vehicle in Pakistan to a person who is resident in Pakistan and non-resident in those territories, is exempt from income tax.

Tax Holiday for Pioneer Industrial Undertakings

Income derived by a taxpayer from a pioneer industrial undertaking[43] which has been set up by June 30, 1997, enjoys a tax holiday for a period of 5 years from the date of commencement of commercial production.

Tax Holiday for Electronic Equipment and Component

An industrial undertaking engaged in the manufacture of electronic equipment or component thereof which was set up in the North West Frontier

Province or in the Islamabad Capital Territory by June 30, 1997 is exempt from income tax for a period of 5 years.

Income from Food Processing, Manufacture of and Soft and Stuffed Toys, Solar Energy Equipment

In Pakistan, income derived by a taxpayer from an industrial undertaking owned and managed by a company and engaged in the food processing and set up between July 1, 1994 and June 30, 2000 enjoys a tax holiday for a period of 5 years from the date of commencement of commercial production. Similarly, income of an industrial undertaking engaged in the manufacture of soft and stuffed toys is also eligible for tax holiday for a period of 5 years from the date of commencement of commercial production. Likewise, industrial undertakings engaged in the manufacture of solar, thermal, photo voltaic equipment for production of solar energy and solar appliances and set up between July 1, 1997 and June 1, 2000 is eligible for tax holiday for a period of 5 years from the date of commencement of commercial production.

Income from the Export of Computer Software

Income from the export of computer software and tax-related services developed in Pakistan are exempt from income tax.

Income of Industrial Undertakings in Export Processing Zone

Income of industrial undertakings in export processing zone is also exempt for a period of 5 years from the date of commencement of production. Income of certain agro-based industrial undertaking is also allowed a 5-year holiday. Profits and gains derived by the assessee in the Karachi Export Processing zone upto June 30, 1997 is also exempt.

Profits and gains of industrial undertakings in special industrial zones set up from 1 July, 1995 to June 30, 1999, is allowed a tax holiday for a period of 10 years beginning with the month in which the undertaking is set up or commercial production is commenced, whichever is later.

Exemption to Power Projects

Profits and gains derived by an assessee from an electric power generation project set up in Pakistan on or after July 1, 1998 and from the transmission line project set up in Pakistan on or after July 1, 1995 shall be exempt if the project is owned by a company in Pakistan and not more than 50 per cent shares of the company are owned by the government or local authority.

Income from Ships Registered in Pakistan

Income from ships registered in Pakistan is exempt from tax.

Tax Credit for Purchase of Plant and Machinery

A company taxpayer is entitled to a tax rebate against tax payable by it at

10 per cent of the amount invested in purchase of plant and machinery for installation at any time between July 1, 2000 and June 30, 2002 in an industrial undertaking set up in Pakistan and owned by the tax payer. The plant and machinery installed includes plant and machinery for the purposes of balancing, modernisation and replacement.

Tax Rebates for Furnishing National Tax Number

1. In Pakistan, a rebate of 5 per cent of tax is allowed to a taxpayer other than a company who derives income from business or profession in case the name of the customer, his address and national tax number (NTN) is stated on each transaction of sale or receipt.
2. Similarly, a taxpayer who derives income from import of goods or wholesale business is entitled to a rebate of 5 per cent of tax if he furnishes complete details of sales giving the namc, NTN and full address of the purchaser.
3. A taxpayer incurring any personal expenditure on legal services is entitled to a tax rebate at the average rate of the tax on the total amount of such payment made in case he furnishes along with his return of income, the receipt, NTN and complete address of the legal practitioners.

Deduction of medical expenditure incurred and allowance for books as discussed earlier in this chapter in Pakistan is also allowed only on furnishing NTN and address of the payee.

Tax rebates on furnishing NTN appear to be more as tax avoidance measures. The income tax department on the basis of information submitted by the taxpayer for claiming the rebate can follow-up and verify the income of the persons whose particulars are thus submitted.

Other Incentives

Reliefs are also given to various classes of income by reducing the tax rate as follows:

1. For companies engaged in exploration and extraction of mineral deposits, the tax rate applicable is reduced by 50 per cent for a period of 5 years immediately following the exemption period of 5 years.
2. An industrial undertaking set up in an area declared by the Federal Government to be a zone is charged to tax at the rate equal to 25 per cent of the rate for a period of 5 years after the expiry period of full exemption.

INDIA

In India, a large number of incentives are available which are meant to promote industrial growth and exports. These incentimes allowed under the Act for the income year 2000-01 are as follows:

Tax Incentives to Promote Certain Industries

Many industries have been earmarked as priority industries to be promoted through tax reliefs by the Government of India. The following industries enjoy tax holiday subject to the fulfilment of necessary conditions under Sec. 80-1B:

1. Industrial undertakings set up in industrial backward state.
2. Industrial undertakings set up in category A, notified backward district.
3. Industrial undertakings set up in category B, notified backward district.
4. Industrial undertakings manufacturing items other than specified in the Eleventh Schedule.
5. Small scale industrial undertaking.

All these industrial undertakings, if set up within the specified time are entitled to claim exemption. In the case of first two categories of industrial undertakings, 100 per cent exemption from tax on profit is given to all the assessees for the first 5 years, and 30 per cent exemption to a company and 25 per cent exemption to other assessees is given for the next 5 years. In the case of category B notified backward district, the exemption is the same except that instead of the first 5 years, it is for the first 3 years. In the remaining two categories, 30 per cent exemption from tax in respect of profits for first 10 years is given to companies and 25 per cent exemption is given to other assessees for the same period.

Companies Engaged in the Operation of Ship

An Indian company deriving profits from the business of operation of a ship, if set up before April 1, 1995 is entitled to exemption of 30 per cent of profits for the first 10 years (Sec. 80 1B).

Hotel Industry

If a hotel industry is located in specified area, i.e. hilly area, rural area or a place of pilgrimage and set up between April 1, 1990 and March 31, 1994. (At a place other than Delhi, Mumbai, Calcutta, Chennai, if started between April 1, 1997 and March 31, 2001), 50 per cent of profits will be deductible for the first 10 years. If that hotel is situated in any other non-specified area, then 30 per cent of profits will be deductible for the first 10 years (Sec. 80 1B).

Infrastructure Facility

Any enterprise carrying on the business of developing, maintaining and operating any infrastructure facility is allowed deduction of 100 per cent of profits for the first 5 years and 30 per cent for the next 5 years (Sec. 80 1A).

Companies engaged in Industrial Research

Approved companies engaged in scientific and industrial research and development activities are entitled to a deduction of 100 per cent of profits for the first 5 years (Sec. 80-1B).

Telecommunication Services

Considering the growing demand of telecommunication services in the fast changing world, undertakings providing telecommunication services, radio paging, domestic satellite service, network of linking and electronic data interchange service will be entitled to a deduction of 100 per cent of profit for first 5 years and 30 per cent in case of a company and 25 per cent in case of other taxpayers for the next 5 years (Sec. 80 1A).

Industrial Parks

Undertakings approved under the scheme for industrial parks by the Ministry of Industry enjoys deduction similar to the one available to telecommunication services above (Sec. 80 1A).

Production of Mineral Oil

Undertakings engaged in the production of mineral oil, and in refining of the oil are entitled to a deduction of 100 per cent of profits for the first 7 years (Sec. 80 1B).

Housing and Other Development Activities, which are Integral Part of Highway Project

Profits earned by an undertakings engaged in housing or other activities which are integral part of a highway project shall be exempt if transferred to a special reserve account and utilised for highway project excluding housing and other activities before the expiry of 3 years following the previous year in which such amount was transferred (Sec. 80 1A).

Developing and Building Housing Projects

Undertakings engaged in developing and building housing project are entitled to a deduction of 100 per cent of profit if the project is approved by a local authority (Sec. 80 1B).

Incentive for Tea Growing and Manufacturing

A taxpayer engaged in the business of growing and manufacturing tea in India is entitled to a deduction upto 20 per cent of the profits of such business in case the same is deposited in Tea Deposit Account in accordance with a scheme. The amount can be used later on for the purpose specified in the scheme approved by the tea board (Sec. 33 AB).

Incentive for Site Restoration to Business of Prospecting Petroleum or Natural Gas

A taxpayer engaged in the business of prospecting for, or extraction or production of petroleum or natural gas or both in India and with whom the Government of India has entered into an agreement, is eligible for a deduction of upto 20 per cent of profits of such business in case the same is deposited in Site Restoration Account in accordance with a scheme framed by Petroleum Ministry. The amount can be withdrawn later on for utilisation for the purposes of the scheme (Sec. 33 ABA).

Incentive for Shipping Business

A taxpayer being a public company or a government company formed and registered in India with the main object of carrying on the business of operation of ships is eligible for a deduction upto 50 per cent of the profits derived from much operation if the same is transferred to a reserve account. The amount in reserve account is to be used for acquiring a new ship for the purpose of the business of the assessee within a period of the next 8 years (Sec. 33 AC).

Incentive for Expenditure on Scientific Research

A taxpayer in India is entitled to deduct the entire expenditure including capital expenditure incurred on scientific research related to the business. Contribution by a taxpayer to approved scientific research association, university, college or institution for the use of scientific research whether related or unrelated to the business of the taxpayer or to a national laboratory, Indian Institute of Technology is eligible for a weighted deduction of one and one fourth times the contribution. Weighted deduction equal to one and one half times the expenditure including capital expenditure (other than on land) incurred on in-house research and development is allowed to company taxpayers engaged in the business of manufacture or production of drugs, pharmaceuticals, electronic equipments, computers, telecommunication equipments, chemicals, etc. provided the research and development facility are approved by the prescribed authority (Sec. 35).

Incentive for Rural Development Programmes and Conservation of Natural Resources

A taxpayer is entitled to claim by way of business expenditure any amount paid to associations and institutions carrying out approved rural development programmes (including training of personnel for implementation of a rural development programme) and conservation of natural resources (Sec. 35 CCA, Sec. 35CCB)

Incentive for Providing Long-term Finance

In India, a financial corporation engaged in providing long-term finance for industrial or agricultural development or development of infrastructure facility and a public company carrying on the business of providing long-term finance for construction or purchase of residential houses are allowed a deduction upto 40 per cent of the profits derived from such business, if transferred to a special reserve account. However, the balance in the special reserve account cannot exceed twice the amount of the share capital and the reserve. The amount withdrawn from the special reserve account is treated as income of the year in which the amount is withdrawn [Sec. 36(i)(viii)].

Export Incentives

Profits and gains derived either by an Indian company or a resident non-corporate taxpayer from the export of specified goods and merchandise computer software, films, television software, and music software, were totally exempt up to the income year 1999-2000.

However, from the income year 2000-01, the above exemptions are being phased out. Only 80 per cent income will be exempt for the income year 2000-01, 70 per cent for the income year 2001-02, 50 per cent for the income year 2002-03 and 30 per cent for the income year 2003-04. No exemption will be available from the income year 2004-05 onwards.

Tax Reliefs Granted to Earn Foreign Exchange

To encourage the inflow of more and more foreign exchange in India, many other incentives are provided to a resident assessee who earn income in foreign currency. A resident assessee who enters into a contract with the foreign government or a foreign enterprise for the construction of any building, road, dam or any other approved project is allowed a deduction up to 40 per cent (for the income year 2000-01) of profits derived from the project outside India, provided at least 40 per cent of the profits are brought into India in convertible foreign exchange. (Sec. 80-HHB) A similar deduction up to 40 per cent of profits derived by a resident assessee from a housing project aided by the World Bank is also allowed (Sec. 80 HHBA). To give boost to tourist business as well as to earn foreign exchange from foreign tourists, deduction is allowed to a resident taxpayer or an Indian company engaged in the business of hotel, tour operators, or of travel agents. The deduction is allowed only in respect of profits derived from services provided to foreign tourists and is restricted to 40 per cent of the eligible profits derived from such business (Sec. 80 HHD).

Royalty received by a resident assessee from foreign enterprise is deductible to the extent of 40 per cent of the income received in, or brought into India in convertible foreign exchange within 6 months from the end of the previous year (Sec. 80-O). Similarly, remuneration received by Indian citizens being professors, and teachers from foreign university or educational institution or income from foreign sources received by an author, an actor, an artist, a musician, sportsmen and remuneration received by a technician from outside India are deductible up to 60 per cent of such amount as is brought in India in convertible foreign exchange within a period of 6 months from the end of the previous year (Sec. 80 R, 80 RR and 80 RRA). The exemption has been reduced proportionately in the subsequent income years as in the case of export income and is finally meant to be phased out by income year 2004-05.

Tax holiday in Respect of Newly Established Industrial Undertaking in Free Trade Zones

All taxpayers are entitled to tax holiday in respect of profits and gains derived from a newly established industrial undertaking, established in any *free trade zone* (FTZ) or any electronic hardware technology park (Sec. 10A). An eligible unit is entitled to full tax exemption in respect of profits and gains for a period of 10 consecutive assessment years beginning with the assessment year, relevant to the previous year in which the undertaking starts its production activity. The benefit under section 10A is available only if the exports by the undertakings are not less than 75 per cent of the total sales during the previous year.

Tax Holiday for Newly Established 100 per cent Export-oriented Undertakings

Profits and gains of newly established 100 per cent *export oriented undertakings* (EOU) are eligible for exemption in respect of 10 consecutive assessment years beginning from the year in which the industrial undertaking commences production (Sec. 10B). However, export should not be less than 75 per cent of the total sales.

To claim the above two exemptions it is necessary that the unit should not be formed by splitting up or reconstruction of business already in existence, and it should not be formed by transfer of old plant and machinery. The tax holiday period for industrial undertaking in FTZ and EOU has been limited up to the income year 2008-09. As such, new units set up will not be able to claim exemption of full 10 years.

Where exemption is claimed under Sec. 10A and 10B, the deduction on account of depreciation allowance, investment allowance, capital expenditure on scientific research and capital expenditure on family planning shall be deemed to have been fully allowed. Such allowances, even if unabsorbed, shall be deemed to have been fully allowed. Unabsorbed business loss or capital loss with respect to any assessment year forming part of the tax holiday period shall not be allowed to be adjusted in any subsequent assessment years.

Conclusion

A study of the business-related incentives shows that developing countries are providing a maximum number of incentives. In these countries, releifs are being provided for various industries, various zones, and specified areas. In all the three developing countries, incentives are available for a new industry, shipping industry and to some other specific industries, which are special to each country. Not only that, tax incentives are provided for export and for other services, which earn foreign exchange.

As against this, no business-related incentive have been found in the U.K. income tax legislation. This shows that no priority is given to any business nor to any area in the U.K. In the U.S., business-related incentives are very few and are meant only for rehabilitation, research and low income housing. Certain incentives in the U.S. are provided for economic revitalisation of distressed urban and rural areas and to create work opportunities for individuals who are economically disadvantaged. Tax concessions in Australia are allowed mainly to primary producers, for research and development expenditure and some concession by way of rebate to residents of isolated areas. In contrast, incentives provided in the developing countries are very large and the objectives are to promote industrial growth, to stimulate economy and to bring economic parity and to achieve regional balance.

In Malaysia, income of some industries are wholly exempt from tax. This include income from Sea transport business, research companies and institutions, income of tour operators, income from repairs and maintenance of luxury boats and yachts. Many industries enjoy deduction up to 70 per cent of statutory total income. These include construction projects outside Malaysia, pioneer industries engaged in priority products or engaged in promoted areas, or companies engaged in incurring capital expenditure on infrastructure. Double deduction is allowed in respect of certain expenses related to exports including insurance premium for import/export overseas advertising, supply of free samples abroad, export market research.

Further, to promote tourist business, exemption is granted on income from repair and maintenance of luxury boats and yachts in Langakawi, an island of Malaysia. Many incentives are provided in Malaysia reflecting the priority given to cultural development. Exemption up to a specified limit is granted to organisers of sports, cultural and art activities at certain specified places.

In Pakistan, agricultural income is wholly exempt from tax and export income is taxed at a negligible rate, around one per cent. Besides, tax holiday for 5 years is provided in respect of income from: (1) industrial undertakings in Export Processing Zone, (2) to certain new establishment industrial undertakings, (3) pioneer industrial undertakings, (4) industries engaged in the manufacture of electronic equipment component, or food processing or industries engaged in manufacture of soft and stuffed toys, solar energy equipment, (5) income from certain power projects, and (6) income from ships registered in Pakistan.

In India, besides exemption granted to agricultural income, tax reliefs are provided to promote various industries set up within a specified time. Industries engaged in the generation, distribution of electricity or power or undertaking set up in industrially backward state or set up in notified backward area are and small scale industries granted tax holiday. Further, hotel industry, shipping industry, industrial undertakings engaged in developing, maintaining and operating infrastructure facilities, telecommunication services, industrial undertaking engaged in industrial research, housing and other projects, are also granted exemption. Export incentives and incentives to earn foreign exchange are also available though the same are being reduced gradually.

Although, it is true that the tax revenue gets affected as a result of these incentives, the loss of revenue can be a temporary phase. The long-term benefits of these industries are likely to be permanent in nature. While social incentives are need based, business incentives are meant to be growth-oriented. The former affect the existing tax base and current tax revenue, the latter affects the future tax base and are meant to broaden the tax base in future and are likely to lead to a broadening of it. Moreover, it does not affect the existing tax base as the income is not in existence rather relief is given to earn income through the setting up of industries.

Impact of Tax Reliefs on Tax Revenue

Analysis of tax reliefs and incentives reveals that while the developed countries provide more social reliefs, the developing countries provide more business-related incentives. To find out the impact of tax reliefs and incentives on tax revenue, the statistical data from different countries has been collected. Although, the data in different countries is given in different forms, an attempt has been made to present the data in a comparable form. Some of the incentives including retirement benefits, depreciation and the amount of dividend imputation benefit in the U.K. could not be incorporated in the Table on account of non-availability of data. It however, covers most of the reliefs available in India except depreciation.

The impact of various tax incentives including social welfare investment, business and other incentives on tax revenue is shown in Table 6.5.

It emerges from Table 6.5 that the social welfare reliefs and incentives have affected tax revenue to the maximum degree. These reliefs constituted 95.99 per cent of reliefs in the U.S. In Australia, investment-related incentives have been found to be the highest, i.e. 52.83 per cent. It appears that these were high due to dividend imputation system and inter-corporate dividend rebate. Business incentives have been found to be the highest in India, i.e. 29.57 per cent. Although Malaysia and Pakistan also provide a large number of such incentives, the data of these countries is not available.

Tax Relief as Percentage of Total Tax Liability

The total incentives as shown in Table 6.6 have been found to be maximum in the U.K., i.e. 35.96 per cent and the least in India, i.e. 20.44 per cent. (The data of Malaysia and Pakistan is not available. Thus, as against the general view, it is clear that tax incentives actually provided in India have been even less than the tax incentives provided in all the three developed countries.

TABLE 6.5. AMOUNT OF TAX INCENTIVES AND REBATES

(for the income year 1997-98, amount in millions)

Type of Incentives	U.K. £	U.S. $	Australia AUD	Malaysia RM	Pakistan	India Rs.
Social welfare Incentives	45,745 (86.62)	364,231 (95.99)	17,867 (43.19)	1,999	n.a.	63,997 (56.48)
Investment Incentives	4,435 (8.40)	8,065 (2.12)	18,205 (52.83)	n.a.	n.a.	14,834 (13.69)
Business Incentives	nil	7,070 (1.86)	1,086 (3.16)	n.a.	n.a.	33,531 (29.57)
Other Incentives	2,630 (4.98)	85 (0.02)	263 (0.76)	n.a.	n.a.	1,015 (6.895)
Total Incentives	52,810	379,451	34,421	n.a.	n.a.	113,377

Notes: 1. Figures in bracket represent incentives as percentage of total tax.
2. n.a. means not available.

Source: Same as in Table 6.3.

TABLE 6.6. TAX RELIEFS AS PERCENTAGE OF TOTAL TAX LIABILITY

(for the income year 1997-98)

Country	Currency	Tax Reliefs	Total Tax Liability	Tax Reliefs as per cent of Total Tax Liability
U.K.	£	52,810	146,847	35.96
U.S.	$	379,451	1,354,700	28.00
Australia	AUD	34,421	122,388	28.12
Malaysia	RM	n.a	24,261	n.a
Pakistan	PKR	n.a	n.a	n.a
India	Rs.	113,377	554,765	20.43

Source: As in Table 6.3.

It is quite obvious that tax incentives and reliefs are a part of tax system of different countries reflecting the priorities, economic and political compulsions and social objectives intended to be achieved by the governments. An overall analysis of the tax incentive provisions show that the developed countries, i.e. the U.K., the U.S. and Australia, are using social-welfare incentives to improve the social conditions, whereas developing countries, namely, Malaysia, Pakistan and India are using business-related incentives to promote industrial and economic growth.

NOTES

1. Ken Messere, *Tax Policy in OECD Countries; Choices and Conflicts* (Amsterdam: IBFD Publications, 1993), p. 465.
2. Charles E. McLure Jr, 'Tax Holidays and Investment Incentives: A Comparative Analysis' *International Bureau of Fiscal Documentation*, Vol. 53, No, 819 (Aug.-Sep. 1999), pp. 326-38.
3. Alan Melville, *Taxation Finance Act:* 2000 (Harlow, England: Pearson Education Ltd., 2001), p. 33.
4. A deed of covenant is a legally binding agreement where the payer agrees to pay a certain amount to the charity annually.
5. Adjusted gross income is the sum arrived at after deducing certain expenditures from the 'gross income'. These expenses are: trade or business expense, rental and royalty expenses, capital loss deductions, alimony paid, contribution to individual retirement accounts (IRAs), moving expenses, reimbursed employee business expenses and one-half of the self-employment taxes paid.
6. A single taxpayer is an individual who is not married on the last day of the tax year and does not have any dependents to support.
7. The head of the household is a single taxpayer who provides support to a relative. To qualify as a head of household, the unmarried taxpayer must pay more than half the cost of maintaining a home that is the principal residence for more than half the year of (1) a qualified dependent, including children, parents and other relatives, or (2) an unmarried child or other direct linear descendent who does not qualify as a dependent.
8. A capital gain property is one that would result in long-term capital gain if sold at its fair market value on the date of contribution.
9. An ordinary income property is a property that would give rise to an ordinary income or short-term capital gain if sold at its FMV on the date of contribution.
10. Qualifying expenses include expenses paid for household services and for the care of qualifying individual.

11. Earned income includes salary income for personal services, and net self-employment income, etc.
12. Qualified adoption expenses include reasonable and necessary adoption fees, court costs, attorney fees and other expenses which are directly related to the legal adoption of an eligible child.
13. An eligible child is an individual who has not attained the age of 18 as on the time of the adoption or who is physically or mentally incapable of caring for himself.
14. Spouse includes a legal or *de facto* husband or wife, but not a divorced husband or wife.
15. Invalid relative means a person aged 16 or more who is a child (including an adopted child, step-child or ex-nuptial child), brother or sister of the taxpayer and who is in receipt of a disability support pension or is certified by an appropriate medical practitioner as having a continuing inability to work.
16. Parents of a taxpayer or taxpayer's spouse includes the parents of the taxpayer and the parents of the taxpayer's (legal or *de facto)* spouse, but does not include a grand parent.
17. *CCH Australian Master Tax Guide: 2001* (Sydney: CCH Australia Ltd., 2001), p. 828.
18. The separate net income is the dependant's gross income including social security payments less expenses which in accordance with the ordinary accounting and commercial principles are direct costs against that income
19. Veerinderjeet Singh and Teoh Boon Kee (eds.), *CCH, Malaysian Master Tax Guide (*Singapore: CCH Asia PTE Ltd., 2000), p. 141.
20. Adjusted gross total income means gross total income less (a) amount deductible under section 80CCC to 80U, excluding section 80G, (b) Long term capital gains, (c) such income on which income tax is not payable, i.e. share from association of persons, and (d) income referred to in Sections 115A, 115AB, 115AC, 115AD and 115D. (These are incomes of non-resident Indian and foreign companies.)
21. For details, see Chapter 3
22. For details, see Chapter 7
23. Qualifying companies are the unlisted U.K. trading companies whose gross assets are not more than £15 million immediately before the investment is made and no more than £16 million immediately afterward and the taxpayer is not connected with the company at any time during the two years prior to the date of investment and five years after that date.
24. Venture capital trust (VCT) is a company listed on the stock exchange having income wholly or mainly from shares or securities and at least 70 per cent of its total investment of which is in shares or securities newly issued to VCT and is approved as such by the Board of Inland Revenue.
25. Qualified residence includes the principal residence of the taxpayer and one other residence, i.e. vacation home.
26. Acquisition indebtedness is debt incurred in acquiring, constructing or substantially improving a qualified residence and secured by such residence.
27. Home equity indebtedness is all debt other than acquisition debt that is secured by a qualified residence to the extent it does not exceed the fair market value of the residence reduced by any acquisition indebtedness.
28. The investee companies are referred to as small-medium enterprises.
29. An eligible issue of capital means an issue by a public company formed in India where the entire proceeds is utilised for developing, maintaining and operating an infrastructure facility or for generating and distributing power or for providing telecommunication services whether basic or cellular.
30. Certified historic structures are structures certified by the Department of Treasure and located in a registered historic district or listed in the National Register.

31. Base amount is the product of the fixed-base percentage and the taxpayer's average annual gross receipts for the four tax years before the current year.
32. A qualified low-income housing project is any project for residential rental property that meets the requirements for low-income tenant occupancy, gross rent restrictions, state credit authority and IRS certification.
33. An eligible small business is a person that elects to claim the disabled access credit and had in the preceding tax year either gross receipts that did not exceed $1,000,000 or no more than 30 full time employees.
34. Eligible access expenditure includes reasonable and necessary amounts paid or incurred for the purpose of removing architecture, communication, physical or transportation barriers that prevent a business from being accessible to or usable by disabled individuals.
35. Empowerment zones and enterprise zones that have a condition of pervasive poverty, employment and general distress are designated by the Secretary of Housing and Urban Development and the Secretary of Agriculture.
36. Labuan is a Federal Territory administered by the Federal Government of Malaysia.
37. Promoted activity means an activity in agriculture, integrated agriculture, hotel, tourist or other industrial or commercial activity determined by the Minister.
38. Promoted areas are defined as the Eastern Corridor of Peninsular Malaysia.
39. A small scale manufacturing company is a company incorporated in Malaysia and which is resident in Malaysia and whose shareholder funds do not exceed RM500,000 and of which at least 70 per cent of the equity shareholding is held by Malaysian citizens.
40. Qualifying services include services in respect of general management, administration, planning, coordination, procurement, training and personnel management, etc.
41. Infrastructure means any construction, reconstruction, extension or improvement of any permanent structure including bridge, jetty, port or road in respect of a business or businesses in operation in a promoted area.
42. An approved project means a project for manufacture or processing undertaken by a company expanding, modernizing or automating its business.
43. A pioneer industrial undertaking is an undertaking which is owned and managed by a company formed and registered in Pakistan which is based on a highly sophisticated technology and the technology employed has fast obsolescence and the investment involves high risk and the goods produced or to be produced are such that neither these goods nor identical substitutes thereof are being produced in Pakistan and is approved as such by the Central Board of Revenue.

CHAPTER 7

Corporate Taxation and Dividend Income

A company is an artificial entity created under the state law and plays a significant role in the economic growth of a country. As a separate statutory entity, it can enter into contracts in its name, own property and be sued, and is required to pay income tax based on its taxable income. A special tax on the corporate form of doing business is considered appropriate because corporations enjoy special privileges and benefits. These include perpetual life, limited liability of shareholders, liquidity of ownership through marketability of shares, growth through retention of earnings and possibilities of inter-corporate affiliations.[1] These non-tax factors act as an impetus for operating a business in the corporate form. That is why in almost all the countries, the 'company form' of organisation represents most of the big projects and major industries. The corporate income tax is one of the most fascinating species produced by the process of economic legislation around the world.[2]

In the search for revenue to meet the ever-expanding government expenditure, taxation of corporations has been looked upon as an important source for further revenues. At the same time, the taxation system has to be so adjusted and modified as to serve the respective governmental evaluations and policies regarding the need for foreign exchange, for foreign capital, for private investment, and for protection to domestic corporations.[3] As a major part of income tax comes from the corporate sector in many countries, it is imperative for every country to have a corporate tax structure which is conducive to corporate growth, is equity-based and at the same time generates enough revenue for the exchequer. This chapter examines the provisions relating to taxation of companies under the following heads:

1. Company as a tax entity
2. Computation of taxable income
3. Tax rates
4. Adjustment for loss relief
5. Taxation of dividend income
6. Minimum alternate tax.

Company as a Tax Entity

Determination of what constitutes a company as a tax unit is an important issue in the corporate tax structure. There can be various forms of business entities depending upon the commercial set-up and the laws of the country which are subjected to corporate tax. Entities that are formed under the domestic corporate laws of the country are treated as company in all the countries. In some countries, entities which have not been formed under the domestic corporate laws, but have certain characteristics typical of a company, are also treated as 'a company' for levying tax.

The concept of company under the income tax law of the selected countries is explained below:

THE U.K.

A company in the U.K. means any corporate body or unincorporated association, excluding partnerships, local authorities and local authority associations. Types of organisations other than limited companies that are included in the definition of a company for corporation tax are clubs, societies, political associations, building societies and nationalised corporations. Organisations excluded from the definition of a company are trade unions, scientific research associations, approved pension schemes, charities, friendly societies and agricultural societies. The companies resident in the U.K. are liable to pay tax on all their chargeable profits[4] of the world, whereas companies which are not U.K. residents but which have their branch in the U.K. are liable to pay tax on the chargeable profits of the branch. The U.K. or foreign companies that are incorporated in the U.K. are U.K. resident companies. Foreign incorporated companies are treated as residents of the country where their central management and control exist and therefore are non-resident companies for the U.K.

THE U.S.

In the U.S., business may be organised and operated as a sole proprietorship, a partnership, a limited liability partnership, or as a corporation. The term 'corporation' includes associations, joint stock companies and insurance companies. 'Domestic corporations' means a corporation created or organised in the U.S. or under the law of the U.S. or of any of the states. The term 'foreign corporation' signifies a corporation, which is not domestic. Domestic corporations are taxed on world-wide income irrespective of whether the income arose from a transaction or activity originating within or outside its geographic borders. Foreign corporations are taxed on the income that is effectively connected with a trade or business conducted within the U.S. or fixed and determinable annual or periodic income from sources within the U.S. Under the Income Tax Regulation, the entities formed under a corporation statute are automatically classified as corporations.

Other entities with more than one member, such as a partnership, a limited liability company or a limited liability partnership, can also choose to be taxed as a corporation. Similarly, a corporation which is a domestic corporation which does not have more than 75 shareholders, does not have non-resident alien as shareholders, has only one class of stock, and which has individuals, estates, certain kinds of trusts and exempt organisations as shareholders, can choose to be taxed as a flow-through entity. Such corporations are called 'S' corporations. Other corporations are called 'C' corporations. In the U.S., 'S', corporations, partnerships, and limited liability companies are called flow-through entities for the purpose of taxation as they entail only one level of taxation at the ownership level. These entities themselves are not taxed and the income or the loss passes through to the shareholders of an 'S' corporation, the partners of the partnership or the members of a limited liability company and is taxed in their hands. On the other hand, a 'C' corporation entails two levels of taxation. It is first taxed directly on its income and, in addition, shareholders are taxed on the dividend received from a 'C' corporation and on any gain from selling the stocks.

AUSTRALIA

In Australia, a company means a body corporate or any other unincorporated association or a body of persons, but it does not include a partnership [(ITAA 97, Sec. 995-1, corresponding to ITAA 36, Sec. 6(1)]. Incorporated clubs and associates, co-operative companies, limited partnerships and friendly societies are all treated as companies. Although the definition of a 'company' and 'partnership' is mutually exclusive, the limited partnerships are still taxed as companies. Unincorporated clubs and associations fall within the term 'company' and fall outside the definition of 'partnership' as they are not run with a view to earning profit. Resident companies are liable to tax on the total income from sources both in and out of Australia, whereas non-resident companies are liable only on income from Australian sources.

Under the statutory definition, a company is resident in Australia if it is incorporated in Australia, or although not incorporated in Australia, carries on business in Australia and has either its central management and control in Australia or its voting power is controlled by shareholders who are residents of Australia.

MALAYSIA

A company under the Malaysian Income Tax Act means a body corporate and includes any body of persons established with a separate legal entity by or under the laws of a territory outside Malaysia. A resident company in Malaysia is liable to tax on its income accrued or derived in Malaysia only, not on its total income unlike other countries. Any income earned outside Malaysia by a resident company is not taxable. A non-resident company is taxed only on its Malaysian source of income. However, banks, shipping, air transport enterprises and insurance companies, which are resident in Malaysia, are taxed on their global income. A company is resident if at any time during the basis year, the management and control of its business or any one of its businesses is exercised in Malaysia or the management and control of its affairs are exercised in Malaysia by its directors or any other controlling authority. A company in Malaysia may change its residence. It can be resident in Malaysia for one year and non-resident in another year.

PAKISTAN

In Pakistan, the expression 'company' is defined to mean, 'a company as defined under the Companies Act, a body corporate formed under any law, body corporate incorporated under the law of any other country relating to the incorporation of companies, a foreign association declared as a company by the *Board of Revenue of Pakistan* and includes a trust formed under any law and a Modarba'[5] Resident companies are liable to pay tax on all income from whatever source derived, which includes income which accrues or arises outside Pakistan during the year. Non-resident companies are liable to pay tax on all income which is received or accrues to, and which is deemed to be received or deemed to accrue to or arise in Pakistan. These companies are not liable to pay tax on income earned outside Pakistan.

A company is 'resident' in Pakistan in the relevant income year if the control and management of its affairs is situated wholly in Pakistan in that year. A Pakistani company is always a resident in Pakistan irrespective of the fact where its control and management is situated. A Pakistani company means a company registered under the Companies Act of Pakistan or a body corporate formed under the law of Pakistan and includes any trust formed under the Pakistan law. Such a Pakistani company is called a 'domestic company'. The term 'domestic company' is wider than Pakistani company as it includes a company, which in respect of its income was liable to income tax of Pakistan and has made arrangements for the declaration and payment of dividends within Pakistan out of such income and for the deduction of tax from such dividends.

Companies other than domestic companies are treated as foreign companies. If the control and management of a company other than a Pakistani company is even partially situated outside Pakistan, then such a company will be a non-resident company and taxed only on that income which is received or which accrues to or arises in Pakistan. In Pakistan trusts formed under the 'Pakistan Law' are also taxed as a company.

INDIA

In India also, a company is a separate legal entity and is liable to pay tax on its taxable income. A company here means and includes (1) an Indian company; or (2) a body corporate incorporated under the laws of a foreign country; or (3) an institution, association or a body which is assessed or was assessable as a company for any assessment year commencing on or after April 1, 1970; or (4) an institution, association or a body, whether incorporated or not, whether Indian or non-Indian, which is declared by general or special order of the Central Board of Direct Taxes (CBDT) to be a company.

A resident company is taxed on its global income, whereas in the case of a non-resident company, only the income, which is received or is deemed to be received in India and the income, which accrues or arises or is deemed to accrue or arise in India are taxable. A company is said to be resident if it is an

Indian company or the control and management of its affair is situated wholly in India during the year. An Indian company means 'a company formed and registered under the *Companies Act*, 1956 of India and includes a corporation established under any Indian law and also an institution or association which is declared by the CBDT to be a company'. An Indian company is also called a domestic company. The term 'domestic company' is wider than 'Indian company' as it also includes a company other than Indian company, which in respect of its income is liable to pay tax under the Income Tax Act of India, and which has made arrangement for the declaration and payment of dividend within India. A company, other than a domestic company, is treated as a foreign company. As in the case of Pakistan, in India, also it is important to note that a company other than an Indian company shall be resident only if the control and management of its affair is wholly situated in India during the relevant income year. If the control and management of its affairs are partially situated in India, then such a company will be a non-resident company and will not be taxed on the income that accrues or arises outside India. Trusts are not included in the definition of a company in India.

A closely-held company in India is one in which the public has no substantial interest. A company in which the public has a substantial interest includes companies owned by the government or the Reserve Bank of India, or formed for promoting art, science, commerce, religion, and charity, or a company having no share capital, or listed companies, or companies owned by a co-operative society.

Conclusion

In all these countries, a corporation is an artificial juridical person distinct from its shareholders and is treated as a separate taxable entity. In the U.K., a company includes club and societies also but excludes trade unions and friendly societies, while in Australia, even friendly societies are taxed as a company. In the U.S., partnership and limited liability partnership can opt to be taxed as a company, called a 'C' corporation. In Pakistan, a company includes a trust. In India, trusts are not treated as companies.

Resident companies are taxed on their global income in all these countries except in Malaysia where income earned outside Malaysia is not taxable. Non-resident companies are taxed on income which has a source in Malaysia or which arises from that country only. The residential status of the company depends on the country of incorporation and the country where its control and management is situated. In all these countries if a company has been incorporated in a particular country, the company is treated as a resident company. In addition, if the control and management of the affairs of company is even partially situated in Australia or Malaysia, the company is a resident company of that country, whereas in Pakistan and India, the company is a resident if the control and management is wholly situated in that country. In the U.K., foreign incorporated companies are treated as resident companies if the central management and control are in the U.K. In the U.S., the residential status depends upon its creation and organisation in the U.S. Any company, which is not created or organised in the U.S., is treated as a foreign corporation.

COMPUTATION OF TAXABLE INCOME

Companies are generally treated differently from individuals for purposes of taxation. The question whether a business is a separate entity from its owner or owners has a long history in the thought and practice of disciplines such as accounting, company law and economics. Italian accountants had decided by the thirteenth century that they wished to separate the business from its owners so that the latter could see clearly how the former was doing.[6] In the case of company, different rules apply for the computation of income as compared to those applicable to individuals. Moreover, a company does not need a minimum exemption limit as is allowed to individuals to fulfil their basic minimum requirements. The provisions relating to the computation of taxable income of companies in the selected countries are given below.

THE U.K.

The profit chargeable to corporation tax in the U.K. is computed by aggregating all the income and chargeable gains of the company for an accounting period and deducting charges on income paid during the same period. The income of each type is calculated in accordance with the rules of the particular source of income. Trading income is calculated under the rules of Schedule D, Case I as in the case of a sole trader. Capital allowance, i.e. depreciation is treated as a trading expense in the accounting period. Bank interest, and building societies interest gross received by the companies are taxed under Schedule D, Case III. Overseas income assessed under Schedule D, Cases IV and V, is grossed up for the overseas tax deducted and then relief is granted for the foreign tax paid. The miscellaneous income of the company is assessed under Schedule D, Case VI. Rental income is assessed generally under Schedule A.

Companies are liable to pay corporation tax on capital gains. Chargeable gains or allowable losses are calculated using the specific provisions contained in the *Taxation of Chargeable Gains Act*, 1992. There is no annual exemption of capital gains for companies. The distinction between long-term and short-term gain is not applicable to companies as it is the case of individuals but indexation is given in full to companies also.

Charges actually paid in the accounting period are deductible. But no deduction is allowed for accrued charges. Interest on loan which prior to the *Finance Act*, 1996, was treated as a charge on income, is now charged on accrual basis. Certain types of income received by a company are received net of income tax. A charge on income by the paying company is taxed income for the receiving company. The main sources of such incomes are patents, royalties, debentures, and other loan interest and interest from gilt-edged securities. A company receiving such income is entitled to claim the income tax deducted at source and gross up such income for inclusion in its total income. Income from patents and royalties are assessed as unfranked investment income on the receipt basis. Debenture interest, loan interest and interest on gilt-edged securities, all are assessed usually on the accrual basis. Credit for tax deducted at source can be claimed on the amount of income actually received during the chargeable accounting period.

THE U.S.

In the U.S., the taxable income of a corporation is computed in a manner similar to that of a sole proprietorship or a partnership business. Corporations are permitted to deduct ordinary and necessary business expenses and exclude items such as tax-exempt interest and life insurance proceeds from the gross income. However, they are not entitled to deduction by way of personal or dependent exemption, or itemized or standard deduction. Charitable contributions are limited in any given year to 10 per cent as against 50 per cent in the case of individuals of the taxable income. Unused contributions are carried forward for 5 years.

Dividend income is deductible in the hands of a corporation up to 70 per cent, 80 per cent, and 100 per cent, depending upon the percentage of its holding. If the holding in the company is 80 per cent or more, the dividend income is 100 per cent deductible. If it is 20 per cent or more, then 80 per cent of the dividend income is deductible, and if it is less than 20 per cent, then 70 per cent of the dividend income is deductible.

Companies do not get any preferential treatment in respect of long term capital gains. Neither a net long-term capital loss nor a net short-term capital loss is deductible against ordinary income in the year in which it is incurred. However, they are subject to a 3 year carry-back period and 5 year carryover as an offset against capital gains for those years. For corporations, both net long-term capital losses and net short-term capital losses are treated as short-term capital losses for the purpose of carry-back and carryover rules.

Consolidated Returns

In the U.S., corporations that are members of a parent subsidiary affiliated group[7] can file a consolidated group return if an election is made under the consolidated group regulations. The consolidated return has the advantage of offsetting net operating losses, capital losses and profits and gains of one or more members against operating income, capital gains, profits and gains of other members in the group.

AUSTRALIA

In Australia, the taxable income of a company is computed just like the taxable income of an individual. From the assessable income, i.e. gross income, all ordinary business deductions, special incentive deductions and any relevant non-business deductions are made. [(ITAA 97, Sec. 4-15, corresponding to ITAA 36, Sec. 48)]. However, there is no basic exemption as in the case of individuals.

Resident companies are entitled to tax rebate on inter-corporate dividend received from resident companies except unfranked dividend in the case of private companies. As such, the dividend income becomes tax free in the hands of residents companies. Non-resident companies are not entitled to the rebate. Certain class of companies that get special treatment are co-operative companies, friendly societies, trade unions and life assurance companies.

The assessable income of a company includes a net capital gain for the income year. Capital gain tax is not a tax separate from income tax. Capital gain income is taxed like ordinary income at the rate applicable on companies and there is no special rate as in the case of an individual where it is taxed at progressive rates.

MALAYSIA

The income of a company is computed in accordance with the ordinary rules laid down under the Malaysian income tax law as applicable to other taxpayers. Income tax is charged in respect of any trade or business carried on in Malaysia. The tax laws do not distinguish between companies by the types of trade they carry on or by their constitution. Dividends received from another company are included in the total income. However, imputation credit by way of tax deducted at source on the dividend is allowed. In Malaysia, capital gains tax, called the real property gains tax is chargeable in the hands of companies only on gains from real property and shares in real property companies, referred to as chargeable assets. There is no tax on the sale of other capital assets. Real property gains tax is imposed on a scale of rates depending on the length of time the chargeable asset is held. Allowable losses arising from the sale of capital assets are not set off like business losses. The relief for such losses is given as a deduction from the total tax assessed on the capital gains of the company for the year of assessment in which the loss occurs. This is so as different rates of tax are applicable to different categories of disposals in an assessment year depending upon the period for which the chargeable asset was held.

Controlled Companies

In Malaysia, the Director General has the power to disregard transactions of a controlled company[8] if it has the effect of altering the incidence of tax or relieving any person from any liability to pay tax, and for the purpose to treat the gross income of a controlled company as having been distributed to its members or to make computation or re-computation of any gross income of any person or persons.

PAKISTAN

The income of a company is computed in a manner similar to the one adopted for computing the income of an individual. First, the gross total income is ascertained under each head of income, excluding income to which

Sec. 80C or Sec. 80CC applies. Sec. 80C provides for the computation of income of certain contractors and importers and Sec. 80CC provides for the computation of income of exporters. These are two special provisions for computing the tax liability of taxpayers engaged in such businesses. If a company is working as contractors, importers and exporters, it has to compute income from such business in the manner provided under these sections. Admissible deductions are made from the gross total income. The total income so arrived at is adjusted against the brought forward loss, if any. From the total income remaining after adjustment of loss, deductions on account of Zakat paid, donation etc are deducted. The total income remaining after the above deductions have been made is income chargeable to tax. Dividend income is included in the total income of the company, but is taxed at concessional rates. Income from capital gains is included in the total income. However, concessional rate is applicable if it arises by the disposal of a capital asset held for more than 12 months from the date of acquisition.

INDIA

The income of a company in India is computed in a manner similar to one adopted for computing the income of an individual. The income is first computed under each head of income. The total income so arrived at is adjusted against any brought-forward loss. From the total income remaining after the adjustment of loss, deductions on account of donation, export allowance, backward area allowance, rural project, and infrastructure project are made. The balance income remaining after these deductions is income chargeable to tax. However, certain deductions and rebates which are allowed to individuals such as deduction under Sec. 80L of the Income Tax Act in respect of, interest from bank and government securities and rebate under Sec. 88 on account of investment in long-term savings are not allowed to a company. Dividend income is not included in the total income of a company as the same is exempt under the Indian Income Tax Act with effect from June 1, 1997. Special provisions apply for the computation of income of retail business and civil construction, in case the turn-over/gross receipt of a company is less than Rs.4 million from such business. Similarly, a special provision applies for computing the income of plying and hiring goods carriages. Income from capital gain is included in the total income. However, a concessional rate of tax is applicable to long-term capital gain, i.e. where the asset is held for more than the specified period.

Conclusion

An analysis of the provisions for the computation of income of the countries under study reveals that no basic exemption or relief is allowed to companies in any of these countries as is allowed to individuals. In the U.S., companies are not entitled to itemized or standard deduction which are allowed to individuals. The taxation in the case of a company starts from the very first amount of income earned. Income arising from all sources including business or trading income as well as non-business income is normally included in the taxable income. All expenses incurred wholly and exclusively in earning taxable income are, in principle, deductible except to prevent tax avoidance. Companies, in all these countries, are also liable to pay tax on capital gains. However, computation of capital gains is different from that of individuals in the U.K. and the U.S. In the U.S., dividend income is deductible in the hands of a company depending upon the percentage of holding, and the companies of parent subsidiary affiliated group are allowed to compute income of the consolidated group with the result, loss of one company can be set off against income of the other company in the group. Similar provisions are proposed to be introduced in Australia.

Tax Rates

Corporation income tax is much more important than the personal income tax and more so in developing countries. From the point of view of theory, which sees changes in welfare in terms of effects on households, the corporation income tax has a limited role.[9]

The most important argument for taxing corporations is as a means of collection of tax on personal incomes. Due to the poor taxation system, personal income tax gets easily evaded. However, the most significant issue is tax rates for companies. Should it be progressive or should it be proportionate? Also, should the tax rate applicable to corporation be aligned with the individual income tax rates? The issue in levying proportionate single tax rate is—what should be the basis to decide that tax rate? Should it be the highest individual rate or the lowest individual rate? A company, despite being an artificial entity, plays a very significant role in the economic growth of a country. As such, the tax rate applicable to a corporate body has a direct bearing on the economic growth of a country. A lower rate of tax may not generate sufficient revenue and at the same time, may be inequitable from the point of view of fixed income earners who may be paying high rate of tax, whereas a higher rate of tax on the company may be inequitable for owners of the companies and may result in encouraging taxpayers to remain unincorporated, which may ultimately affect economic growth.

An analysis of the tax rates applicable to companies in the selected countries is given below.

THE U.K.

Corporate tax structure has undergone several changes in the U.K. Important amongst these are: the adoption of dividend imputation system in 1973, and the reduction in the tax rates which were as high as 52 per cent in the case of large companies and 40 per cent in the case of small companies.

In the U.K., corporate tax rates are applicable for the financial year of a corporation which runs from April 1 to the following March 31. From the income year 2000-01, there are three rates of corporation tax, known as *the starting rate*, *the small companies rate* and *the full rate*. Till the income year

1999-2000, there were only two rates of corporation tax, known as the small companies rate and the large companies rate. Whether a company is small or large it depends upon whether the profits of the company are more or less than the given lower or upper limit. For the income year 1998-99 and 1999-2000, the lower limit was £300,000 and the upper limit was £1,500,000. If the profit of the company were up to £300,000 it would be treated as a small company and if the profit of a company exceeded the upper limit of £1,500,000, it would be treated as a large company.

The corporate tax rate for the financial year 1999-2000 for a small company was 20 per cent and for a large company, 30 per cent. However, for the income year 2000-01, the starting rate of 10 per cent applies to companies with profits not exceeding the starting rate lower limit, which is £10,000 for the year 2000-01. The small companies rate of 20 per cent applies to companies with profits, which lies between the starting rate lower limit and the small companies rate lower limit, which is £300,000 for the year 2000-01. However, the tax liability is reduced by an amount known as marginal relief if profits do not exceed the starting rate upper limit, which is £50,000. The full rate of 30 per cent applies to companies with profits, which exceed the small companies rate lower limit. However, as in the case of small companies, the tax liability is reduced by marginal relief if profits do not exceed the small companies rate upper limit, which is £1,500,000. In spite of the fact that three separate tax rates are applicable depending upon the profit of a company, still a flat tax rate system applies in respect of companies in the U.K. as against individuals where the progressive tax rate system applies.

The profits, which are compared with upper and lower limits in order to determine the applicable rate, are not the company's chargeable profits. The term *profit* for this purpose is a company's chargeable profit plus grossed up franked investment income (FII). Though FII is not charged to corporation tax, the FII received by the company is taken into account while determining the rate of tax applicable to the company.

Marginal Relief

Companies with profits which lie between the starting rate lower and the starting rate upper limits and between the small companies rate lower limit and the small companies rate upper limit are charged to corporation tax at the small companies rate and the full rate respectively, but such companies are provided marginal reliefs from the income year 2000-01. First, tax on the basis of the small companies rate or the full rate as may be applicable is computed for such companies and from that tax liability, marginal relief is subtracted and the balance amount is the actual tax liability. The purpose of providing marginal relief is to charge companies a rate that falls in between the two rates. The formula to compute marginal relief is as follows:

Marginal Relief = Fraction × (Relevant upper limit – Profits) × Chargeable Profits / Profits

The fraction called marginal relief fraction is set for each year and is 1/40 for the financial years 1999-2000 and 2000-01.

Corporation tax rates in the U.K. are low for companies earning lower profits and are high for companies earning high profits. Thus, in the U.K., corporation tax rates are to some extent based on the ability-to-pay principle.

Close Investment Companies

A close investment[10] holding company is not entitled to small companies' rate of corporation tax no matter how small its chargeable profit be, and in certain cases, the Inspector of Taxes may restrict the repayment of tax credit to a person who receives a distribution from a close investment company where the main purpose of the payment was to obtain a tax advantage. However, the above restrictions are not applicable to close investment companies whose main purpose is carrying on a trade on a commercial basis or investment in land to be let out on a commercial basis.

THE U.S.

Corporate tax rates in the U.S. are applicable only to a C corporation. Unlike individual tax rates, these rates are not subject to inflation indexing. The corporate rate structure in the U.S. for the income year 2000 is given in Table 7.1.

The corporate tax structure in the U.S. as shown above is so designed that the lower rates of 15 per cent and 25 per cent are applicable to corporate taxpayers having taxable income up to $50,000 and $75,000, respectively. By imposing 5 per cent surtax on corporate income of more than $100,000 and less than $335,000, the government takes away the benefit of the lower tax rate brackets (15 and 20 per cent) from the higher income corporations. The impact of this 39 per cent rate is that when the income is more than $335,000 and less than $10,000,000, it is taxable at a flat rate of 34 per cent. Further, the impact of 3 per cent surtax on income above $15,000,000 is that the income above $18,333,333 is taxable at a flat rate of 35 per cent.

TABLE 7.1. CORPORATE TAX RATE STRUCTURE IN THE U.S.

(for income year 2000)

Income Level ($)		Tax Rates
Over	But not over	(Percentage)
0	50,000	15
50,000	75,000	25
75,000	100,000	34
100,000	335,000	39
335,000	10,000,000	34
10,000,000	15,000,000	35
15,000,000	18,333,333	38
18,333,333	35	

Source: The Internal Revenue Code as on December 1, 2000 (U.S.)

Thus, the corporate tax rate structure of the U.S. is such that it is neither completely progressive, nor is it a flat rate system. It combines the benefit of both. Companies having income up to $50,000 are taxable at a rate of 15 per cent. Although high tax rates of 39 per cent and 38 per cent have been imposed in between, the effective tax rate never exceeds 35 per cent. Foreign corporations are taxed in the same manner as domestic corporations on all incomes which are effectively connected with their conduct of a trade or business in the U.S. However, fixed or determinable periodic incomes from U.S. sources are taxed at a flat rate of 30 per cent.

Tax for Controlled Groups

The progressive rate of taxation on a corporation could lead to tax savings by splitting the corporation into smaller corporations. To meet such a situation, a controlled group[11] in the U.S. has to apportion the lower tax rates among the group members as if only one corporation existed. An equal apportionment to each corporation is done unless all the members in the controlled group agree to the unequal allocation.

Accumulated Earnings Tax

To discourage retaining excessive amounts of earnings by a closely held corporation and a publicly held company where effective control is in the hands of a few related shareholders and to avoid payment of tax by shareholders on dividend income, an accumulated earnings tax at the rate of 39.6 per cent is imposed on a corporation's accumulated taxable income of a particular year.

Personal Holding Company Tax

In the U.S., a personal holding company[12] is liable for another tax, called personal holding company tax, to prevent closely held companies from converting an operating company into a non-operating investment company by reinvesting substantial amount of earnings into passive investments. The rate of personal holding company tax is 39.6 per cent times of undistributed personal holding company income. Various adjustments are made in the taxable income to arrive at the tax base similar to those required for the accumulated earnings tax. These include adding the dividend-received deduction and the net operating loss deduction to the taxable income and deducting net capital losses, federal income tax liability, charitable contribution exceeding 10 per cent, deductions for dividends paid or deemed paid and accumulated earnings credit.

Special Rules for Regulated Investment and Real Estate Investment Corporations

Regulated Investment Corporations[13] (RICs) are not taxed on the amount distributed to its shareholders. Tax rates for the RICs are the same as for a corporation. Tax rates are computed on income after excluding capital gains and without allowing deduction for any net operating loss.

Real Estate Investment Corporations[14] (REICs) can elect to be taxed as an REIC, if at least 95 per cent of their gross income is from dividend, interest, rents from real property, gains from the sale of stocks and securities and real properties, and if 75 per cent of gross income is from rents, interest on mortgages, gains from the sale of real properties and mortgages interests.

An REIC that distributes at least 95 per cent of its taxable income of the tax year is taxed at the regular domestic corporate tax rate on retained earnings other than capital gains only. The distributed earnings are taxed in the hands of the beneficiaries, and shareholders and the REIC is allowed dividend-paid deduction. Taxable income that is distributed is taxable as ordinary income in the hands of the beneficiaries. Capital gains to the extent distributed are taxed as long-term capital gain in the hands of the beneficiaries. In the case of retained net long-term capital gains, an REIC will have to pay tax on such gains, while the shareholders have to include their proportionate share of the undistributed long-term capital gain in income and are entitled to receive credit for their share of the tax paid by the REIC on such gains.

RICs are not taxed on the amounts distributed to their shareholder so as to avoid triple taxation as these companies receive income from other companies who have already paid tax on their income, and shareholders of RIC will be paying tax on its dividend income. Similarly, REICs are allowed dividend paid deductions to avoid double taxation on income from real estate. As such, REIC, in fact is a flow through entity to the extent of income distributed as dividend.

AUSTRALIA

In Australia, a flat rate of 34 per cent for the income year 2000-01, is applicable in the case of both private and public companies. However, special rates apply to life assurance companies and registered organisations.

Although tax rates for private and public companies both are the same in Australia, it is still important to distinguish between the two as certain payments made by private companies to associated persons are treated as dividends and inter-corporate dividend rebate is not allowed to private companies in respect of unfranked portion of the dividends received from a company.

The meaning of public and private companies for tax purposes and under company law differs. Many companies which are not private companies under the corporation law, may be private companies for tax purposes. Public companies for tax purposes include listed companies, government companies, co-operative companies, and friendly societies.

MALAYSIA

There is a single rate of tax applicable to all the companies in Malaysia. Malaysian companies are subject to income tax at 28 per cent for the income year 2000 on their chargeable income. This rate of 28 per cent is applicable from the year of assessment 1998. Previously, the rate of tax on companies was 30 per cent. Rates of tax applicable to chargeable capital gains vary from 5 to 30 per cent.

PAKISTAN

Tax rates in Pakistan differ substantially for private and public companies.[15] The tax rate applicable to a public company other than a banking company for the assessment year 2000-01, is 33 per cent, and for other companies, it is 43 per cent. The tax rate applicable to a banking company is 38 per cent. There is gradual reduction in tax rates applicable to companies in Pakistan over the years. In the income year 1992-93, tax rate for a public company was 42 per cent, for other companies, 52 per cent, and for a banking company, 64 per cent. In Pakistan, tax rates for private companies are high as compared to public companies. Banking companies are also being taxed at a very high rate in Pakistan.

Under Sec. 80C, the total amount received by a resident taxpayer from a contract or for the supply of goods is considered income, and the same is taxable at a presumptive rate of tax which for the year commencing on or after July 1,1999 were from 1.5 per cent to 10 per cent, depending upon the nature of contract and income.

Similarly, under Sec. 80CC, in the case of a taxpayer engaged in export, the total amount realised on account of export of goods is deemed as income and is taxed for the income year 2000-01 at a rate which ranges from 0.50 per cent to 1.00 per cent, depending upon the nature of the goods exported. For the assessment year commencing on or after July 1, 2001, these tax rates have been increased from 0.50 to 0.75 per cent and 1 per cent to 1.25 per cent respectively.

The tax rate applicable on the income of capital gains arising from the disposal of a capital asset held for more than 12 months from the date of acquisition is 25 per cent.

Dividend income is taxable in the hands of the company. The tax rate applicable on dividend income in the hands of a public company is 5 per cent and 20 per cent in other cases. However, in the case of a company incorporated outside Pakistan, including foreign associations, dividend income is taxable at the rate of 15 per cent. Dividends received from a company set up for power generation and transmission line project are taxable at the rate of 7.5 per cent in the hands of companies other than public companies where they are taxable at the rate of 5 per cent. Dividend income in the hands of insurance companies is taxable at the normal rate of tax applicable to the company.

Tax on Issue of Bonus Shares

In Pakistan, a company has also to pay tax on the issue of bonus shares at the rate of 10 per cent in the case of a public company and at the rate of 15 per cent in the case of other companies on the face value of the bonus shares issued. Thus in Pakistan, bonus shares issued are considered as dividend and the company issuing bonus shares is liable to pay tax. However, no income is included in the hands of the shareholders. This provision of paying tax on the issue of bonus shares is peculiar to Pakistan only among the selected countries.

Tax on Lower Distribution of Profits

A company is also liable to pay tax in case it does not distribute dividend within the prescribed period to an extent, whereby its reserves exceed 50 per cent of its paid-up capital. The tax rate applicable on so much of its reserves as exceed 50 per cent of its paid-up capital is 10 per cent.

INDIA

There is only one tax rate applicable to all domestic companies. The tax rate for the income year 2000-01, is 35 per cent. In addition, a surcharge is also levied on the tax. The rate of surcharge for the income year 2000-01 is 13 per cent. Hence, the effective rate of tax on a company is 39.55 per cent. The rate of surcharge has been reduced to 2 per cent for the income year 2001-02, resulting in the effective tax rate of 35.70 per cent. However, the tax rate applicable to a foreign company is 48 per cent for the income year 2001-02 without any surcharge as applicable to a domestic company.

The tax rate applicable on a long-term capital gain is 20 per cent plus 10 per cent surcharge. However, the long-term capital gain arising from listed shares and securities is chargeable at the rate of 10 per cent without the benefit of indexation of the cost.

As dividend income is exempt from tax with effect from June 1, 1997, no tax is payable on the dividend income in the hands of a company. However, a company has to pay a distribution of profit tax on the payment of dividend to its shareholders. The tax rate on the distribution of dividend declared or paid after June 1, 2000, is 20 per cent (earlier it was 10 per cent) with a 13 per cent surcharge. This has again been reduced to 10 per cent with 2 per cent surcharge thereon from June 1,2001. Therefore, the effective tax on the distribution of profit is 10.20 per cent. This distribution tax is applicable on the total dividend declared by the company irrespective of whether the shareholder is an individual or a company. Every company distributing dividend out of its dividend income has to pay a dividend distribution tax. As such, in India there can be not only double but also multiple taxation of dividend income in the hands of companies. There is, however, no tax on the issue of bonus shares. The cost of acquisition in the case of bonus shares is taken as nil while computing gain on the sale of bonus shares.

In India, a company is free to decide whether or not to declare dividend, or to declare dividend at a lesser rate. No tax is payable if no dividend is declared. However, if dividend is declared, a distribution tax, as mentioned above, has to be paid by the company.

Conclusion

Except in the U.K. and the U.S., all the selected countries have adopted flat rate of tax applicable to companies. In the U.K. although there are different rates of tax applicable to different type of companies, there is only one flat rate applicable to one company. In the U.S., the tax rate is partly progressive. As the income of the company increases, the tax rate applicable to the company also increases. A comparative corporate rate structure applicable in these countries is shown in Table 7.2.

As shown in the table, corporate tax rates are the highest (i.e. 43 per cent) in Pakistan. However, the tax rate for public companies in Pakistan is 33 per cent, which is 10 per cent less than the tax rate applicable to private companies. The corporate rates in Australia were also high, but have been reduced to 34 per cent for the income year 2000-01 and will be reduced to 30 per cent in the income year 2001-02. The tax rate in India is 35 per cent, but including surcharge of 13 per cent, the effective company tax rate is 39.55 per cent for the income year 2000-01 and will get reduced to the effective rate of 35.70 per cent in the income year 2001-02.

In the U.S., the maximum tax rate is 35 per cent payable by very high income earning companies. Low-income companies which earn income up to $ 50,000 have to pay just 15 per cent tax on their income. There are a total of 8 slabs with fluctuating tax rates to deprive the benefit of low tax rates to high-income companies.

In the U.K., the minimum rate of 10 per cent is applicable in the case of companies having profits of less than or up to £10,000, and the maximum rate of 30 per cent is applicable in the case of companies which are earning profits of £1,500,000 or more. Malaysia is the only country among the selected countries, which has the lowest tax rate of 28 per cent applicable to all companies irrespective of the income of the company.

Thus, tax rates in India, Pakistan and Australia are the highest. In the U.S.

TABLE 7.2. CORPORATE TAX RATE STRUCTURE IN THE SELECTED COUNTRIES

Country	Multiple Tax Rates (in percentage) (Minimum)	(Maximum)	Flat Tax Rates (in percentage)	Income Year
U.K.	10 (If profits are up to £10,000)	30 (If profit exceeds £1,500,000)	n.a.	2000-01
U.S.	15 (Up to taxable income of US$50,000)	35 (income above US$18,333,333)	n.a.	2000
Australia	n.a.	n.a.	34	2000-01
Malaysia	n.a.	n.a.	28	2000
Pakistan	n.a.	n.a.	43	2000-01
India	n.a.	n.a.	35	2000-01

Note: n.a. means not applicable.

Source: Income Tax Act and Taxation Statistics of Selected Countries, as given in Table 2.2.

tax rates being partly progressive appears to be reasonable. In Malaysia, tax rates are low despite the small number of corporate taxpayers. Tax rates in the U.K. are also low.

A comparison of the minimum and maximum tax rates applicable to individuals and companies in the selected countries is given in Table 7.3.

As shown in the table, the highest tax rate applicable to the individual is higher than the highest tax rate applicable to a company in the U.K., the U.S. and Australia. The difference in the maximum tax rates is maximum in Australia, where it is 13 per cent and next is U.K where it is 10 per cent, followed by the U.S. where it is 4.6 per cent. Therefore, it is more beneficial in these countries to get the business corporatised as compared to Pakistan and India, where the corporate rate is higher than the maximum rate applicable to an individual. In Malaysia, the maximum rate for individual and a company is almost same and, therefore, there is full alignment of corporate tax rate with individual tax rate.

In the U.K., the minimum corporate tax is 10 per cent and in the U.S., it is 15 per cent. Hence, it may be beneficial to organise trade in small companies rather than having higher income in the hands of individuals. In the U.S. however, there are provisions to check this type of tax planning. A controlled group in the U.S. has to apportion the lower tax rates among the group members. Moreover, there is accumulated earnings tax levied at the rate of 39.6 per cent, which is the maximum tax rate applicable to individuals.

The lower tax rate for companies earning lower income with accumulated earning tax in the case of retained earnings in the U.S., appears to be more equitable and aligned to individual tax rates. Thus, in the U.S., there will not be much impact on tax liability, if individuals having low income, get their trade corporatised. As against this, a single high rate of tax on all companies in Pakistan and India, there will be increase in tax burden if individuals with low income get their trade corporatised. In Australia and Malaysia, though the minimum tax rate applicable to individuals are much lower than the minimum tax rate applicable to companies, because of full imputation credit as discussed in this chapter later, there is otherwise alignment of corporate tax rate with the individual tax rates.

TABLE 7.3. MINIMUM AND MAXIMUM TAX RATES APPLICABLE ON INDIVIDUAL TAXPAYERS AND COMPANIES

Country	Income Year	Maximum Tax Rate (%)		Minimum Tax Rate (%)	
		Individual	Company	Individual	Company
U.K.	2000-01	40	30	10	10
U.S.	2000	39.6	35	15	15
Australia	2000-01	47	34	17	34
Malaysia	2000	29	28	1	28
Pakistan	2000-01	30	43	5	33
India	2000-01	30	35	10	35

Source: Same as for Table 7.2.

ADJUSTMENT FOR LOSS RELIEF

Losses incurred by a company raise some additional issues other than those arising from income earned. A company is owned by its shareholders. Hence, losses incurred by the company belong to the shareholders who owned it at the time when the loss was incurred. According to this view, the company should not be allowed the benefit of loss relief in case of change of shareholders. That may be theoretically possible but practically difficult as change in the shareholders of a company is usually an ongoing process. The other view is that a company is an independent entity, taxed on its income and should be entitled to loss relief on its own irrespective of the change in its shareholders. These issues do not arise in the case of individuals. The loss incurred by an individual belongs to him and he is only entitled to claim loss relief, as the loss cannot be transferred. As such, the provisions of loss relief applicable to companies are different from those applicable to individuals. The provisions for loss relief applicable to companies in the selected countries are examined below.

THE U.K.

Loss relief is available when a company incurs a loss. The type of relief available depends on whether the loss is a trading loss or a non-trading one. Trading losses can be carried forward indefinitely and set-off against the first available trading income of the same trade. The company may set off the trading loss against its other income and gains of the same period before deducting charges on income. Any loss still unrelieved may be carried back and set off against the total profits for the 12 months prior to the accounting period in which the loss was incurred after deducting trade charges. Claim for the current year must be made first. The claim can be made only if the trade was carried on a commercial basis with a view to earning profit. Companies which are engaged in the trade of farming or market gardening and which have incurred losses in each of the 5 years prior to the year for which the loss relief is claimed, are not entitled to loss relief. Losses incurred prior to July 2, 1997 could be carried back and set off against the total profits for the 36 months prior to the accounting period in which the loss was incurred on a First In First Out basis after deducting trade charges. However, the *Finance Act*, 1997 reduced the carry-back facility to 12 months, a situation that existed before 1991. However, the 3 year carry-back facility will continue to be available to a company incurring loss in its final year of trading.

Restrictions on Loss Relief

The right to carry forward or carry back losses is not available if within a period of 3 years, there is both a change in ownership of the company and a major change in the nature of trade or the state of activity of the company becomes negligible and there is a change of ownership before there is any considerable revival of the trade. These restrictions are to prevent tax planning by sale/purchase of a company purely for its tax losses.

THE U.S.

While computing the net operating loss of corporations, no adjustment is required for non-business deductions and capital gains and losses. Net operating losses can be carried back for 3 years and carried forward up to 15 years, and net capital losses can be carried back to 3 years and carried forward up to 5 years. However, after a change in corporate ownership or reorganisation, the amount of income that a corporation may offset each year by pre-acquisition net operating loss carry-forwards is limited to an amount determined by multiplying the value of the equity of the corporation just prior to the change of ownership by the federal long-term tax exempt rate[16] in effect on the date of change. Federal long-term exempt rate for the month of January 1999 was 5.26 per cent. Any unused limitation is carried forward and added to the next year's limitation. The above limitation applied when a change involved a 5 per cent shareholder whereby one or more of the 5 per cent shareholders have increased their percentage of ownership in the corporation by more than 50 per cent over their lowest pre-change ownership percentage. Similar rules are applicable for the carry forward of net capital losses, unused business credits and foreign taxes. Net operating loss/income and capital loss/gain for the change year are allocated between the pre-change period and post-change period either by allocating the same according to the number of days in each period or by making accounts of each period.

Net operating loss carry-forward is not allowed after an ownership change if a shareholder with 50 per cent or more control claims within 3 years a worthless stock deduction with respect to the stock of the corporation. Moreover, if an acquisition is made to acquire control of a corporation directly or indirectly to evade or avoid income tax by securing the benefit of a deduction, credit or other allowance that would not otherwise be available, then such deduction, credit or other allowance will not be allowed.

AUSTRALIA

A loss is incurred in any income year if the taxpayer's allowable deductions exceed the assessable income and the net exempt income of the year. A tax loss cannot be increased by deductions of gifts. Companies, like any other taxpayer, are entitled to carry forward losses incurred in one income year for claiming deduction in subsequent years. Domestic losses, including primary production losses, are allowed to be carried forward indefinitely until absorbed.

A loss brought forward must first be offset against the net exempt income, if any, and then against the income remaining after all current year deductions are allowed. However, if in the year of recoupment the deduction exceeds the total assessable income, that excess is first set off against the net exempt income of the year, and the brought-forward loss is deducted from the remaining net exempt income.

To avoid misuse of accumulated losses, where existing shareholders sell their holding to a purchaser who could use these accumulated losses against his income to reduce tax liability, and to claim the deduction of 'prior year' losses, a company has to satisfy either a 'continuity of ownership'[17] test or the 'same business test'.[18] It is important to note that, in Australia, the ownership test is of a group and change of holding within the group is permissible for claiming the deduction of the prior year losses. Where the continuity of the ownership test is satisfied in relation to part of the loss year under the current year loss rules, part of the prior year losses are allowed.

It is important to note that for claiming deduction of the prior year losses, a company has to satisfy any one of the above two tests. However, provisions of the above two tests are strictly applied and there are anti-avoidance measures to prevent companies circumventing these tests. In Australia, for claiming bad debts also, the company has to satisfy either of the tests.

A capital loss cannot be deducted from a company's assessable income. However, it can generally be offset against capital gains made in the same year or a later income year. Companies can only offset a net capital loss against a capital gain if it passes either the continuity of ownership test or continuity of business test in relation to both the capital loss year and the capital gain year.

Transfer of Losses

In Australia, a resident company which incurs a loss can transfer the right to a deduction for the loss to another resident company if both companies are members of the same wholly owned group.

MALAYSIA

Where a company incurs a business loss in Malaysia, such a loss can be deducted by the company from any other income the company may have in the same basis period. Hence, current business losses can be set off against income from any sources. Business losses incurred, which cannot be set off against the current year income, can be carried forward for deduction against business income in any of the next years. However, unabsorbed business losses cannot be set off against future income from sources other than business sources. In the case of resident companies, losses are computed with reference to Malaysian sources only. Unlike other countries, there is no condition of continuity of ownership for claiming set off of carry-forward losses. In Malaysia, only business losses are allowed to be carried forward and that too indefinitely. There is no provision in Malaysia for allowing the carry-back of losses to earlier years. Unabsorbed tax relief of capital losses called allowable losses under the 'Malaysian Real Property Gains Tax' can be carried forward to future years indefinitely to be set off against the tax liability arising from capital gains.

PAKISTAN

A company can set off a loss under any head of income against income under any other heads of income except loss in speculation business, the capital loss, and loss from a source, which is exempt from tax. Speculation loss can be set off against speculation income. Similarly, capital loss can be set off against capital gain only. Losses from business or profession, speculation losses and capital losses are permitted to be carried forward. Business losses when carried forward can be set off against income from such business or profession. For claiming the business loss, the business from which loss arises must be carried on. The losses can be carried forward for 6 years succeeding the assessment year in which it is first determined. In Pakistan, there is no condition of continuity of ownership for claiming the benefit of brought-forward losses to the shareholders.

INDIA

A company can set off loss under any head of income against income under any other head of income except loss in speculation business and capital loss. Loss in speculation business can be set off against speculation income only. Speculation loss means loss in speculation transaction, i.e. where a contract for the purchase or sale is settled otherwise than by the actual delivery.

Capital loss can be set off against capital gain. Loss from business or profession, speculation loss and capital loss are permitted to be carried forward. Business losses if, carried forward can be set off against income from business. Earlier, there used to be a condition that the business in which loss has been incurred must be continued to be carried on in the year in which the set off of such loss is claimed. However, this condition has been withdrawn from the assessment year 2000-01. The loss can be carried forward for 8 years succeeding the assessment year in which it is incurred.

Continuity of Ownership

A company in which the public has no substantial interest can claim the set-off of carry-forward losses only if the shares of the company on the last date of the year in which the set-off is claimed, carrying not less than 51 per cent of the voting power, are held by persons who beneficially held shares of the company, carrying not less than 51 per cent of the voting power on the last day of the year in which the loss was incurred.

Conclusion

In all the countries under study, losses incurred by the company are allowed to be carried forward and set off against the income of subsequent years. Carry back of losses is allowed in the U.K. and the U.S. only. In the U.K., loss can be carried back and set off against the total profit for 12 months prior to the accounting period in which the loss was incurred, whereas in the U.S., losses can be carried back for 3 years.

In the U.K., Malaysia and Australia, there is no time limit for carrying forward trading losses, whereas in the U.S., net operating losses can be carried forward for 15 years and net capital losses for 5 years. In Pakistan, losses can be carried forward for 6 years succeeding the assessment year in which it is first determined, whereas in India losses can be carried forward for 8 years succeeding the assessment year in which it is incurred

For claiming the set off of carry forward losses, in all these countries except in Malaysia and Pakistan, there is a restriction on the change of ownership of the company. In the U.K., the restriction is for 3 years when there is both a change in the ownership of the company and a major change in the nature of the trade. In the U.S., on change of the ownership, the amount of the set off is limited by applying a formula based on federal long-term exempt rate. In Australia, losses are also adjusted against the net exempt income and they cannot be increased by deduction of gifts. For claiming the set off and carry-forward losses, the company has to satisfy one of the two tests, i.e. 'continuity of ownership test' or 'same business test'. In India, the continuity of ownership for claiming the benefit of carry-forward losses is required in the case of a company in which the public is not substantially interested. However, there is no condition of the continuity of the same business. On a comparison of provision of loss relief and systems of company tax in Malaysia and the U.S., one interesting issue emerges. Malaysia follows the full imputation system as it allows full credit of the tax paid by the company to its shareholders. Thus, it accepts the principle that a company belongs to the shareholders. But for loss relief, no restriction has been provided in the case of change of shareholders, with the result that the loss incurred by the company, which belonged to its shareholders at the time when it was incurred, gets transferred to those who were not shareholders at that point of time. On the contrary, the U.S. follows the classical system of company taxation. However, the loss relief is restricted in case of change of ownership. The classical system is based on the principle of separate entity, which means that a company and its shareholders are two distinct entities and that both should be taxed independently on their income. For loss relief, however, this principle is not followed, as loss is restricted on the change of ownership following the principle that a company is owned by the shareholders. Thus, more time is allowed for the adjustment or losses in the U.K., Australia, Malaysia and the U.S. However, the rules are strict in the U.K., U.S. and Australia with regard to the change of ownership.

Share of Corporate Income Tax in the Total Income Tax

While analysing the corporate tax structure, it is important to examine the contribution of corporate tax in the total income tax revenue of a country. The total number of corporate taxpayers, corporate income tax and percentage of corporate income tax to total income tax in the selected countries are shown in Table 7.4.

TABLE 7.4. CORPORATE TAXPAYERS AND THE RATIO OF CORPORATE INCOME TAX TO TOTAL INCOME TAX

Country	Currency	Year	No. of corporate taxpayers	Corporate income tax (in billions)	Total income tax (in billions)	Corporate income tax as % of total income tax
U.K.	£	1997-98	431,158	34.138	107.097	31.9
U.S.	$	1997	4,710,083	182.78	920.25	19.9
Australia	AUD	1997-98	576,951	23.222	90.436	25.7
Malaysia	RM	1997	57,164	16.896	23.663	71.4
Pakistan	PKR	1996-97	19,954	66.863	81.155	82.4
India	Rs.	1996-97	260,312	213.6	509.1	42

Sources: 1. For corporate income tax and total income tax, *IMF Government Finance Statistics Year book*, 1991 and 1999.
2. For number of corporate taxpayers, taxation statistics of the selected countries as given in Table 6.3.

As shown in the table, among the six countries, the maximum number of corporate taxpayers are in the U.S., where the number of corporate taxpayers in the year 1997, was far in excess of the total corporate taxpayers in all the other selected countries. Corporate income tax was also the highest in the U.S. However, the percentage of corporate income tax to total income tax was lowest in the U.S. among the selected countries. The percentage of corporate tax to total income tax reveals that it was very high in developing countries as compared to developed countries despite the low number of corporate taxpayers. In Pakistan, corporate tax contributed 82.4 per cent of the total income tax whereas in Malaysia, corporate tax contribution was 71.4 per cent and in India, it was 42 per cent. The higher percentage of corporate tax to total income tax indicates that the contribution of individual income tax to total income tax in these countries was very low. Among the developed countries, the percentage of corporate tax to total income tax was high in the U.K. The high percentage of corporate income tax to total income tax in developing countries, despite the lesser number of corporate taxpayers seems to be due to lower income tax collection from individuals. The per capita GDP in the selected developing countries was less than the basic exemption in these countries, with the result that there was lesser number of individual taxpayers and lower collection of income tax from individual taxpayers. As against this, for corporate taxpayers there was no basic exemption and a flat rate of tax was applicable. This meant that every corporate taxpayer had to pay corporate tax with the result that there was better collection of corporate tax despite lesser number of corporate taxpayers.

Thus, two observations emerge out of the above analysis:

1. The major part of income tax revenue comes from corporate sector in the developing countries as against developed countries where the major share comes from individual tax.
2. The large share of corporate tax in the total income tax also seems to be

due to the fact that, as compared to the tax rates applicable on individuals, the rates for companies are higher and that every part of taxable income is charged to tax.

Growth in Corporate Income Tax Revenue as Compared to the Growth in GDP

The growth in corporate income tax may not be a true indicator as the growth in the absolute amount gets affected by inflation and appreciation or fall in the value of currency of the country concerned. Hence, it is better to compare the growth in the corporate income tax with the growth in GDP over a period. A comparative analysis of the growth in GDP and corporate income tax during the period 1984 and 1997 is shown in Table 7.5.

As shown in the table above, the corporate income tax has grown in absolute terms in all these countries. However, the percentage growth was more in India and Australia as compared to the growth in the U.S., the U.K. and Malaysia. Separate data for corporate income tax for the year 1984 is not available for Pakistan. The difference in the percentage growth in corporate income tax between 1984 and 1997 and the growth in GDP between the same periods was the highest in Australia, i.e. 260.71 per cent followed by India where it was 158.51 per cent, whereas in the U.S., it was 112.54 per cent. In Malaysia and the U.K., the difference in the percentage growth in corporate tax and the percentage growth in the GDP was negative, which indicates that corporate income tax growth has not been in proportion to the growth in the GDP in these countries.

TAXATION OF DIVIDEND INCOME

A company is owned by its shareholders. After paying tax on its income it distributes its income to its owners, i.e. shareholders. The distribution of income by the company to its shareholders is called 'dividend'. If business

TABLE 7.5. PERCENTAGE GROWTH IN GROSS DOMESTIC PRODUCT (GDP) AND PERCENTAGE GROWTH IN CORPORATE INCOME TAX (CIT)

(from the year 1984 to year 1997)

Country	Currency	GDP (in billions) 1984	GDP (in billions) 1997	% Growth in GDP	C.I.T in (billions) 1984	CIT (in billions) 1997	% Growth in CIT	Difference in % growth in CIT and GDP
U.K.	£	325.85	800.94	145.80	14.41	32.138	136.90	-8.9
U.S.	$	3902.4	8110.9	107.84	57.05	182.78	220.38	112.54
Australia	AUD	214.35	549.29	156.25	4.492	23.222	416.96	260.71
Malaysia	RM	79.95	275.367	244.42	6.007	16.896	181.27	-63.15
Pakistan	PKR	419.8	2404.6	472.79	n.a.	66.863	n.a.	n.a.
India	Rs.	2313.4	15635.5	575.86	25.6	213.6	734.37	158.51

Note: n.a. not available

Sources: 1. *IMF Government Finance Statistics Yearbook*, 1991 and 1999.
2. *IMF International Financial Statistics Yearbook*, 1999.

income is taxed at the level of companies only when it is earned, then different shareholders will not pay different rates of personal income tax. If its income is taxed only on distribution, taxation may be postponed indefinitely. On the other hand, if income is taxed both when it is earned and when it is distributed, it means double taxation.

Few pieces of tax tangle pose a greater challenge in explaining tax policy to a general audience than does the corporation income tax. The corporate tax is variously viewed—as a pernicious double tax on savings, a tax shelter for the small businessman, a critical instrument to preserve the progressivity of the individual tax, and a fundamentally just way to compel institutions that control a large share of the nation's wealth to contribute to the collective expense.[19]

Systems of corporation tax are of three types, namely, classical, imputation and split rate.[20]

In the *classical system,* there is double taxation. Income is first taxed at company level when it is earned and then again taxed in the hands of shareholders when distributed. In this system, all individual owners of the company bear the same rate of tax and there is bias against the distribution of dividends to avoid payment of personal income tax.

The second system is *imputation system.* In this system, the tax paid at company level when income is earned, is allowed to be imputed to the shareholders while levying personal income tax. The owner of the company, i.e. the shareholders, get credit of the tax paid by the company. The imputation system removes double taxation and the bias against distribution. However, there can still be some bias against distribution if the personal income tax is more than the imputation credit.

In the *split rate method*, the preferential treatment for distributed profits takes the form of a lower rate rather than a deduction from the base. The tax treatment of dividend varies in the selected countries. As dividend income arises from the company income, it is important to examine the taxation of dividend income in the selected countries.

THE U.K.

The taxability of dividend income has been subject to frequent changes in the U.K. Prior to 1965, there was no separate tax on corporations and such tax was payable along with tax on other incomes. Corporation tax was introduced in the U.K. in 1965. From 1965 till 1973, corporate income was taxable according to the classical system.

As a result, there was double taxation in the U.K. Debt finance was preferred to equity finance as interest was allowable as expense, but not the dividend. Due to severe criticism in 1973, the country introduced partial imputation system of corporate tax. Under this system, dividends received by individuals from the U.K. companies were imputed with a tax credit equal to 20/80 of the amount of the dividends received. Dividends received after April 6, 1999 had an imputation credit of 10/90 of the amount of the dividends received. In the U.K., the due date for the payment of corporation tax falls

9 months and 1 day after the end of the chargeable accounting period. But companies were required to make payment of 'Advance Corporation Tax' (ACT) at the time of the distribution of dividends to take care of the imputation credit attached to the dividend distributed. This ACT payment by the company satisfied the company's tax liability against its income. However, with effect from April 6, 1999, ACT has been abolished as it was considered to have affected the cash flow of the companies, thus affecting growth. A system of shadow ACT was introduced to enable companies to relieve the surplus ACT accumulated on April 6, 1999. In the U.K., irrespective of the tax rate applicable to a company, credit is allowed to shareholders on dividend income at the rate of 10 per cent only. As such, for starting rate companies, which are chargeable to tax at the rate of 10 per cent, there is full imputation of tax paid by the company to the shareholders. However, for small companies and full rate companies, which are chargeable to tax at the rate of 20 and 30 per cent, respectively, there is partial imputation.

Many changes have been made in the U.K. regarding the taxation of investment income during the income year 1999-2000. Dividend income, which was previously a part of savings income, is separated from it. Investment incomes are divided into three categories: (1) Income from savings, (2) Dividend income, and (3) Other investment income.

Tax is deducted at source at the rate of 20 per cent from the savings income. Though no tax is deducted at source from the dividend income, a tax credit equal to 1/9 of the dividend received (10 percent of the gross dividend) is allowed. Savings income excluding dividends is taxable as it was taxable earlier either at the rate of 20 per cent or 40 per cent. Dividend income is taxable at the rate of 10 per cent or 32.5 per cent. All other investment incomes are taxable at the normal rates of 20, 23 or 40 per cent applicable in the case of individual taxpayers.

Since different tax rates are charged on different investment incomes, tax is calculated first on the total income excluding income from savings and dividends. Then tax is computed on income from savings excluding dividend income. Thereafter, tax on dividend income is calculated. Tax computed on different incomes is added. The impact of these changes on the taxability of dividend income is as follows: Where the total income including the dividend income does not exceed the personal allowances available to the individual, no refund can be claimed in respect of the tax credit which could not be claimed. Where dividend income including savings income and other income exceeds £28,000, then tax credit at the rate of 10 per cent will be allowed, thus leaving the remaining tax of 22.5 per cent, i.e. 32.5 per cent less 10 per cent to be borne by the individual on dividend income.

Close Company Status

The benefits-in-kind provided to participators and their associates and loans made to participators by a close company[21] in the U.K. are treated as distribution and are assessed to tax.

Any benefit provided for a participator or an associate, which does not fall within the Schedule E (income from employment) rules for benefits in kind is treated as distribution and is disallowed in computing the company's profits and is charged in the hands of the recipients as dividend income.

Loan to a participator or an associate by a close company is charged to tax on the amount of loan. For periods before April 6, 1999, the company had to pay ACT on the amount of loan, which could be reclaimed by the company on the repayment of the loan. For the period after April 6, 1999, a tax equal to 25 per cent of the loan is charged on the company, which is repaid if the loan is repaid. However, these rules do not apply if the loan is made by the company in the normal course of its business, i.e. whose business is that of lending money or loans not exceeding £15,000 made to a participant who is a full-time employee or director of the company and does not own more than 5 per cent of the ordinary small capital.

THE U.S.

The term 'dividend' in the U.S. means any distribution made by a corporation to its shareholders, whether in money or other property out of earnings and profits of the tax year or out of accumulated earnings.

If the dividend is received partly as cash and partly as non-cash property, the amount of the dividend will be equal to the amount of the cash plus the fair market value of the property distributed.

The U.S. follows the classical system of corporate taxation. No credit is allowed to the shareholders in respect of the tax paid by 'C' corporations on their income. Of the various types of business organisations, 'C' corporations are subject to the toughest tax bite. Their earnings are taxed twice.[22] First, a corporation pays tax on its income and then the shareholders pay tax again on the dividend income distributed out of profits remaining after the payment of tax by the company. Hence, there is no imputation system in the U.S. However, 'S' corporations are entitled to opt for a flow-through entity status. 'S' corporations are a special form of corporation and their income is not taxed as in the case of a partnership. The income, deductions, losses and credits of 'S' corporations flow through to the shareholders. As such, there is no double taxation on 'S' corporations. Regulated Investment Corporation (RIC) and Real Estate Investment Corporation (REIC) are entitled to deduct the amount of dividend distributed to its shareholders and taxed on the remaining income. The credit for the tax paid on the net long-term capital gain retained by such corporations is allowed in the hands of the shareholders.

In the U.S., no tax is deducted at source from the dividend income. However, to ensure that the taxpayer reports this income, the U.S. government has made it compulsory for the taxpayer to supply his taxpayer-identification number (TIN) to the payer of the dividend. If the TIN is not supplied to the payer or the Internal Revenue Service (IRS) finds that the taxpayer has under-reported the dividend income, then such income will be subject to a back-up withholding tax at a flat 31 per cent rate.

Dividend income is included in the gross income in the U.S. and is taxable like any other income. No rebate is allowed in respect of this income. The tax burden on dividend income depends on the taxable income of an individual. The higher the income, the higher will be the tax burden. Thus, dividend income is subject to double taxation in the U.S.

AUSTRALIA

Dividend in Australia includes any distribution made by a company to its shareholders, whether in money or other property (including shares in that or another company) and any amount credited by a company to its shareholders as such [ITAA 36, Sec. 6(1)]. Any distribution by way of redemption or cancellation of a redeemable preference share to the extent the value of the distribution exceeds the amount paid-up on the share is also a dividend. A distribution of capital is also a dividend to the extent it exceeds the amount debited to the share capital account.

Dividend income in Australia is added to the assessable income (gross income) and is taxable like any other income. Tax is not deducted at source. The imputation system applies to dividends paid by Australian resident companies to resident individual shareholders. In the case of franked dividend, the tax paid at the company level is allocated to shareholders by way of imputation credits attached to the dividends they receive. The dividend paid to the shareholder is grossed up to include the amount of company tax attributable to the dividend, i.e. imputation credit. A tax rebate equal to the amount of company tax attributable to the dividend is allowed to the shareholders. Therefore, dividend paid to shareholders may either become tax- free or taxable at very low rates.

The tax rate for companies in Australia is 34 per cent for the income year 2000-01. Therefore, a credit of 34/66 of the dividend received will be given to the shareholder receiving franked dividend. For example, if a company earns income of AUD200,000 and pays a tax of AUD68,000, i.e. 34 per cent of AUD200,000, the distributable profit will be AUD 132,000. If a shareholder receives net dividend of AUD3,300, his dividend will be grossed up as 3,300 x 100/66 = 5,000. Thus, AUD5,000 will be added to his income. Tax will be levied on the dividend income of AUD5,000 at ordinary tax rates applicable to individuals, ranging from 15 per cent to 47 per cent tax. The shareholder receiving a gross dividend of AUD5,000 will be allowed a tax credit of AUD1,700.

The impact of franking rebate varies according to the income earned by a shareholder. For small income earners, the dividend normally becomes tax-free, as the tax rate applicable is equal to or less than 34 per cent tax credit, while for higher income groups, the effective tax rate on the dividend is reduced to 13 per cent (i.e. 47 per cent less 34 per cent). In Australia, tax credit can be used to reduce the tax liability on other income, but no refund of tax credit is not allowed.

An unfrankable dividend (dividend received by shareholder without adding any amount of imputation credit) is taxable like ordinary income. Unfranked dividends paid to non-residents in Australia are liable to a flat withholding tax. Dividend withholding tax is generally imposed at a flat rate of 30 per cent. However, if Australia has a double taxation agreement with any country, the withholding rate of 15 per cent will be applicable in respect of dividends paid to the residents of such countries.

The extent to which a company may frank a dividend depends on the credit balance in its franking accounts at the time of payment of the dividend. All companies in Australia must keep a franking account. Credit in franking account arises when a company pays company tax and also when a company receives franked dividend from another company. Debit to franking account arises when the dividend is distributed. A company must frank dividends to the extent permitted by its franking account balance at the date of payment of the dividends. The franking account balance is the difference between a company's franking credit of a particular class and its franking debit of the same class.

When determining the extent to which particular dividends are to be franked, future dividends, dividends on preference shares, and the interim dividend paid including additional franking credits expected to be received later in the year, are considered. Where a company has over franked a dividend, i.e. has paid franked dividend in excess of its franking credits for the year, the company is required to make a non-refundable payment shortly after the end of the year to make good this deficit. This payment is known as the franking deficit tax. In Australia, special rules apply to prevent tax avoidance through franking credit-trading schemes. While only partial imputation is applicable in the U.K., full imputation is allowed in Australia.

Inter-Corporate Dividend

In Australia, companies which receive dividends are entitled to two types of benefits. First, these companies get credit in respect of franked dividend received from other companies. The credit will increase the franking account surplus and may be imputed to the shareholders when the company receiving it distributes it to its shareholders.

Secondly, companies are also entitled to inter-corporate dividend rebate. The amount of the rebate is calculated by applying the companies' average tax rate to that part of the companies' taxable income, which represents dividends. While in the case of public companies, rebate is allowed in respect of both franked and unfranked dividends, in the case of private companies, rebate is allowed when a company receives a franked dividend only. The rebate is allowed only to resident companies in respect of dividends received from resident companies.

Payment to Associates—Deemed Dividend

In Australia, amounts paid, lent or forgiven by a private company to associated persons[23] to the extent of its distributable surplus are treated as dividends except those which fall within the specified exclusions. This deemed dividend is not frankable although franking debit will be made in the franking account of the company. Payments and loans excluded are loans made in the ordinary course of business on ordinary commercial terms and a loan meeting a specified minimum interest rate and maximum term criteria. To prevent double taxation, where a private company distributes a subsequent dividend and the dividend is set off against the deemed dividend, the amount set off is not taken to be a dividend income.

Similarly, if the Income Tax Commissioner thinks that any payment by a private company as remuneration for services rendered or a retirement or terminal allowance, gratuity or compensation to an associated person exceeds what is reasonable, the excess is deemed as dividend. This excess is also not deductible to the company. Such excess is deemed to have been paid out of the company profits and to have been paid to the recipient as a shareholder, though the recipient may not be a shareholder. This deemed dividend is not frankable under the imputation system.

MALAYSIA

The term 'dividend' in Malaysia means any sum distributed amongst its shareholders by a company which is not in liquidation or which is not reducing its capital. In Malaysia, a company can declare dividend out of its reserves, which may comprise of untaxed capital profits. Sec. 14(1) of the *Income Tax Act*, 1967, provides that where a company resident for the basis year for a year of assessment, pays, credits or distributes a dividend in that basis year, the dividend shall be deemed to be derived from Malaysia.

Where a company was not resident for the basis year, for a year of assessment only dividends paid, credited or distributed by the company on or after the day on which the management and control of any business of the company were first exercised in Malaysia, shall be deemed to be derived from Malaysia.

In case a dividend is distributed in a form other than money it shall be taken to be an amount equal to the market value of the property at the time of the distribution of the dividend.

Money given as loan has been held to be a deemed dividend in Malaysia under certain circumstances. A bonus issued by a company is not deemed as dividend distribution.

In Malaysia, as in Australia, full imputation system is applicable. There is no double taxation. First, tax is paid by the company on its income at the prescribed rate of 28 per cent (for the year of assessment 2000). The dividend when paid to a shareholder is also taxable in his hands at the rates applicable for the individual taxpayer. However, full credit at the company rates of 28 per cent is allowed to the shareholders.

A company in Malaysia is entitled to deduct tax at the rate applicable to the company for the year of assessment. This tax is, however, not required to be paid by the company. In case no deduction of tax is made, the dividend is deemed to be a dividend of a gross amount, which after the deduction of tax, would be equal to the net amount paid.

A company is required to prepare a statement working out the tax credit in the hands of shareholders on the dividend income distributed by it and compare the same with the tax liability on its chargeable income for that year. In case the tax liability on the chargeable income is more than the total tax credit on dividend, the balance is allowed to be carried forward for credit to a subsequent year. However, in case the tax credit allowed is more than the total tax liability on the company after allowing the carry-forward benefit, the difference is a debt due by the company to the government and is required to be paid by the company. As such, in Malaysia, a company can recover its tax from a shareholder by deducting tax on the dividend distributed and using the same towards the tax liability on its income.

Dividend income is included in the total income in the hands of shareholders and is taxed at the appropriate rates applicable to the shareholders, which vary from 2 to 30 per cent. The shareholder is entitled to offset his tax liability against the tax credit on dividend income and also claim refund if the tax credit is more than the tax payable on its total income.

The Malaysian tax system relating to dividend income is similar to the Australian system. In both the countries, full tax credit is allowed in the hands of the shareholder without deduction of tax at source. However, in Australia, tax credit is allowed only to the extent of tax on total income but if it could not be fully availed of, the balance is non-refundable. In Malaysia, however, tax credits which cannot be set off, is refundable.

PAKISTAN

In Pakistan, the term 'dividend' means any distribution by a company of accumulated profits to its shareholders if such distribution entails the release of all or any part of the assets of the company and includes distribution made to the shareholders of a company in liquidation or on the reduction of its capital to the extent to which distribution is attributable to the accumulated profits of the company. Dividend in its ordinary connotation means the amount paid or received by a shareholder in proportion to his shareholding in a company out of the total sum so distributed.

The tax paid by a company is not imputed to its shareholders. All shareholders including the company are liable to pay tax on their dividend income. However, lower tax rates are applicable on dividend income. As such, Pakistan follows the modified classical system by providing relief to the shareholders in the form of concessional tax rate on dividend income. Every company is liable to pay tax individually. There is no system of filing a consolidated return of companies forming a group as is in the U.S. and Australia.

With effect from the assessment year 1992-93, the tax treatment of dividend income in respect of an individual has been changed. The dividend income in the case of an individual from the assessment year 1992-93 onwards is to be taxed as a separate block of income. The rate of tax on dividend income in respect of an individual is 10 per cent for the income year 2000-01.

Tax is deducted at source from the dividend income in Pakistan at the rate of 10 per cent. However, the gross dividend is taxable in the hands of the shareholders. Grossing up is done by multiplying the dividend received by 100/90. The shareholder is entitled to get tax credit in respect of the tax so deducted. Credit, if not fully availed of, however, is not refundable.

Payment to Shareholders—Deemed Dividend

In Pakistan, any payment by way of loan or advance by a private company to a shareholder or on his behalf or for his individual benefit to the extent of accumulated profits is deemed as dividend and is taxable in the hands of the shareholder except advance or loan mode to a shareholder by a company in the ordinary course of business where money-lending is a substantial part of the business of the company. This provision of deemed dividend is not applicable in the case of a public company.

Inter-corporate Dividend

Dividend income of companies, including profits received by Modarba shareholders, is also taxable as a separate block of income. Dividend income in the case of companies is taxable at the rate prescribed in Para D, Part V of the First Schedule to the *Income Tax Ordinance,* 1979. In the case of dividend received by a public company, the tax rate is 5 per cent and in the case of any other company, the tax rate is 20 per cent. However, the rate of 20 per cent shall be reduced to 7.5 per cent in the case of dividend declared or distributed on shares of a company set up for power generation and transmission line projects.

INDIA

The system of taxation of dividend income in India is different from that in Pakistan, but the meaning of dividend and deemed dividend is the same. Dividend in India can be paid out of current profits, and the undistributed profit of the previous accounting year and the money provided by the Central or State Government for the payment of dividends in pursuance of the guarantee by the government. Dividend income is taxable whether it is paid out of revenue profits or capital gains, out of taxable income or tax-free income, and whether it is paid in cash or in kind.

The mode of computation of tax liability on dividend income in India has changed in recent years. In India, no credit is allowed to the shareholder of a company for the tax paid by the company on its income. Moreover, the company is required to pay tax at the time of distribution of dividend. However, no tax is chargeable on dividend income in the hands of the shareholder. As such, India follows a modified classical system.

Prior to June 1997, companies in India were required to pay tax on their total income and the dividend paid out of post-tax income was again taxable in the hands of shareholders. Tax was required to be deducted at source at the rate of 20 per cent from dividend income. A tax rebate equal to the tax deducted at source was allowed. Hence, there was double taxation on dividend income. However, dividend income in the hands of company was exempt to the extent of the dividend declared by such company under Sec. 80M of the Income Tax Act. Besides, individual shareholders were also entitled to the benefit of deduction up to Rs.12,000 of the dividend income including bank interest under Sec. 80L of the Income Tax Act.

From 1997, the dividend income in the hands of shareholders is exempt. However, tax at the rate of 10 per cent on dividend distribution was imposed on companies with the purpose that the company should withhold funds for its growth. Any amount declared, distributed, or paid by a domestic company by way of dividend was subject to an additional tax of 10 per cent (the effective tax rate being 11 per cent including 10 per cent surcharge up to May 31, 2000). *The Finance Act*, 2000, has increased the tax rate on the distribution of dividend from 10 per cent to 20 per cent with effect from June 1, 2000. After taking into account, the surcharge of 13 per cent of income tax, the effective tax rate comes to 22.6 per cent. However, this rate has been again reduced to 10 per cent with surcharge of 2 per cent of income tax (effective rate being 10.20 per cent) with effect from June 1, 2001.

Loan and Advances to Shareholders: Deemed Dividend

In India, any loan or advance paid by a company in which the public is not substantially interested to the extent of its accumulated profit is deemed as dividend if paid:

1. to an equity shareholder, holding not less than 10 per cent of the voting power;
2. to any concern in which such shareholder (holding not less than 10 per cent of voting power) is a member or a partner and in which he has a substantial interest;[24] or
3. to any person on behalf or for the individual benefit of any such shareholder

However, any advance or loan by a company in the ordinary course of business where the lending of money is a substantial part of business of the company is not considered deemed dividend. Such dividend is taxable at the normal rate in the hands of the shareholder and there is no dividend distribution tax applicable on the company. The above provisions are meant to curb the tendency of making advances to interested persons by way of loan or advance instead of declaring dividend and paying tax thereon.

Conclusion

There is a great deal of variation in the taxation of dividend income in the selected countries. The U.S. is the only country, amongst the selected countries, which follows the classical system, and consequently, there is double taxation. This classical system is not equity based as the same income is taxed twice. However, due to the multi-rate system and the existence of 'S' corporations being flow-through entities, the impact of classical system is only on those corporations which have high income. Full credit is allowed to the shareholders for the tax paid by the company in Australia and Malaysia. In Malaysia, the shareholder is entitled to claim even a refund of the tax paid by the company and transferred to him by imputation credit. In Australia, credit of tax paid by the company is allowed to a shareholder by way of franked dividend credit, but a refund of franked dividend credit is not allowed to the shareholders. The system in Australia and Malaysia appears to be equity-based as there is no double taxation and with full imputation of tax paid by the company, there is an incentive to the taxpayer to declare full dividend income in order to obtain tax credit, which may result in better compliance in these countries. Tax laws for corporate bodies in Malaysia and Australia recognise that a company is owned by its shareholders and that the income earned by the company is income earned by the shareholders and that the company is an artificial entity for carrying business only. The corporate tax structure in the U.K. partially recognises this idea. In the U.K., there being multi-rate system and imputation credit to the extent of 10 per cent of dividend income only, the provisions are more equitable for individual taxpayers having small income but are discriminatory for individual taxpayers having income above a certain level when dividend income is taxed at a higher rate. No imputation credit is allowed in Pakistan and India. These countries have followed a modified classical system. In Pakistan and India, although there is double taxation of income earned by the company, the rates applicable on dividend income are lower. There is also a very interesting contradiction. In Pakistan, there is tax on the company if it does not distribute its income whereas in India, there is tax on the company if it distributes dividend. The reason for levying tax in Pakistan if the company does not distribute dividend is that the government does not get tax, which it otherwise would have got, had the dividend been distributed from the shareholders on their income from such dividend. On the other hand, the reason for levying tax on distribution of dividend in India is the recovery of tax from company on such dividend income instead of recovery of tax from the shareholders, since the dividend distributed after paying tax on distribution by the company is exempt in the hands of the shareholders. Another reason stated by the Finance Minister while levying dividend distribution tax in India was that 'Some companies distribute exorbitant dividends. Ideally, they should retain the bulk of their profits and plough them into fresh investments. I intend to reward companies who invest in future growth. Hence, I propose to levy a tax on distributed profits at the moderate rate of 10 per cent on the amount so distributed'.[25]

Overall Tax Liability on Company Income and Dividend Income

A company is an artificial entity created and owned by its shareholders. The taxes paid by the company are an *indirect* payment of taxes by the shareholders whereas the taxes paid on dividend income is a *direct* payment of taxes by the shareholders. Therefore it is important to compare the overall corporate tax liability by consolidating the tax rate applicable on the company income and the tax rate applicable on the dividend distributed to shareholders out of the income remaining after payment of taxes by the company.

The minimum overall tax liability in the selected countries as regards the taxation of the income of the company and dividend income is given in Table 7.6.

As shown in the table, the overall tax burden of 5 per cent was the lowest in Malaysia, where the shareholder could get refund of tax paid by the company in case the tax liability of the shareholder is lower than the company tax imputed on his dividend income. The overall tax burden in the U.K. was 10 per cent, including company tax and dividend tax, followed by the U.S. (27.75 per cent). In Australia, the overall tax liability was 34 per cent, as the shareholder is not entitled to claim refund of excess tax. In Pakistan, the overall minimum tax burden of 39.70 per cent has arisen in the case of public companies where the tax rate on such companies was 33 per cent. In India, the overall minimum tax burden has been the highest, i.e. 50.70 per cent.

The maximum overall tax liability in the selected countries as regards the taxation of the income of the company and dividend income is given in Table 7.7.

The maximum overall tax liability, including company tax and the tax on dividend, as shown in Table 7.7, indicates that the effective rate of 60.74 per cent in the U.S. was applicable on company income of above US$10 millions when the maximum company rate of 35 per cent would be charged and on income of individual shareholder above U.S.$288,350, when the maximum individual tax rate of 39.6 per cent was applicable. Though the effective tax rate of 60.74 per cent has been the maximum in the U.S., it was applicable only in the case of very high-income group, but in India, the highest tax rate of 50.70 per cent is applicable on every rupee. In Pakistan, the maximum tax rate of 48.70 per cent was applicable only in the case of private companies, where the tax rate on company income was 43 per cent. The next highest liability of 47.5 per cent was on the U.K. shareholder, when his total income exceeded £28,400 in which case the dividend income would be taxable at the rate of 32.5 per cent (though the highest rate for individuals in U.K. is 40 per cent), and the effective rate on dividend would be 32.5 per cent less credit of 10 per cent, i.e. 22.5 per cent. In Australia, the maximum liability arose when the total income of the shareholder, including dividend income, exceeded AUD60, 000 when the effective tax rate on dividend income would have been 47 per cent less 34 per cent, i.e. 13 per cent. The overall tax rate in Malaysia has been the lowest among all these countries, i.e. 29 per cent. This was the maximum tax liability in Malaysia, which arose when the income of the shareholder exceeded RM150,000.

Thus, the tax liability on the shareholder was the maximum in the U.S. only when the shareholder was in the higher income bracket group. On the

TABLE 7.6. MINIMUM TAX LIABILITY ON COMPANY INCOME INCLUDING DIVIDEND INCOME[1]

Country	Income year	Income level	Tax Rate on Company (%)	Tax Liability on Company (%)	Balance	Tax Rate on Distribution (%)	Tax Liability on Dividend Distribution	Amount in the hands of Shareholders	Tax Liability of Share-holders	Net Balance	Overall Tax Liability
U.K	2000-01	10,000	10	1,000	9,000	Nil	Nil	9,000	1000[2] -1000[3]	9,000	10
U.S.	2000	10,000	15	1,500	Nil	Nil	Nil	8,500	12,75	7,225	27.75
Australia	2000-01	10,000	34	3,400	6,600	Nil	Nil	6,600	1700 -3400 1700[4]	6,600	34
Malaysia	2000	10,000	28	2,800	7,200	Nil	Nil	7,200	500 -2,800 +2,300	7,200 2,300[5] 9,500	5
Pakistan	2000-01	10,000	33	3,300	6,700	10%	Nil	6,700	670	6,030	39.70
India	2000-01	10,000	39.55	3,955	6,045	22.6%	1,115	4,930	Nil	4,930	50.70

Note:
1. Assuming company has income of amount 10,000 (amount is presumed to be in individual country currency) and all income after paying tax by the company is distributed as dividend.
2. Tax liability of shareholder is calculated on the basis of minimum tax rates applicable on individual taxpayers, as given in Table 2.3.
3. This represents tax credit allowed to shareholders on dividend income.
4. In Australia, refund of excess tax credit of dividend income is not allowed to the shareholders presently, but the excess tax credit can be adjusted against tax liability of other income during the year, if any.
5. In Malaysia, refund of excess tax credit of dividend income is allowed to the shareholders, as such the same has been deducted from the overall tax liability.

Source: Author's Calcuations, Income Tax Acts and taxation statistics of the selected countries.

TABLE 7.7. MAXIMUM TAX LIABILITY ON COMPANY INCOME INCLUDING DIVIDEND INCOME[1]

Country	Income year	Income Level	Tax Rate on Company (%)	Tax Liability on Company (%)	Balance	Tax Rate on Distribution (%)	Tax Liability on Dividend Distribution	Amount in the hands of Shareholders	Tax Liability of Share-holders	Net Balance	Overall Tax Liability
U.K.	2000-01	1,000,000	30	300,000	700,000	Nil	Nil	700,000	252,777[2] - 77,777 175,000	525,000	47.5
U.S.	2000	1,000,000	35	350,000	650,000	Nil	Nil	650,000	257,400	392,600	60.74
Australia	2000-01	1,000,000	34	340,000	660,000	Nil	Nil	660,000	470,000 - 340,000 130,000	530,000	47
Malaysia	2000	1,000,000	28	280,000	720,000	Nil	Nil	720,000	290,000 -280,000 10,000	710,000	29
Pakistan	2000-01	1,000,000	43	430,000	570,000	10	Nil	570,000	57,000	513,000	48.70
India	2000-01	1,000,000	39.55	395,500	604,500	22.6	111,440	493,060	Nil	493,060	50.70

Notes: 1. Assuming company has income of amount 1,000,000 (amount is presumed to be in individual country currency) and all income after paying tax by the company is distributed as dividend and both company and shareholders fall in the highest tax brackets.

2. In the U.K., dividend income is grossed by 9/10 and tax credit is allowed 1/9th of dividend received. Tax liability of shareholders is calculated on the basis of maximum tax rates applicable on individual taxpayers as given in Table 2.3.

Source: Same as given in Table 7.6.

other hand, in India, the overall tax liability was applicable, whatever the income of the shareholder. However, the tax rates on dividend distribution in India have been reduced.

MINIMUM ALTERNATE TAX

The government levies taxes to collect revenues for public expenditure and at the same time allow concessions and benefits to taxpayers to promote social and economic objectives. However, over a period, concessions on account of socially and economically desirable activities have proliferated and taxpayers have tended to plan their affairs in a manner where they avail themselves of the maximum concessions on account of these transactions and pay zero tax or minimal tax despite their ability to pay. The purpose of allowing concessions for undertaking socially and economically desirable activities is not to defeat the fundamental concept that tax system should reflect the taxpayers' ability to pay. Accordingly, in some countries a minimum tax is levied on the income earned by the taxpayer ignoring some of the deductions, incentives. Amongst the selected countries, the U.S., and India have introduced a minimum tax system[26].

In Pakistan, the minimum tax liability is linked to the turnover. If the tax payable is nil or the total tax payable is less than one-half per cent of the total turnover from all sources, then the total turnover is deemed as income, and tax at the rate of one half per cent less tax payable on regular income is the minimum tax, which a taxpayer will have to pay. The minimum tax provisions are applicable to all taxpayers including companies.

In 1969, the U.S. Congress introduced the 'Add on Minimum Tax'. The amount of the tax was 10 per cent of tax preference in excess of $30,000 statutory exemption. Such tax was added to the taxpayer's regular income tax liability. As this tax did not serve the purpose of assuring that all taxpayers pay their fair share of taxes, the alternative minimum tax (AMT) system was introduced in 1978. The AMT is not an add-on tax, but a separate and parallel tax system. The AMT is applicable on individuals, corporations, estates and trusts in the U.S.

The base of AMT is the alternative minimum taxable income (AMTI), which is calculated by making certain adjustments to the regular taxable income. The first step in the calculation of AMTI is to: (1) add or subtract adjustments; (2) add tax preferences in the regular taxable income.

AMT Adjustments

The AMT adjustments include adjustment of depreciation and itemized deductions. While the depreciation adjustment is applicable both to corporate and individual taxpayer, the itemized deduction adjustments are applicable only to individuals. The manner in which some itemized deductions including medical expenses, qualified interest and state and local taxes and miscellaneous deductions are allowed, differ for the AMT and for regular tax liability. Most of the other itemized deductions, casualty and theft losses;

charitable contributions are allowed on similar basis in both the cases.

The most common adjustment due to timing differences applicable both to individual and corporate taxpayers is depreciation. This adjustment is required because the rules for calculating taxable income permit the taxpayer to temporarily defer the recognition of income or to accelerate deductions. In the U.S., while a higher depreciation based on a shorter recovery period is allowed for regular tax purposes, on the other hand, alternative depreciation system (ADS) with straight line method and a longer recovery period is allowed for AMT purposes. This may cause a huge gap between the two depreciation amounts in the initial years. Although the trend will reverse in the future years, the difference in the amount of depreciation is adjusted either by adding to or subtracting from the regular taxable income, depending upon whether the depreciation under AMT is more or is less than the depreciation under regular tax liability.

Tax Preference Items

After making the AMT adjustments, the following tax-preference items are added in the regular taxable income:

1. Excess of accelerated depreciation over hypothetical straight-line depreciation for real property, placed in service before 1987.
2. Tax-exempt interest on certain private activity bonds.
3. Exclusion of gain on the sale of certain small business stock.

From the amount arrived at after making the above adjustments, deduction by way of a minimum exemption amount is allowed. The initial exemption is given to eliminate taxpayers with a relatively moderate amount of taxable income. The initial exemption amount is, however, reduced by 25 per cent of every dollar when the AMTI exceeds a specified level. And further, no initial exemption is available when the AMTI reaches a particular level.

The initial exemption amount and the level of the AMTI at which the phase out begins or at which exemption is withdrawn are given in Table 7.8.

Thus, as shown in Table 7.8, although the initial exemption of $40,000 to companies and $33,750 to individual taxpayers are allowed, no such exemption is allowed to companies, if the AMTI exceeds $310,000 and in

TABLE 7.8. AMOUNT OF INITIAL EXEMPTION AND THE LEVEL OF AMTI AT WHICH PHASE OUT BEGINS OR EXEMPTION IS WITHDRAWN

Type of Entity	Initial Exemption	Phase out begins at AMTI of	No Exemption if AMTI exceeds
Corporation	$40,000	$150,000	$310,000
Individual (single)	$33,750	$112,500	$247,500
Individual (head of household)	$33,750	$112,500	$247,500
Individual (married filing jointly)	$45,000	$150,000	$330,000
Individual (married filing separately)	$22,500	$75,000	$165,000

the case of individual taxpayers if the AMTI exceeds $247500. The balance amount after making the AMT adjustments to the regular taxable income and adding tax preference items and subtracting the initial exemption, is AMTI. The tentative AMT is found out by applying tax rates to such income. The AMT tax rate is 20 per cent in the case of corporations and 26 percent on the first $175,000 of AMTI and 28 per cent in excess of $175,000 in the case of the individual taxpayer. Subtraction of foreign tax credit, subject to the maximum of 90 per cent of the tentative AMT (no other tax credit is allowed to be deducted) provides the tentative AMT. The tentative AMT is compared to the regular tax liability. The excess of the tentative AMT over the regular tax liability is called AMT. Thus, the AMT is payable in addition to the regular tax liability in the U.S. No AMT is payable where the regular tax liability exceeds the tentative AMT.

Credit for AMT

While credit for the AMT is allowed in the U.S. for an indefinite period of time, the credit is allowed only for those adjustments which take place due to timing differences, namely depreciation. No credit is allowed in case the AMT is payable due to any tax preference item, or due to disallowance of any tax credit.

Minimum Alternate Tax in India

Minimum alternate tax (MAT) in India is applicable in the case of companies only. The purpose of this tax is to ensure that at least some minimum tax is paid by those companies which earn substantial profit as per the *Companies Act*, but are zero tax companies or are paying little tax under the Income Tax Act due to large number of exemptions and tax preferences. The first attempt to tax these companies was made in 1983 by introducing Sec. 80VV under the *Income Tax Act*, 1961, whereby deductions on account of certain exemptions under the Act were restricted to 70 per cent of the gross total income. The MAT provisions in India were introduced in a proper form with the induction of Sec. 115J in the Income Tax Act from the assessment year 1988-89. Under Sec. 115J, MAT was charged on 30 per cent of the book profit of the companies, calculated after making certain adjustments. However, due to opposition from the corporate sector, the provision was withdrawn from the assessment year 1991-92.

MAT was reintroduced after a gap of 6 years with the insertion of Sec. 115JA from the assessment year 1997-98. For the assessment year 1997-98, no exemption was allowed in respect of export income exempt under Sec. 80HHC and 80HHE of the Act, while computing MAT liability. However, from the assessment year 1998-99, exemption of export income was also allowed. An important change brought about by the *Finance Act*, 1998 was the provision of carry-forward of tax credit in respect of MAT paid under Sec. 115JAA. If the tax payable under MAT was in excess of the tax payable on the total income under the Income Tax Act, the tax credit under Sec. 115JAA was allowed upto a period of 5 years.

With a view to making MAT provisions more purposeful and effective, the *Finance Act*, 2000 has replaced Sec.115JA by new Sec. 115JB of the Income Tax Act effective from the assessment year 2001-02.

With effect from the assessment year 2001-02, MAT is levied at the rate of 7.5 per cent of the book profits, whereas until the assessment year 2000-01, MAT was payable at the ordinary company tax rate of 10.5 per cent, i.e. 35 per cent on 30 per cent of the book profit. Thus, the effective tax rate is now 7.5 per cent as against the rate of 10.5 per cent on the book profits earlier. Relief available to the industrial undertakings engaged in infrastructure projects will no longer be allowed. Credit for MAT paid in excess of the tax liability under the Income Tax Act will not be available from the assessment year 2001-02. However, the credit for the tax paid under MAT in excess of the tax liability on the total income under the Income tax Act, in earlier years will still be available over the remaining period of 5 years.

Computation of Minimum Alternate Tax in India

The base of calculating MAT in India is the book profit. The book profit is calculated after making adjustment to the net profit as shown in the profit and loss account prepared in accordance with the provisions of Parts II and III of the Sixth Schedule to the *Companies Act*, 1956. The profit as shown in the profit and loss account, is increased by the following amounts if debited to the profit and loss account:

1. the amount of Income tax paid, payable, or provided,
2. the amounts carried to any reserve
3. the provision for meeting uncertain liabilities
4. the provision for losses of subsidiary companies
5. the amount of dividends paid or proposed
6. the amount of expenditure relatable to any income which is exempt under Sections 10, 10A, 10B, 11 or 12 of the Income Tax Act.

The following amounts are subtracted from the profit as per profit and loss account.

1. the amounts withdrawn from reserves or provisions, it any such amount is credited to the profit and loss account
2. the amount of Income exempt under Sections 10, 10A, 10B, 11 or 12 of the Income-tax Act
3. the amount of loss brought forward or unabsorbed depreciation,which ever is less, as per books of account
4. the amount of profit eligible for deduction under Sec. 80 HHC, 80 HHE or 80 HHF
5. the amount of profits of sick industrial company starting from the year in which the said company has become a sick industrial company and ending with the year during which the entire network (i.e. paid-up capital plus free reserves) of such company becomes equal to or exceeds the accumulated losses.

The balance amount after the above adjustment is the book profit.

The MAT is payable in full if the regular tax liability is nil and to the extent of MAT, if any regular tax is payable by the company. In the case of a domestic company, the tax rate of 7.5 per cent is levied along with a surcharge of 13 per cent for income year 2000-01, thus, making the effective tax rate equal to 8.47 per cent. In the case of a non-domestic company, the MAT is payable at the rate of 7.5 per cent as no surcharge is applicable to a non-domestic company.

Difference in the Computation of MAT in the U.S. and India

The major points of difference in the computation of MAT in the U.S and India are given in Table 7.9.

Thus, it is clear from Table 7.9 that the AMT provisions in the U.S., though extremely complicated, are equity based. These provisions are so designed that all taxpayers pay fair part of their taxes, and that the benefit of tax preference is availed of by the taxpayers only up to a certain level of income. The income level up to which the benefit of tax preference is available is represented by the fixed amount of exemption. Only those taxpayers whose adjusted income exceeds the exemption amount are supposed to pay AMT, and are deprived of the tax preferences. Also, as the exemption amount is phased out if the adjusted total income (AGI) exceeds a certain level, and is reduced to nil beyond a certain level of AGI, very high income earners are neither provided the benefit of fixed exemption tax preferences, nor of the tax credits except foreign tax credit.

Another important aspect of AMT provisions in the U.S. is that although tax credit is allowed for an indefinite period, it is confined to only those adjustments which have a reversal impact like depreciation.

It also shows that once the benefit of tax preference is disallowed, the same is not allowed in future years in the form of credit. Another feature of the AMT provision is that tax rates applicable on alternate minimum taxable income (AMTI) in the case of individuals and corporations both are higher than the lower tax rate of 15 per cent levied on the ordinary taxable income in both the cases. In the case of individuals with 5 tax slabs, the minimum tax rate is 15 per cent and the maximum tax rate is 39.6 per cent. In the case of corporations, with 8 tax slabs, the minimum tax rate again is 15 per cent but the maximum tax rate is 35 per cent.

The MAT provision in India is still very controversial and is subject to a lot of criticism. The basic purpose of MAT in India is to charge a minimum tax from those companies which earn enormous or substantial profits, but due to a large number of tax incentives these companies are not liable to pay any tax or pay very small tax. On the other hand, the scope of AMT is wide in the U.S., where not only corporations but also high-income individuals are also required to pay AMT.

The basis of levying MAT in India is the net profit as per the Companies Act. As against it, in the U.S., the basis of computation of AMT is taxable

TABLE 7.9. DIFFERENCE IN THE COMPUTATION OF MAT IN THE U.S. AND INDIA

U.S.	India
(a) Known as alternative minimum tax (AMT)	(a) Known as minimum alternate tax (MAT)
(b) Initially started in 1969, method of computation changed in 1978, continuously in operation since then, without any major change.	(b) Initially started in 1983, method of computation changed from the income year 1987-88, withdrawn from the income year, 1990-91, again reintroduced from the income year, 1996-97, with frequent changes.
(c) Applicable to individual, corporate taxpayers and estates and trusts	(c) Applicable to corporate taxpayers only.
(d) Basis of computation is taxable income under the Income-tax regulations or under the Internal Revenue Code provisions.	(d) Basis of computation is net profit as per the provisions of the Companies Act.
(e) Tax preference items not eligible for deduction are added to the taxable income.	(e) Tax preference items eligible for deduction are subtracted from the net profit.
(f) Depreciation is either added or subtracted	(f) No adjustment of depreciation.
(g) A fixed amount of exemption is deducted from the alternate minimum taxable income	(g) No exemption is allowed from the minimum alternate taxable income (MATI)
(h) Tax incentives available in the form of tax credits are not deductible from the tentative AMT, except the foreign tax credit. Tax rates applicable on AMTI for the income year 2000 are: 1. 20% in the case of corporate taxpayers 2. 26% on the first $1,75,000 and 28% on the balance in the case of individuals.	(h) Tax incentives available in the form of deductions are not deductible except certain export incomes while calculating book profit. Tax rate applicable in the case of domestic company is 7.50 per cent plus 13 per cent surcharge for the income year 2000-01, thus effective tax rate is 8.47 per cent while in the case of non-domestic company, tax rate is just 7.5 per cent.
(i) Tax credit is allowed against AMT for an indefinite period but only in respect of those adjustments, which have reversal effect or impact, mainly depreciation.	Tax credit in respect of MAT in excess of regular tax liability paid for income year upto 1999-2000 can be claimed within next five years. No such credit allowed in respect of MAT paid for income year 2000-01 onwards.

income under the income tax regulation, to which certain deductions and exemptions are added.

Under the new provisions of MAT in India, tax credit against MAT has been withdrawn. But tax credit against MAT is allowed in the U.S. in respect of those adjustments which have a reversal impact, mainly depreciation. Similar is the position of depreciation in India. The charge of depreciation in initial years under the *Companies Act* is usually low, as companies prefer to charge a lower rate of depreciation and adopt straight-line method for book profit as against a higher rate of depreciation and written-down value methods adopted under the Income Tax Act for computing the regular taxable income. This results in payment of MAT in the initial years, which has a reversal effect in later years when the charge of depreciation under the Companies Act is higher and under Income Tax Act is lower. Thus, there is regular tax liability in later years on account of the difference in depreciation on which MAT has been paid in the earlier years. Therefore, to make MAT equity-based, as in the U.S., tax credit against MAT needs to be allowed in India in respect of depreciation which has a reversal effect.

In India, the lower of brought-forward loss or depreciation as per the book of accounts is allowed to be set-off against the current year book profit for computing MAT liability, whereas in the U.S., recomputed net operating losses (i.e. net operating loss after the adjustment of tax preferences that are subject to adjustment for AMTI) are allowed to be set off against the current year AMTI. Allowing the set off, the lower of brought-forward loss or depreciation in India is not equitable. The basis of computing the set off of losses of earlier years should be same as is the basis of computing MAT income in the current year. Both loss and depreciation are considered while computing the book profit of the current year for determining MAT. Thus, to make the provision equity-based, both carry-forward loss and depreciation should be allowed to be set off for MAT as is done in the U.S., where the recomputed net operating loss which is in fact adjusted minimum taxable loss is allowed to be set off against the current year.

NOTES

1. Joseph A. Pechman, *Federal Tax Policy* (Washington D.C.: The Brookings Institution, 1971), p. 105.
2. Arnold C. Harberger, in Walker and Bloomfield's, 'New Directions in Federal Tax Policy for the 1980s', as quoted in David F. Bradford's, *Untangling the Income Tax* (Massachusetts: Harvard University Press, 1986), p. 100.
3. Richard M. Bird and Oliver Oldman (eds.), *Readings on Taxation in Developing Countries* (Baltimore: The Johns Hopkins Press, 1967), p. 140.
4. Chargeable profits consist of income plus capital gains less charges on income. Dividends received from other U.K. companies known as franked investment income do not form part of chargeable profits. Investment income forms part of chargeable profits.
5. Modarba company has the meaning assigned in the Modarba Companies and Modarba (Floatation and Control) Ordinance, 1980.
6. Simon James and Christopher Nobes, *The Economics of Taxation: Principles, Policy and Practice* (Great Britain: Prentice-Hall Europe, 1997-98), p. 246.
7. Parent subsidiary affiliated group means where 80 per cent of the stock of each other member of the controlled group is owned by other members of the controlled group or where a common parent corporation owns at least 80 per cent of the stock of at least one subsidiary corporation.
8. A 'controlled company' means a company having not more than fifty members and controlled by not more than five persons in the manner described in the Act.
9. Ehtisham Ahmad and Nicholas Stern, *The Theory and Practice of Tax Reform in Developing Countries* (New Delhi: Foundation Books, 1991), p. 81.
10. A close company is defined as a U.K. resident cmpany which is under the control of either five or fewer participators, or any number of participators who are also directors

of the company. An 'investment company' in the U.K. means any company whose business consists wholly or mainly in the making of investments and the principal part of whose income is derived there from. Income of such a company is normally income from house property, interest from bank, building society, net credits on non-trading loan relationship, besides franked investment income which is otherwise not chargeable to corporation tax.

11. A controlled group is a group of corporations that have 80 per cent common ownership.
12. A personal holding company is any corporation, if at least 60 per cent of adjusted ordinary gross income for the tax year is personal holding company income, i.e. dividends, interest, royalties and annuities and at any time during the last half of the tax year, more than 50 per cent in value of its outstanding stock is owned, directly or indirectly by or not more than 5 individuals.
13. Regulated Investment Corporation is a domestic corporation that derives at least 90 per cent of its gross income from dividend, interest, payments with respect to certain securities, loans and gains on the sale of stock and securities and distributes 90 per cent of its dividend, interest income.
14. Real Estate Investment Corporation (REIC) including trusts, or associations are those that specialize in investments in the real estate and real estate mortgages.
15. 'Public company' according to Part IV of the First Schedule to The *Income Tax Ordinance*, 1979 includes the following:
    (a) a company in which not less than 50 per cent of the shares are held by the Government;
    (b) a company whose shares were listed in a registered stock exchange in Pakistan at any time during the year and remained listed till the close of the year.
    (c) a trust formed under any law for the time being in force. The above definition of a public company shall be applicable only for the purposes of First Schedule to the Income Tax Ordinance, which prescribes the rate of tax applicable to taxpayers and is different from the definition of a public company given under the *Companies Ordinance*, 1984 of Pakistan.
16. The long-term tax exempt rate for purposes of net operating loss carry-forwards is the highest of the adjusted federal long-term rates for the three months ending with the month in which the particular ownership change occurs.
17. 'Continuity of ownership' means that shares carrying more than 50 per cent of all voting, dividend and capital rights be beneficially owned at all times during the claim year by one or more persons who individually or together held any shares (not the same shares) carrying similar rights at all times during the loss year. Ownership during the intervening years is not relevant.
18. 'Same business test' is satisfied if throughout the same business test period, the company carries on the same business as it carried on immediately before a change in the ownership occurred.
19. David F. Bradford, *Untangling the Income Tax* (Boston, Massachusetts: Harvard University Press), p. 100
20. A.J.van den Tempel, *Corporation Tax and Individual Income Tax in the EEC* (Brussels, 1974).
21. A 'close company' is defined as a U.K. resident company, which is under the control of either five or fewer participators or any number of participators who are also directors of the company. Persons are deemed to have control over a company if taken together they own over 50 per cent of the company's issued share capital or have over 50 per cent of the company's voting power or would receive over 50 per cent of the company's income or assets.
22. *2000 U.S. Master Tax Guide* (Chicago: CCH Incorporated, 2000), p. 112
23. 'Associated person' is a shareholder, an associate of a shareholder or a person who was formerly such a shareholder or an associate.
24. A person shall be deemed to have a substantial interest in the company, if he holds

20 per cent of the equity capital or voting power of the company. In the case of any other concern, if he is entitled to not less than 20 per cent income of such concern.

25. Budget 1997-98, Speech of Minister of Finance, as reported in *Current Tax Reporter*, 1997, Vol. 138, p. 17 (statutes).
26. The U.K., Australia and Malaysia have not so far introduced minimum tax system.

CHAPTER 8

Assessment of Income

The most challenging task before a government is to design an appropriate administration and assessment system so that every person pays the tax due from him and pays the tax at the appropriate time and reports the correct income to the tax authorities. The law provides for the due date of filing tax returns, the mode of payment, the collection of tax, the information required to be given by the taxpayer to the tax authorities, examination of the information submitted by the taxpayer, and investigation of the affairs of the taxpayer. While formulating these policies, the government must ensure that the tax system is equity-based, i.e. it does not place undue burden on the taxpayer and at the same time helps the revenue authorities in collecting proper tax and is easy to administer. Various countries have enacted different provisions in the income tax laws for the proper administration and assessment. These provisions are amended from time to time, based on past experiences, administrative difficulties and convenience of taxpayers as well. This chapter examines the provisions relating to the income tax administration in the selected countries under the following heads:

1. Tax administration
2. Filing of tax returns
3. Assessment procedure
4. Rectification/Amendment of returns
5. Failure to file returns
6. Income-escaping assessment
7. Search at taxpayer's premises
8. Collection of income tax

TAX ADMINISTRATION

THE U.K.

In the U.K., there is a separate Act, known as, the *Taxes Management Act*, 1970 (TMA, 1970), which, deals with the provisions of administration of income tax and capital gains tax. The Act is managed by the Inland Revenue Board (IRB), which consists of Commissioners of Inland Revenue. The TMA, 1970 has authorised officers of the Board to exercise the power of assessment and determination of tax and penalty interest. The *Finance Act*, 1994, introduced a self-assessment system for individuals, trustees, personal representatives and some others liable to account for income tax and capital gains other than companies effective from the tax year (income year) 1996-97, the biggest change in the system of direct taxation in the U.K. since the introduction of the 'Pay as You Earn' (PAYE) scheme in 1944. Although in respect of interest income and employment income, tax is deducted at source, the taxpayer is required to pay tax under self-assessment scheme in respect of all other incomes including investment income liable to higher rate of income tax. With the introduction of self-assessment system in the U.K., there is a shift in the responsibility for the assessment of direct taxes from the IRB to the taxpayer. One of the main aims of self-assessment is to simplify the tax system. However, in reality, the compliance costs for the taxpayers are likely to increase and the cost of administration will decrease. As such, the IRB will be more benefited rather than the taxpayers with this self-assessment scheme.

THE U.S.

In the U.S., the administration and levy of income tax is governed by the *Internal Revenue Code (IRC)*, 1986. The Internal Revenue Service (IRS), which is the branch of the Treasury Department, is responsible for the administration of income tax law. The Commissioner of Internal Revenue is the head of IRS. The IRC, 1986 has authorised the Secretary for assessment and determination of tax, interest, penalty and other enforcement measures. The term 'secretary' includes his delegate, which means any officer, employee of the treasury department duly authorised by the Secretary.

The U.S. also follows a system based on self-assessment and voluntary compliance. The taxpayer is expected to compute his tax liability, pay the same and file income tax return as per the provisions of the IRC, 1986.

AUSTRALIA

In Australia, provisions dealing with the administration of the tax laws are contained in the *Taxation Administration Act*, 1953 (TAA) and the regulations made there under. Besides, there are two principal Acts called, the *Income Tax Assessment Act*, 1936 (ITAA 36) and the *Income Tax Assessment Act*, 1997 (ITAA 97). Since the ITAA 36 has become complicated due to the several amendments, it is being gradually replaced by the ITAA 97. The income tax system is administered in Australia by the Australian Taxation office (ATO), which, is headed by the Commissioner of Taxation. All powers of assessment, determination of tax and penalty under the Act are with Commissioner of Taxation. But these powers are delegated to Deputy Commissioners for the assessment, determination of tax and penalty of the taxpayers.

MALAYSIA

In Malaysia, the management of tax is governed by the provisions of the *Income Tax Act*, 1967. The Director General (DG) of Inland Revenue is the person who has the management of the income tax in Malaysia. Chief executive officer of the Inland Revenue Board (IRB), Malaysia is appointed as the Director General. Under the Malaysian Income Tax Act, all powers of assessment, determination of tax and penalty have been given to the DG. However, the Act has authorised Senior Assistant and Assistant Directors of Inland Revenue to exercise the functions of the DG. Malaysia has an official assessment system whereby the IRB does the assessment based on the tax return filed by the taxpayers as against the self-assessment system in other countries. However, the official assessment system is going to be changed progressively to the self-assessment from the income year 2001.

PAKISTAN

In Pakistan, the law relating to income tax is known as the *Income Tax Ordinance*, 1979. As per the provisions of this Ordinance, the administration of income tax is with Central Board of Revenue (CBR) that is headed by its chairman. All officers employed for the implementation of the Income Tax Ordinance have to follow the orders, instructions and directions of the CBR. The assessment of the taxpayer in Pakistan is done by the Deputy Commissioners who have got various powers under the Ordinance.

INDIA

In India, the levy of income tax is governed by the *Income Tax Act*, 1961. The administration of income tax in India is with Central Board of Direct Taxes (CBDT), which has the powers to issue circulars and clarifications. The CBDT is headed by a Chairman. However, the assessment of the taxpayer is done by the Assessing Officer (AO), whose status depends upon the level of income declared by the assessee. It can be an Income Tax Officer, a Deputy Commissioner or a Joint Commissioner. The AO has got very wide discretionary powers under the Indian Income Tax Act, which, are to be exercised judiciously. The AOs are under the administrative supervision of the Commissioners of Income Tax, but the Commissioners cannot interfere in the functioning of AOs while exercising the judicial power of assessment.

FILING OF TAX RETURNS

THE U.K.

In the U.K., income tax is levied for a fiscal year that runs from April 6 to April 5 of the following year. The fiscal year is also referred to as the tax year.

The Inland Revenue issues tax forms in the month of April following the tax year. (For tax year 1999-2000, forms were issued in the month of April, 2000). These forms are issued to all individuals, including the self-employed, members of a partnership and company directors having liability to discharge income tax. Sec. 8 (TMA 1970), provides that the tax returns should show the net amount of any income and gains for the fiscal year concerned and is in two parts.

1. Part one is compulsory and requires the taxpayers to submit details of their net income and gains and claim allowance for the fiscal year.
2. Part two is voluntary and enables the taxpayer to calculate the tax due for the fiscal year.

If the taxpayer opts to calculate the tax due, the tax return must be submitted by January 31 following the fiscal year to which the return relates or 3 months after the return is issued. If the taxpayer asks the IR to calculate the tax due, the return must be submitted by September 30 following the fiscal year to which the return relates or two months after the return is issued, whichever is later.

Where the taxpayer either makes a request or does not complete part two, and files the return within the prescribed limits, the IR will calculate the tax due based on the information recorded and advise the taxpayer of this amount. Taxpayers having a liability to discharge income tax or capital gain tax but who do not receive a tax return form should notify the IR of their liability no later than October 5 following the end of the year of assessment.

Tax Returns by Companies

The self-assessment system for companies has come into effect from the accounting periods ending after July 1, 1999 as against for other assesses for whom it came into operation on April 6, 1996. Earlier, a company had to pay its estimated Corporation Tax (CT) liability by the normal due date, i.e. 9 months after the end of accounting period and file the return together with the tax computation and supporting documentary evidence 12 months after the end of the accounting period or if later, three months after notice to file the return is made.

The introduction of self-assessment system for companies has not affected the date on which a company must file corporation tax returns. The annual filing date for corporate tax self-assessment return remains unchanged, i.e. 12 months after the end of accounting period or if later, three months after notice to file the return is made. It should be noted that IR does not issue tax forms to companies as are issued to other taxpayers usually in the month of April. The computation of corporation tax submitted with the tax return will constitute the tax self-assessment. There is no law requiring the IR to calculate the tax if the return is submitted early as there is for individuals.

A company must notify its chargeability to corporation tax within 12 months of the end of the accounting period.

THE U.S.

For each tax year, a return must be filed by a US citizen or a resident alien who has at least a minimum specified amount of gross income. The income year normally runs from January 1 to December 31. But the taxpayers may adopt a fiscal year of 12 months ending on the last day of month other than December. The income year is also known as the Accounting Year. The income levels at which individuals must file income tax returns depend on the status under which the return is being filed. For the income year 1999, the income level at which individuals must file returns was $7,050 for single taxpayer, $2,750 for married individual filing return separately, and $12,750 for married couple filing joint return. The income level at which the returns must be filed is higher for aged persons.

Similarly, there are prescribed income levels for the head of the household, qualifying widow(er), dependent child and dependents who are blind.

Even if income levels mentioned above are not reached, an individual is required to file a return if the net earnings from self-employment in 1999 are $400 or more, or if there is liability for alternative minimum tax, or if tax is due from the recapture of an investment credit. The income level test applies to the gross income and not to the adjusted gross income.

The individual income tax return is due on or before the 15th day of the 4th month following the close of the tax year. In case the taxpayer follows the calendar year as the tax year, April 15 is the due date for filing the return. In case the tax year opted by the taxpayer is 12 months ending June 30, then the due date for filing the income tax return is October 15. Corporate tax returns are due on or before the 15th day of the 3rd month following the close of the corporation's tax year. For companies following the calendar year, March 15 is the due date for filing the return. If the due date falls on a Saturday, Sunday or a legal holiday, the return may be filed on the succeeding day that is not Saturday, Sunday or a legal holiday. There is no fixed due date of filing the return for all taxpayers in the U.S. It is round the year depending upon the tax year (accounting year) opted for by the taxpayer although most taxpayers have opted for the calendar year as their income year.

An individual, however, can obtain an automatic extension of 4 months for filing the tax return, if he files on or before the due date of the return an application in the prescribed form (Form 4868) accompanied by a proper estimate of tax. Except in cases of undue hardship, no additional extension of time is granted. However, the total extension of period may not exceed 6 months including the 4 months' automatic extension.

Corporations are allowed an automatic 6-month extension whereas partnership and trusts can automatically extend their filing date by 3 months. Filing an application for an extension does not extend the time for paying the tax. Applications for extension must show and include payment of the estimated amount due.

AUSTRALIA

In Australia, income tax returns are filed on an annual basis. The taxable year for most taxpayers is the 12 months period from July 1 to June 30. However, in certain circumstances, a substituted accounting period of 12 months closing on a date other than June 30, may be adopted. Income tax is levied for each tax year on the taxable income earned during the income year.

Tax is payable initially by the taxpayer under the self–assessment system. The taxpayer calculates his/her own tax inability and deposits the tax along with the filing of the return of income. Resident individuals whose taxable income exceeds the tax-free threshold limit are required to file a return. (For the Income year 1998-99, the threshold limit is AUD5,400.) The last date for filing income tax returns is specified in the Commissioner's gazette notice calling for the lodgement of returns every year. The last date for individual taxpayers, partnerships and trusts is usually October 31, immediately following the income year. Individuals with taxable incomes below the tax-free threshold, in case they carry on a business during the income year and non-resident individuals who derive any assessable income from an Australian source are also required to file return. Every resident company which derives Australian source income or foreign income, and every non-resident company, which derives Australian source income, is required to lodge a return.

Companies are generally required to lodge returns by the date on which they are required to pay their final tax liability. The due dates for companies for 1998-99 returns were as under:

1. Small taxpayers whose likely tax liability was less than AUD8,000–December 1, 1999
2. Medium taxpayers whose likely tax liability was between AUD8,000–AUD300,000–March 1, 2000
3. Large taxpayers whose likely tax liability was more than AUD300,000–December 1, 1999.

The Commissioner can grant a further period of time for filing an annual return. An application for additional time to file the return need to be made before the due date and should state the reason. Usually there is no difficulty in getting a short period extension.

The return forms are simpler and require the taxpayer to provide only limited information. The taxpayer is not required to submit records and statements showing how the taxpayer's taxable income is calculated, although these records must be retained by the taxpayer and may have to be produced before the ATO later. Returns are not treated as filed until they have been completed, signed, and received by the ATO. However, the returns must contain such information and particulars and be accompanied by such documents, accounts and statements as are indicated in the instruction booklets to the relevant return forms. The ATO provides instruction booklets to help taxpayers complete their returns.

MALAYSIA

The present Malaysian law requires the DG to issue a notice in writing requiring the taxpayer to furnish a return of income. Every person who is chargeable to tax for a year of assessment and does not receive any notice from the DG to file return, is required to give notice to the DG that he is so chargeable before April 15 of the following year of assessment. The normal income year, called 'basis year' in Malaysia runs from January 1 to December 31, except in the case of business income where the basis year can be a period of 12 months or less ending on a day other than December 31.

Every person chargeable to tax is sent early in the year a tax return form. Normally, unmarried individuals with an annual income of RM18,000 and married individuals with an annual income of RM21,000 are considered chargeable. Every individual carrying on a trade or profession, ought to file a return whether or not he is chargeable to tax to get a tax loss from trade or profession established for deduction against income earned in future years.

The due date for filing returns is within 30 days of the issue of the notice by the DG for non-residents and residents in West Malaysia and within 60 days for residents in East Malaysia.

Extension of time for filing returns is granted by the DG on application. Normally extension is granted up to May 31. In cases where the accounting year ends after September 30, extension up to July 31 is allowed. Further extension is generally not allowed except in genuine and exceptional circumstances. Where returns are prepared and submitted by tax agents, requests for extensions are favourably considered.

The *Income Tax (Amendment) Act*, 1999, has introduced provisions for self-assessment for companies to be implemented from the year of assessment 2001. As per these amendments, every company is required to furnish a return for each year of assessment within 6 months from its financial closing without any notice from the DG and the tax return submitted by the company is deemed to be a notice of assessment served on the company.

PAKISTAN

In Pakistan, every person whose total income for any income year exceeds the maximum amount not chargeable to tax under the Ordinance is required to file a return of income. The income year for all assesses from the assessment year 1995-96 is from July 1 to June 30, except where a special income year is notified by the CBR. So, all taxpayers in Pakistan have a uniform income year and this facilitates information matching and cross verifications. The assessment year is the year following the income year in which income is taxed and assessed. This is a period of 12 months and runs from July 1 to June 30. The period of assessment is fixed by law and remains so irrespective of the income year even for special income year notified by the CBR. The applicability of provisions in the Ordinance is by and large with reference to the assessment year. Any person who has been charged to tax for any of the 4 income years preceding the current income year is also required to file a return though his income for the current year may not exceed the maximum amount not chargeable to tax. Besides, every person who fulfils any one of the following criteria is also required to file a return though the income may not be chargeable to tax:

1. ownership of immovable property with a land area of 250 square yards or more;
2. ownership of a motor vehicle;
3. subscriber to a telephone;
4. foreign travel.

Moreover, the Deputy Commissioner can ask any person to file the return of income. Also, a return of wealth is to be filed along with the income tax return. In the absence of a Wealth Tax return, the return of income is treated as invalid.

The due date for filing returns of income is September 30 next following the income year. However, in the case of a company whose income year ends any time between January 1 to June 30, the due date for filing return is December 31 next following the income year. The Deputy Commissioner can grant extension for not more than fifteen days.

INDIA

In India, every person whose total income during the income year, called 'the previous year' exceeds the maximum amount not chargeable to tax, is required to furnish a return of income. The previous year means the financial year immediately preceding the assessment year. With effect from April 1, 1989, the previous year has been fixed starting from April 1 to March 31. The assessment year means the period of 12 months commencing on April 1, immediately following the income year. No flexibility has been given to any class of taxpayer in choosing the income year as is available in other countries. The income year is 12-month period ending on March 31 and every taxpayer is required to submit his income computation for that period irrespective of the accounting year followed by him. The maximum amount not chargeable to tax for an individual for the income year 1999-2000 is Rs.50,000. In the case of other taxpayers such as partnership firms and companies, no basic exemption is provided and these entities have to file their return of income even if their income is negligible. Taxpayers who suffer loss in any year are also required to file a return in case they want to claim the set-off of such losses against income in subsequent years. With a view to increasing the tax base and ensuring better compliance, the filing of returns of income has been made mandatory even for those persons whose income is below the maximum amount not chargeable to tax, if they fulfil any one of the following criteria during the income year.

1. Ownership/lease of a motor vehicle;
2. Occupation of immovable property;
3. Foreign travel (other than neighbouring countries);
4. Subscription of a telephone;
5. Holder of a credit card;
6. Membership of a club.

Moreover, the Assessing Officer (AO) can ask any person who has not filed a return of his income to do so.

The last date of filing returns is different for different class of assessees. For the income year 1999-2000, the last date for filing returns is as under:

1.	Companies	November 30
2.	Taxpayers other than companies who are required to get their accounts audited under the provisions of the Act.	October 31
3.	Taxpayers whose income includes income from business and profession but are not required to get their accounts audited.	August 31
4.	Other taxpayers	June 30

The above due dates have been changed from the income year 2000-01 (assessment year 2001-02) as under:

All companies and taxpayers who are required to get their accounts audited	October 31
All other taxpayers	July 31

The AO does not have any power to extend the date of filing of returns. However, belated returns can be filed by the taxpayer at any time before the expiry of the 1 year from the end of the relevant assessment year, i.e. within 2 years from end of the income year. The, penalty and interest are leviable for late returns.

Conclusion

The tax management and filing of return provisions have been summarised in Table 8.1.

As shown in the table, all the selected countries have enacted detailed provisions for ensuring compliance of income tax laws. All these countries have prescribed the time period for which the income will be computed for the purpose of income tax. Though this time period is of 12 months in all the countries but the period is different in different countries. While the U.S. and Malaysia by and large follow the calendar year, Australia and Pakistan follow the year from July 1 to June 30. The U.K. follows the year from April 6 to April 5, and India follows the year from April 1 to March 31. All countries except India have given an option to business taxpayers to follow an income year different from the prescribed year. In Pakistan, it can only be when notified by the CBR.

The period allowed for filing returns, however, varies. In the U.S., only 2 months and 15 days are allowed to companies and 3 and 15 days to individuals after the end of income year, whereas in the U.K., it is almost 10 months from the end of income year. In Malaysia and Australia, 4 months period is allowed while in Pakistan, 3 months period is normally allowed. In India, with the proposed amendment effective from the income year 2000-01, a 4 months period will be allowed except for those taxpayers who are

TABLE 8.1. A SUMMARY OF PROVISIONS RELATING TO INCOME TAX ADMINISTRATION AND FILING OF RETURNS

Sl. No.	Particulars	U.K.	U.S.	Australia	Malaysia	Pakistan	India
1.	Act under which assessment is done	The Taxes Management Act, 1970	Internal Revenue Code, 1986	Taxation Administration Act, 1953	Income Tax Act, 1967	Income Tax Ordinance, 1979	Income Tax Act, 1961
2.	Name of Administrative Department	Inland Revenue Board (IRB)	Internal Revenue Service (IRS)	Australian Taxation Office (ATO)	Inland Revenue Board (IRB)	Central Board of Revenue (CBR)	Central Board of Direct Taxes (CBDT)
3.	Head of Department	Commissioners of Inland Revenue	Commissioners of Internal Revenue	Commissioner of Taxation	Director General (DG)	Chairman	Chairman
4.	Designation of officer making assessment	Officer of the Board	Secretary and his delegate which means any officer or employee duly authorised by the secretary.	Commissioner, delegation to Deputy Commissioner	Director General but delegation to Assistant Director	Deputy Commissioner	Assessing Officer
5.	Liability to file Income Tax Return	All person having a liability to discharge income tax. Return forms are issued to taxpayer by IR	All US citizens and resident aliens having minimum specified amount of gross income.	Liability is fixed by notification and includes individual whose taxable income exceeds tax-free threshold, or who carry on business and all companies who have an Australian source income.	All persons chargeable to tax. Notice issued by DG. Those chargeable to tax but not receiving the notice are required to send information of chargeability to DG.	All persons having income exceeding the maximum amount not liable to tax and also those who own immovable property motor vehicle, telephone or who have undertaken foreign travel.	All persons having income exceeding the maximum amount not chargeable to tax and also those who occupy immovable property, own or lessee of motor vehicle, telephone subscriber, holders of credit card, members of club, or have incurred expenditure for foreign travel.

6.	Income Year	Fiscal year i.e. April 6 to April 5 of following year.	Usually from January 1 to December 31. Option to have a fiscal year of 12 months ending on last day of month.	Usually from July 1 to June 30. Substituted accounting period of 12 month allowed. Fixed by Notification	January 1 to December 31. In case of business income it can be different.	July 1 to June 30 except where special year is notified by CBR.	April 1 to March 31 (No exception).
7.	Due date of filing returns	January 31 following the income year or three months after the return is issued, whichever is later.	15th day of the 4th month following the close of the year. Normally April 15, for income year January 1 to December 31. In case of companies 15th day of the third month following the close of the year.	Usually October 31 but filing date for company varies according to tax liability	Within 30 days of issue of notice for West Malaysia and 60 days for East Malaysia. Notice generally issued before April 15. Normal date of filing April 30. Company to submit return within 6 months of its closing.	September 30 following the income year. For companies having income year between January 1 to June 30 due date is December 31.	With effect from income year 2000-2001, October 31 for companies and taxpayer required to get their accounts audited July 31 for other taxpayers.
8.	Tax payer required to compute tax	Optional. In case taxpayer does not compute tax, return to be filed by September 30 or two months after the return form is issued.	Yes, however taxpayer can ask the IRS to compute tax.	Yes.	Yes.	Yes.	Yes.

required to get their accounts audited, in which case 7 months period after the end of income year is allowed to file income tax return. Though the period allowed for filing returns in India is more as compared to other countries except the U.K., it must be noted that the extension of time is not allowed for filing returns in India under any circumstances, whereas in the U.S., Australia, Malaysia and Pakistan, extension of time is allowed under certain circumstances. The period of 7 months in India may be justified as these taxpayers are required to get their accounts audited and enclose a copy of audit report along with certain other information certified by the auditor called the tax audit report. Considering the computerised maintenance of accounts by almost all the taxpayers, the period of almost 10 months from the end of income year for filing return in the U.K. seems too prolonged.

As regards liability to file returns in developed countries, i.e. the U.S., the U.K. and Australia, it arises by and large only in case of persons liable to pay tax. However, in India and Pakistan, the liability to file income tax returns extends to persons other than those liable to pay tax, such as those having immovable property, motorcar, and foreign travel. The objective of extending the scope of persons liable to file tax returns in these countries appears to be to increase the tax base.

Assessment Procedure

Different countries follow different methods to verify the returns filed by the taxpayers to ensure that taxpayers report their income correctly. These assessment procedures are as follows:

THE U.K.

On receiving a completed tax return form, the Inland Revenue (IR) can carry out revisions in the return at any time during the following nine-month period. This revision can be for correcting arithmetical and other obvious errors. But it does not cover any thorough or detailed examination of the information recorded on the return.

Prior to the introduction of self-assessment in the 1996-97 tax year, there was no statutory procedure in case of inaccurate and incomplete return filed by the taxpayer. Sec. 9 TMA 1970, gives statutory powers to inquire into any tax return at random, to check its accuracy and completeness, without the need to justify the inquiry. However, the officer of the IR must notify about the inquiry to the taxpayer in writing within 12 months of the fixed date for filing returns and if the return is filed after the due date then, by the end of the quarter following the anniversary of the actual filing date, the quarter dates being given as January 31, April 30, July 31, and October 31. For tax year 1998-99 tax return, if filed on March 1, 2000, then notice may be given up to April 30, 2001.

Besides making inquiries on the basis of a random selection, the officer may make inquiry on the basis of any information received by the IR, or on the basis of the return. As a result of inquiry, the officer may issue a notice requesting the taxpayer to provide documentary evidence, to support the accuracy and completeness of the return under enquiry. After completing the inquiry, the officer of the board must issue a notice to inform him:

1. that the inquiry is complete and
2. of the corrections to be made in the self assessment.

The taxpayer must then amend the assessment within 30 days of this notice. After the 30 day limit has expired, the officer may further amend the assessment already amended by the taxpayer within 30 days.

The taxpayer has the right to appeal against such amendments. The appeal is to be filed within 30 days of the assessment being notified. On an appeal being filed, an officer of the Board tries to reach an agreement with the taxpayer to settle the matter. Where the appeal is not settled, on request either by the taxpayer or the officer, the appeal is heard by the Commissioner of Inland Revenue (CIR). The CIR may be a general commissioner or a special commissioner. General Commissioners are local businessmen and if in their opinion the case requires special knowledge, they can refer the appeal to special commissioners. Special Commissioners are civil servants and must be barristers, solicitors or advocates of at least ten years standing and are tax specialists. On question of facts, the decision of the CIR is final. The taxpayer or the officer of the Board can file appeal on point of law within 30 days to the High Court against the decision of CIR.

THE U.S.

The U.S. income tax system is based on self-assessment, and the taxpayers are required to report and pay their taxes correctly. IRS examination or audits can vary from asking supporting information by mail to full-scale continuous examination.

Almost all returns are checked for mathematical tax calculation and clerical errors during the initial processing of the returns. If an error is discovered under this, the IRS recalculates the amount of tax due and sends an explanation to the taxpayer.

Audit is also conducted in respect of selected returns filed to ensure accuracy and to detect any error or fraud. Prior to October 23, 1995 complete (line-by-line) audit of some taxpayers selected on a stratified random sampling basis was conducted. Such audit known as, the Taxpayer Compliance Measurement Program (TCMP) was discontinued due to budget constraints. However, the IRS uses a Discriminant Function System (DIF) to select individual returns for audit. Cases where DIF is used includes the following.

(a) Investments and trade or business expenses that produce significant tax losses,

(b) Itemized deductions in excess of an average amount for the person's income level.
(c) Filing of a refund claim by a taxpayer who has been previously audited, where substantial deficiencies have been assessed.
(d) Individuals who are self-employed with substantial business income or professional income.

For the purpose of ascertaining the correctness of any return and determining the liability of any person, the Secretary is authorised to examine any books, papers, records or other data which may be relevant or material to such inquiry and to summon the person liable for tax or an officer or employee of such person or any other person and to ask such person to produce such books, papers, records and to give testimony on oath as may be relevant or material to such inquiry. The examination of books and records may be either at the place of business where the books and records are maintained, i.e. field examination or at an IRS office. The type of examination affects the internal appeals procedure. Taxpayers cannot be subjected to unnecessary examination or investigations and only one inspection of taxpayers' books of accounts can be made for each taxable year unless the Secretary after investigation notifies in writing that an additional inspection is necessary. The officer of the IRS at the time of the in-person interview of the taxpayer is required to provide a written explanation of the audit process and taxpayers' rights under such a process. The taxpayer has a right to consult with an attorney at any time during the interview. The taxpayer also has a right to make an audio recording of any in-person interview conducted by the IRS upon ten days' advance notice.

After the examination, the revenue agent prepares a report describing how the issues have been settled and the amount of any additional tax or refund due to the taxpayer.

A taxpayer who does not agree with the agent's report may ask for a meeting with agents from the IRS Appeals Division within 30 days of the date of the letter. This process allows taxpayers one additional opportunity to reach a settlement before resorting to the courts. After lengthy negotiations, the appeals division and taxpayer may or may not reach an agreement.

Taxpayers unable to reach an agreement in the appeals division, or who have not opted for appeals division as stated above, are issued a statutory notice of deficiency. This letter is the official notification by the IRS for additional taxes. Taxpayers who want to litigate must file a petition with the U.S. Court within 90 days of the date of the letter. An appeal against the decision of Tax Court can be filed in the U.S. Court of Appeals by filing a notice of appeal within 90 days after the Tax Court decision.

Filing of appeal with the U.S. Court of Appeals does not operate as a stay of assessment or collection of deficiency tax determined by the Tax Court. A taxpayer if he wants the assessment postponed he has to file an appeal bond with the tax court guaranteeing payment of the deficiency as finally determined.

The judgement of the U.S. Court of Appeals is final except that a review can be sought by either party through a petition for a *writ of certiorari* by the Supreme Court.

In the U.S., certain procedures have been developed for unbinding mediation of any unresolved issues after unsuccessful attempts to enter into closing agreements. Procedure for binding arbitration of unresolved issued are also being developed.

AUSTRALIA

In Australia, ITAA 36, Sec. 169 A, provides that while making an assessment, the commissioner may accept any statement made in a return, including a statement of the assessable income derived by the taxpayer. The ATO makes post-assessment checking and auditing to determine whether a taxpayer has disclosed all assessable income and whether deductions and rebates have been property claimed. In case he finds that the income has been understated, he has the power to amend assessments. Wide powers are given to the ATO to find out the accuracy of the assessable income and tax liability. These include audit and access power, the power to negotiate settlement.

Audits and Access Powers

In Australia, to promote voluntary compliance with the tax laws, the ATO is authorised to conduct tax audit. It also helps the ATO in identifying areas of law which may need clarification and where existing rules and practices make compliance difficult. Tax audits are not in general governed by any particular statutory provisions. The Commissioner can randomly select any taxpayer for audit. The introduction of self-assessment system has resulted in a substantial expansion in the ATO audit programs. Depending upon the requirement, the following types of audit may be conducted.

Income-matching audit. Under this, certain incomes including interest, dividend, social security benefits and rental income shown in the return are matched with the data received from external sources (e.g. financial institutions, government departments).

Desk audits. A desk audit is conducted to check the accuracy of the returns of salary and wage earners, property income earners and small business taxpayers through interviewing the taxpayers along with documentary evidence in support of their claim.

Business audit. A business audit involves an examination of the taxpayer's business operations, records, accounting systems and other matters. It also includes examination of private financial transactions to enable the auditor to determine the accuracy and consistency of any information in the return with the expenditure.

Complex audits. Such audits cover large corporate groups, companies that operate internationally also and banking and insurance industries. The ATO has issued guidelines on the conduct of complex audits. The taxpayer will generally be given one month written notice of an intention to audit and will be informed about the intended scope and duration of the audit. The focus of audit is on royalties, intra-company loans, and transfer pricing arrangements and double taxation treaty matters.

Special audits. This type of audit is conducted in the case of fraud and tax avoidance cases.

Source deduction audits. These audits are conducted to check the employers' and prescribed payment payers' records to ensure compliance with PAYE, PPS, and RPS arrangements.

Commissioner's Power to Obtain Information

Under ITAA Sec. 264, the Commissioner has wide powers to obtain information from a taxpayer or any other person. This power can be exercised even after an assessment or amended assessment has been made. Under Sec.264, the Commissioner may by notice in writing require any person to provide such information as is necessary to attend and give evidence, to produce relevant documents and books and give the information or evidence on oath either verbally or in writing.

The power to require production of documents does not authorise him to require persons to make copies of documents. A person who fails to comply with a Sec. 264 notice may be guilty of an offence and may be subject to fine, or imprisonment and fine both.

On the basis of the annual return filed by the taxpayer and from any other information in his possession, the Commissioner is required to make an original assessment of the taxpayer's taxable income and the amount of tax payable (ITAA 36, Sec. 6(1): 166). The assessment process is treated as complete only after a notice of assessment is served on the taxpayer. ITAA 36, Sec.174 provides that a written notice of an assessment should be served on the person liable to pay the assessed tax as soon as convenient after the making of the assessment. Though there is no time limit on making an original assessment, an individual taxpayer who has not received a notice of assessment within 12 months of filing a return may request the Commissioner in writing to make an assessment. If an assessment notice is not received within 3 months of the receipt of that request, the notice is treated as served on the last day of the 3-month period. In the case of companies and fund, the Commissioner does not issue an assessment at all and the taxpayer's return is deemed a notice of assessment.

A taxpayer dissatisfied with an assessment or in the case of companies and fund, etc., where the filing of return is considered a deemed assessment, the company may also file an objection with the Commissioner within 4 years of service of the notice of assessment. The ATO officers who are independent of the original assessor, consider the objections. The Commissioner issues within 60 days his decision allowing in whole or in part or disallowing the objection altogether. If no decision is made within 60 days, the taxpayer may require the commissioner to make a decision within a further period of 60 days. A taxpayer dissatisfied with the decision of Commissioner on his objection can either file a review with the Administrative Appeals Tribunal (AAT) or Small

Taxation Claims Tribunal (STCT) or may appeal to the Federal Court against the decision within 60 days of the service of notice of the decision on the objection. For appeal before the Federal Court, a filing fee, setting down fee and a daily hearing fee are payable. In case review is filed, an appeal to the Federal Court can be lodged against the decision of AAT or STCT as the case may be within 28 days. An appeal to the full Federal Court can also be filed against the decision of a single judge of the Federal Court within 21 days. An appeal to the High Court can also be filed with the special leave of the High Court against the decision of the full Federal Court.

Negotiated Settlements

In Australia, the ATO has the power to negotiate settlement with the taxpayer on the tax payment. Negotiations may occur before or after the issue of an assessment, or upon issue of a request for an amended assessment or after the lodgement of an objection or appeal. Factors which may justify a settlement, include the amount of tax in dispute, the cost of litigation and whether the case is of a precedent value. The 'Draft Code' released by the ATO states that settlement would not be appropriate where;

1. there is clearly settled and articulated ATO view on the issue;
2. judicial clarification of the issue is in the public interest;
3. pursuit of the issue through the courts could have a significant effect on compliance by the wider community; or
4. the taxpayer has a consistent record of involvement in tax avoidance schemes or tax evasion and the contested issues are of that nature.

In settlement negotiations, the ATO officers cannot use threat of either prosecution or imposition of severe penalties. The ATO officers do not have power to exclude prosecution and as such conditions to exclude prosecution cannot form part of settlement.

MALAYSIA

According to Sec. 90(1), where a person has delivered a return under Sec. 77, the DG may either accept the return and make an assessment accordingly, or may refuse to accept the return and determine the chargeable income of that person for that year to the best of his judgement. If the DG is of the opinion that a person who has not delivered a return under Sec.77 for a year of assessment, is chargeable to tax for that year, he may according to the best of his judgement determine the amount of chargeable income of that person also and make an assessment accordingly.

For obtaining full information and for ascertaining whether a person is chargeable to tax or not and for determining his tax liability, the DG can ask any person to produce books, accounts and other documents. He may also require a statement containing particulars of all bank accounts, whether held solely or jointly, assets possessed by him, all sources of his gross income from such sources and all facts affecting his present and past tax liability.

Under Sec. 82(a), every person carrying on a business is required to keep and retain sufficient records to find out business income and/or to adjust business loss and under sub section (b), to issue printed receipt in case gross takings from the business for the basis year exceeds RM150,000 from the sale of goods or RM100,000 from the performance of services, and to retain a duplicate of every receipt so issued.

The DG may require the employer under Sec. 83 to give information about the name and gross income of the persons employed by him. If any employee intends to leave Malaysia for more than three months with no intention of returning, the DG may direct the employer to pay the full amount or part of the money payable to the employee towards payment of the tax payable by the employee. Similarly, the occupier of any land or premises may be required to furnish a return containing the name and address of the person registered as the proprietor of the landlord's premises or whom he pays rents and a statement of rent payable in respect of the occupation.

After an assessment has been made, the DG serves a notice of assessment. The notice of assessment shall indicate the amount of chargeable income, the amount of tax charged thereon and additional tax, if any.

A person aggrieved by an assessment can appeal to the special commissioner against the assessment. The notice of appeal is to be given to the DG within 30 days after the service of the notice of assessment.

The DG can on receipt of a notice of appeal, reviews the assessment and for that purpose ask the appellant to produce further information, produce books of accounts and summon any person to give evidence. As a result of the review, the DG and appellant can come to an agreement and the assessment against which the appeal is made gets modified accordingly and the appeal gets abated. If there is no agreement, the appellant after a period of six months from the notice of appeal can ask the DG to send the appeal to the special commissioners and the DG within three months after such request shall forward the appeal to special commissioners to decide the same. The taxpayer or the DG, if dissatisfied by the decision of special commissioners as being erroneous in law or of mixed law and fact can ask the commissioners to refer the case to the High Court for appeal. The High Court will determine the question of law on a stated case and can reduce, amend or annual an assessment. In Malaysia, proceedings in High Court are heard *in camera* unless otherwise ordered on request. This practice is different from that in other countries where proceedings before courts are open unless otherwise ordered. The decision of the High Court on question of fact is final. However, appeals against High Court can be filed to the Court of Appeals and against the Court of Appeal's decision to the Federal Court.

PAKISTAN

The return filed by the taxpayer is accepted if the same is correct and complete. The Deputy Commissioner (DC) in such cases assesses the total income on the basis of the return filed by the taxpayer by an order in writing. However, certain adjustments such as any arithmetical error and disallowance of excess deduction can be done while doing summary assessment.

The DC when not satisfied with the return of income filed by the taxpayer may ask him to produce books of accounts and evidences in support of his return. For this purpose, the DC is authorised to make his own inquiry. After considering the evidences produced, the DC determines the total income of the taxpayer and tax payable thereon by an order in writing.

The time limit for completing assessment where a return is filed within the relevant assessment year is 2 years from the end of the relevant assessment year and if the return is filed beyond the relevant assessment year, is 2 years from the end of the financial year in which the return is filed.

Any taxpayer who wants to object to the assessment order passed can make an appeal within 30 days from the date of service of the notice of demand relating to the said assessment to the Appellate Additional Commissioner (AAC). The AAC after hearing the taxpayer may pass an order confirming, reducing, enhancing or cancelling the assessment.

The Commissioner and the taxpayer both are entitled to file an appeal against the order of the AAC within 60 days from the date of order before the tribunal called, the Income Tax Appellate Tribunal (ITAT). The ITAT which is an independent body has power to pass such order as it may deem fit while hearing an appeal against the order of the AAC. The ITAT is the final fact finding authority. Only questions of law arising from the order of ITAT can be referred to the High Court.

Settlement

Any taxpayer who wants to settle his tax disputes arising out of an assessment order can make an application before the Settlement Commission constituted by the Government of Pakistan to settle tax disputes, giving full and true disclosure of his income which has not been disclosed, the manner in which such income has been earned and the tax payable on such income. The Settlement Commission after obtaining a report from the Commissioner may either reject the application for settlement or proceed with the settlement. The Settlement Commission after examination of records and evidences and hearing both the taxpayer and the Commissioner may pass an order of settlement including the amount of tax, penalty and interest payable by the taxpayer. The order passed by the Settlement Commission is conclusive.

INDIA

India follows the system of self-assessment. As such, every taxpayer is required to compute his income and compute tax on such income and file the return showing such income and tax paid thereon. Prior to June 1, 1999, the Assessing Officer (AO) was authorised to calculate the tax liability on the basis of the return filed by the assessee after making prima facie adjustment of arithmetical errors, loss carried forward, deduction, allowance or relief allowed more or less than admissible. The assessee was also required to pay additional tax of 20 per cent of the difference between tax on income after adjustment and tax on returned income. As the assessee was not given opportunity of being heard before making adjustments, there were a large number of appeals against such adjusted income and additional tax. With effect from June 1, 1999, the provision of prima facie adjustment of income by the AO without giving the assessee the opportunity of being heard has been abolished. The AO has the power only to calculate the tax liability and interest on the basis of the information given in the return and to issue notice of demand, if any tax or interest is found due on the basis of such return. No adjustment can be made by the AO.

Regular Assessment

Where a return has been made and the AO on verification of the return considers it necessary to ensure that the taxpayer has not understated the income or has not underpaid tax in any manner, he may ask the taxpayer to produce evidence on which the taxpayer relies in support of the return. For this purpose, the AO issues a notice. Such notice has to be issued before the expiry of 12 months from the end of the month in which the return is furnished. The AO may make such inquiry as he may deem fit. For the purpose of inquiry, the AO has the power to ask the taxpayers to produce books of accounts and documents. The AO also has the power to issue summon to any person to get information and documents. After taking into consideration the evidence produced by the assessee and all relevant material gathered by the AO, the latter makes an order in writing, called, the assessment order determining the total income or the loss of the assessee and the tax payable or refund if any due to the assessee.

Any taxpayer aggrieved by the assessment order passed by the AO can file an appeal before the Commissioner of Income Tax (CIT) (Appeals) within 30 days from the date of service of the notice of demand of such order. The CIT (Appeals) has the power to confirm, reduce, enhance or annul the assessment. The CIT (Appeals) can also set aside the assessment back to the AO for making fresh assessment in the light of directions given by him. These powers of setting aside the assessment has been withdrawn from June 1, 2001 by the amendment carried out by the *Finance Act*, 2001, mainly to reduce the number of pending old cases and give finality to the order of the assessing officer. The CIT (Appeals) has the power not only to reduce but also to enhance the income computed by the AO. The taxpayer or the AO, if aggrieved by the order passed in appeals by the CIT (Appeals) can file an appeal before the tribunal called, the Income Tax Appellate Tribunal (ITAT) within 60 days of the receipt of appeal order of CIT (Appeals). The ITAT is an independent body and it has the power to pass such order as it may deem fit after hearing both the parties. It is the final fact finding authority. No further appeal can be filed against the order passed by ITAT on the question of facts. However, an appeal on a question of law can be filed before the High Court and in Supreme Court against the decision of the High Court.

Settlement Scheme

In India, there is no scheme for assessment by agreement. However, there is a provision whereby a taxpayer can make an application for settlement of disputes before a commission called 'Settlement Commission' (SC), which is an independent body. The SC on receipt of application calls for a report from the CIT under whose jurisdiction the case of the taxpayers is assessed. The SC after taking into consideration the report and having regard to the complexity of the investigation involved may accept the application or reject the same after giving an opportunity to the taxpayer to represent his case. If the application for settlement is accepted then all the proceedings for which the application has been made gets abated and the taxpayer is required to pay such tax, interest and penalty as are finally determined by the. SC. Under the Act, the SC has got very wide powers and can even grant immunity to the taxpayer from prosecution and penalty not only under the Income Tax Act but under other Acts also.

RECTIFICATION/AMENDMENT OF RETURNS

THE U.K.

The Board may correct any obvious errors in a tax return within 9 months of the return being filed, e.g. arithmetical errors, which may reduce or increase the tax liability. The taxpayer can also correct a self-assessment within 12 months from the filing date. Errors discovered after the time limit may still be corrected within 5 years of the annual filing date where the error results in an overpayment of tax and the taxpayer can claim refund.

THE U.S.

If the taxpayer has failed to report some income or has claimed excessive deductions or credits or has claimed less deductions or credits, he can amend the return by filing a form called, Form 1040X. This amendment can be done within 3 years from the later of the date the tax return was actually filed or its due date. He is supposed to write his income, deductions and credits as reported originally on the return, the changes required and the corrected amounts. Then tax on the corrected amount of taxable income is calculated and shown on the return along with the amount of additional tax or refund if any. If any tax is payable, it should be paid along with the filing of Form 1040X. If any refund becomes due because of amendment, then one can either apply for refund or apply it towards estimated tax of next year.

AUSTRALIA

A taxpayer can 'self-amend' an assessment at any time within 4 years of the due date for payment. ITAA 36, Sec. 170 provides that the Commissioner has the power to amend an assessment or to further amend an amended assessment by making such alterations and additions, as he considers necessary, even though tax under that assessment has been paid. The Commissioner is required to amend an assessment where this is necessary to give effect to an Administrative Appeals Tribunal (AAT) or a court decision. Such an amendment must be made within 60 days of the decision becoming final.

MALAYSIA

In Malaysia, a taxpayer can claim relief in respect of any error or mistake in the tax return of his taxable income. The error that can be rectified is one that is by chance not conscious one. The time limit for correcting any mistake is 6 years after the end of the year of assessment within which the assessment is made.

PAKISTAN

If any person having furnished a return discovers any omission or wrong statement therein, he may furnish a revised return. The revised return is without prejudice to liability one may incur for providing wrong information or concealment.

Any apparent mistake in the assessment order can be rectified by the income tax authority that passed the order suo-motto or on the application of the taxpayer. The limitation for rectification is 4 years from the date of the order sought to be amended.

The assessment order made by the DC can also be revised by the Inspecting Additional Commissioner (IAC) if the order passed by the DC is erroneous or prejudicial to the interest of revenue.

INDIA

In India, a taxpayer can revise tax return in case he discovers any omission or any wrong statement therein before the expiry of one year from the end of the relevant assessment year or before the completion of assessment, whichever is earlier. The omission or wrong statement must have a bearing on the assessment of the assessee itself. The return cannot be revised in cases of concealment or false statements.

The AO is also empowered to rectify any mistake apparent from the record and amend any order passed by him within 4 years from the end of the financial year in which the original order is passed (the order sought to be amended). Mistakes that can be rectified include an error of law or fact, a clerical or arithmetical mistake. Rectification shall be made by the income tax authorities on its own or if the mistake is brought to its notice by the assessee.

The assessment in India is completed by the AO. To safeguard the interest of revenue, there is provision in the Act for revision by the Commissioner of the order passed by the AO. The taxpayer can also ask the Commissioner to revise the order. The revision can be suo motto by the Commissioner if in his opinion the order is erroneous or prejudicial to the interest of revenue.

FAILURE TO FILE RETURNS

THE U.K.

In the U.K., where the taxpayer fails to submit a return, the officer of the IR has the power to estimate the tax due. He must make the assessment to the best of his information and must state the date by which tax is payable by the taxpayer. Determinations made by the IR in this way are treated as self-assessments. The time limit for making a determination is 5 years from the original filing date. Actual self-assessments can only replace the determination if they are made within the five-year limit or if later, within 12 months of the determination. When the taxpayer files an actual self-assessment, i.e. income tax return, it replaces the determination made by the IR. As such, an appeal against the determination is unnecessary.

THE U.S.

In the U.S., in case of failure to file return by the taxpayer, the tax may be assessed and court proceedings to collect tax may be commenced at any time against the taxpayer.

AUSTRALIA

In Australia, where the taxpayer has failed to furnish a return and the Commissioner has reason to believe that such person who has not filed a return has earned taxable income or he is dissatisfied with the return filed, he may make a default or an arbitrary assessment. In such a case, he will find out the taxable income and tax liability based on his judgement. This power is generally used where following an investigation into a taxpayer's financial affairs, the increase in net assets over a fixed period is found to be inconsistent with the taxpayer's disclosed income. The ATO will generally provide a statement as to the taxpayer's assets, liabilities and such other information which helped them in the determination of the taxable income on an assets betterment basis, unless the taxpayer has failed to co-operate with the investigating officers.

MALAYSIA

In Malaysia, in case of failure to file tax return, the DG has power to raise an assessment on an estimated income of the taxpayer. There is procedure to make composite assessment also. Sec. 96A provides that where a person either makes default in furnishing a return or fails to give notice of his chargeability or makes an incorrect return by omitting or understating any income or gives any incorrect information in relation to any matter affecting his tax liability for one year or years of assessment, the DG and that person may come to an agreement in writing as to the payment by that person of a sum of money being:

1. the amount of tax which has been undercharged or not charged and
2. the amount of any penalty or penalties that a person may be required to pay.

After the completion of the composite assessment, the DG shall cause a notice to be served on the person in respect of whom the composite assessment was made. A composite assessment is final and conclusive and no appeal can be made against it.

PAKISTAN

In Pakistan, under Sec. 60, if no return of income has been furnished by the assessee and if under Sec. 60-A, a concealed asset of any person is impounded by any department or agency of the government, the DC may, at any time, assess provisionally the total income of such person and the tax payable by him on the basis of the assessment.

The D.C. under Sec. 63 may by an order in writing, assess the total income of the assessee to the best of his judgement and determine the tax payable in case any person fails to furnish a return of his total income or to furnish his wealth statement or fails to comply with the notice issued for submitting information and evidence in support of the return.

INDIA

In India, where the assessee does not file a return on his own or after receiving a notice from the AO, or fails to produce accounts or documents if required or fails to appear before AO, the AO is authorised to make an assessment of the total income or loss to the best of his judgement on the basis of material and information available on record. While doing so, he is expected to be fair, and impartial.

INCOME-ESCAPING ASSESSMENT

THE U.K.

In the U.K., Sec. 29 TMA 1970, provides that once a self-assessment has become final, the IR can only make a discovery assessment when there has been:

1. an incomplete disclosure; or
2. fraudulent or negligent conduct;

The time limits for making a discovery assessment are;

(a) 5 years from the January 31 following the year of assessment;
(b) 20 years where fraudulent or negligent conduct is involved.

THE U.S.

In the U.S., if any error or concealment of income is found after audit, then the IRS may amend the return by doing supplemental assessment. There is a time limit within which the IRS can make corrections to a return after it has been filed. This time period is called the 'statute of limitations'. The statute of limitation is 3 years from the later of the date the tax return was actually filed or its due date. The period is extended to 6 years if the taxpayer omits an item of gross income that exceeds 25 per cent of the gross income reported on the return. A return can be amended at any time if a fraudulent return is filed or if no return is filed.

AUSTRALIA

In Australia, in case of avoidance of tax, the Commissioner can amend an assessment (to increase the taxpayers liability) within 4 years from the date the tax becomes due and payable under the assessment. In case avoidance of tax is due to fraud or evasion, the commissioner can amend the assessment (to increase the taxpayer's liability) at any time. An amendment to reduce taxpayer's liability may only be made within 4 years from the date the tax became due and payable under the assessment being amended. To improve the administration of tax laws and to reduce the compliance burden for taxpayers, the *Tax Reform Plan* of 1998 intends to reduce the period within which the ATO can amend an assessment from 4 years to 2 years. An unlimited period will, however, continue to apply in case of fraud or evasion.

MALAYSIA

1. Where no assessment or no sufficient assessment has been made on a person chargeable to tax, the DG may in that year or within 6 years after its expiration, make an assessment or additional assessment, and determine the tax or additional tax according to the best of his judgement. Before January 1, 1999, the DG had the power to make additional assessment within 12 years after its expiration.
2. If any refund has been paid to a person in excess, the DG may make an assessment in respect of that person in the amount of tax.
3. Where any fraud or wilful default has been committed by or on behalf of any person; or any person is found to be negligent in relation to the payment of tax, the DG may at any time make an assessment for the purpose of making good any loss of tax attributable to the fraud, wilful default or negligence.

A matter, which has been settled in appeal, cannot be reopened, but the discovery of new facts would allow for the raising of additional assessments.

PAKISTAN

In Pakistan, Sec. 65 provides that in case any income chargeable to tax has escaped assessment or the total income of an assessee has been under-assessed, or assessed at too low a rate, or excessive relief or refund has been granted, the DC may issue a notice and may proceed to assess or determine by an order in writing the total income of the assessee or the tax payable by him. The tax shall be charged at the rate or rates applicable to the assessment year for which the assessment is made. No proceedings shall be initiated unless definite information has come into the possession of the DC and he has obtained the approval of Inspecting Additional Commissioner (IAC) in writing to do so. Notice in respect of any income year may be issued within ten years from the end of the assessment year in which the total income of the said year was first assessable.

INDIA

In India, the AO is authorised to assess or reassess any income, which he believes has escaped assessment. Such a situation arises where either

1. no return of income has been furnished although the total income of the assessee is above the taxable limit;
2. where the assessee is found to have understated his income or claimed excessive loss, deduction in the return; or
3. where though the assessment has been made, the income has been assessed at too low a rate.

In case any reassessment or recomputation is done, the tax is chargeable at the rate or rates at which it would have been charged had the income not escaped assessment. Before any reassessment, notice is served on the assessee requiring him to furnish a return of income within a specified period, along with the reasons for doing so. There is a time limit within which such a notice can be issued. The time limit of issuing notice under Sec. 148 is 4 years, 7 years or 10 years from the end of the relevant assessment year depending upon whether the income which escaped assessment is less than Rs.50,000 or Rs.50,000 or more or Rs.100,000 or more for that year. With effect from 1 June 2001, this time limit has been reduced to 6 years where the income escaping tax is Rs.100,000 or more and 4 years where the income escaping tax is less than Rs.100,000.

SEARCH AT TAXPAYER'S PREMISES

THE U.K.

In the U.K., search at the premises of the taxpayer is not ordinarily allowed. However, the search by an officer of the Board can be done after a search warrant is issued by the appropriate judicial authority (circuit judge) on being satisfied by the information given on oath by an officer of the Board, with the specific prior approval of the Board to make such an application that there is reasonable ground for suspecting that an offence involving serious fraud in connection with tax is being, has been or is about to be committed. An offence which involves fraud is serious if its commission will cause serious prejudice to the proper assessment or collection of tax. As such, in the U.K., the power to search cannot be exercised by the Board independently. It can be exercised only after satisfying the judicial authority and obtaining a warrant from such authority.

THE U.S.

In the U.S., the Secretary is authorised to enter any building or place where any article or object subject to tax are made, produced or kept for the purpose of examining such articles or objects in the daytime. However, if these premises are open at night, the Secretary can enter such premises at night also.

AUSTRALIA

In Australia, under ITAA Sec. 263, the Commissioner and his duly authorised ATO officer have the right of full and free access to all buildings, places, books, documents and other papers. The officers can even obtain tax-related information from the offices of solicitors and accountants, whose clients are being investigated for tax avoidance. He can even obtain documents from a bank for use in proceedings to recover the unpaid tax. The commissioner can even have access to documents held at premises of a person acting for or advising the taxpayer. The access powers in general does not entitle officers to take possession of a taxpayer's records but they are entitled to make extracts or copies.

MALAYSIA

Under Sec. 80, the DG is authorised to have free access to all lands, buildings, and to all books and other documents and may search such lands, buildings and may inspect, copy and make extracts from any such books or documents. He may further ask any information to be given in writing within a specified time.

PAKISTAN

In Pakistan, tax authorities have the power to enter and search the premises in which a person carries on or is believed to carry on his business or profession. The power is to enter and search business premises only and not the residential premises. The powers include: (i) to search such premises; (ii) to inspect accounts; (iii) to take copies of such accounts; (iv) to impound accounts or documents; and (v) to make inventory of any articles found in such premises. There is no power to impound or seize the assets during search. However, there is provision under Sec. 60A to make a provisional assessment where a concealed asset is impounded by any department or agency of the Government.

INDIA

In India, if the tax authorities have a reason to believe that any person is in possession of undisclosed assets, or has not produced the books of accounts or is not likely to produce the books of accounts which are relevant or useful to any proceeding under the Income Tax Act, they can enter and search any building, place, including vehicle, where there is reason to suspect that such assets or books of accounts are kept and even to break open the lock of any door, box, locker or safe. The tax authorities have powers to search any person at such building, place and even to seize books of accounts and undisclosed assets found as a result of the search.

Thus, the powers of search in India as compared to other countries extend not only to business premises but to any premises including residential premises and tax authorities are empowered to seize the books of accounts and undisclosed assets. Separate provisions exist under the Indian Income Tax Act for the assessment of undisclosed income found as a consequence of the search. A block assessment is done of the last 10 years (reduced to 6 years for search after June 1, 2001) of undisclosed income detected as a consequence to search and such income is taxed at a flat rate of 60 per cent.

Conclusion

The assessment procedure of the selected countries have been summarised in Table 8.2

As shown in the table, all the countries have now gradually adopted the self-assessment system. Under this system, the taxpayer is required to compute his own income, compute tax thereon and pay the same before filing the return and is required to file return accordingly. India, Pakistan, Australia and the U.S. were already following this self-assessment system. The U.K. introduced this system from the income year 1996-97 and Malaysia is also switching over to this system progressively from the year 2001. This system is administratively more convenient to tax authorities. With the increasing number of taxpayers, it has become practically impossible for tax authorities in all the countries to verify individual returns, compute tax thereon and then to intimate the same to the assessee. Accordingly, all countries have adopted the system of self-assessment delegating obligation on the taxpayers to compute income and tax thereon correctly. This system is administratively convenient for tax authorities but it places an extra responsibility and financial burden on the taxpayers. With the complicated nature of tax provisions it is difficult for a taxpayer to compute his income and tax liability thereon properly without the help and assistance of tax consultants. All the onus and responsibility has now been shifted on the taxpayers with the tax authorities only to make a random or selective examination of returns to ensure that taxpayers are reporting correct income and paying tax thereon. Accordingly, the system of checking and verification of returns filed has been modified. Now only certain selective returns are examined in all the selected countries. The powers of examination and

TABLE 8.2. A SUMMARY OF PROVISIONS RELATING TO INCOME ASSESSMENT PROCEDURES

Sl. No.	Particulars	U.K	U.S.	Australia	Malaysia	Pakistan	India
1.	Self-assessment system	Yes.	Yes.	Yes.	Yes, for companies from year 2001	Yes.	Yes.
2.	Time period for making inquiry	Inquiry to be notified within 12 months from due date of filing returns.	3 years from the due date of filing returns.	No time limit. But a taxpayer can apply for assessment, if no assessment is received within 12 months.	No time limit, but overall limit of 6 years will apply.	2 years from the end of relevant assessment year.	2 years from the end of relevant assessment year.
3.	Time period for reassessment of income escaping tax	5 years from the January 31 following the income year, 20 years in case of fraud or negligent conduct.	6 years if the item of gross income omitted exceeds 25 per cent of gross income reported in the return. No limitation in case of no return and fraudulent return.	4 years, proposed to be reduced to 2 years. However, in case of fraud or evasion unlimited period.	6 years, but at any time in case of fraud or willful default.	10 years from the end of relevant asstt year.	10 years from the end relevant asstt year. Proposed to be reduced to 6 years with effect from 1 June 2001.
4.	Search at taxpayers premises	Only after search warrant is issued by judicial authority on being satisfied of serious fraud in connection with tax.	Search only at building or place where articles or objects subject to tax are made, produced or kept.	Full and free access to all buildings, places. Records cannot be seized but authorities entitled to make extracts or copies.	Free access to all lands, buildings and to copy, make extracts from books or documents.	Power to enter and search business premises only. To make inventory of articles found and to take copies of accounts and even to impound accounts or documents found in search.	Power to enter and search business, and residence premises and to seize documents, books of accounts and undisclosed assets found during search.

investigation are very wide in all the countries. The tax officers in all the countries are authorised to examine books of accounts, records and even to summon the taxpayer and any other person whose statement may be relevant for the purpose of inquiry. The process of selection of returns however, varies. In the U.S. and Australia, there is scientific method and the criteria for selection of returns to be verified. No such scientific method has been adopted by other countries, i.e. Malaysia, Pakistan and India. Even in the U.K. there is no prescribed method, though a time period has been fixed for initiating an enquiry.

After completion of inquiry, there is a system of settlement in the U.K., the U.S., Australia and even in Malaysia. The taxpayer in these countries is informed of the deficiency and wherever the taxpayer objects, an effort is made to settle or decide the issue by negotiations. Though there is settlement commission in India and Pakistan, it can be approached only when there is complexity as against in the above countries where the settlement procedure is adopted invariably in all cases where the taxpayer objects to the deficiency in the tax return, pointed out by the revenue officer. The procedure of having negotiated settlement in all cases of differences is administratively more convenient as it expedites the proceedings and avoids unnecessary wastage of time and money in litigation and gives opportunity to the taxpayer to come forward and settle all issues without going into technicalities.

Income tax laws in all these countries provide for a procedure of appeal in case the taxpayer is not satisfied with the assessment of income completed by the tax officer. The first appeal in all the selected countries lies with a senior officer of the tax department itself except in the U.K. where the appeal is heard by general commissioners who are businessmen or by special commissioners who are experienced solicitors, advocates and civil servants. In the U.S., in case of failure of settlements before the IRS appeals division, the appeal lies with the Tax Court. Further appeal against the decision on the first appeal are allowed in all the selected countries and questions of law are allowed to be appealed to the highest court of the country. As such, in all the selected countries, a fair and reasonable opportunity is provided to the taxpayer to present his case in case of any dispute.

The time period for the re-opening of a completed assessment in case of income-escaping assessment also varies in these countries. While it is 6 years in the U.S. and Malaysia, 5 years in the U.K., 4 years in Australia (proposed to be reduced to 2 years) and 10 years in India and Pakistan. In India, it has been reduced to 6 years from June 1, 2001. However in case of fraud, there is no time limit in the U.S., Australia and Malaysia. In the U.K. there is a time limit of 20 years in case of fraud or negligent conduct.

Another important provision for the assessment of proper income is search. This provision also varies to a great extent in these countries. Provisions of search at the taxpayer's premises in India are widest. These tax authorities can search not only business premises but also the residential premises of the taxpayer, any vehicle, or ship. They are not required to obtain any prior approval of any court as is required in the U.K. where search warrants have to be obtained by tax authorities from the court after satisfying it of serious fraud in connection with tax. In Australia, and Malaysia, the tax authorities have free access to all buildings; they cannot seize any asset or documents but can take extracts or copies only. In the U.S., search can be conducted at a building or place where articles or objects subject to tax are produced or kept, which in a way means business premises. Similarly, in Pakistan, power to search is for business premises. However, accounts and documents found at the time of search can be impounded, but assets cannot be seized, though an inventory can be made of such assets.

Thus, it appears that powers in India are discriminately high and allow the tax authorities power even to seize the assets. The power to search is required for the proper determination of income of a delinquent taxpayer, but it needs to be reasonable considering the fact that this process affects the privacy of a person. Tax authorities could be allowed to invoke these powers in the rare cases only on reaching the conclusion that all the available remedies available under the Act have been exhausted as it is in the U.K. where the court has to be satisfied before issuing a search warrant.

COLLECTION OF INCOME TAX

In any system of taxation, it is crucial to devise a system of collection of tax which is convenient for the taxpayer and which helps mobilise tax to the maximum extent. The system should also ensure that it is not only convenient for the taxpayer but also administratively cost-effective for the revenue. In order to achieve this objective, these countries have by and large adopted four methods for the collection of income tax. The scope and timing of payments, however, differs. The methods adopted are:

1. Pay as you earn or tax deduction at source.
2. Payment on account or advance tax.
3. Self- assessment tax.
4. Additional tax or assessed tax.

The scope and timing of each method in the countries selected are examined below.

THE U.K.

In the U.K., the collection of income tax is effected through the following modes.

Pay as You Earn and Tax Deduction at Source

The majority of income tax payable under Schedule 'E' income, i.e. income arising from employment pensions and certain social security benefits, is collected under the Pay As You Earn (PAYE) system. Under this system, the employer is responsible for collecting the income tax and National Insurance

Contributions (NICs) due for each tax month during the fiscal year and the amounts collected are due and payable 14 days after the end of the tax month. However, where income tax and NICs due on an average are £1,000 per month or less (for small employers), an election is available to pay the amounts due on a quarterly basis.

Investment income is subject to tax deduction at source (TDS). Persons making payments of interest, annuities and patent royalties are required to deduct tax at source. The main categories of interest taxed at source are building society interest, bank interest, debentures and other loan interest from companies in the U.K. The tax rate for deduction on interest payment is 20 per cent, whereas the tax rate for deduction on payment of annuities and patent royalties is 23 per cent. The gross equivalent of the income received during an income year is included in the taxpayer's total income for that year and a tax credit is given for the tax deducted at source.

Payment on Account or Advance Tax

Under the self-assessment system, income tax, along with Class 4 NIC is payable in three stages namely:

(a) First payment on account on or before January 31.
(b) Second payment on account on or before the following July 31 and
(c) A balancing payment on the January 31 following the end of the income year.

For the income year 1999-2000, these stages were:

(a) First payment on account January 31, 2000, i.e. about 2 months before the end of the income year.
(b) Second payment on account July 31, 2000, i.e. about 4 months after the end of the income year.
(c) A balancing payment January 31, 2001.

As the final tax liability may not be known prior to the end of the income year, the tax liability of the year immediately preceding the income year will be the basis for determining the payment on account. For the income year 1999-2000, the income tax liability of the income year 1998-99 along with NIC, less income tax deducted at source, PAYE deductions and tax credit on dividends will be the basis. Of this liability, 50 per cent is paid at the time of the first payment on account, i.e. January 31 and the balance 50 per cent is paid at the time of the second payment on account, i.e. July 31.

No payment on account will be due if either:

(a) income tax and Class 4 contribution liability for the tax year, calculated net of tax deducted at source and tax credit on dividends is less than £500; or
(b) more than 80 per cent of income tax and Class 4 contribution liability for the tax year was met by deduction of tax at source or from tax credits on dividends.

If the tax paid in both instalments of payment on account exceeds the actual tax liability, then the excess may either be refunded or adjusted against future liabilities.

Payment on Account by Companies

Large companies, which have annual profits of at least £1.5 million, are required from the income year 1999-2000 to pay quarterly instalments on account of their expected corporation tax liability for the current year. Payment by instalments system is applicable for the accounting period on or after July 1, 1999 with payments starting in the 7th month of the accounting period. Where an accounting period extends throughout 12 months, payment dates for the 4 instalments after the commencement of that period will be as follows:

1. 6 months and 13 days.
2. 9 months and 13 days
3. 12 months and 13 days
4. 15 months and 13 days.

The first two instalments must be discharged before the end of the accounting period, with the third instalment due a few days later. The final instalment will be due more than 3 months later.

During the first 4 years of the instalment system (introduced from July 1, 1999) only part of the total tax liability is to be paid in instalments. 60 per cent was to be paid in the first instalment and 72 per cent was to be paid in the second instalment. In the third instalment, it is 88 per cent and in the fourth 100 per cent of the total tax which is to be paid in instalments, the balance being due 9 months after the company's accounting year has ended. The above system of instalment is confined only to large companies. Small and medium companies will continue to make payments of corporation tax on a date falling nine months after the end of the accounting period.

Balancing Payment (Self-assessment Tax)

A balancing payment will represent the final tax liability based on the actual return of income calculated in a similar manner as the payment on account is calculated, and after deducting the amount of tax paid in two instalments of payment on account.

Capital gain tax is not discharged by instalments. The entire liability for a tax year must be discharged on or before January 31, following the end of the income year in which the gain or gains arose.

Additional Tax

Liability of tax arising on account of amendment to self-assessment or because of discovery assessment is called additional tax liability and the taxpayer is required to make the payment of the same in 30 days from the date of notification.

THE U.S.

Collection of tax in the U.S. is done through the following modes:

Withholding of Income Tax

Income tax payable on the employees' wages is collected by withholding of income tax by the employer. An employer is required to withhold tax on salaries, fees, bonuses, commission, taxable fringe benefits, pensions, and retirement pay. The term 'employer' includes organisations exempt from income tax. An employer is required to deposit the withholding tax on a monthly basis or semi-weekly. If the amount of aggregate employment taxes is $50,000 or less during the lock-back period, i.e. ending on June 30 of the preceding year, then the employer is required to deposit withholding tax on a monthly basis, i.e. each month's taxes on or before the 15th day of the following month. Where the aggregate employment taxes are more than $50,000, the withholding tax is deposited semi-weekly.

Withholding of tax is also required in the case of taxable payments from an employer sponsored pension annuity, profit-sharing and stock bonus. Withholding is required unless the recipient elects not to have taxes withheld. Withholding is also required on an annuity, endowment or life insurance contract issued by a life insurance company.

A payer is required to deduct and withhold income tax on payments of interest or dividends at a rate of 31 per cent if the payee fails to furnish his Tax Identification Number (TIN).

Estimated Tax/Advance Tax

In the U.S., payment on account is known as estimated tax. The U.S. law requires individuals whose tax liability for the year beginning after January 1, 1998, is $1,000 or more after credit for withheld taxes, to estimate tax liability and to pay estimated tax in 4 instalments. An individual whose income year is the calendar year is required to pay 4 instalments of 25 per cent each in the income year.

These instalments are payable as follows:

First instalment by	April 15
Second instalment by	June 15
Third instalment by	September 15
Fourth instalment by	January 15

Similarly a corporation that anticipates a tax liability of $500 or more has to estimate its income tax liability for the current year and pay 4 quarterly estimated tax instalments as in the case of the individual. The estimated tax payable to avoid penalty is at least 90 per cent of the tax shown on the current years return or 100 per cent of the tax shown on the prior year's return. However, a large corporation is prohibited from using its prior year's tax liability except in determining the first instalments of its tax year. The 4th tax instalment of estimated tax for an income year need not be made if a taxpayer files Form 1040 for tax return and pays the balance of the tax on or before January 31, 2000, if it follows the calendar year as the income year, or for a fiscal year on or before the last day of the month following the close of the fiscal year. This will however not avoid addition to tax for underpayment of any of the first three instalments that were due for the year.

Self-assessment Tax

Any tax shown on the tax return is to be paid without assessment or notice and demand at the time fixed for filing the return. The taxpayer is required to compute tax on his income and make a balance payment after adjusting credit for tax withheld and estimated tax paid for the tax year. If the taxpayer asks the IRS to compute tax for him, he receives a bill for any tax due which should be paid within 30 days from the date the demand is sent, or the due date of return if later.

Deficiency

Although tax in the U.S. is payable under the self-assessment system, strict measures are taken to ensure the correct payment of tax. All tax returns are initially checked for mathematical accuracy and errors. A deficiency is the excess of the correct tax liability over the income tax shown on the return and is payable within 30 days after notice of the same.

AUSTRALIA

In Australia, the income tax is collected through the following methods.

Pay As You Earn and Prescribed Payment System

The Pay As You Earn (PAYE) system was introduced in Australia in 1941. It is the main tax system affecting individuals. Employees are required to pay tax on their salary or wage income progressively as they earn it. Every employer is required to withhold tax instalment deductions at prescribed rates from each payment of salary or wage made to an employee in order to cover their employee's anticipated tax liability at the end of the year and pay them directly to the Australian Taxation Office (ATO). This is how the majority of tax is collected in Australia. In 1998-99, AUD71.158 billion of income tax was collected through this system out of the total gross collection of AUD107.572 billion, which is about 66 per cent.

In order to ensure collection in Australia and to minimise administrative burden to taxpayers and the ATO, a withholding tax system applies in respect of the Australian origin interest, unfranked dividend and royalties paid to non-residents. Interest, unfranked dividends and royalties derived by non-residents are generally not taxed according to the normal process of assessment but are subject to a flat rate withholding tax. To collect tax at source from certain prescribed payments for work or services in specified industries, a separate system known as, the Prescribed Payment System (PPS) applies. It ensures that people in certain prescribed industries pay their tax as they earn. A payer is required to deduct tax at the rate of 20 per cent from the prescribed payment and forward the deduction to the ATO.

Provisional Tax/Advance Tax

The individual taxpayer is liable to pay provisional tax on all income excluding salary and wages. Provisional tax is generally calculated by applying current year rates to the preceding year's adjusted income, increased by a certain percentage known as the provisional tax uplift factor. This factor is determined on an annual basis by reference to the percentage increase in Australia's GDP. The provisional tax factor for 1998-99 was 5 per cent. Taxpayers who expect to earn a lower income than in the preceding year may assess their provisional tax liability using their own estimate of taxable income for the current year. Provisional tax is payable in a single lump sum where the previous year's provisional tax did not exceed AUD8,000 and is payable on the date specified in the notice issued by the Commissioner and is not earlier than March 31 in the provisional tax year. In other cases provisional tax is payable in 4 instalments each payable on September 1, December 1, March 1 and June 1 in the provisional tax year, the first three instalments being 25 per cent of provisional tax and the 4th instalment being the balance provisional tax.

Companies pay tax depending on the real or pre-determined level of tax liability. This level determines whether the company pays in a single lump sum or in instalments. Small taxpayers where the likely tax is less than AUD8,000 are to pay their estimated tax liability on the 15th day of the 18th month from the start of their income year in one lump sum.

Medium taxpayers where the likely tax is between AUD8,000 and AUD300,000 are to pay their estimated tax liability in 4 quarterly instalments starting from the first day of the 12th month from the start of their year of income.

Large taxpayers whose likely tax liability is more than AUD300,000 are also to pay their estimated tax in 4 quarterly instalments but starting from the 1st day of the 9th month from the start of their year of income.

If after paying an instalment, an estimate lodged by a medium taxpayer or a large taxpayer increases or decreases the taxpayer's tax likely for the year, the taxpayer must pay the shortfall.

With effect from July 1, 1997, the ATO has started a voluntary advance payment system. Payments made in advance of an assessment are credited to a taxpayer's account and applied against primary tax or provisional tax assessment. Any excess is refunded. Payments in advance are also refundable on request.

Assessed Tax

In the case of individuals, any assessed income tax is due for payment on the date specified in the notice of assessment or on the 30th day after service of the notice on the taxpayer, whichever is later. This rule also applies on the payment of penalty imposed. The 30-day period is the minimum period and the Commissioner often specifies a date which is more than 30 days. In the case of companies, income tax is due and payable on the later of the due date for payment of the final instalment of tax or on the day the relevant annual return is lodged. Liability to pay tax assessed is not suspended pending the Commissioner's consideration of the taxpayer's objection against the assessment, nor during the pendency of appeal. The Commissioner however, has the power to grant an extension of time for payment of tax.

MALAYSIA

Collection of tax in Malaysia is done in the following ways:

Tax Deduction at Source

In Malaysia, the employer deducts tax while making payment of salaries to his employees. This is done by a Scheduler Tax Reduction System that requires employers to pay stipulated amounts from the employees' emoluments to the Director General (DG) on a monthly basis. Tax is also deducted from interest or royalty paid to non-residents. Tax is deducted at the rate of 15 per cent on interest income and 10 per cent on royalties. Tax is also deducted while making payments for services, technical advices, assistance, rental or other income.

Instalment Payment/Advance Tax

Individuals and companies are required to pay tax under an instalment payment scheme. Employed individuals, whose tax is deducted from salaries, are excluded. Under this scheme, all taxpayers are issued a notice of instalment payment before the start of the basis year, i.e. income year requiring them to make 5 bi-monthly payments beginning from the month of January or February, depending upon whether taxpayer's income tax reference number ending is odd or even. The estimated tax payable by instalments is based on the preceding year's assessment. However, in the case of individual taxpayers, only those with an estimated tax liability of RM 1,000 or more are covered by this scheme. For the year of assessment 2000, the instalments are on a monthly basis instead of a bi-monthly basis.

Excess Tax

In Malaysia, where the tax payable under an assessment exceeds the tax payable under the instalment scheme, the excess tax is to be paid in the month subsequent to the final instalment.

Assessment Tax

The taxpayer is required to make the payment of tax under an assessment or a composite assessment within 30 days after service of the notice of assessment. This tax has to be paid, notwithstanding any objection or appeal filed against the assessment. However, in certain circumstances, an extension of 30 days is allowed. There are also circumstances where the DG may require an immediate payment within 7 days of the issue of notice.

PAKISTAN

Pakistan also follows the self-assessment system. All taxpayers are required to compute their income and tax thereon and make payment of the same before filing the return of income. The payment of tax is affected through following modes:

Deduction of Tax at Source

As in other countries, the employer here is required to deduct tax from the payment of salaries and wages to his employees.

Moreover, tax is required to be deducted while making the payment for interest to non-residents, payment for technical services, contracts, supply of goods, brokerage and commission. The rate of deduction varies for different payments. Tax deducted is required to be deposited within the prescribed period. Tax is to be deducted at source not only on the above-mentioned payments but also in respect of following payments:

(a) Tax deduction at the import stage;
(b) Tax deduction at exports;
(c) Payment of dividends;
(d) Issue of bonus shares;
(e) Sale by public auction;
(f) Rental income;
(g) Approval of site plan;
(h) Electricity consumption bill;
(i) On mobile phones;
(j) Gas bills of industrial and commercial consumers;
(k) Petroleum products to petrol pump operators.

The list of payments in Pakistan on which tax is required to be deducted at source is quite exhaustive.

Advance Payment of Tax

In Pakistan, advance payment of tax is required to be made by all companies, registered firms and other assessees whose total income assessed for the latest assessment year is PKR150,000 or more. The total income excludes capital gain and income chargeable under the head salary, dividend income and income from imports and exports liable for deduction at source.

The advance tax is to be paid in 4 equal instalments in the income year as under:

First instalment by	October 7
Second instalment by	January 7
Third instalment by	April 7
Fourth instalment by	June 21

The tax to be paid in each instalment is one-fourth of the full amount of tax determined to be payable less tax deducted at source. The liability to pay tax in Pakistan becomes due within 7 days from the end of the first quarter. Moreover, in the fourth quarter, it has to be paid even 9 days before the end of the year irrespective of the fact whether the payer has been able to realise his income, though the same may have accrued. Advance tax is to be paid on the basis of the latest assessment year for which the tax has been determined. However, an option has been given to taxpayers other than companies and registered firms to make their own estimate of the amount of tax payable and to pay tax accordingly at any time before the last date of the last instalment. This option is not available to companies and registered firms which are required to pay advance tax in proportion of their turnover to the tax payable on the turnover of the latest assessment year for which tax has been determined. The option to make an estimate for companies was withdrawn from the financial year 1997-98, causing hardship to many taxpayers who may have been running into losses but were yet required to pay advance tax. No advance tax is, however, payable by new taxpayers even if their estimated income exceeds the prescribed limit.

Payment of Tax with Returns

Every taxpayer in Pakistan is required to make payment of tax on the basis of returns of income before filing them. The payment of tax is to be made before the due date of furnishing of such returns.

Payment of Tax on Demand

Tax determined on the basis of assessment is required to be paid within such time as is allowed by the officer making an assessment from the date of issue of the notice of demand. The usual time allowed for making a payment is 35 days from the date of issue of the notice of demand.

INDIA

In India, tax is collected through the following modes:

Tax Deduction at Source

As in other countries, law requires every employer in India to deduct tax from the payment of salaries and wages to its employees. Similarly, tax is required to be deducted by the person making payment for interest, contract works, professional services, technical services, commission and rent. Different rates of deduction have been prescribed for different types of payments. The deductor is required to deduct the tax at the prescribed rate and make payment of the same to the government and submit a return of such deduction and payment to the income tax department.

Advance Tax

Every taxpayer in India is required to estimate his/her tax liability after deducting credit for tax to be deducted at source for the income year and pay the same in instalments in case the same exceeds Rs.5000. Taxpayers other than companies are required to make payment of advance tax in 3 instalments in the income year as given in Table 8.3.

Companies are required to make payment of advance tax in 4 instalments in the income year as given in Table 8.4.

No declaration or intimation of tax or estimated income is to be filed by the taxpayer for advance tax purposes. The taxpayer is required to simply deposit the instalments in bank by due dates.

In India, advance tax payments start as early as 2 months and 15 days from the start of income year and the total tax gets deposited 15 days before the end of the income year. In case of non-payment/short payment of advance tax on due date, penalty in the form of interest is leviable.

Self-assessment Tax

Every person, who is liable to pay tax, is required to compute tax liability at the time of filing of return and pay the balance tax, if any, before filing the return. This tax is called self-asscssment tax. Any interest payable for late

TABLE 8.3. ADVANCE PAYMENT OF TAX BY NON-CORPORATE TAXPAYERS IN INDIA

Instalment	Percentage of Tax on Estimated Income	Due Date
First Instalment	30 per cent	September 15, i.e. after 5 months 15 days from the beginning of income year
Second Instalment	30 per cent (Total 60 per cent)	December 15, i.e. after 8 months 15 days from the beginning of income year.
Third Instalment	40 per cent (Total 100 per cent)	March 15, i.e. after 11 months 15 days from the beginning of tax year.

Source: The *Income Tax Act*, 1961 as on June 1, 2001 (India).

TABLE 8.4. ADVANCE PAYMENT OF TAX BY CORPORATE TAXPAYERS IN INDIA

First Instalment	15 per cent of tax on estimated income for the income year.	June 15, i.e. within 2 months and 15 days from the beginning of the income year.
Second Instalment	30 per cent of tax on estimated income (total 45 per cent of tax on estimated income).	September 15, i.e. within 5 months and 15 days from the beginning of the income year.
Third Instalment	30 per cent of tax on estimated income (total 75 per cent of tax on estimated income).	December 15, i.e. within 8 months and 15 days from the beginning of the income year.
Fourth Instalment	25 per cent of tax on estimated income. Total 100 per cent of tax on estimated income.	March 15, i.e. within 11 months and 15 days from the beginning of the income year.

Source: Same as in Table 8.3.

filing of return or for non-payment or short payment of advance tax is to be paid at the time of filing of the return of income. The return of income is to be accompanied by proof of payment of both tax and interest. If the total amount paid falls short of the total tax and interest, the amount paid is attributed first towards interest and the balance towards the tax liability.

Post-assessment Tax

Any tax including interest and penalty payable in consequence to any assessment or any order passed by the AO is to be paid within 30 days from the time when notice of demand is served on the person concerned. This period of 30 days can be reduced if the AO has reason to believe that it will be detrimental to revenue.

Conclusion

Table 8.5 gives a summary of the various provisions of collection of taxes in the selected countries.

The collection of tax in all the selected countries is by way of withholding tax (i.e. tax deduction at source, PAYE), advance payment of tax, self-assessment tax and tax on demand. The provisions regarding withholding tax in these countries are almost similar except in Pakistan and India, where the scope is too wide and TDS provisions are applicable on a large number of payments to possibly plug revenue leakages either by way of not reporting of the income or non filing of return by the recipient. In the U.S., the scope of withholding tax is very limited and for payments other than salaries, is applicable when the recipient does not submit the Tax Identification Number (TIN) to the deductor. This indicates the effectiveness of TIN and the computer system by which income declared in the return is matched with the income distributed or paid by various corporations, banks and other organisations.

The collection of TDS may be good from the point of view of tax collection and revenue, but administratively, it places an extra burden on a person who is required to deduct and pay the tax of others and comply with all the relevant rules and procedure in this regard. The deductor is discharging the obligation of others at his own cost and in a way rendering service to the revenue without any monetary compensation. The U.S., however, has very narrow applicability, and TDS is required only when the TIN of the payee is not available. India and Pakistan on the other hand are progressively widening the scope of applicability of deduction of tax at source every year by bringing more and more kinds of payment within its scope. With growing computerisation in India and Pakistan and applicability of a tax number for every taxpayer, these countries can exclude this mode of collection of tax like the U.S. for taxpayers who submit their tax number.

All the selected countries have gradually introduced the collection of tax through advance tax. The countries have named this payment system differently. In the U.S., Australia and Pakistan, it is payable in 4 instalments.

TABLE 8.5. A SUMMARY OF PROVISIONS RELATING TO COLLECTION OF INCOME TAX

Sl. No.	Particulars	U.K.	U.S.	Australia	Malaysia	Pakistan	India
1.	Tax deduction at source	On salaries, investment income, payment of interest, annuities, patent royalties	On salaries. On interest and dividend if payee does not provide tax identification number.	On salaries and on payment for work or services in specified industry. Also on interest, unfranked dividend and royalties paid to non-residents.	On salaries, services, rental, royalty, interest.	On salaries, import, export, dividends, rent, mobile phone, electricity bill, gas bill, petroleum products	On salaries, interest, rent, professional, technical services, contracts, commission.
2.	Advance payment of tax	Yes, known as payment on account: payable in two instalments on the basis of tax liability of preceding year. 50 per cent - January 31, about 10 months from the beginning of year. 50 per cent - July 31, about 4 months after the end of year.	Yes, known as estimated tax in four equal instalments every quarter starting from 15 April in case of calendar year. The estimated tax either to be 100 per cent of preceding year tax or 90 per cent tax of current year.	Yes, known as provisional tax on the basis of preceding year income adjusted by a percentage linked to gross domestic product. Usually payable in 4 quarterly instalments starting from September 1 of income year. Large taxpayers company pay starting from 9th month from start of the income year i.e. March 1.	Yes, known as instalment payment payable in monthly instalment in income year on the basis of previous year's liability.	Yes, payments in 4 instalment in the income year. October 7 January 7 April 7 June 21	Yes, payable in 4 instalments for companies and in 3 instalments for other assesses within the income year. Companies Others June 15 15% — Sep. 15 30% 30% Dec. 15 30% 30% Mar. 15 25% 40%
3.	Additional tax	30 days from the date of notification	Within 30 days after notice of demand	Within 30 days from the date of service of notice or date specified whichever is later.	Within 30 days after the service of notice.	Within 35 days from the date of notice.	Within 30 days from the date of receipt of notice of demand.

In India, it is payable in 3 instalments (for taxpayers other than companies) and in 4 instalments (for companies). However, the date of start of instalment in these countries varies. In the U.K., it is payable in 2 instalments one of which is after the end of the income year whereas in Malaysia, it is payable in 12 monthly instalments as against the earlier system of 6 bi-monthly instalments. The basis for estimating advance tax in the U.K., the U.S., Australia, Malaysia and Pakistan is the preceding year's taxable income. However, in India, the basis of advance tax is the current year's income.

The liability to pay it in India starts as early as after only 2 months and 15 days in the case of companies and after 5 months and 15 days in the case of other taxpayers from the start of the income year. The provision to pay tax on the basis of the current year's income appears to be too strict. On the other hand, in the U.K., the due date of 50 per cent payment of the second instalment of advance tax (called payment on account) after almost 4 months from the end of the income year seems to be too liberal and in a strict legal sense cannot be called advance tax.

Provisions in Australia are similar, where the payment of advance tax called provisional tax starts within the income year but quarterly payments go beyond the end of the income year, estimated on the basis of the preceding year's income, though increased by a percentage linked to increase in the GDP of Australia. In Malaysia, the advance tax called instalment tax is payable in 12 monthly instalments starting from the first month of the income year on the basis of the preceding year's liability.

The monthly instalment system may be good for collection of revenue on the principle of pay as you earn, but administratively it is inconvenient to both the taxpayers as well as tax administrators. Not only that, in Malaysia, tax authorities are required to issue an instalment notice to the taxpayers liable to pay instalment tax as compared to other countries where no such notices are required to be issued and taxpayers have to pay advance tax on the due date.

The other system of self-assessment tax and tax on demand is by and large similar in the selected countries. The taxpayer is usually required to make payment of tax demanded within 30 days from the date of demand. In Pakistan, 35 days period is given for making payment of additional tax. However, all these countries have provisions to reduce the period of 30 days if there are reasons to believe that it will be detrimental to the revenue.

CHAPTER 9

Compliance and Enforcement

Enforcement provisions are an integral part of a tax statute. The law provides for the submission of returns by the taxpayer on his own, the manner in which the returns should be filed, the information which the taxpayer should supply in the returns, and the time limit by which returns should be filed. The law also provides for the maintenance of books of accounts, and to produce them for inspection when called for. The law has also placed an obligation on the taxpayer to declare correct income. Though there is a voluntary compliance of the law by and large, there is a tendency to circumvent the law to gain a monetary advantage, or there can be non-compliance of the law because of negligence. To ensure the compliance of provisions, the law prescribes punitive measures for a delinquent taxpayer. These punitive measures can take the form of levy of interest, penalty and even prosecution leading to imprisonment.

Tax compliance depends very much on the efficacy of sanctions against non-compliance. However, sanctions prescribed in the law alone cannot ensure compliance unless there is a credible threat of being caught and punished in the event of default. Stiff penalties lose their teeth if detection is lax and conviction happens to be rare. While factors like the values of the society also play a vital role in influencing people's attitude towards taxes, the climate of compliance in a country depends very much on the credibility of the sanctions laid down in the law against the non-compliance. Confiscatory penalties by themselves do not lend credibility. In fact, statutory penalties, if too stiff, often generate adverse reactions both among the people and the judiciary. Tax systems which have been successful in securing a high degree of compliance depend more on mechanisms which help detection and a judicial process, which while assuring justice, does not allow defaulters to frustrate the law through prolonged litigation.[1]

The income tax law in all the selected countries provide for penalties both in the shape of imposing additional monetary burden on the defaulting taxpayers for breach of law and by providing imprisonment and fine in case of certain defaults. Like other provisions of the income tax, the provisions relating to penalties have been subject to considerable changes because of the liberalisation of administrative procedures. There are basically three types of punitive provisions, i.e. interest, penalty and imprisonment. This chapter examines the extent of variations in these penal provisions for late payment of tax, late filing of returns and reporting of incorrect income and also examines to what extent the penal provisions are reasonable and commensurate with the nature of default committed by the taxpayer. Although there are number of provisions relating to interest, penalty and prosecution, only common provisions have been taken for study purposes to make a comparative analysis. The chapter is divided into three parts;

1. Interest provisions
2. Penalty provisions
3. Tax offences and prosecution provisions

Interest Provisions

In case of default by the taxpayer in furnishing the return or in paying the tax on due date or in paying the full amount of tax, the taxpayer is charged with interest on the tax underpaid. A taxpayer is also entitled to claim interest on the overpayment of tax in many countries. The interest provisions of the selected countries arc reviewed in this part.

THE U.K.

In the U.K., after the introduction of the self-assessment system, interest and penalty provisions have been amended. For ensuring the compliance of tax provisions, interest and surcharge is payable for default in making payment at due date.

Interest is charged on any tax that is paid after the due date. The interest payment on account of the first and second instalments of tax and balancing payment runs from the due date to the date of payment. Interest on additional tax due as a result of an amendment or a discovery assessment runs from the annual filing date to the date of actual payment. Interest on unpaid surcharges is also payable and runs from the due date to the date the surcharge is paid. The rates at which interest is levied have been changed many times. It was 5.5 per cent for the period from January 6, 1994 till October 5, 1994, went upto 9.5 per cent for the period from August 6, 1997 till January 5, 1999 and again reduced to 7.5 per cent for the period beginning March 6, 1999. Interest is calculated for the exact number of days of default.

Interest on Overpaid Tax

The taxpayer is entitled to interest on overpaid tax from the due date of payment of tax or the date the payment is made, whichever is later, to the date it is repaid by the tax authorities. The rate of interest on overpaid tax has also been amended from time to time. Until February 5, 1997, the rate of interest on excess payment was same as chargeable on short payment. However, from February 6, 1997, the rate of interest payable on excess payment has been reduced and is almost half of the rate leviable on short payment. It was 4.75 per cent for the period from August 6, 1997, to January 5, 1999, and was reduced to 3 per cent for the period from March 6, 1999.

Surcharge on Late Payment of Tax

Besides interest, surcharge is also leviable on the late payment of tax with respect to balancing payments, amendments, and discovery assessments. Surcharge is payable as follows:

(a) If all or part of a balancing payment remains unpaid more than 28 days after the due date, a surcharge equal to 5 per cent of the tax unpaid.
(b) If all or part of any additional tax payable (because a self-assessment has been amended or because a discovery assessment has been raised) remains unpaid more than 28 days after the due date, a surcharge equal to 5 per cent of the tax unpaid arises.
(c) Any tax that remains unpaid more than 6 months after the due date is subject to a surcharge equal to 10 per cent of the tax unpaid

The surcharge is payable within 30 days after the date on which it is imposed. But it is not applicable to payment on account (Instalment payments).

THE U.S.

Interest on underpayments of tax is imposed at the federal short-term rate plus 3 percentage points. Interest accrues from the date the payment was due until it is received by the Internal Revenue Service (IRS). Interest rates are adjusted quarterly. Interest rate for the first quarter of 1999 was 7 per cent and for subsequent quarters of 1999, it was 8 per cent. On underpayment by a corporation that exceeds $100,000 for any tax period it is imposed at the federal short-term rate plus 5 percentage points.

Interest is also charged on the tax not paid by the due date of return. Interest is charged even if one get an extension of time for filing the return. However, if the IRS calculates tax for the taxpayer, interest cannot start earlier than the 31st day after the IRS sends you a bill.

Interest on Penalties

Interest is also charged on the failure to file penalty, fraud penalty and accuracy-related penalty from the due date of the return (including extensions) till the date of payment. Interest on other penalties start on the date of notice and demand.

Interest due to IRS Error or Delay

Interest can be forgiven wholly or partly if it is due to an unreasonable error or delay by an officer or employee of the IRS in performing a ministerial or managerial act. A ministerial act is a procedural or technical act that occurs during the processing of a taxpayer's case. Interest and certain penalties may also be suspended for a limited period if the taxpayer filed the return by the due date (including extensions) and the IRS does not provide a notice stating the liability and the basis for it before the close of the 18 month period beginning on the later of the date the return is filed, or the due date of the return without regard to extensions.

Interest on Refund

Interest is also payable on refund to the taxpayer. No interest is payable if the refund is made within 45 days after the due date of return. If the refund is not made within this 45-day period, interest will be paid from the due date of return or from the date the return is filed, whichever is later. The interest rate that the IRS pays for the overpayment of taxes in the case of non-corporate taxpayers is equal to the federal short-term rate plus 3 percentage points and in the case of corporate taxpayers is, the short-term federal rate plus 2 percentage points. For large corporate overpayments that exceed $10,000, the interest rate is plus one half of 1 percentage point over the federal short-term rate. These rates are also adjusted quarterly. The rate for the first quarter of 1999 was 7 per cent for non-corporate taxpayers and 6 per cent for corporate taxpayers. For the last 3 quarters of 1999 was 8 per cent for non-corporate taxpayers and 7 per cent for corporate taxpayers.

One good feature of the U.S. system is global interest netting. Under this system no interest is imposed to the extent that underpayment and overpayment interest run simultaneously on equal amounts. Moreover, a taxpayer that has made an overpayment of tax can ask for adjustment of such tax against the payment of tax for the next year.

AUSTRALIA

Interest on Underpayment of Tax

In Australia, a taxpayer is liable to pay interest on the amount that remains unpaid after the due date for payment. Where an assessment is amended to increase one's tax liability, interest is payable on the amount of increase. The period for which interest is payable is the period starting from the day on which the underpaid tax should have been paid and ending on the date on which the assessment is made. The rate at which interest is payable has been revised from time to time. It was 8.8 per cent per annum for the period from January 1, 1998 until June 30, 1999.

From July 1, 1999 it is proposed to replace the existing late payment interest with a uniform tax deductible interest charge, based on the outstanding balance called, the general interest charge (GIC). The GIC will apply in the same situation where interest applies. The GIC rate for a day is the rate worked out by adding 8 per cent to the weighted average yield for the 13 week Treasury Note yield rate for that particular day and dividing the total by the number of days in a calendar year.

Interest on Tax Early Paid

In Australia, interest is allowed where income tax is paid by the taxpayer more than 14 days before the day on which the relevant amount becomes due and payable. The interest rate for early payment was 4.8 per cent per annum for the period from January 1, 1998 until June 30, 1999. From July 1, 1999, early payment interest shall be payable on the GIC. A taxpayer can ask for the payment of the interest on early payment of tax or can claim the interest as a credit in the return for the income year in which entitlement to the interest arises. Early payment interest is assessable to tax. The rate of interest on tax paid early in Australia is much less than the interest payable on the tax unpaid.

Interest on Overpayments

Interest is also payable if any refund is due under different circumstances, such as refund as a result of successful objection against an assessment or as a result of a successful review of an appeal against the Commissioner, or if refund is due in ordinary assessment process. As the provisions are detailed, all the cases are not taken up here. The period for which the refund is due differs in different circumstances. The rate of interest on overpayment during the income year 1999-2000 was 4.72 per cent in the first quarter and it rose to 5.65 per cent in the last quarter of the year.

MALAYSIA

Malaysia being an Islamic country, no interest is levied for the late/short payment of tax nor is any interest allowed for the excess payment of the tax.

PAKISTAN

Pakistan like Malaysia, being an Islamic country, interest is not levied for the late payment of taxes. However, additional tax is charged for failure, or delay in the payment of taxes.

Additional Tax in Pakistan

Additional tax at the rate of 18 per cent per annum is leviable for failure to pay the tax deducted at source and failure to pay the advance tax. The additional tax is calculated from the date on which the amount was payable to the date on which it is paid in case of tax deducted at source. However, in the case of advance tax it is calculated upto the date of actual payment or September 30 of the financial year next following, whichever is earlier.

Additional tax at the rate of 18 per cent per annum is also levied for failure to pay tax with return. The additional tax is calculated from the first day of October or the date on which tax is payable, whichever is later to the date on which the tax is paid or the date on which the order of assessment is made. An additional tax at the rate of 18 per cent per annum is also levied for failure to pay the tax levied or penalty levied within the time allowed in the notice of demand. The additional tax is calculated from the date on which such tax or penalty was originally payable to the date on which it is paid.

INDIA

Interest is payable by the assessee under the Indian Income Tax Act in the following cases;

Interest for Default in Furnishing Return of Income

If the taxpayer fails to furnish the return or furnishes return after the due date, he shall be liable to pay interest under Sec. 234A at the rate of 1.5 per cent (reduced to 1.25 per cent from June 1, 2001) per month or part of the month, from the due date of filing the return of income and ending on the date of furnishing the return and if no return is filed, then ending on the date of completion of assessment. Interest shall be payable on the tax payable on the assessment less any advance tax paid or tax deducted at source. Tax paid under self-assessment is not deducted.

Interest for Default in Payment of Advance Tax

Every taxpayer in India whose advance tax payable is Rs.5,000 or more is required to pay advance tax in fixed instalments. If any person by whom advance tax is payable has failed to pay it then he shall be liable under Sec. 234B to pay interest on the assessed tax[2] at the rate of 1.5 per cent (reduced to 1.25 per cent from June 1, 2001) for every month or part thereof or part of month. If the advance tax paid is less than 90 per cent of the assessed tax, then interest at the above rate is payable on the amount by which the advance tax falls short of the assessed tax. No interest is payable if the advance tax paid is equal to 90 per cent of the assessed tax or exceed such amount. Interest is payable from April 1 of the assessment year to the date of determination of income under Sec. 143(1) and where a regular assessment is made, to the date of such regular assessment. If any self-assessment tax is paid then interest on such tax paid is computed from April 1 till the date on which tax is so paid.

Interest for Deferment of Advance Tax

In India, advance tax is payable in 3 instalments by a non-corporate taxpayer and in 4 instalments by a corporate taxpayer. If any instalment of advance tax is not paid or is not fully paid, then interest at the rate of 1.5 per cent per month (reduced to 1.25 per cent from June 1, 2001) is charged under Sec. 234C on the amount of advance tax instalment not paid or on the shortfall of advance tax instalment paid and actually due on any instalment payment date.

Interest for Late Payment of Income Tax

In case of failure on the part of any person to pay tax within 30 days of the service of notice of demand, such person shall be required to pay interest at the rate of 1.5 per cent for every month or part of month (reduced to 1.25 per cent from June 1, 2001) from the expiry of 30 days of the service of the demand notice.

Interest on Refunds

Where any taxpayer is entitled to refund due to excess payment of tax, interest shall be payable to such taxpayer at the rate of 1 per cent per month or part of the month (reduced to 0.75 per cent per month with effect from June 1, 2001) from the first day of the assessment year to the date of grant of refund. If the amount of refund is less than 10 per cent of the tax determined, no interest is paid. In India, also the rate of interest on tax excess paid is less than the interest levied on tax underpaid.

Conclusion

Interest provisions in the selected countries have been summarised in Table 9.1

As shown in the table, interest for late payment or underpayment is payable in all the selected countries except Malaysia. In Pakistan, no interest is levied but additional tax is levied which in fact is a substitute of interest. Rates of interest are comparatively higher in Pakistan and India. Interest is payable in respect of non-payment or underpayment of regular tax in the U.K., the U.S., Australia, Pakistan and India. As regards interest on the overpayment of tax, i.e., refund of excess tax is concerned, it is also payable in all these countries except Malaysia and Pakistan. However, the rates on extra payment are lower than rates of interest on underpayments in the U.K., Australia, Pakistan and India. Rates are however, much lower (nearly half of the rates on underpayments) in the U.K. and Australia. The position of the U.S. is different in two ways, i.e. while rates in the U.S. for individual taxpayers are same, both for overpayments and underpayments, the rates for corporate taxpayers are less by 1 per cent.

Two observations emerge out of the above discussion:

1. Interest rates for the non-payment or underpayment of taxes are in general higher except for the U.S. as compared to interest rates for the overpayment of taxes.
2. The U.S. is the only country amongst the selected countries, which has provided for separate rate of interest for individual and corporate taxpayers.

As such, different rates for levying and allowing interest are not equitable. Interest being a monetary compensation, the rate should be the prevalent rate both for levying and allowing interest. There should not be any hidden penalty as there are separate provisions for levying penalty. Levy of interest should be limited to compensate loss to the revenue arising from late payment.

PENALTY PROVISIONS

The penalty provisions applicable in the selected countries in respect of various defaults of the taxpayers are analysed below:

TABLE 9.1. A SUMMARY OF PROVISIONS RELATING TO INTEREST ON UNDERPAYMENT AND OVERPAYMENT OF TAX

Particulars	U.K.	U.S.	Australia	Malaysia	Pakistan	India
Rate of interest levied for late payment or underpayment of tax	7.5 per cent per annum	Federal short-term late plus three percentage point adjusted every quarter (Interest was 8 percent for 1999).	8.8 per cent per annum (for July 1, 1998 to June 30, 1999).	n.a.	Additional tax at the rate of 18 per cent per annum.	15 per cent per annum with effect from June 1, 2001
Rate of interest on overpaid tax	3 per cent	Federal short term rate plus three percentage points (Interest was 8 per cent for 1999)	4.8 percent (for July 1, 1999 to June 30, 1999)	n.a.	15 per cent per annum from the expiry of 3 months of the date refund become due a	9 per cent per annum with effect from June1, 2001.

THE U.K

In the U.K., besides interest on overdue tax and surcharge for late payment of tax, a taxpayer is subject to the following penalties under different circumstances.

Failure to File a Return on Time

A fixed penalty of £100 is imposed if the return is submitted late. If the return is late by more than 6 months then a further £100 fixed penalty may be imposed. If the return has not been filed 12 months after the filing date, a penalty of 100 per cent of the tax liability may be imposed. If the fixed penalty of £100 is insignificant compared with the tax involved, the Commissioner may direct that a penalty of upto £60 per day be imposed, while the return remains outstanding.

In the case of companies, a fixed penalty of £100 is imposed for delay in filing the return upto 3 months. This amount is increased to £500 if the return is late for 3 consecutive accounting periods. If there is delay of over 3 months, the fixed penalty is £200 which is increased to £1,000 if the return is late for 3 consecutive accounting periods. However, if the delay is more than 6 months, penalty as percentage of tax due is applied which is 10 per cent of tax due if the delay is between 6 to 12 months and 20 per cent of tax due if the delay is over 12 months.

Failure to Notify Chargeability to Tax

An individual to whom the return has not been issued by the Inland Revenue (IR), but is liable to tax for an income year, should notify the IR. In case he fails to notify within 6 months of the end of the income year, he would be liable to a maximum penalty equal to 100 per cent of the tax unpaid by the annual filing date.

Submission of an Incorrect Tax Return

If a taxpayer either negligently or fraudulently, submits an incorrect tax return (or submits incorrect information), a penalty may be imposed of upto 100 per cent of the amount of tax underpaid as a consequence of the incorrect return.

Fraud or Negligence when Claiming Reduced Payment on Account

A taxpayer who makes a claim for reduced payment on account (POA), instalment payments fraudulently, may be subjected to a maximum penalty equal to the difference between the POA actually made and the correct POA.

Failure to Keep Records

A penalty of upto £3000 may be imposed for the failure to maintain adequate records in support of the year's tax return.

Failure to Produce Documents

A penalty of £50 can be imposed for failure to produce documents after a formal notice is given by the revenue authorities during an enquiry and where failure continues then penalty of £30 per day can be imposed. This amount of daily penalty can be increased to £150 per day if so determined by the Commissioner.

THE U.S.

In the U.S., interest as well as penalty is required to be paid in respect of default in filing returns of income or paying tax after the due date, or for underpayment of tax, or for fraud. The following penalties are levied for various defaults.

Failure to File a Return

A taxpayer who does not file his return by the due date is required to pay penalty of 5 per cent of the unpaid tax for each month or part of a month that the return is late but the penalty shall not exceed more than 25 per cent of the unpaid tax. The penalty is based on the tax not paid by the due date without regard to extension on the net amount of tax due on the return after credit of withholding tax, estimated tax and any other credits. If failure to file the return is due to fraud, the penalty is 15 per cent for each month or part of a month that the return is late, up to a maximum of 75 per cent. If the return is filed more than 60 days after the due date or extended due date, the minimum penalty is the lesser of $100 or 100 per cent of the unpaid tax. This penalty is not imposed if the taxpayer can show that failure to file was due to a reasonable cause.

Failure to Pay Tax

Penalty is imposed for failure to pay the taxes as shown by a taxpayer on his return. The penalty is also imposed for failure to pay additional taxes determined to be due on audit. This penalty runs for the period of non-payment beginning after the 21st calendar day following the demand, if the amount demanded is less than $100,000 and after 10th business day if amount demanded is at least $100,000. The penalty is one-half of 1 per cent, i.e. 0.5 per cent of the tax not paid for each month or part of a month it remains unpaid. The maximum penalty is 25 per cent of tax not paid. This penalty increases to one per cent per month after the notice of levy of this penalty is given beginning with the 10th day after the notice of levy.

In case the return is filed late and both the failure to file and the failure to pay penalties are leviable, then penalty for the failure to file will be reduced by penalty for the failure to pay. However, if no return is filed or if a late return understates the amount required to be shown on the return or the penalty for failure to file beyond 60 day applies, then the failure-to-payment penalty attributable to additional tax may not be offset against the penalty of failure to file.

If both the failure-to-file penalty and the failure to pay penalty apply in any month, both the penalties may not be payable if the taxpayer had a reasonable cause. Penalty must be abated if penalties result from reliance on incorrect IRS advice.

Accuracy-related Penalty

In case a taxpayer underpays tax because of either 'negligence' or 'disregard' of rules or regulations or substantially understates his income tax, he shall be required to pay penalty equal to 20 per cent of the underpayment. However, this penalty will not be levied on any part of an underpayment on which a fraud penalty is charged. The penalty is based on the part of the underpayment due to negligence or disregard of rules and regulations and not on the entire underpayment on the return. (Negligence includes a failure to make a reasonable attempt to comply with the tax law or to exercise ordinary and reasonable care in preparing a return. Disregard includes any careless, reckless, or intentional disregard.) A substantial understatement exists when the understatement for the year exceeds the greater of 10 per cent of tax required to be shown on the return or $5,000 ($10,000 for corporation other than 'S' corporations. However, penalty is not levied if the taxpayer shows that he acted in good faith and there was reasonable cause for understatement or understatement was based on substantial authority.

Frivolous Return Penalty

There is a penalty of $500 for filing a frivolous return. A frivolous return is one that omits information necessary to determine the taxpayer's tax liability, shows a substantially incorrect tax, or is based upon the taxpayer's desire to impede the collection of tax.

Fraud Penalty

Where underpayment of tax is attributable to fraud, a penalty at the rate of 75 per cent on the portion of underpayment is imposed. If any portion is attributable to fraud, it is presumed that the entire payment is attributable to fraud. The fraud penalty will not apply, if no return is filed except when a return is prepared by the IRS when a person fails to make required return.

AUSTRALIA

In Australia, taxpayers may be liable to pay interest and in some cases penalty as well as interest for not complying with the provisions relating to the furnishing of returns of income, or for the failure to pay the tax or for the tax shortfall or for the failure to keep records or to provide information or for the failure to notify penalty under Sec.163A to 163C. The Commissioner has the discretion to remit penalties and interest in whole or in part in accordance with the established guidelines set out in the Taxation Rulings.

Penalties are imposed under the following circumstances:

Failure to Lodge Returns

Penalty imposed on a person for failure to file a return depends upon on whether he is a non-instalment taxpayer or an instalment taxpayer, and whether the return is due before July 1, 1999 or after July 1, 1999.

Non-instalment Taxpayers:
Return due before July 1, 1999

Non-instalment taxpayers whose tax returns were required to be filed before July 1, 1999 are required to pay the late payment penalty tax at the rate of 8 per cent per annum on the lesser of the assessed income tax[3] and the taxpayer's net tax payable.[4]

Late filing penalty tax is payable from the date after the due lodgement date to the earlier of the day the return is actually lodged and the day the assessment is made. The taxpayer liable to pay penalty tax for failure to file returns is also liable to pay penalty interest under ITAA 36, Sec. 163C on the amount on which and for the same period for which the penalty tax is payable. Interest is payable at the rate provided for under ITAA 36, Sec. 214 A.

Non-instalment Taxpayers:
Return due on or after July 1, 1999

The Government has proposed General Interest Charge (GIC) instead of penalty tax and penalty interest in case the taxpayer fails to file a return which is due after July 1, 1999. The GIC is also calculated on the lesser of the assessed income tax and the net tax payable. The GIR is worked out on a daily compounding basis. The GIC for a day is the rate worked out by adding 8 per cent to the weighted average yield for the 13 week Treasury Note yield rate for that day (determined in accordance with the TAA proposed Sec.8AAD), and dividing that total by the number of days in the calendar year. The daily effective rate will be adjusted each quarter to reflect quarterly movements in the 13 week Treasury Note Yield. The GIC will be deductible under ITAA 97, Sec. 25-5 (1).

Instalment Taxpayer

The amount of late lodgement penalty payable by an instalment taxpayer under Sec.163A is AUD10 for each week or part of a week occurring after the due date and upto the filing of return. The maximum penalty is AUD200. The penalty is payable irrespective of whether any tax is payable.

Failure to Provide Information

The taxpayer is required to pay under ITAA Sec. 222, a penalty equal to 200 per cent of the tax payable for the failure to provide information relating to the taxpayer's affairs in relation to an income year. Thus, no penalty is payable if the tax is not payable.

Failure to Keep Records

A taxpayer (companies and funds or others also) who fails to keep a record containing particulars of the basis of the calculation of a taxpayer's taxable income and tax liability or refuses or fails to produce such a document, is liable to pay penalty under ITAA Sec. 222(1A) or (1B) of an amount equal to 200 per cent of the tax payable for that year.

Tax Shortfalls and Tax Avoidance Penalty

In Australia, penalty is also levied at different rates if there is a tax shortfall caused by a particular behaviour of the taxpayer. A tax shortfall is the difference between the proper tax and tax calculated on the basis of 'taxation statements' made by the taxpayer. A taxation statement includes information in written, oral or other form given to an ATO officer or to another person for taxation purposes. The provisions of penalty for the tax shortfall are given in ITAA Sec. 222A to 226ZB. The penalty for different reasons causing the tax shortfall are shown below:

Penalty caused by	*Amount of penalty*
(a) Tax evasion	75% of the tax shortfall
(b) Recklessness	50% of the tax shortfall
(c) Tax avoidance	50% of the tax shortfall
(d) No reasonable care	25% of the tax shortfall
(e) No reasonably arguable case	25% of the tax shortfall
(f) Private ruling disregarded	25% of the tax shortfall

In case the shortfall results from a statement made by the taxpayer treating the tax law as applying in a particular way where the position taken is not reasonably arguable, the penalty applies only when the shortfall exceeds the greater of the AUD10,000 or one per cent of the taxpayer's return tax for the year (i.e. tax payable based on the taxpayer's return of income).

Penalty tax on shortfall is increased by 20 per cent where the taxpayer takes steps to prevent or hinder the commission or from becoming aware that a tax shortfall exists. To encourage voluntary compliance and to reduce enforcement costs, there is provision under ITAA 36, Sec. 226E, 226Z for 80 per cent reduction in penalty tax payable due to tax shortfall or tax avoidance schemes, where the taxpayer voluntarily notifies the commissioner of the shortfall before being informed of a tax audit and the penalty tax is reduced to 20 per cent if the taxpayer notifies about the shortfall after being informed of a tax audit.

Penalty for Late Payment

Where the tax including provisional tax or the franking deficit tax (in respect of dividend distribution) remains unpaid after the due date for payment, the taxpayer is liable to pay on the unpaid amount or balance; (1) late payment penalty tax at the rate of 8 per cent per annum (ITAA36, Sec. 207); and (2) late payment penalty interest at the statutory rate. From January 1, 1998 until June 30, 1999 the rate was 8.8 per cent (ITAA Sec. 207A).

Late payment penalty tax and penalty interest may also be imposed for late payment of interest and penalty tax and late lodgement penalties, and are computed on a daily basis from the date the unpaid amount becomes due and payable. The penalty interest payable under Sec. 207A is deductible but not the penalty tax.

MALAYSIA

In Malaysia, penalty and prosecution rules and regulations are merged and in many cases where prosecution is not instituted, a higher penalty is normally payable under the same provisions. Penalties are levied for short/delay in payment of tax. These provisions applicable in Malaysia are analysed below.

Failure to Furnish Return and give Notice of Chargeability

The Director-General (DG) may under Sec. 77(1) require any person by notice in writing to furnish him within a time specified a return of income and under Sec. 77(2) every person who has not been issued notice but who is chargeable to tax shall give notice within 14 days after the expiry of the first 3 months of assessment that he is so chargeable. Accordingly, under Sec.112, any person who makes default in furnishing a return in accordance with Sec. 77(1) or in giving a notice under Sec. 77(2) without any reasonable cause, he shall be guilty of an offence and shall on conviction, be liable to a fine of not less than RM200 and not more than RM2,000 or to an imprisonment of maximum up to 6 months or both.

Where no prosecution is instituted under sub-sec.(1), the DG may require that person to pay a penalty equal to treble the amount of that tax which, before any set off, repayment or relief under this Act, is payable for that year.

Thus, both prosecution and penalty provisions are given under same section. However, penalty is an alternative to prosecution. It obviates such prosecution.

Late Payment of Tax

If a tax demanded in a notice of assessment is not paid within the stipulated 30 days, (time limit is increased to 44 days from the year of assessment 1999), after the service of the notice of assessment, a penalty of 10 per cent shall be added to the tax payable. A notice is issued showing tax and penalty payable. The tax and penalty both are to be paid within one month of the issue of the notice. A further penalty of 5 per cent on the balance shall be levied where the taxpayer does not pay the 10 per cent penalty and balance tax within 60 days from the date of levy of the 10 per cent penalty. Both the 10 per cent and 5 per cent penalties are automatic without any notice being served on the taxpayer. However, penalty can be remitted by the DG, if he is satisfied that delay in payment is caused by the taxpayer's illness.

Similarly, if an instalment payment under the 'Payment by Instalment Scheme' is not made within 30 days from the due date, a penalty of 10 per cent is imposed. This penalty is also automatic without any notice being served on the taxpayer. The notice levying the late payment penalty is issued after the date of the final instalment. Where an approval is given to change the amount of the instalment and the tax payable for the year of assessment exceeds the total of the instalment payable, then the difference that exceeds 30 per cent of the tax payable is liable to a penalty of 10 per cent.

Incorrect Returns

Any person who files an incorrect return by writing or understating any income or gives any incorrect information in respect of his own income or income of any other person, otherwise than in good faith, he shall be guilty of an offence and shall, on conviction be liable to a minimum fine of RM 1,000 and a maximum fine of RM10,000 and shall pay a special penalty of double the amount of tax undercharged due to incorrect return or incorrect information under Sec. 113(1). If no prosecution under sub-sec.(1) has been instituted in respect of the incorrect return, the DG may require that person to pay a penalty equal to the amount of tax undercharged due to incorrect return or incorrect information under Sec. 113(2).

Wilful Evasion

Omission of any income in a return, or making a false statement in the return, or preparing or maintaining or authorising the preparation or maintenance of false books of accounts by any person wilfully and with intent to evade tax or assist any other person to evade tax shall be an offence, and such person shall, on conviction, be liable under Sec. 114(1) to a minimum fine of RM1,000 and a maximum fine of RM20,000 or to imprisonment upto maximum of 3 years or to both and also a penalty of treble the amount of tax undercharged due to such offence.

Obstruction of Officers

Any person who obstructs the DG or any authorised officer or refuses to permit their entry or obstructs them from performing their duty or refuses to produce any books or other document required by them or fails to give reasonable assistance to them shall under Sec. 116 be guilty of an offence and shall on conviction, be liable to a maximum fine of RM4,000 or to imprisonment up to 1 year or both.

No proceedings for an offence due to incorrect return (Sec. 113), or due to obstruction of officers (Sec. 116) can be instituted more than 12 years after the offence was committed. Any person who aids, abets or incites another person to commit the offences mentioned above under Sec. 113, 115 and 116 is deemed to have committed the same offence and is liable to the same penalty.

Power to Compound Offences and Abate or Remit Penalties

Where any person has committed any offence under the Act, the DG may at any time before conviction, compound under Sec. 124(1) the offence and order that person to pay such sum of money, not exceeding the amount of the maximum fine and any special penalty to which that person would have been liable if he had been convicted of the offence, as he thinks fit. The DG may under Sec. 124 (3) abate or remit any penalty imposed under the Income-tax Act 1967 except a penalty imposed on conviction.

PAKISTAN

Provisions for the levy of penalty for late filing of returns, late payment of tax and concealment of income in Pakistan are examined below.

Penalty for Failure to Furnish Returns of Total Income

A penalty equal to one tenth of 1 per cent (0.1 per cent) of the tax payable for each day of the default subject to a minimum of PKR500 and a maximum of 25 per cent of the tax payable is imposable on any person who fails to file a return himself or after receiving a notice, or for failure to file the return in case of discontinued business, or when he is about to leave Pakistan and is required to file his return.

Penalty for Non-payment of Tax

A penalty not exceeding an amount equal to tax (100 per cent of tax) in default may be imposed on a taxpayer when there is default in making payment of any tax. This penalty can be imposed by one order and in case of continuing default by several orders. However the total amount of penalty cannot exceed the amount of tax in default.

Penalty for Concealment of Income

Where any person has concealed his income or furnished inaccurate particulars of such income, a penalty equal to the amount of tax (100 per cent of tax) undercharged due to concealment or furnishing of inaccurate particulars is imposable.

Penalty for Failure to Maintain Prescribed Accounts

The Deputy Commissioner (DC) may under Sec.109 impose a penalty equal to 15 per cent of the tax payable subject to a minimum of PKR200, on any person who without reasonable cause fails to maintain the prescribed accounts as required under Sec. 32(2).

Penalty for Non-compliance with Notice

Where any person has without reasonable cause, failed to give a wealth statement as required under Sec. 58, or failed to attend office or produce books of accounts or documents on the demand of the DC under Sec. 61, the DC may impose under Sec. 110 on him a penalty equal to 15 per cent of the amount of tax, which would have been avoided, if the income as returned by such person had been accepted as the correct income.

INDIA

Penalty provisions applicable in India for the most common defaults by the taxpayer are as follows:

Penalty for Late Furnishing Return of Income

In India, penalty for the filing of returns beyond the due date was merged with the interest for late filing in the year 1989. From the income year 1989 till the income year 1997-98, there was no separate penalty for late filing of return. However, from the income year 1998-99, i.e. the assessment year 1999-2000, penalty provision for late filing of return has been re-introduced. The penalty leviable for late filing of returns on those taxpayers, who have taxable income, is Rs.1,000, where the delay extends beyond the end of the assessment year. No penalty is leviable in such cases if the return is filed after the prescribed due date but before the end of the assessment year. However, those people who do not have taxable income but are required to file a return by virtue of fulfilling one of the six criteria such as owning a motor vehicle, occupation of immovable property are liable for penalty of Rs.500 in case of delay beyond the due date. Both the above penalties have been increased to Rs.5,000 with effect from June 1, 2001.

Penalty for Default in Making Payment of Tax within Prescribed Time

Where any taxpayer makes default in making payment of tax within the time specified, a penalty under Sec. 221(1) maximum to the extent of tax in arrears may be imposed on him. This penalty is payable along with interest for the non-payment of tax under Sec. 220(2).

Penalty for Concealment of Income or Furnishing Inaccurate Particulars of Income

A minimum penalty equal to 100 per cent and maximum 300 per cent of tax sought to be evaded may be imposed on any person who has concealed the particulars of his income or furnished inaccurate particulars of such income. The penalty is in addition to the tax payable by the assessee.

Penalty for Failure to Produce Documents or Accounts, to Attend Office, or to get the Accounts Audited

If a taxpayer has been asked under Sec. 142(1) to produce documents/accounts or to furnish any information in writing or under Sec.143(2) to attend the office or to produce any other evidence or under Sec.142(2A) to get the accounts audited by an accountant and he fails to comply with these requirements, he may be asked to pay a minimum penalty under Sec.271(1)(b) of Rs.1,000 for each failure subject to a maximum of Rs.25,000 for each failure. The amount of penalty leviable for this default has been fixed at Rs.10, 000 with effect from June 1, 2001.

Penalty for concealment and other penalty may be waived under Sec.273A

(4) by the Commissioner on receiving an application by the taxpayer, after considering the circumstances of the taxpayer. A penalty exceeding Rs.100,000 can be reduced or waived under Sec. 273A(4) only with the previous approval of Chief Commissioner or Director-General. The penalty can be imposed only after the taxpayer has been given a reasonable opportunity of being heard and no penalty is imposed if the taxpayer proves that there was reasonable cause for any failure.

Conclusion

Penalty provisions in the selected countries are summarised in Table 9.2 As shown in the table, penalties have been prescribed for various defaults in the selected countries. Monetary penalties can be imposed where the default, attracting penalty is proved without the necessity of the authorities establishing criminal intent on the part of the defaulter. All these countries have provisions for excluding penalty in case the taxpayer is able to show reasonable cause for the occurrence of a default. The penalty for late filing is most severe in Malaysia where the penalty equal to treble the amount of the tax before any set off or repayment can be levied. Penalty for late filing of return in India is Rs.1,000 (increased to Rs.5,000 if the delay is beyond the year of assessment, Penalty for late filing in Pakistan comes to about 3 per cent per month (one tenth of one per cent for each day) of tax payable subject to minimum of Rs.500 and maximum of 25 per cent of tax payable, which means that penalty for late filing for delay of 8 months and more will be same as it gets frozen at 25 per cent of tax. In the U.K., there is a fixed penalty without any relation to the amount of tax and period of delay. For a delay of less than 6 months, a fixed penalty of £100 and for more than 12 months delay, a fixed penalty of £200 is levied. However, for delay beyond 12 months, there is a very severe penalty linked to the tax liability, i.e. 100 per cent of tax liability.

Penalty for late filing of return in Australia is very low. It is just 8 per cent per annum for the delay computed on a daily basis. On the other hand, in the U.S., penalty as high as 5 per cent of the tax underpaid is imposed for each month of delay, which is increased to 25 per cent of the tax underpaid in case of fraud. As such, the penalty of 5 per cent per month for delay in filing a return is highest in the U.S. amongst the selected countries except in Malaysia where the penalty up to treble the amount of tax can be imposed. However, there is overall ceiling of 25 per cent in the U.S. As such, penalty for delay of 5 and more than 5 months will be same.

Accordingly, penalty in the U.S. is more severe for initial period of default but gets frozen for the later part of default and its severity gets diluted. On the other hand, there is a nominal penalty in the U.K. for the initial period of default but becomes more severe for a longer period of default, i.e. 100 per cent of tax if delay is for more than 12 months. So there is no similar pattern for the levy of penalty in the selected countries, except in Australia, and Pakistan where this penalty has a direct connection with the amount of tax

TABLE 9.2. A SUMMARY OF PENALTY PROVISIONS IN THE SELECTED COUNTRIES

Particulars	U.K.	U.S.	Australia	Malaysia	Pakistan	India
For late filling of return	Fixed penalty of £100. If delay more than 6 month, a penalty of £200. If delay more than 12 months, then penalty of 100 percent of the tax liability.	5 per cent of the underpaid tax per month (subject to a maximum of 25 per cent) increased to 15 per cent per month in case failure to file is due to fraud (subject to a maximum of 75 per cent).	8 per cent per annum on lesser of assessed income tax or net tax payable for the period from due date of return.	A penalty equal to treble the amount of the tax payable before any set off, repayment or relief.	One tenth of one per cent (0.1 per cent) of tax payable for each day of default subject to a minimum of PKR 500 and maximum of 25 per cent of the tax payable.	A fixed penalty of Rs.1,000 (increased to Rs.5,000 with effect from June 1, 2001) impossible if the return is not filed within the assessment year.
For failure to pay tax	No penalty. Surcharge levied for tax remaining unpaid more than 28 days after the fixed due date. Fixed rate of surcharge, 5 per cent of tax unpaid. Fixed 10 per cent if tax remains unpaid more than 6 months after due date.	0.5 per cent of tax not paid for each month or part of month it remains unpaid.	Late payment penalty tax at the rate of 8 per cent per annum computed on daily basis from the due date.	Automatic penalty of 10 per cent of tax payable if not paid within 44 days. Further penalty of 5 per cent on balance tax and 10 percent penalty if not paid within 60 days from the levy of 10 per cent penalty.	Total penalty equal to the tax in default can be imposed by one order or by several orders.	Total penalty equal to the tax in default leviable either by one order or by several orders.
For submission of incorrect return	100 per cent of the amount of tax underpaid as a consequence of the incorrect return.	20 per cent of tax underpaid if it is because of negligence or disregard of rules. 75 per cent of tax underpaid if under payment is attributable to fraud.	From 25 per cent to 75 per cent of tax shortfall depending upon the reasons.	A penalty equal to 100 per cent of tax undercharged due to incorrect return. In case of wilful evasion, a penalty of treble the amount of tax undercharged.	A penalty equal to the amount of tax undercharged (100 per cent of tax under paid) due to incorrect return.	Minimum penalty is 100 per cent of tax under paid and maximum penalty is 300 per cent of tax underpaid.

involved, the period of default and the rate of penalty is in accordance with rate of interest. Penalty for late filing in the U.K. for delay beyond 12 months appears to be too high considering the nature of default.

Penalty for failure to pay tax is levied in all the selected countries. In the U.K. and Malaysia, this penalty is automatic. In the U.K., it is a fixed surcharge of 5 per cent of tax unpaid and in case it remains unpaid more than 6 months then a fixed surcharge is 10 per cent. In Malaysia, it is an automatic penalty of 10 per cent of tax payable if not paid within 44 days and a further penalty of 5 per cent if not paid within 60 days from the levy of earlier penalty of 10 per cent. In the U.S. and Australia, this penalty is computed for the period of delay. In the U.S., it is 0.5 per cent per month (with a maximum penalty of upto 25 per cent of tax unpaid increased to 1.00 per cent per month after notice of levy of 0.5 per cent penalty) whereas in Australia, it is computed at the rate of 8 per cent per annum computed on a daily basis from the due date. In India and Pakistan, this penalty is not automatic. The total penalty equal to the amount of tax can be imposed by several orders or by one order. This penalty is on the lower side in the U.K., the U.S., Australia and Malaysia where the maximum penalty is from 15 per cent to 25 per cent whereas in India and Pakistan, it can go upto 100 per cent of the tax unpaid. The objective of this penalty is to achieve tax payment on due date and as such, the penalty has to be such which creates a fear in the mind of taxpayer. Accordingly, a fixed automatic penalty, as in the U.K. and Malaysia, may act as a counter productive after the date of default but may be helpful before the due date in forcing the taxpayer to pay. On the other hand, discretionary penalty, as in India and Pakistan, may not act as a strong deterrent but the fear of levy of penalty may force the taxpayer to pay unpaid taxes. Recurring penalty, as in the U.S. and Australia, for the period of default may be revenue generating but can make the taxpayer complacent and may not act as a strong deterrent.

Penalty for the submission of incorrect returns declaring incorrect income is the most important penalty. The late filing of return, and late payment of tax can be by negligence or by factors beyond the taxpayer's control, whereas chances of intentional default are greater in returns declaring incorrect income. Different amounts of penalties have been prescribed in different countries. In the U.K, Pakistan and Malaysia, it is 100 per cent of tax undercharged due to incorrect return. In India, it is a minimum 100 per cent but the maximum can be upto 300 per cent of tax underpaid. In Malaysia also, this can be upto 300 per cent in case of wilful default. On the other hand, this penalty is very low in the U.S. and Australia. In the U.S., it is 20 per cent and can be 75 per cent if the tax underpaid is due to fraud whereas in Australia, it is levied a minimum of 25 per cent to a maximum of 75 per cent, depending upon the reason for shortfall of tax. As such, there is very large variation in the levy of penalty on account of declaration of incorrect income. In India and Malaysia it goes as high as 300 per cent as against maximum penalty of 75 per cent in the U.S. and Australia. Accordingly, the penalty for incorrect income in India and Malaysia is four times the penalty leviable in the U.S.

and Australia. A penalty tends to serve its purpose only so long as it is within reasonable limits. Once it crosses that limit, it is more likely to increase the rigidity of a taxpayer's recalcitrance than to reform him. Undue harsh penalties tend to breed only defiance of law.

Penalty for submission of incorrect return in India and Malaysia is not commensurate with the nature of default. The penalty need to be one which acts as a deterrent but at the same time helps in a better compliance of law and increases the taxpayer's confidence in the taxation system. Moderate penalty as in the U.S. and Australia, commensurate with the nature of default are more equity-based, revenue productive and administratively good.

TAX OFFENCES AND PROSECUTION PROVISIONS

Penalties by way of imprisonment and/or fine can be imposed when behind the default there is a guilty mind and guilty intent. All the selected countries follow the legal concept of *'mens rea'*—of criminal intent on the part of the wrongdoer for imposing criminal penalties.

THE U.K.

In the U.K., the *Taxes Management Act* (TMA), 1970, prescribes only civil monetary penalties. It does not prescribe any criminal penalty except for Scotland. However, the TMA provides to not to effect any criminal proceedings for any misdemeanour. The Board of Inland Revenue is the prosecuting authority and as such has the option of prosecuting the offender in the criminal courts for offences involving fraud where it considers that it is in the public interest to do so. The Board's practice is not to impose civil penalty where for the same default the taxpayer is being prosecuted. However in case of acquittal, a civil penalty may be imposed.

In Scotland, a person who knowingly makes any false statement or false representation in any return made with reference to tax, may be imprisoned for a term not exceeding 6 months.

THE U.S.

In the U.S., in addition to the levy of interest and penalties, the taxpayer may incur the following criminal penalties:

1. If a person wilfully attempts to evade or defeat any tax imposed or the payment thereof, then upon conviction he shall be fined not more than $100,000 ($500,000 in the case of corporation), or imprisoned for not more than 5 years, or both, together with the cost of prosecution.
2. If a person required under the Code to make a return, keep any records or supply any information or to pay any estimated tax, wilfully fails to make such return, keep such records, or supply such information or pay such estimated tax at the time or times required by law or regulations, shall be fined not more than $25,000 ($100,000 in case of a corporation) or

imprisoned for not more than 1 year or both together with the cost of prosecution.

3. Any person who wilfully delivers any return, account, statement or other document known by him to be fraudulent or to be false in any material matter, or fact, shall be fined not more than $10,000 ($50,000 in the case of corporation) or imprisoned for not more than 1 year or both. These include:
   (a) The suppression of any item of receipt liable to tax in whole or in part, or failure to disclose income chargeable to tax,
   (b) Claiming any deduction for or showing any expenditure not actually incurred, and
   (c) Any investment not disclosed.

AUSTRALIA

In Australia, both penalty and prosecution provisions are applicable in case of failure to file a return, to provide information, to produce documents or evidence. However, if prosecution is instituted, penalty tax is not payable.

The *Taxation Administration Act*, 1953 (TAA) contains offence and prosecution provisions that are applicable where there is a breach of the income tax laws. The offences in some cases carry fines only, while in others carry fine and/or imprisonment. The fine in many cases is higher for second or subsequent offences. Company officers and managers may be liable for taxation offences committed by their companies. In Australia, it is the Audit Prosecution Unit which considers prosecution and if appropriate, refers the matter to the Director of Public Prosecution. The ATO officers are not authorised to use the threat of prosecution nor to advise a taxpayer that there is no intention to prosecute. The offences and prosecution provisions of Australia are shown in Table 9.3

The table shows that the minimum fine is AUD2,200 for individuals as well as companies in respect of the first offence arising due to failure to furnish return, or information or to produce document or for making false or misleading statements. For second such offence, the fine is AUD4,400 both in the case of individual and companies. In respect of some of the above offences, the maximum fine may be AUD5,500 and/or 12 months imprisonment for an individual and AUD27,500 in the case of companies. Besides this, a convicted person may also be ordered to pay up to double or for subsequent offences, treble the amount of tax avoided.

The maximum fine of AUD11,000 and/or 2 years imprisonment in the case of an individual and AUD55,000 in the case of companies is applicable in the case of second offence of falsifying, concealing destroying and altering records or concealing identity with the intent to deceive or obstruct.

In some cases including the failure to file a return or in the case of tax shortfall, because income is omitted from the return or excessive claims are made, the Commissioner may prosecute the offender as an alternative to imposing penalty tax. If a prosecution is instituted, the person ceases to

TABLE 9.3. TAX OFFENCES AND PENALTIES IN AUSTRALIA

Offence	Maximum Penalty, if committed by	
	Natural Person	Corporation
Refusal ro failure to comply with a requirement of a tax law to furnish a return or information, produce (or permit access to) document, answer questions, attend before the Commissioner or give evidence on oath or affirmation (Sec. 8C; 8D; 8E)	1st Offence: AUD2,200 fine 2nd Offence: AUD4,400 fine 3rd and each subsequent offence; AUD5,500 fine and/or 12 months imprisonment	1st Offence: AUD2,200 fine 2nd Offence: AUD4,400 fine 3rd and each subsequent offence; AUD27,500 fine.
	A convicted person may also be ordered to pay up to double or, for subsequent offences, treble the amount of tax avoided.	
Refusal or failure to comply with a court order to give evidence or furnish a return or information (Sec. 8G; 8H)	Fine of AUD5,500 and/or 12 months imprisonment	AUD27,500 fine.
	A convicted person may also be ordered to pay up to double or, for subsequent offences, treble the amount of tax avoided.	
Making a false or misleading statement or an omission which makes the statement misleading, subject to a statutory defence (Sec. 8K; 8M). Incorrectly keeping records, subject to a statutory defence (Sec. 8L; 8M).	1st Offence: AUD2,200 fine 2nd and each subsequent offence: AUD4,400 fine. 1st offence: AUD2,200 fine.	2nd and each subsequent offence: AUD4,400 fine.
	A convicted person may also be ordered to pay the Commissioner up to double the amount of tax avoided (Sec. 8W)	
Recklessly or knowingly making a false or misleading statement or recklessly or knowingly omitting something from a statement which makes it misleading (Sec. 8N; 8P; 8R) Recklessly or knowingly incorrectly keeping records (Sec. 8Q; 8R)	1st Offence: AUD3,300 fine. 2nd and each subsequent offence; AUD5,500 fine and/or 12 months imprisonment.	1st Offence: AUD3,300 fine. 2nd and each subsequent offence: AUD27,500 fine.
	A convicted person may also be ordered to pay the Commissioner up to double or, for second and subsequent offences, treble the amount of tax avoided (Sec. 8W)	
Falsifying, concealing, destroying or altering records with intent to deceive or obstruct (Sec. 8T; 8V) Falsifying or concealing identity or address with intent to deceive or obstruct (Sec. 8U; 8V)	1st Offence: AUD5,500 fine and/or 12 months imprisonment. 2nd and each subsequent offence; AUD11,000 fine and/or 2 years imprisonment.	1st offence; AUD27,500 fine. 2nd and each subsequent offence: AUD55,000 fine.
	A convicted person may also be ordered to pay the Commissioner up to double or, for second and subsequent offences, treble the amount of tax avoided (Sec. 8W).	
Obstructing ATO officers (Sec 8X)	AUD2,200 fine and/or imprisonment for 6 months. AUD11,000 fine.	

Note: Sections referred to in the table are Sections of the Taxation Administration Act.
Source: CCH, 1999, *Australian Master Tax* Guide, pp. 1216-17.

be liable to pay the penalty tax, even if the prosecution is later withdrawn (TAA, Sec. 82E). In such a case, any amount paid or applied by the Commissioner to discharge that liability for the penalty tax must be refunded or applied towards any other tax liability of the person. As such, in Australia, both civil penalty and criminal prosecution cannot be invoked. It can be either of the two.

MALAYSIA

Prosecution provisions in Malaysia are merged with penalty provisions which have been examined under the head 'Penalty' earlier.

PAKISTAN

Prosecution for Non-compliance of Certain Statutory Obligations

Where any person without reasonable cause, fails to deduct tax at source, or pay advance tax if required or fails to file a return after getting notice under Sec. 56, or file a return in case of discontinued business or furnish a return if he intends to leave Pakistan with no intention of returning back, or fails to file his wealth statement if required under Sec. 58, or to produce documents and books of accounts if required under Sec. 61 or obstructs any income tax authority in the discharge of functions, he may be subject to an imprisonment for a term up to 1 year or with fine or both.

Prosecution for False Statement in Verification

A person may be punishable with imprisonment for upto 3 years or with fine or with both for making a statement in any verification in any return or any other document furnished which is false or which he does not believe to be true.

Prosecution for Concealment of Income

For any concealment of income or deliberate furnishing of an inaccurate return, any person may be punishable with imprisonment for a term of upto 5 years or with fine or with both.

Prosecution for Abatement or Assistance to Deliver False Return, Statement or Certificate

Any person who knowingly and wilfully aids, abates, assists or induces another person to make or deliver a false return, account, statement or certificate or wilfully delivers such false return, statement or certificate on behalf of another person, he shall be punishable with imprisonment for a term of upto 3 years or with fine or with both.

The Commissioner has the power under Sec. 126 to compound any offence either before or after the institution of proceedings and to ask the person concerned to pay the amount for which the offence may be compounded.

TABLE 9.4. OFFENCES AND PROSECUTION PROVISIONS IN INDIA

Section Number	Nature of Offence	Rigorous Imprisonment	
		Minimum Period	Maximum Period
1	2	3	4
276C(1)	Wilful attempt to evade tax, penalty or interest imposable under the Act.	If tax evaded exceeds Rs.100,000: 6 months; otherwise: 3 months and fine	If tax evaded exceeds Rs.100,000: 7 years; otherwise: 3 years (and fine)
276C(2)	Wilful attempt to evade the payment of any tax, penalty or interest.	3 months and fine at the discretion of court	3 years (and fine)
276CC	Wilful failure to file return of income before expiry of the assessment year and where tax payable after credit of tax deducted at source and advance tax exceed Rs.3,000	If tax evaded exceeds Rs.100,000: 6 months; otherwise: 3 months and fine	If tax evaded exceeds Rs.100,000: 7 months; otherwise: 3 years (and fine)
277	Making a false statement in verification or delivering a false account or statement.	If tax evaded exceeds Rs.100,000: 6 months; otherwise: 3 months (and fine)	If tax evaded exceeds Rs.100,000: 7 months; otherwise: 3 years (and fine)
278	Abatement to make a false statement or declaration.	If tax evaded exceeds Rs.100,000: 6 months; otherwise: 3 months (and fine)	If tax evaded exceeds Rs.100,000: 7 months; otherwise: 3 years (and fine)
278A	Punishment for second and subsequent offences under Sec. 276C(1), 276CC, 277 or 278	6 months for every offence.	7 years for every offence.

Source: Dr. Vinod K. Singhania and Kapil Singhania, *Direct Taxes, Law and Practice* (Delhi: Taxmann, 2001).

INDIA

In India, the *Income Tax Act*, 1961, gives the power of prosecution to the income tax authorities in respect of offences committeed by the taxpayers. Proceedings for the offences can be started only at the instance of the Commissioner or Commissioner (Appeals). A penalty can be imposed and at the same time prosecution can also be launched. These include failure to furnish a return of income or failure to produce books of accounts and documents or failure to comply with a direction to get the accounts audited or concealment of income. While a penalty is imposable for these defaults in general, prosecution is executed only if the above defaults are wilful. Provisions relating to prosecution for offences are given in Table 9.4.

As shown in the table, the imprisonment of minimum 6 months and maximum 7 years is imposed along with a fine in case the tax evaded exceeds Rs.100,000 in the following circumstances:

1. Wilful attempt to evade tax, penalty, or interest imposable under the Act.
2. Wilful failure to file return of income.

3. Making a false statement in verification or delivering a false account or statement.
4. Abatement to make a false statement or declaration.

Where the tax evaded in the above circumstances is up to Rs.100,000, imprisonment shall be of a minimum of 3 months and a maximum of 3 years and a fine. If the tax evaded exceeds Rs.100,000, the imprisonment is a minimum 6 months and maximum 7 years for every offence.

The Chief Commissioner or a Director-General either before or after the institution of proceedings can compound any such offence.

Tax offences and prosecution provisions in selected countries are summarised in Table 9.5

Conclusion

The income tax laws of the selected countries not only provide for monetary penalties but also criminal penalties by way of imprisonment and fine. In the U.S, India and Pakistan, both monetary penalty and prosecution can be invoked for the same default. However, in the U.K., Australia and Malaysia, monetary penalty is not imposed where the taxpayer is prosecuted for the same offence.

Different countries have provided different punishment for various offences in the income tax laws. In the U.K., Board of Internal Revenue can prosecute a person under the criminal law of the U.K. for any misdemeanour in the criminal courts. Though there is no legal provision for not levying penalty where prosecution is initiated, the Board's practice is not to impose civil penalty where prosecution is initiated. In the U.S., punishment for attempt to evade tax or payment thereof is more severe as compared to the punishment for the filing of incorrect return. The maximum punishment is in India, where it can be imprisonment of 7 years and fine if tax evaded exceeds Rs.100,000. In the U.S., it is imprisonment of not more than 5 years and fine of $100,000 for attempt to evade tax. For filing an incorrect return in the U.S., the punishment is imprisonment of not more than 1 year, whereas in Australia, it is 12 months for the first offence and 24 months for the second offence. In Malaysia, it is 3 years imprisonment, in Pakistan, it is 5 years imprisonment and in India it is up to 7 years imprisonment.

In prosecution, it is not necessary that punishment should be by way of imprisonment only. It can be by way of fine and or both, i.e. fine and imprisonment. The amount of fine is stated in the tax laws of U.S., Australia and Malaysia. However, no amount has been stated in the tax laws of India and Pakistan and criminal courts have the power to impose fine as it may deem fit looking to the facts and circumstances of the case. For the same offence, the penalty in India is most severe, i.e. 7 years, whereas in the U.S. and Australia, it is for one year only. In India, the punishment is same for all the 3 offences shown in Table 9.5, though there is less severe penalty for failure to file return and attempt to evade tax in other countries.

TABLE 9.5. A SUMMARY OF TAX OFFENCES AND PROSECUTION PROVISIONS

Particulars	U.K.	U.S.	Australia	Malaysia	Pakistan	India
Attempt to evade tax or payment thereof	No specific criminal penalty prescribed in U.K. income tax law. However, U.K. income tax law provides to not to effect criminal proceedings for any misdemeanor.	Imprisonment of not more than 5 years or fine of not more than $100,000 ($500,000 in the case of corporation) or both.	12 months imprisonment and/or fine of AUD5,500 for first offence and 24 months imprisonment and/or fine of AUD11,000 for 2nd offence.	Imprisonment for a maximum of 3 years or minimum fine of RM1,000 and a maximum fine of RM20,000 or both.	Imprisonment up to one year or fine or both	Imprisonment of minimum 3 years and maximum 7 years and fine if tax evaded exceeds Rs.100,000. Otherwise imprisonment of minimum 3 months and maximum 6 months and fine.
Failure to file return	No criminal penalty prescribed in U.K. income tax law except for Scotland.	Imprisonment of not more than 1 year or fine of not more than $25,000 ($100,000 in the case of corporation) or both.	Fine of AUD2,200 and 4,400 in 1st and 2nd offence. 12 months imprisonment and/or fine of AUD5,500 in case of 3rd offence.	Maximum imprisonment up to 6 months or minimum fine of RM200 and a maximum fine of RM 2,000 or both.	Imprisonment up to one year or with fine or both.	Same as above.
Filing of incorrect return	In Scotland, imprisonment for a term up to 6 month for false statement. However, U.K. income tax law provides to not to effect criminal proceedings for any misdemeanor.	Imprisonment of not more than 1 year or fine of not more than AUD10,000 ($50,000 in case of corporation) or both.	12 months imprisonment and/or fine of AUD5,500 for first offence and 24 months imprisonment and/or fine of AUD11,000 for 2nd offence. Convicted person may be asked to pay double the tax avoided in case of 1st offence and treble the tax avoided in case of 2nd and subsequent offence.	Minimum fine of RM1,000 and maximum fine of RM10,000 and also a penalty of double the amount of tax undercharged.	Imprisonment up to 5 years or fine or both.	Same as above.

NOTES

1. Report of the Expert Group to Rationalise and Simplify the Income Tax Law, *Current Tax Reporter*, Vol. 138, 1997, p. 128 .
2. Assessed tax means tax on total income determined under summary assessment under Sec. 143(1) (excluding additional tax) or on regular assessment under Sec. 143(3) as reduced by tax deducted or collected at source on any income which is subject to such deduction or collection and which is taken into account in computing such total income.
3. Assessed income tax means income tax for the year after allowing any deduction under Sec.100(2) or any rebates, but before crediting or applying any amounts under the PAYE and other tax collection systems or any advance payment of tax.
4. Net tax payable means the sum of the taxpayer's tax liabilities (i.e. assessed income tax, penalty tax, interest, higher education contribution and financial supplement assessment debts.) less the sums of amounts credited or applied against the assessed income tax (i.e. amounts deducted under the PAYE, PPS and RPS provision amounts deducted under TFN or other withholding tax arrangements, provisional tax payments and foreign tax credits) and any advance payments of tax.

CHAPTER 10

Conclusions

A comparison of income tax system of the six selected countries has been a formidable task. Many issues have arisen which point out the unique characteristics of the tax system of some countries and which raise issues of vital importance. These need further discussion and debate.

The U.S. system of levying tax on the world-wide income in the hands of the U.S. citizen as against the system prevailing in other countries where such income is taxable only in the hands of resident taxpayers, appears to be discriminating. On the other hand, the Malaysian system of levying tax in the hands of resident taxpayers those incomes which arise outside Malaysia only when these are remitted to Malaysia seems to narrow the scope of taxable income in that country. Such difference in the tax system may affect the taxpayers liability differently in these countries. This requires a debate as to which system should be adopted so that it is equitable as well as administratively convenient.

As regards the tax unit is concerned, the tax is levied on individual basis in most of these countries. In the U.S., however, the married taxpayers have the option either to file return jointly or separately. While on the one hand, the married couples earning unequal incomes in the U.S. will bear less burden if they file returns jointly, the difference in the tax rate structure of married individuals filing separately and filing jointly complicates the tax system.

While the progressive tax rate structure in the case of individual taxpayer is adopted in all these countries, the tax rates in the developed countries are found to be higher than that of the developing countries.

Individual income tax structure of India does not seem to be truly progressive, and the gap in the levels of income at which different rates are applicable also does not appear to be reasonable considering the gap in the income levels of other countries. As the level of income at which the maximum marginal rate is applicable in India is very low, the income tax at maximum tax rate is payable even by individual taxpayers whose taxable income is not very high. Thus, it needs some readjustment so that the medium income group taxpayer do not bear the maximum burden at the cost of the high income earners.

Although the agricultural income in Pakistan and India is exempt from tax, yet the taxable agricultural income has been found to form a small part of taxable income in those countries where agricultural income is taxable. Losses from farm activity in the U.S. have been found to be more than the income from farm activity there in the case of individual taxpayers. Thus, it appears that levying tax on agricultural income in India may not result in higher tax revenue. Rather, it may increase the administrative cost.

While personal exemptions are meant to provide relief to the low income earner taxpayers, the system of inflation adjustment in the U.K. and U.S. in respect of fixing the amount of personal, spouse and dependent exemptions, appears to be rational. The system in the U.S. of phasing out exemptions and tax credits as the gross income exceeds a certain level, and of withdrawing completely the exemption if such income reaches another fixed higher level, appears to be equity-based. It requires minimum changes in the income tax policy.

Fringe benefits are taxable in the hands of employees in all these countries except in Australia, where these benefits are taxable in the hands of the employer. This system is used by Australia to prevent employers from giving a large part of salary in the form of benefits-in-kind in respect of which either full or partial exemption could be claimed earlier. Fringe benefits in the U.K. and Malaysia are taxable on the basis of the cost of the facility to the employer, while in the U.S., these are taxed on the basis of the fair-market value of the benefit. Some fringe benefits are exempt altogether in all these countries. There are other specified fringe benefits, which are taxable in the U.K. and India only in the hands of specified employees who earn income above a certain level. In Pakistan, some fringe benefits are taxable at a much higher value in the case of those employees whose taxable salary exceeds a certain level of salary income.

In all the countries, the historical cost is used as the basis for computation of depreciation. These countries, except Australia, allow deduction on account of depreciation as a tax incentive rather than as actual business charge. To encourage investment in productive assets, an additional deduction is allowed in the form of either the first year allowance or the annual deduction in the U.K., Malaysia, Pakistan and the U.S. Pooling of assets system for allowing depreciation which is being followed by the U.K., Australia and India, though administratively convenient, lacks equity

The system of allowing loss on sale of assets in India at the time of sale of all the assets in block rather than on the sale of individual asset alone, appears to be inequitable. Further, treating such loss which arises on the sale of entire block of assets as short-term capital loss is not only against equity, it is also against the general trend prevailing in other countries.

Although the debate continues, on whether the capital gains should be taxed or not, yet all these countries have opted to levy tax on capital gains. However, many variations have been found in the manner in which the capital gains tax is levied. In Malaysia and Pakistan, the base itself, i.e. the items included in the definition of capital asset is very narrow. Besides, concession in tax rates, relief in the form of market-value substitution, indexation and annual exemptions are also provided in different ways. Another common method of providing relief as well as encouraging investment is to either exempt or defer capital gains tax on the investment of either the entire sales consideration or only the capital gain in the like-kind assets or in the specified assets. Thus, so many concessions are likely to affect not only the revenue, these provide unnecessary benefit to those persons who hold such capital assets and have the capacity to pay taxes.

In spite of so many authors pleading for the reduction or elimination of tax reliefs and incentives, these continue to be allowed in various forms and manner. Social reliefs in the form of personal allowance, spouse allowance, children allowance, dependent allowance and medical allowance are allowed in large number in the developed countries. The business-related allowance, in the form of tax holiday in respect of industrial undertakings set-up in either specific zones, areas or manufacturing certain specified goods, are accorded a high priority in the developing nations. While social-welfare incentives are need-based, the business incentives are meant to be growth oriented. While the former reduces the current income tax base, the latter on the other hand may increase the future tax base. These business-related incentives appear to be useful for the economic growth of the developing countries.

As regards the dividend income, the maximum burden is in the U.S., which follows the classical system. The tax is levied both in the hands of the company and the shareholders. This system is not equity based as the same income is taxed twice. The full imputation system of dividend taxation in Australia and Malaysia and partial imputation system in the U.K. provide relief from double taxation. The imputation system may prove to be useful in encouraging the investment in the companies. In Pakistan, there is tax on the company if it does not distribute its income, while in India, there is tax on the company if it distributes dividend.

The system of allowing adjustment of loss suffered by a company in future in the U.K., U.S., Australia and India, subject to the continuity of the company ownership is different from the rule applicable in Malaysia, where adjustment is allowed without any such condition. The alternative minimum tax provisions are applicable in the U.S. on individual and corporate taxpayers both. As against this, the minimum alternative tax provisions are applicable in India only in respect of individual taxpayers. Although, the U.S. system is equity-based, it seems to complicate the system more rather than generating additional revenue.

The self-assessment system is being gradually adopted in all the countries. The process of selection of returns for scrutiny assessment appears to be more systematic in the U.S. and Australia. The system of negotiated settlement at an early stage applicable in the U.S., Australia may be helpful in resolving disputes and in avoiding unnecessary litigation.

Search provisions in India appear to be harsh as it is the only country among the selected countries which empowers its officials to seize assets and books of accounts.

While the deduction of tax at source system is used in Pakistan and India in respect of a large number of incomes including salary and interest, it is used in developed countries mainly in respect of salary income. This may be partly due to the poor compliance system and party due to efforts made by the revenue authorities to generate the revenue at the earliest.

The system of payment of advance tax in India on the basis of current year income does not appear to be rational. The requirement to pay last instalment, even before the end of the year, i.e. before such income has been earned, does not seem to be justified.

Penalty and prosecution provisions applicable in India in respect of various defaults of the taxpayers appear to be harsh. The system in Australia not to impose penalty, if the prosecution is instituted, appears to be rational. The objective of levying penalty should be to penalise the defaulting taxpayers to the extent of his default, and not to raise revenue.

Bibliography

I. Books

Aaron, Henry J., and Michael J. Boskin (eds.), *The Economics of Taxation* (Washington, D.C.: The Brookings Institution, 1980).

Aggarwal, Manju, *Tax Incentives and Investment Behaviour* (Delhi: Indian Institute of Finance, 1988).

Aggarwal, Pawan K., *India: A Review of its Tax System and Recent Tax Reform Proposals* (New Delhi: NIPFP, 1995).

Ahmad, Ehtisham, and Nicholas Stern, *The Theory and Practice of Tax Reform in Developing Countries* (New Delhi: Foundation Books, 1991).

Ault, Hugh J., *Comparative Income Taxation: A Structural Analysis* (The Netherlands: Kluwer Law International, 1997).

Australian Master Tax Guide (Sydney: CCH Australia Ltd., 2001).

Bagchi, Amaresh, and Nicholas Stern, *Tax Policy and Planning in Developing Countries* (Delhi: Oxford University Press, 1994).

Bird, Richard M., and Oliver Oldman (eds.), *Readings on Taxation in Developing Countries* (Baltimore: The Johns Hopkins Press, 1967).

Bird, Richard M., 'Tax Administration and Tax Reform: Reflections on Experience', in Shirazi, Javad Khalilzadeh and Anwar Shah, *The Tax Policy in Developing Countries* (Washington, D.C.: The World Bank, 1994).

Borkar, V.V., *Income Tax Reform in India* (Bombay: Popular Prakashan, 1971).

Boskin, Michael J., and Charles E. Mclure, Jr. (eds.), *World Tax Reform: Case Studies of Developed and Developing Countries* (San Francisco: ICS Press, 1990).

Bradford, David F., *Untangling the Income Tax* (Boston, Massachusetts: Harvard University Press, 1986).

Broadway, Robin W., Dale Chua, and Frank Flatters, 'Investment Incentive and the Corporate Tax System in Malaysia', in Anwar Shah (ed.), *Fiscal Incentives for Investment and Innovation* (New York: Oxford University Press for the World Bank, 1995).

Chaturvedi and Pithisaria, *Income Tax Law* (Nagpur: Wadhwa and Co, 1998).

Chelliah, Raja J., *Towards Sustainable Growth: Essays in Fiscal and Financial sector Reforms in India* (Delhi: Oxford University Press, 1996).

Dasgupta, Arindam, and Dilip Mookherjee, *Incentives and Institutional Reform in Tax Enforcement. An Analysis of Developing Country Experience* (Delhi: Oxford University Press, 1998).

Davies, David G., *United States Taxes and Tax Policy* (Cambridge, London: Cambridge University Press, 1986).

FICCI, *Direct Taxes: An International Comparison* (New Delhi: FICCI, 1969).

Gale, William G., 'What Can America Learn From the British Tax System?' in Joel Slemrod (ed.), *Tax Policy in the Real World* (Cambridge: Cambridge University Press, 1999).

Gandhi, Ved P., *Some Aspects of India's Tax Structure: An Economic Analysis* (Bombay: Vora & Co. Publishers Pvt. Ltd., 1970).

Gillis, Malcolm (ed.), *Tax Reforms in Developing Countries* (Durham: Duke University Press, 1989).

Goode, Richard, 'A New Method of Taxing Capital Gains and Losses', in Richard M. Bird and Oliver Oldman (eds.), *Readings on Taxation in Developing Countries* (Baltimore: The Johns Hopkins Press, 1967).

———, *The Individual Income Tax* (Washington, D.C.: The Brookings Institution, 1976).

Haq, Ikramul, *Practical Handbook of Income Tax* (Lahore: Lahore Law Publications, 1999).

Harberger, Arnold C. and Martin J. Bailey (eds.), *The Taxation of Income from Capital* (Washington, D.C.: The Brookings Institution, 1969).

Harberger, Arnold C., 'Principles of Taxation Applied to Developing Countries: What We Have Learned', in Michael J. Boskin and Charles E. McLure, Jr. (eds.), *World Tax Reform: Case Studies of Developed and Developing Countries* (California: ICS Press, 1990).

Hellawell, Robert (ed.), *United States Taxation and Developing Countries* (N.Y.: Columbia University Press, 1980).

Heller, Walter W., 'Fiscal Policies for Under-developed Countries', in Richard M.Bird and Oliver Oldman (eds.), *Readings on Taxation in Developing Countries* (Baltimore: The Johns Hopkins Press, 1967).

Illersic, A.R., *The Taxation of Capital Gains* (London: Staples Press Ltd, 1962.).

IMF, *Government Finance Statistics Yearbook* (Washington D.C.: IMF, 1999).

———, *International Financial Statistics Year Book* (Washington D.C.: IMF, 1997).

———, *World Economic Outlook*, May 2001 and May 1996

Jain, Anil Kumar, *Some Aspects of Income Tax Administration in India* (New Delhi: Uppal Publishing House, 1983).

———, *Taxation of Income in India: An Empirical Study since 1939* (Delhi: The Macmillan Company of India Ltd., 1975).

James, Simon and Christopher Nobes, *The Economics of Taxation: Principles, Policy and Practice* (New York: Prentice-Hall, 1998).

Kaldor, Nicholas, 'Tax Reform in India', in Richard M. Bird and Oliver Oldman (eds.), *Readings on Taxation in Developing Countries* (Baltimore: The Johns Hopkins Press, 1967).

Kay, J.A., and M.A. King, *The British Tax System* (London: Oxford University Press, 1990).

Keen, Michael, 'Peculiar Institutions: A British Perspective on Tax Policy in the United States', in Joel Slemrod (ed.), *Tax Policy in the Real World* (Cambridge: Cambridge University Press, 1999).

Kumar, D., *The Cambridge Economic History of India*, Vol. II (Cambridge: Cambridge University Press, 1982).

McLure, Jr., Charles E., 'Appraising Tax Reforms', in Michael J. Boskin and Charles E. McLure, Jr. (eds.), *World Tax Reform: Case Studies of Developed and Developing Countries* (San Francisco: ICS Press, 1990).

Melville, Alan, *Taxation Finance Act:* 2000 (Harlow, England: Pearson Education Ltd., 2001).

Messere, K., (ed.), *The Tax System in Industrialised Countries* (Oxford University Press, 1998).

Messere, Ken, *Tax Policy in OECD Countries: Choices and Conflicts* (Amsterdam: IFBD Publications, 1993).

Mongia, J.N., *Tax Patterns around the Globe: A Treatise on Comaprative Taxation System* (New Delhi: Neera Enterprises, 1984).

Murphy, Kevin E. and Mark Higgins, *Concepts in Federal Taxation* (Cincinnati, Ohio: South-Western College Publishing, 1999).

Musgrave, Richard, 'Tax Reform in Developing Countries', in David Newbery and Nicholas Stern (eds.), *The Theory of Taxation for Developing Countries* (Washington, D.C.: Oxford University Press, 1987).

National Institute of Public Finance and Policy, *Direct Taxes in Selected Countries: A Profile* (New Delhi: NIPFP, December 1989).

National Tax Research Center, *The Fiscal Incentives of Selected Countries in Asia and the Pacific* (Phillippines: National Tax Research Center, 1986).

Newbery, David and Nicholas Stern (eds.), *The Theory of Taxation for Developing Countries*, A World Bank Research Publication (N.Y.: Oxford University Press, 1987)

Nightingale, Kath, *Taxation, Theory and Practice* (Harlow, England: Pearson Education Ltd., 2000).

O.E.C.D., *International Comparison of Tax Depreciation Practices* (Paris: O.E.C.D., 1975).

———, *The Personal Income Tax Base-A Comparative Survey* (Paris: O.E.C.D., 1999).

———, *The Taxation of Fringe Benefits* (Paris: O.E.C.D., 1988).

Panchmukhi, P.R., *Tax Rate and Tax Revenue: A Quantitative Study* (New Delhi: Har Anand Publications, 1996)

Palkhivala, N.A. and B.A. Palkhivala, *The Law and Practice of Income Tax*, Vol. *I* (Bombay: N.M. Tripathi Pvt Ltd, 1990).

Pandey, A.T., 'A Study of Changing Dimensions of Taxation of Income in India' (an unpublished Ph.D. thesis, Faculty of Commerce: Amravati University, 1992).

Pechman, Joseph A. (ed.), *Tax Reform and the U.S. Economy* (Washington, D.C.: The Brookings Institution, 1987).

——— (ed.), *What should be Taxed: Income or Expenditure?* (Washington D.C.: The Brookings Institution, 1980).

——— (ed.), *World Tax Reform: A Progress Report*, (Washington, D.C.: The Brookings Institution, 1988).

———, *Federal Tax Policy* (Washington D.C.: The Brookings Institution, 1971).

———, *Tax Reform: The Rich and the Poor* (New York: Harvester Wheatsheaf, 1989).

Pope, Thomas R. and John L. Kramer (eds.), *Prentice-Hall's Federal Taxation:* 1998 (Upper Saddle River, NJ: Prentice-Hall, 1998).

Puttaswamaiah, K. (ed.), *Economic Policy and Tax Reform in India* (New Delhi: Indus Publishing Co., 1994).

Rotterdam Institute for Fiscal Studies, *International Tax Avoidance*, Country Reports, Vol.B (The Neitherlands: Kluwer, 1978).

Sabine, B.E.V., *A History of Income Tax* (London: George Allen and Unwin Ltd., 1966).

Sandford, Cedric (ed.), *Key Issues in Tax Reform* (Great Britain: Fiscal Publications, 1993).

Shah, Anwar (ed.), *Fiscal Incentices for Investment and Innovation* (New York: Oxford University Press for the World Bank, 1995).

——— (ed.), *Fiscal Incentives for Investment in Developing Countries* (Washington D.C.: World Bank, 1992).

Shah, Anwar and Whalley John, *Tax Incidence Analysis for Developing Countries* (Washington D.C.: Discussion Paper, World Bank, 1990).

Shirazi, Javad Khalilzadeh and Anwar Shah, *The Tax Policy in Developing Countries* (Washington, D.C.: The World Bank, 1994).

Shome, Parthasarthi (ed.), *Tax Policy Handbook* (Washington, D.C.: IMF, 1995).

Shome, Parthasarthi, Pawan K. Aggarwal and Kanwarjit Singh, 'Papers on Tax Evasion and Tax Adminsitration: A Focus on Tax Deduction at Source', in *Symposium on Fiscal Policy, Public Policy and Governance* (New Delhi: NIPFP, 1996).

Singh, Veerinderjeet and Teoh Boon Kee (eds.), *CCH, Malaysian Master Tax Guide* (Singapore: CCH Asia PTE Ltd., 2000).

Singhania, Vinod K., and Kapil Singhania, *Direct Taxes: Law and Practice* (Delhi: Taxmann Publications (P) Ltd., 2001).

Slenırod Joel, and Jon Bakija, *Taxing Ourselves, A Citizen's Guide to the Great Debate Over Tax Reform* (Massachusetts: The MIT Press, 2000).

Slemroed, Joel, *Tax Policy in the Real World* (Cambridge: University of Cambridge, 1999).

Sorenson, Peter (ed.), *Public Finance in a Changing World* (Hampshire, London: MacMillan Press Ltd., 1998).

Surrey, Stanley S., 'Tax Administration and Technical Assistance', in Richard M. Bird and Oliver Oldman (eds.), *Readings on Taxation in Developing Countries* (Baltimore: The Johns Hopkins Press, 1967).

Surrey, Stanley S., and Paul R. McDaniel, *Tax Expenditures* (Cambridge, Massachusetts: Harvard University Press, 1985).

Tanzi, Vito, *Taxation in an Integrating World* (Washington D.C.: The Brookings Institution, 1995).

———, *The Individual Income Tax and Economic Growth: An International Comparison* (Baltimore: The Johns Hopkins Press, 1969).

The World Bank, *Lessons of Tax Reform* (Washington D.C.: The World Bank, 1991).

———, *World Development Report, 1999-2000* (New York: Oxford University Press, 2000).

Thornton, Richard, *MLJ Tax Handbook* (Kuala Lumpur: Malaysian Law Journal Sdn Bhd, 1998).

Tingley, Kenneth, *Income Tax Guide 1999-2000* (London: Orion Business Book, 1999).

U.S. Master Tax Guide (Chicago: CCH Incorporated, 2000).

Williamson, J. Peter, *Federal Taxation: Cases and Notes* (Illinois: Scott Foresman and Co., 1967).

Wiseman, Jack, *Comparative Aspects of the Taxation of Business in the United Kingdom and Germany* (Great Britain: David Green Printers Ltd., 1980).

II. Articles

Adhikari, Ramesh, 'Tax Policy and Adminstration in Asian Countries: A Review of Key Issues and Options', *Bulletin for International Fiscal Documentation*, Vol. 56, No. 2, February 2002, pp. 46-59.

Azzi, John, 'Budget and Other Developments', *Asia-Pacific Tax Bulletin*, Vol.5, No.7, 1999, pp. 256-58.

Bagchi, Aamresh, 'Strengthening Direct Taxes, Some Suggestions', *Economic & Political Weekly*, Vol. XXX, Nos. 7&8 (Feb 18-25), pp. 380-4.

Bird, Richard M., 'Why Tax Corporations', *Bulletin for International Fiscal Documentation*, Vol. 56, No. 5, May 2002, pp. 194-203.

Dirkis, Michael, 'Observations on the Development of Australia's Income Tax Policy and Income Tax Law', *Bulletin for International Fiscal Documentation*, Vol. 56, No. 10, October 2002, pp. 522-33.

Easson, Alex, 'Tax Incentives for Foreign Direct Investment, Part I: Recent Trends and Counter Trends', *Bulletin for International Fiscal Documentation*, Vol. 55, No. 7, July 2001, pp. 266-74.

———, 'Tax Incentives for Foreign Direct Investment, Part II: Design Considerations', *Bulletin for International Fiscal Documentation*, Vol. 55, No. 8, August 2001, pp. 365-75.

Haq, Ikramul, 'Constitutionality of Agricultural Income Tax', *Asia-Pacific Tax Bulletin*, Vol. 7, No. 2, February 2001, pp. 28-30.

Har Govind, 'India: Important Fiscal and Tax Changes in 1999-2000', *International Tax Review. Inter Tax*, Vol. 28, No. 10 (October 2000), pp. 381-94.

———, 'Minimum Alternate Tax in India', *Asia-Pacific Tax Bulletin*, Vol. 7, No. 3 (March 2001), pp. 61-66.

———, 'Tax Treatment of Capital Gains with Special Reference to Non-residents', *Bulletin for International Fiscal Documentation*, Vol. 53, No. 5 (May 1999), pp. 200-7.

Henegbi, Rami, 'Tax Concessions Available to Small Business in Australia', *Bulletin for International Fiscal Documentation*, Vol. 55, No. 11, November 2001, pp. 571-79.

Jain, Anil Kumar, Tax Evasion, Economic Reforms and Corruption in India', *International Tax Review. Inter Tax*, Vol. 25, No. 1 (January 1997), pp. 18-22.

Jain, Indu, 'A Comparative Analysis: Minimum Alternative Tax', *The Chartered Accountant*, Vol. XLIX, No. 9, March 2001, pp. 33-38.

Jain, Indu, 'Taxation of Dividend Income: A Global Perspective', *Taxman*, Vol. 115, Part 6, April 2001, pp. 255-62.

Jain, Ved, 'Changing Perspectives: Minimum Aletrnative Tax', *The Chartered Accountant*, Vol. XLIX, No. 3, September 2000. pp. 16-21.

James, Simon, 'Self Assessment and the U.K. Tax System' *Australian Tax Forum*, Vol. 13, No. 2, 1997.

Kobetsky, Michael, 'Tax Reform in Australia—The New Tax System', *Bulletin for International Fiscal Documentation,* Vol. 54, No. 2 (February 2000), pp. 67-79.

McLure, Jr., Charles E., 'Globalization, Tax Rules and national Sovereignity', *Bulletin for International Fiscal Documentation*, Vol. 55, No. 8, August 2001, pp. 328-41.

———, 'Tax Holidays and Investment Incentives: A Comparative Analysis', *Bulletin for International Fiscal Documentation*, Vol. 53, No. 819 (Aug.-Sep. 1999), pp. 326-39.

Messere, Ken, 'Half a Century of Changes in Taxation', *Bulletin for International Fiscal Documentation*, Vol. 53, No. 819 (Aug.-Sept. 1999) pp. 340-65.

Pandey, T.N., 'How Direct Taxes are Administered in Japan' in *Current Tax Reporter*, Vol. 131 (1996), pp. 109-17.

———, 'Future Tax Policy Concerning Exemptions, Deductions and Incentives in the IT Act, 1961", *Current Tax Reporter*, Vol. 173, 2002, pp. 178-90.

Passant, John, 'A Comparison of Some Aspects of the French and Australia Tax Systems', *Bulletin for International Fiscal Documentation*, Vol. 49, No. 1, January 1995.

Pope, Jeff and Prafula Fernandez, 'Current Tax Reform in Australia: An Ambitious Programme', *British Tax Review, 2001*, Number 2 (85-152), pp. 135-51.

Rothschild, Leonar W. and Michael G. Shinner, 'Determining Residency for Federal Income Tax Purposes', *Bulletin for International Fiscal Documentation*, Vol. 47, No. 2 (Feb 1993), pp 84-89.

Singh, Veerinderjeet, 'Malaysia, Recent Tax Developments', *Bulletin for International Fiscal Documentation,* Vol. 53, No. 2 (Feb 1999), pp. 80-89.

Verma, D.P.S. and Indu Jain, 'Tax Changes in the Finance Act 2000—An Analysis', *Asia-Pacific Tax Bulletin,* Vol. 6, No. 11 (November 2000), pp. 47-50.

———, 'Growth in Income Tax Base–A Comparison of developed and Developing Countries', *The Chartered Accountant*, Vol. 51, No. 1, July 2002, pp. 99-104.

———, 'Income Tax, A World Turned Upside Down', *Business Standard*, April 22, 2002, p. 10.

Vito, Tanzi and Howell H. Zee, 'Tax Policy for Emerging Markets: Developing Countries', *National Tax Journal*, Vol. LIII, No. 2, pp. 299-322.

III. LEGISLATIONS

The *Income Tax Act,* 1961, as on June 1, 2001 (India).

The *Income Tax Act,* 1967 *(Act 53),* as on November 1, 1999 (Malaysia).

The *Income Tax Assessment Act,* 1936, as on January 1, 2000 (Australia).

The *Income Tax Assessment Act,* 1997, as on January 1, 2000 (Australia).

The *Income Tax Ordinance,* 1979, as on July 10, 2000 (Pakistan).

The *Income Tax Rules,* 1962, as on June 1, 2000 (India).

The *Income Tax Rules,* 1982, as on July 10, 2000 (Pakistan).

The *Internal Revenue Code,* 1986 as on December 1, 2000 (The U.S.).

IV. OFFICIAL REPORTS

Commonwealth of Australia, Ministry of Finance, Australian Taxation Office, *Taxation Statistics, 1997-98.*

———, Commissioner of Taxation, *Annual Report, 1997-1998 and 1998-1999*

Government of India, Ministry of Finance, 'Report of the Expert Group to Rationalise and Simplify the Income-Tax Law', reported in *Current Tax Reporter*, Vol. 138, 1997.
———, Ministry of Finance, 'Budget 1997-98', Speech of Minister of Finance, reported in *Current Tax Reporter*, Vol. 138, 1997.
———, Ministry of Finance, Directorate of Income Tax, *All India Income Tax Statistics:* Assessment Year 1997-98 (New Delhi).
———, Ministry of Finance, *Economic Survey,* 1998-99, 1999-2000, 2000-01.
———, Planning Commission, 'Report of the working group on Tax Policy of the Steering Group on Financial Resource', Chairman Parthasarthi Shome, in *India: Tax Policy for the Ninth Five Year Plan.*
———, Union Government, *Report of the Comptroller and Auditor General of India, for the year ended March 1998* (No. 12 of 1999).
Government of Malaysia, Inland Revenue Board of Malaysia, *Annual Report,* 1997.
———, Ministry of Finance, Board of Inland Revenue, *Taxation Statistics,* 1998.
———, Ministry of Finance, *Economic Report, 1998-99* (Kuala Lumpur, 1998).
Government of Pakistan, Directorate of Research and Statistics, Central Board of Revenue, *CBR Year Book, 1997-98* (Islamabad).
———, Economic Adviser's Wing, Finance Division, *Economic Survey,* 1999-2000, 2000-01 (Islamabad).
Government of U.K., Board of Inland Revenue, *Annual Report for the Year ending March 31, 1998.*
———, Ministry of Finance, Board of Inland Revenue, *Inland Revenue Statistics 1999,* 2000.

Index